Network Security with OpenSSL

Network Security
with OpenSSL

John Viega, Matt Messier, and Pravir Chandra

O'REILLY®

Beijing · Cambridge · Farnham · Köln · Paris · Sebastopol · Taipei · Tokyo

Network Security with OpenSSL

by John Viega, Matt Messier, and Pravir Chandra

Published by O'Reilly Media, Inc., 1005 Gravenstein Highway North, Sebastopol, CA 95472.

O'Reilly Media, Inc. books may be purchased for educational, business, or sales promotional use. Online editions are also available for most titles (*safari.oreilly.com*). For more information, contact our corporate/institutional sales department: (800) 998-9938 or *corporate@oreilly.com*.

Editor:	Robert Denn
Production Editor:	Colleen Gorman
Cover Designer:	Ellie Volckhausen
Interior Designer:	David Futato

Printing History:

June 2002:	First Edition.

 This book uses RepKover™, a durable and flexible lay-flat binding.

ISBN: 978-0-596-00270-1
[M]

To the memory of Arthur J. Zoebelein,
former Chief of the Office of Cryptologic
Archives and History, National Security Agency

Table of Contents

Preface

About This Book

The Internet is a dangerous place, more dangerous than most people realize. Many technical people know that it's possible to intercept and modify data on the wire, but few realize how easy it actually is. If an application doesn't properly protect data when it travels an untrusted network, the application is a security disaster waiting to happen.

The SSL (Secure Socket Layer) protocol and its successor TLS (Transport Layer Security) can be used to secure applications that need to communicate over a network. OpenSSL is an open source library that implements the SSL and TLS protocols, and is by far the most widely deployed, freely available implementation of these protocols. OpenSSL is fully featured and cross-platform, working on Unix and Windows alike. It's primarily used from C and C++ programs, but you can use it from the command line (see Chapters 1 through 3) and from other languages such as Python, Perl, and PHP (see Chapter 9).

In this book, we'll teach developers and administrators how to secure applications with OpenSSL. We won't just show you how to SSL-enable your applications, we'll be sure to introduce you to the most significant risks involved in doing so, and the methods for mitigating those risks. These methods are important; it takes more work to secure an SSL-enabled application than most people think, especially when code needs to run in multithreaded, highly interoperable environments where efficiency is a concern.

OpenSSL is more than just a free implementation of SSL. It also includes a general-purpose cryptographic library, which can be useful for situations in which SSL isn't an appropriate solution. Working with cryptography at such a low level can be dangerous, since there are many pitfalls in applying cryptography of which few developers are fully aware. Nonetheless, we do discuss the available functionality for those that wish to use it. Additionally, OpenSSL provides some high-level primitives, such as support for the S/MIME email standard.

The bulk of this book describes the OpenSSL library and the many ways to use it. We orient the discussion around working examples, instead of simply providing reference material. We discuss all of the common options OpenSSL users can support, as well as the security implications of each choice.

Depending on your needs, you may end up skipping around in this book. For people who want to use OpenSSL from the command line for administrative tasks, everything they need is in the first three chapters. Developers interested in SSL-enabling an application can probably read Chapter 1, then skip directly to Chapter 5 (though they will have to refer to parts of Chapter 4 to understand all the code).

Here's an overview of the book's contents:

Chapter 1, *Introduction*
> This chapter introduces SSL and the OpenSSL library. We give an overview of the biggest security risks involved with deploying the library and discuss how to mitigate them at a high level. We also look at how to use OpenSSL along with Stunnel to secure third-party software, such as POP servers that don't otherwise have built-in SSL support.

Chapter 2, *Command-Line Interface*
> Here we discuss how to use basic OpenSSL functionality from the command line, for those who wish to use OpenSSL interactively, call out to it from shell scripts, or interface with it from languages without native OpenSSL support.

Chapter 3, *Public Key Infrastructure (PKI)*
> This chapter explains the basics of Public Key Infrastructure (PKI), especially as it manifests itself in OpenSSL. This chapter is primarily concerned with how to go about getting certificates for use in SSL, S/MIME, and other PKI-dependent cryptography. We also discuss how to manage your own PKI using the OpenSSL command line, if you so choose.

Chapter 4, *Support Infrastructure*
> In this chapter, we talk about the various low-level APIs that are most important to OpenSSL. Some of these APIs need to be mastered in order to make full use of the OpenSSL library. Particularly, we lay the foundation for enabling multithreaded application support and performing robust error handling with OpenSSL. Additionally, we discuss the OpenSSL IO API, its randomness API, its arbitrary precision math API, and how to use cryptographic acceleration with the library.

Chapter 5, *SSL/TLS Programming*
> Here we discuss the ins and outs of SSL-enabling applications, particularly with SSLv3 and its successor, TLSv1. We not only cover the basics but also go into some of the more obscure features of these protocols, such as session resumption, which is a tool that can help speed up SSL connection times in some circumstances.

Chapter 6, *Symmetric Cryptography*

This chapter covers everything you need to know to use OpenSSL's interface to secret-key cryptographic algorithms such as Triple DES, RC4, and AES (the new Advanced Encryption Standard). In addition to covering the standard API, we provide guidelines on selecting algorithms that you should support for your applications, and we explain the basics of these algorithms, including different modes of operation, such as counter mode. Additionally, we talk about how to provide some security for UDP-based traffic, and discuss general considerations for securely integrating symmetric cryptography into your applications.

Chapter 7, *Hashes and MACs*

In this chapter, we discuss how to use nonreversible (one-way) cryptographic hash functions, often called message digest algorithms. We also show how to use Message Authentication Codes (MACs), which can be used to provide data integrity via a shared secret. We show how to apply MACs to ensure that tampering with HTTP cookies will be detected.

Chapter 8, *Public Key Algorithms*

Here we talk about the various public key algorithms OpenSSL exports, including Diffie-Hellman key exchange, the Digital Signature Algorithm (DSA), and RSA. Additionally, we discuss how to read and write common storage formats for public keys.

Chapter 9, *OpenSSL in Other Languages*

This chapter describes how to use OpenSSL programmatically from Perl using the Net::SSLeay package, from Python using the M2Crypto library, and from PHP.

Chapter 10, *Advanced Programming Topics*

In this chapter, we discuss many of the more esoteric parts of the OpenSSL API that are still useful, including the OpenSSL configuration API, creating and using S/MIME email, and performing certificate management programmatically.

Appendix, *Command-Line Reference*

Here we provide a reference to the many options in the OpenSSL command-line interface.

Additionally, the book's web site (*http://www.opensslbook.com*) contains API reference material that supplements this book. We also give pointers to the official OpenSSL documentation.

Note that we do not cover using SSL from Apache. While Apache does use OpenSSL for its cryptography, it provides its own API for configuring everything. Covering that isn't in the scope of this book. Refer to the Apache documentation, or the book *Apache: The Definitive Guide* by Ben Laurie and Peter Laurie (O'Reilly & Associates).

As we finish this book, OpenSSL is at Version 0.9.6c, and 0.9.7 is in feature freeze, though a final release is not expected until well after this book's publication.

Additionally, we expect developers to have to interoperate with 0.9.6 for some time. Therefore, we have gone out of our way to support both versions. Usually, our discussion will apply to both 0.9.6 and 0.9.7 releases unless otherwise noted. If there are features that were experimental in 0.9.6 and changed significantly in 0.9.7 (most notably support for hardware acceleration), we tend to explain only the 0.9.7 solution.

We've set up a web site at *www.opensslbook.com*. It contains an up-to-date archive of all the example code used in this book. All the examples have been tested with the appropriate version of OpenSSL on Mac OS X, FreeBSD, Linux, and Windows 2000. They're expected to work portably in any environment that supports OpenSSL.

In addition, the web site contains API reference documentation. Because OpenSSL contains literally thousands of functions, we thought it best to offload such documentation to the Web, especially considering that many of the APIs are still evolving.

The book's web site also contains links to related secure programming resources and will contain an errata listing of any problems that are found after publication.

You can contact the authors by email at *authors@opensslbook.com*.

Conventions Used in This Book

The following conventions are used in this book:

Italic
> Used for filenames, directory names, and URLs. It is also used to emphasize new terms and concepts when they are introduced.

`Constant Width`
> Used for commands, attributes, variables, code examples, and system output.

`Constant Width Italic`
> Used in syntax descriptions to indicate user-defined items.

`Constant Width Bold`
> Indicates user input in examples showing an interaction. Also indicates emphasized code elements to which you should pay particular attention.

 Indicates a tip, suggestion, or general note.

 Indicates a warning or caution.

Comments and Questions

We have tested and verified the information in this book to the best of our ability, but you may find that features have changed or that we have made mistakes. If so, please notify us by writing to:

O'Reilly & Associates, Inc.
1005 Gravenstein Highway North
Sebastopol, CA 95472
(800) 998-9938 (in the United States or Canada)
(707) 829-0515 (international or local)
(707) 829-0104 (fax)

To ask technical questions or comment on the book, send email to:

bookquestions@oreilly.com

We have a web site for this book, where you can find examples and errata (previously reported errors and corrections are available for public view there). You can access this page at:

http://www.oreilly.com/catalog/openssl/

For more information about this book and others, see the O'Reilly web site:

http://www.oreilly.com

Acknowledgments

We'd like to thank everyone who has contributed to this book, either directly or indirectly. Everyone at O'Reilly has been very helpful, particularly Julie Flanagan, and Kyle Hart, and our editor Robert Denn.

All of our co-workers at Secure Software Solutions have been extremely tolerant of our work on this book and have helped us out whenever necessary. Particularly, we'd like to thank Zachary Girouard, Jamie McGann, Michael Shinn, Scott Shinn, Grisha Trubetskoy, and Robert Zigweid for their direct support.

As with our co-workers, we'd like to thank all of our family and friends for their tolerance, support and enthusiasm, particularly our parents, Anne, Emily, and Molly Viega, Ankur Chandra, Nupur Chandra, Sara Elliot, Bob Fleck, Shawn Geddis, Tom O'Connor, Bruce Potter, Greg Pryzby, George Reese, Ray Schneider, and John Steven.

We'd particularly like to thank the people who reviewed this book, including Simson Garfinkel, Russ Housley, Lutz Jänicke, and Stefan Norberg. Their input was highly valuable across the board.

Everyone who has contributed to what is now OpenSSL deserves special thanks, including Mark Cox, Ralf Engelschall, Dr. Stephen Henson, Tim Hudson, Lutz

Jänicke, Ben Laurie, Richard Levitte, Bodo Möller, Ulf Möller, Andy Polyakov, Holger Reif, Paul Sutton, Geoff Thorpe, and Eric A. Young.

We also thank Sue Miller for encouraging us to write this book in the first place.

—John Viega, Matt Messier, and Pravir Chandra
March 2002
Fairfax, VA

## CHAPTER 1

Introduction

In today's networked world, many applications need security, and cryptography is one of the primary tools for providing that security. The primary goals of cryptography, data confidentiality, data integrity, authentication, and non-repudiation (accountability) can be used to thwart numerous types of network-based attacks, including eavesdropping, IP spoofing, connection hijacking, and tampering. OpenSSL is a cryptographic library; it provides implementations of the industry's best-regarded algorithms, including encryption algorithms such as 3DES ("Triple DES"), AES and RSA, as well as message digest algorithms and message authentication codes.

Using cryptographic algorithms in a secure and reliable manner is much more difficult than most people believe. Algorithms are just building blocks in cryptographic protocols, and cryptographic protocols are notoriously difficult to get right. Cryptographers have a difficult time devising protocols that resist all known attacks, and the average developer tends to do a lot worse. For example, developers often try to secure network connections simply by encrypting data before sending it, then decrypting it on receipt. That strategy often fails to ensure the integrity of data. In many situations, attackers can tamper with data, and sometimes even recover it. Even when protocols are well designed, implementation errors are common. Most cryptographic protocols have limited applicability, such as secure online voting. However, protocols for securely communicating over an insecure medium have ubiquitous applicability. That's the basic purpose of the SSL protocol and its successor, TLS (when we generically refer to SSL, we are referring to both SSL and TLS): to provide the most common security services to arbitrary (TCP-based) network connections in such a way that the need for cryptographic expertise is minimized.

Ultimately, it would be nice if developers and administrators didn't need to know anything about cryptography or even security to protect their applications. It would be nice if security was as simple as linking in a different socket library when building a program. The OpenSSL library strives toward that ideal as much as possible, but in reality, even the SSL protocol requires a good understanding of security principles to apply securely. Indeed, most applications using SSL are susceptible to attack.

Nonetheless, SSL certainly makes securing network connections much simpler. Using SSL doesn't require any understanding of how cryptographic algorithms work. Instead, you only need to understand the basic properties important algorithms have. Similarly, developers do not need to worry about cryptographic protocols; SSL doesn't require any understanding of its internal workings in order to be used. You only need to understand how to apply the algorithm properly.

The goal of this book is to document the OpenSSL library and how to use it properly. This is a book for practitioners, not for security experts. We'll explain what you need to know about cryptography in order to use it effectively, but we don't attempt to write a comprehensive introduction on the subject for those who are interested in why cryptography works. For that, we recommend *Applied Cryptography*, by Bruce Schneier (John Wiley & Sons). For those interested in a more technical introduction to cryptography, we recommend Menezes, van Oorschot, and Vanstone's *Handbook of Applied Cryptography* (CRC Press). Similarly, we do not attempt to document the SSL protocol itself, just its application. If you're interested in the protocol details, we recommend Eric Rescorla's *SSL and TLS* (Addison-Wesley).

Cryptography for the Rest of Us

For those who have never had to work with cryptography before, this section introduces you to the fundamental principles you'll need to know to understand the rest of the material in this book. First, we'll look at the problems that cryptography aims to solve, and then we'll look at the primitives that modern cryptography provides. Anyone who has previously been exposed to the basics of cryptography should feel free to skip ahead to the next section.

Goals of Cryptography

The primary goal of cryptography is to secure important data as it passes through a medium that may not be secure itself. Usually, that medium is a computer network.

There are many different cryptographic algorithms, each of which can provide one or more of the following services to applications:

Confidentiality (secrecy)
> Data is kept secret from those without the proper credentials, even if that data travels through an insecure medium. In practice, this means potential attackers might be able to see garbled data that is essentially "locked," but they should not be able to unlock that data without the proper information. In classic cryptography, the *encryption* (scrambling) algorithm was the secret. In modern cryptography, that isn't feasible. The algorithms are public, and cryptographic *keys* are

used in the encryption and decryption processes. The only thing that needs to be secret is the key. In addition, as we will demonstrate a bit later, there are common cases in which not all keys need to be kept secret.

Integrity (anti-tampering)

The basic idea behind data integrity is that there should be a way for the recipient of a piece of data to determine whether any modifications are made over a period of time. For example, integrity checks can be used to make sure that data sent over a wire isn't modified in transit. Plenty of well-known checksums exist that can detect and even correct simple errors. However, such checksums are poor at detecting skilled intentional modifications of the data. Several cryptographic checksums do not have these drawbacks if used properly. Note that encryption does not ensure data integrity. Entire classes of encryption algorithms are subject to "bit-flipping" attacks. That is, an attacker can change the actual value of a bit of data by changing the corresponding encrypted bit of data.

Authentication

Cryptography can help establish identity for authentication purposes.

Non-repudiation

Cryptography can enable Bob to prove that a message he received from Alice actually came from Alice. Alice can essentially be held accountable when she sends Bob such a message, as she cannot deny (repudiate) that she sent it. In the real world, you have to assume that an attacker does not compromise particular cryptographic keys. The SSL protocol does not support non-repudiation, but it is easily added by using digital signatures.

These simple services can be used to stop a wide variety of network attacks, including:

Snooping (passive eavesdropping)

An attacker watches network traffic as it passes and records interesting data, such as credit card information.

Tampering

An attacker monitors network traffic and maliciously changes data in transit (for example, an attacker may modify the contents of an email message).

Spoofing

An attacker forges network data, appearing to come from a different network address than he actually comes from. This sort of attack can be used to thwart systems that authenticate based on host information (e.g., an IP address).

Hijacking

Once a legitimate user authenticates, a spoofing attack can be used to "hijack" the connection.

Capture-replay

In some circumstances, an attacker can record and replay network transactions to ill effect. For example, say that you sell a single share of stock while the price is high. If the network protocol is not properly designed and secured, an attacker could record that transaction, then replay it later when the stock price has dropped, and do so repeatedly until all your stock is gone.

Many people assume that some (or all) of the above attacks aren't actually feasible in practice. However, that's far from the truth. Especially due to tool sets such as dsniff (*http://www.monkey.org/~dugsong/dsniff/*), it doesn't even take much experience to launch all of the above attacks if access to any node on a network between the two endpoints is available. Attacks are equally easy if you're on the same local network as one of the endpoints. Talented high school students who can use other people's software to break into machines and manipulate them can easily manage to use these tools to attack real systems.

Traditionally, network protocols such as HTTP, SMTP, FTP, NNTP, and Telnet don't provide adequate defenses to the above attacks. Before electronic commerce started taking off in mid-1990, security wasn't really a large concern, especially considering the Internet's origins as a platform for sharing academic research and resources. While many protocols provided some sort of authentication in the way of password-based logins, most of them did not address confidentiality or integrity at all. As a result, all of the above attacks were possible. Moreover, authentication information could usually be among the information "snooped" off a network.

SSL is a great boon to the traditional network protocols, because it makes it easy to add transparent confidentiality and integrity services to an otherwise insecure TCP-based protocol. It can also provide authentication services, the most important being that clients can determine if they are talking to the intended server, not some attacker that is spoofing the server.

Cryptographic Algorithms

The SSL protocol covers many cryptographic needs. Sometimes, though, it isn't good enough. For example, you may wish to encrypt HTTP cookies that will be placed on an end user's browser. SSL won't help protect the cookies while they're being stored on that disk. For situations like this, OpenSSL exports the underlying cryptographic algorithms used in its implementation of the SSL protocol.

Generally, you should avoid using cryptographic algorithms directly if possible. You're not likely to get a totally secure system simply by picking an algorithm and applying it. Usually, cryptographic algorithms are incorporated into cryptographic protocols. Plenty of nonobvious things can be wrong with a protocol based on cryptographic algorithms. That is why it's better to try to find a well-known cryptographic protocol to do what you want to do, instead of inventing something yourself. In fact, even the protocols invented by cryptographers often have subtle holes.

If not for public review, most protocols in use would be insecure. Consider the original WEP protocol for IEEE 802.11 wireless networking. WEP (Wired Equivalent Privacy) is the protocol that is supposed to provide the same level of security for data that physical lines provide. It is a challenge, because data is transmitted through the air, instead of across a wire. WEP was designed by veteran programmers, yet without soliciting the opinions of any professional cryptographers or security protocol developers. Although to a seasoned developer with moderate security knowledge the protocol looked fine, in reality, it was totally lacking in security.

Nonetheless, sometimes you might find a protocol that does what you need, but can't find an implementation that suits your needs. Alternatively, you might find that you do need to come up with your own protocol. For those cases, we do document the SSL cryptographic API.

Five types of cryptographic algorithms are discussed in this book: symmetric key encryption, public key encryption, cryptographic hash functions, message authentication codes, and digital signatures.

Symmetric key encryption

Symmetric key algorithms encrypt and decrypt data using a single key. As shown in Figure 1-1, the key and the plaintext message are passed to the encryption algorithm, producing ciphertext. The result can be sent across an insecure medium, allowing only a recipient who has the original key to decrypt the message, which is done by passing the ciphertext and the key to a decryption algorithm. Obviously, the key must remain secret for this scheme to be effective.

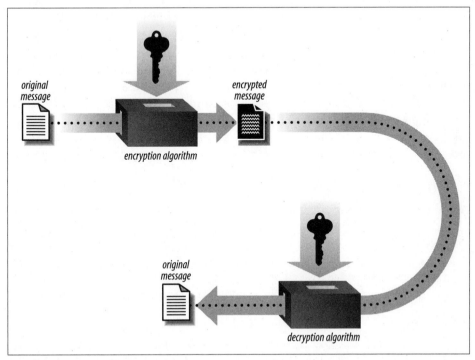

Figure 1-1. Symmetric key cryptography

The primary disadvantage of symmetric key algorithms is that the key must remain secret at all times. In particular, exchanging secret keys can be difficult, since you'll usually want to exchange keys on the same medium that you're trying to use encryption to protect. Sending the key in the clear before you use it leaves open the possibility of an attacker recording the key before you even begin to send data.

One solution to the key distribution problem is to use a cryptographic key exchange protocol. OpenSSL provides the Diffie-Hellman protocol for this purpose, which allows for key agreement without actually divulging the key on the network. However, Diffie-Hellman does not guarantee the identity of the party with whom you are exchanging keys. Some sort of authentication mechanism is necessary to ensure that you don't accidentally exchange keys with an attacker.

Right now, Triple DES (usually written 3DES, or sometimes DES3) is the most conservative symmetric cipher available. It is in wide use, but AES, the new Advanced Encryption Standard, will eventually replace it as the most widely used cipher. AES is certainly faster than 3DES, but 3DES has been around a lot longer, and thus is a more conservative choice for the ultra-paranoid. It is worth mentioning that RC4 is widely supported by existing clients and servers. It is faster than 3DES, but is difficult to set up properly (don't worry, SSL uses RC4 properly). For purposes of compatibility with existing software in which neither AES nor 3DES are supported, RC4 is of particular interest. We don't recommend supporting other algorithms without a good reason. For the interested, we discuss cipher selection in Chapter 6.

Security is related to the length of the key. Longer key lengths are, of course, better. To ensure security, you should only use key lengths of 80 bits or higher. While 64-bit keys may be secure, they likely will not be for long, whereas 80-bit keys should be secure for at least a few years to come. AES supports only 128-bit keys and higher, while 3DES has a fixed 112 bits of effective security.* Both of these should be secure for all cryptographic needs for the foreseeable future. Larger keys are probably unnecessary. Key lengths of 56 bits (regular DES) or less (40-bit keys are common) are too weak; they have proven to be breakable with a modest amount of time and effort.

Public key encryption

Public key cryptography suggests a solution to the key distribution problem that plagues symmetric cryptography. In the most popular form of public key cryptography, each party has two keys, one that must remain secret (the *private key*) and one that can be freely distributed (the *public key*). The two keys have a special mathematical relationship. For Alice to send a message to Bob using public key encryption (see Figure 1-2), Alice must first have Bob's public key. She then encrypts her message

---

* 3DES provides 168 bits of security against brute-force attacks, but there is an attack that reduces the effective security to 112 bits. The enormous space requirements for that attack makes it about as practical as brute force (which is completely impractical in and of itself).

using Bob's public key, and delivers it. Once encrypted, only someone who has Bob's private key can successfully decrypt the message (hopefully, that's only Bob).

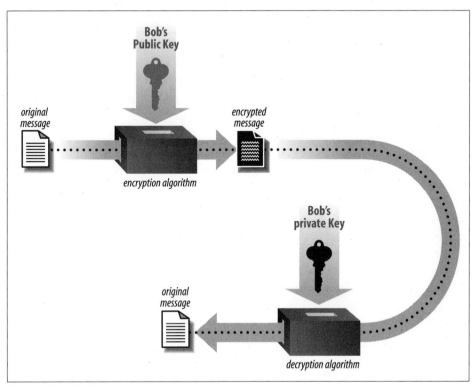

Figure 1-2. Public key cryptography

Public key encryption solves the problem of key distribution, assuming there is some way to find Bob's public key and ensure that the key really does belong to Bob. In practice, public keys are passed around with a bunch of supporting information called a *certificate*, and those certificates are validated by trusted third parties. Often, a trusted third party is an organization that does research (such as credit checks) on people who wish to have their certificates validated. SSL uses trusted third parties to help address the key distribution problem.

Public key cryptography has a significant drawback, though: it is intolerably slow for large messages. Symmetric key cryptography can usually be done quickly enough to encrypt and decrypt all the network traffic a machine can manage. Public key cryptography is generally limited by the speed of the cryptography, not the bandwidth going into the computer, particularly on server machines that need to handle multiple connections simultaneously.

As a result, most systems that use public key cryptography, SSL included, use it as little as possible. Generally, public key encryption is used to agree on an encryption key for a symmetric algorithm, and then all further encryption is done using the symmetric algorithm. Therefore, public key encryption algorithms are primarily used in key exchange protocols and when non-repudiation is required.

RSA is the most popular public key encryption algorithm. The Diffie-Hellman key exchange protocol is based on public key technology and can be used to achieve the same ends by exchanging a symmetric key, which is used to perform actual data encryption and decryption. For public key schemes to be effective, there usually needs to be an authentication mechanism involving a trusted third party that is separate from the encryption itself. Most often, digital signature schemes, which we discuss below, provide the necessary authentication.

Keys in public key algorithms are essentially large numbers with particular properties. Therefore, bit length of keys in public key ciphers aren't directly comparable to symmetric algorithms. With public key encryption algorithms, you should use keys of 1,024 bits or more to ensure reasonable security. 512-bit keys are probably too weak. Anything larger than 2,048 bits may be too slow, and chances are it will not buy security that is much more practical. Recently, there's been some concern that 1,024-bit keys are too weak, but as of this writing, there hasn't been conclusive proof. Certainly, 1,024 bits is a bare minimum for practical security from short-term attacks. If your keys potentially need to stay protected for years, then you might want to go ahead and use 2,048-bit keys.

When selecting key lengths for public key algorithms, you'll usually need to select symmetric key lengths as well. Recommendations vary, but we recommend using 1,024-bit keys when you are willing to work with symmetric keys that are less than 100 bits in length. If you're using 3DES or 128-bit keys, we recommend 2,048-bit public keys. If you are paranoid enough to be using 192-bit keys or higher, we recommend using 4,096-bit public keys.

Requirements for key lengths change if you're using elliptic curve cryptography (ECC), which is a modification of public key cryptography that can provide the same amount of security using faster operations and smaller keys. OpenSSL currently doesn't support ECC, and there may be some lingering patent issues for those who wish to use it. For developers interested in this topic, we recommend the book *Implementing Elliptic Curve Cryptography*, by Michael Rosing (Manning).

Cryptographic hash functions and Message Authentication Codes

Cryptographic hash functions are essentially checksum algorithms with special properties. You pass data to the hash function, and it outputs a fixed-size checksum, often called a *message digest*, or simply digest for short. Passing identical data into the hash function twice will always yield identical results. However, the result gives away no information about the data input to the function. Additionally, it should be practically impossible to find two inputs that produce the same message digest. Generally, when we discuss such functions, we are talking about one-way functions. That is, it should not be possible to take the output and algorithmically reconstruct the input under any circumstances. There are certainly reversible hash functions, but we do not consider such things in the scope of this book.

For general-purpose usage, a minimally secure cryptographic hash algorithm should have a digest twice as large as a minimally secure symmetric key algorithm. MD5 and SHA1 are the most popular one-way cryptographic hash functions. MD5's digest length is only 128 bits, whereas SHA1's is 160 bits. For some uses, MD5's key length is suitable, and for others, it is risky. To be safe, we recommend using only cryptographic hash algorithms that yield 160-bit digests or larger, unless you need to support legacy algorithms. In addition, MD5 is widely considered "nearly broken" due to some cryptographic weaknesses in part of the algorithm. Therefore, we recommend that you avoid using MD5 in any new applications.

Cryptographic hash functions have been put to many uses. They are frequently used as part of a password storage solution. In such circumstances, logins are checked by running the hash function over the password and some additional data, and checking it against a stored value. That way, the server doesn't have to store the actual password, so a well-chosen password will be safe even if an attacker manages to get a hold of the password database.

Another thing people like to do with cryptographic hashes is to release them alongside a software release. For example, OpenSSL might be released alongside a MD5 checksum of the archive. When you download the archive, you can also download the checksum. Then you can compute the checksum over the archive and see if the computed checksum matches the downloaded checksum. You might hope that if the two checksums match, then you securely downloaded the actual released file, and did not get some modified version with a Trojan horse in it. Unfortunately, that isn't the case, because there is no secret involved. An attacker can replace the archive with a modified version, and replace the checksum with a valid value. This is possible because the message digest algorithm is public, and there is no secret information input to it.

If you share a secret key with the software distributor, then the distributor could combine the archive with the secret key to produce a message digest that an attacker shouldn't be able to forge, since he wouldn't have the secret. Schemes for using *keyed hashes*, i.e., hashes involving a secret key, are called *Message Authentication Codes* (MACs). MACs are often used to provide message integrity for general-purpose data transfer, whether encrypted or not. Indeed, SSL uses MACs for this purpose.

The most widely used MAC, and the only one currently supported in SSL and in OpenSSL, is HMAC. HMAC can be used with any message digest algorithm.

Digital signatures

For many applications, MACs are not very useful, because they require agreeing on a shared secret. It would be nice to be able to authenticate messages without needing to share a secret. Public key cryptography makes this possible. If Alice signs a message with her secret signing key, then anyone can use her public key to verify that she signed the message. RSA provides for digital signing. Essentially, the public key and private key are interchangeable. If Alice encrypts a message with her private key, anyone can decrypt it. If Alice didn't encrypt the message, using her public key to decrypt the message would result in garbage.

There is also a popular scheme called DSA (the Digital Signature Algorithm), which the SSL protocol and the OpenSSL library both support.

Much like public key encryption, digital signatures are very slow. To speed things up, the algorithm generally doesn't operate on the entire message to be signed. Instead, the message is cryptographically hashed, and then the hash of the message is signed. Nonetheless, signature schemes are still expensive. For this reason, MACs are preferable if any sort of secure key exchange has taken place.

One place where digital signatures are widely used is in certificate management. If Alice is willing to validate Bob's certificate, she can sign it with her public key. Once she's done that, Bob can attach her signature to his certificate. Now, let's say he gives the certificate to Charlie, and Charlie does not know that Bob actually gave him the certificate, but he would believe Alice if she told him the certificate belonged to Bob. In this case, Charlie can validate Alice's signature, thereby demonstrating that the certificate does indeed belong to Bob.

Since digital signatures are a form of public key cryptography, you should be sure to use key lengths of 1,024 bits or higher to ensure security.

Overview of SSL

SSL is currently the most widely deployed security protocol. It is the security protocol behind secure HTTP (HTTPS), and thus is responsible for the little lock in the corner of your web browser. SSL is capable of securing any protocol that works over TCP.

An SSL transaction (see Figure 1-3) starts with the client sending a handshake to the server. In the server's response, it sends its certificate. As previously mentioned, a certificate is a piece of data that includes a public key associated with the server and other interesting information, such as the owner of the certificate, its expiration date, and the fully qualified domain name* associated with the server.

During the connection process, the server will prove its identity by using its private key to successfully decrypt a challenge that the client encrypts with the server's public key. The client needs to receive the correct unencrypted data to proceed. Therefore, the server's certificate can remain public—an attacker would need a copy of the certificate as well as the associated private key in order to masquerade as a known server.

---

* By fully qualified, we mean that the server's hostname is written out in a full, unambiguous manner that includes specifying the top-level domain. For example, if our web server is named "www", and our corporate domain is "securesw.com", then the fully qualified domain name for that host is "www.securesw.com". No abbreviation of this name would be considered fully qualified.

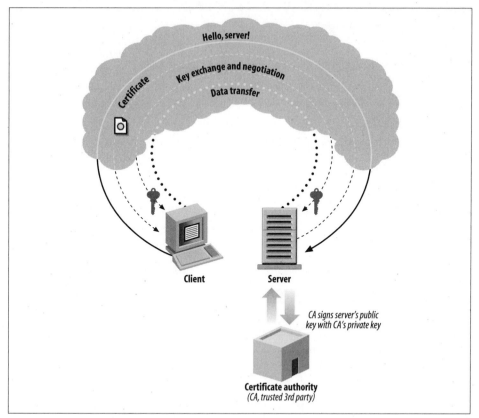

Figure 1-3. An overview of direct communication in SSL

However, an attacker could always intercept server messages and present the attacker's certificate. The data fields of the forged certificate can look legitimate (such as the domain name associated with the server and the name of the entity associated with the certificate). In such a case, the attacker might establish a proxy connection to the intended server, and then just eavesdrop on all data. Such an attack is called a "man-in-the-middle" attack and is shown in Figure 1-4. To thwart a man-in-the-middle attack completely, the client must not only perform thorough validation of the server certificate, but also have some way of determining whether the certificate itself is trustworthy. One way to determine trustworthiness is to hardcode a list of valid certificates into the client. The problem with this solution is that it is not scalable. Imagine needing the certificate for every secure HTTP server you might wish to use on the net stored in your web browser before you even begin surfing.

The practical solution to this problem is to involve a trusted third party that is responsible for keeping a database of valid certificates. A trusted third party, called a *Certification Authority*, signs valid server certificates using its private key. The signature indicates that the Certification Authority has done a background check on the

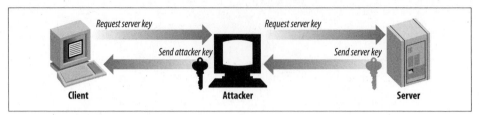

Figure 1-4. A man-in-the-middle attack

entity that owns the certificate being presented, thus ensuring to some degree that the data presented in the certificate is accurate. That signature is included in the certificate, and is presented at connection time.

The client can validate the authority's signature, assuming that it has the public key of the Certification Authority locally. If that check succeeds, the client can be reasonably confident the certificate is owned by an entity known to the trusted third party, and can then check the validity of other information stored in the certificate, such as whether the certificate has expired.

Although rare, the server can also request a certificate from the client. Before certificate validation is done, client and server agree on which cryptographic algorithms to use. After the certificate validation, client and server agree upon a symmetric key using a secure key agreement protocol (data is transferred using a symmetric key encryption algorithm). Once all of the negotiations are complete, the client and server can exchange data at will.

The details of the SSL protocol get slightly more complex. Message Authentication Codes are used extensively to ensure data integrity. Additionally, during certificate validation, a party can go to the Certification Authority for *Certificate Revocation Lists* (CRLs) to ensure that certificates that appear valid haven't actually been stolen.

We won't get into the details of the SSL protocol (or its successor, TLS). For our purposes, we can treat everything else as a black box. Again, if you are interested in the details, we recommend Eric Rescorla's book *SSL and TLS*.

Problems with SSL

SSL is an excellent protocol. Like many tools, it is effective in the hands of someone who knows how to use it well, but is easy to misuse. There are many pitfalls that people fall into when deploying SSL, most of which can be avoided with a bit of work.

Efficiency

SSL is a lot slower than a traditional unsecured TCP/IP connection. This problem is a direct result of providing adequate security. When a new SSL session is being established, the server and the client exchange a sizable amount of information that is required for them to authenticate each other and agree on a key to be used for the session. This initial *handshake* involves heavy use of public key cryptography, which, as we've already mentioned, is very slow. It's also the biggest slowdown when using SSL. On current high-end PC hardware, OpenSSL struggles to make 100 connections per second under real workloads.

Once the initial handshake is complete and the session is established, the overhead is significantly reduced, but some of it still remains in comparison with an unsecured TCP/IP connection. Specifically, more data is transferred than normal. Data is transmitted in packets, which contain information required by the SSL protocol as well as any padding required by the symmetric cipher that is in use. Of course, there is the overhead of encrypting and decrypting the data as well, but the good news is that a symmetric cipher is in use, so it usually isn't a bottleneck. The efficiency of symmetric cryptography can vary greatly based on the algorithms used and the strength of the keys. However, even the slowest algorithms are efficient enough that they are rarely a bottleneck at all.

Because of the inefficiency of public key cryptography, many people decide not to use SSL when they realize it can't handle a large enough load. Some people go without security at all, which is obviously not a good idea. Other people try to design their own protocols to compensate. This is a bad idea, because there are many nonobvious pitfalls that can besiege you. Protocols that aren't designed by a skilled cryptographer inevitably have problems. SSL's design does consider efficiency; it simply isn't willing to sacrifice security for a speed improvement. You should be skeptical of using protocols that are more efficient.

There are ways to ameliorate this problem without abandoning the protocol. SSL does support a connection resumption mechanism so that clients that reconnect shortly after disconnecting can do so without incurring the full overhead of establishing a connection. While that is useful for HTTP,[*] it often isn't effective for other protocols.

Cryptographic acceleration hardware

One common approach for speeding up SSL is to use hardware acceleration. Many vendors provide PCI cards that can unload the burden of cryptographic operations from your processor, and OpenSSL supports most of them. We discuss the specifics of using hardware acceleration in Chapter 4.

---

[*] As is HTTP keepalive, which is a protocol option to keep sockets open for a period of time after a request is completed, so that the connection may be reused if another request to the same server follows in short order.

Load balancing

Another popular option for managing efficiency concerns with SSL is *load balancing*, which is simply distributing connections transparently across multiple machines, such that the group of machines appears as a single machine to the outside world for all intents and purposes. This can be a more cost-effective solution than accelerator cards, especially if you already have hardware lying around. Often, however, load balancing requires more work to ensure that persistent data is readily available to all servers on the backend. Another problem with load balancing is that many solutions route new connections to arbitrary machines, which can remove most of the benefit of connection resumption, since few clients will actually connect to the original machine during reconnection.

One simple load balancing mechanism is round-robin DNS, in which multiple IP addresses are assigned to a single DNS name. In response to DNS lookups, the DNS server cycles through all the addresses for that DNS name before giving out the same address twice. This is a popular solution because it is low-cost, requiring no special hardware. Connection resumption generally works well with this solution, since machines tend to keep a short-term memory of DNS results.

One problem with this solution is that the DNS server handles the load management, and takes no account of the actual load on individual servers. Additionally, large ISPs can perform DNS caching, causing an uneven distribution of load. To solve that problem, entries must be set to expire frequently, which increases the load on the DNS server.

Hardware load balancers vary in price and features. Those that can remember outside machines and map them to the same internal machine across multiple connections tend to be more expensive, but also more effective for SSL.

Version 0.9.7 of OpenSSL adds new functionality that allows applications to handle load balancing by way of manipulating session IDs. Sessions are a subset of operating parameters for an SSL connection, which we'll discuss in more detail in Chapter 5.

Keys in the Clear

In a typical SSL installation, the server maintains credentials so that clients can authenticate the server. In addition to a certificate that is presented at connection time, the server also maintains a private key, which is necessary for establishing that the server presenting a certificate is actually presenting its own certificate.

That private key needs to live somewhere on the server. The most secure solution is to use cryptographic acceleration hardware. Most of these devices can generate and store key material, and additionally prevent the private key from being accessed by an attacker who has broken into the machine. To do this, the private key is used only on the card, and is not allowed off except under special circumstances.

In cases in which hardware solutions aren't feasible, there is no absolute way to protect the private key from an attacker who has obtained root access, because, at the very least, the key must be unencrypted in memory when handling a new connection.* If an attacker has root, she can generally attach a debugger to the server process, and pull out the unencrypted key.

There are two options in these situations. First, you can simply keep the key unencrypted on disk. This is the easiest solution, but it also makes the job of an attacker simple if he has physical access, since he can power off the machine and pull out the disk, or simply reboot to single-user mode. Alternatively, you can keep the key encrypted on disk using a passphrase, which an administrator must type when the SSL server starts. In such a situation, the key will only be unencrypted in the address space of the server process, and thus won't be available to someone who can shut the machine off and directly access the disk.

Furthermore, many attackers are looking for low-hanging fruit, and will not likely go after the key even if they have the skills to do so. The downside to this solution is that unattended reboots are not possible, because whenever the machine restarts (or the SSL server process crashes), someone must type in the passphrase, which is often not very practical, especially in a lights-out environment. Storing the key in the clear obviously does not exhibit this problem.

In either case, your best defense is to secure the host and your network with the best available lockdown techniques (including physical lockdown techniques). Such solutions are outside the scope of this book.

What exactly does it mean if the server's private key is compromised? The most obvious result is that the attacker can masquerade as the server, which we discuss in the next section. Another result (which may not be as obvious) is that all past communications that used the key can likely be decrypted. If an attacker is able to compromise a private key, it is also likely that the attacker could have recorded previous communications. The solution to this problem is to use *ephemeral keying*. This means a temporary key pair is generated when a new SSL session is created. This is then used for key exchange and is subsequently destroyed. By using ephemeral keying, it is possible to achieve *forward secrecy*, meaning that if a key is compromised, messages encrypted with previous keys will not be subject to attack.† We discuss ephemeral keying and forward secrecy in more detail in Chapter 5.

---

* Some operating systems (particularly "trusted" OSs) can provide protection in such cases, assuming no security problems are in the OS implementation. Linux, Windows, and most of the BSD variants offer no such assurance.

† Note that if you are implementing a server in particular, it is often not possible to get perfect forward secrecy with SSL, since many clients don't support Diffie-Hellman, and because using cryptographically strong ephemeral RSA keys violates the protocol specification.

Bad Server Credentials

A server's private key can be stolen. In such a case, an attacker can usually masquerade as the server with impunity. Additionally, Certification Authorities sometimes sign certificates for people who are fraudulently representing themselves, despite the efforts made by the CA to validate all of the important information about the party that requests the certificate signing.* For example, in early 2001, VeriSign signed certificates that purported to belong to Microsoft, when in reality they did not. However, since they had been signed by a well-known Certification Authority, they would look authentic to anyone validating the signature on those certificates.

SSL has a mechanism for thwarting these problems: Certificate Revocation Lists. Once the Certification Authority learns that a certificate has been stolen or signed inappropriately, the Authority adds the certificate's serial number to a CRL. The client can access CRLs and validate them using the CA's certificate, since the server signs CRLs with its private key.

One problem with CRLs is that windows of vulnerability can be large. It can take time for an organization to realize that a private key may have been stolen and to notify the CA. Even when that happens, the CA must update its CRLs, which generally does not happen in real time (the time it takes depends on the CA). Then, once the CRLs are updated, the client must download them in order to detect that a presented certificate has been revoked. In most situations, clients never download or update CRLs. In such cases, compromised certificates tend to remain compromised until they expire.

There are several reasons for this phenomenon. First, CRLs tend to be large enough that they can take significant time to download, and can require considerable storage space locally, especially when the SSL client is an embedded device with limited storage capacity. The Online Certificate Status Protocol (OCSP), specified in RFC 2560, addresses these problems. Unfortunately, this is not yet a widely accepted standard protocol, nor is it likely to become so anytime soon. Additionally, the only version that is widely deployed has serious security issues (see Chapter 3 for more information). OpenSSL has only added OCSP support in Version 0.9.7, and few CAs even offer it as a service. Other authorities have facilities for incremental updates to CRLs, allowing for minimal download times, but that solution still requires space on the client, or some sort of caching server.

These solutions all require the CA's server to be highly available if clients are to have up-to-the-minute information. Some clients will be deployed in environments where

---

* Actually, a Registration Authority (RA) is responsible for authenticating information about the CA's customers. The CA can be its own RA, or it can use one or more third-party RAs. From the perspective of the consumer of certificates, the RA isn't really an important concept, so we will just talk about CAs to avoid confusion, even though it is technically not accurate.

a constant link to the CA is not possible. In addition, the need to query the CA can add significant latency to connection times that can be intolerable to the end user.

Another problem is that there is no standard delivery mechanism specified for CRLs. As a result, OpenSSL in particular does not provide a simple way to access CRL information, not even from VeriSign, currently the most popular CA. One common method of CRL (and certificate) distribution is using the Lightweight Directory Access Protocol (LDAP). LDAP provides a hierarchical structure for storing such information and fits nicely for PKI distribution.

Due to the many problems surrounding CRLs, it becomes even more important to take whatever measures are feasible to ensure that SSL private keys are not stolen. At the very least, you should put intrusion detection systems in place to detect compromises of your private key so that you can report the compromise to the CA quickly.

Certificate Validation

CRLs aren't useful if a client isn't performing adequate validation of server certificates to begin with. Often, they don't. Certainly, for SSL to work at all, the client must be able to extract the public key from a presented certificate, and the server must have a private key that corresponds with that public key. However, there is no mechanism to force further validation. As a result, man-in-the-middle attacks are often feasible.

First, developers must decide which Certification Authorities should be trusted, and must locate the certificates associated with each of those authorities. That's more effort than most developers are willing to exert. As a result, many applications using SSL are at the mercy of man-in-the-middle attacks.

Second, even those applications that install CA certificates and use them to validate server certificates often fail to perform adequate checking on the contents of the certificate. As a result, such systems are susceptible to man-in-the-middle attacks in which the attacker gets his hands on credentials that will look legitimate to the client, such as a stolen set of credentials in which the certificate is signed by the CA that has not yet appeared on any CRLs.

The best solution for thwarting this problem depends on the authentication needs of the client. Many applications can expect that they will only legitimately talk to a small set of servers. In such a case, you can check appropriate fields in the certificate against a white list of valid server names. For example, you might allow any certificate signed by VeriSign in which the fully qualified domain name mentioned in the certificate ends with "yourcompany.com". Another option is to hardcode a list of known server certificates. However, this is a far more difficult solution to manage if you ever wish to add servers.

Additionally, if you do not wish to trust the authentication mechanisms of the established CAs, you could consider running your own CA, which we discuss in

Chapter 3 (of course, we are assuming you control both the client and server code in such a situation). In environments where you expect that anyone can set up their own server, and thus managing DNS space or your own Certification Authority is not feasible, then the best you can do is ensure that the DNS address for the server that the client tried to contact is the same as the one presented in the certificate. If that is true, and the certificate was signed by a valid CA, everything should be fine if the certificate was not stolen or fraudulently obtained.

Poor Entropy

In the SSL protocol, both the client and the server need to generate random data for keys and other secrets. The data must be generated in such a way that a knowledgeable attacker cannot guess anything about it. SSL implementations usually generate such data using a *pseudorandom number generator* (PRNG). PRNGs are deterministic algorithms that produce a series of random-looking numbers. Classical PRNGs are not suitable for use in security-critical situations. Instead, SSL implementations use "cryptographic" PRNGs, which work in security-critical situations, as long as they are "seeded" properly.

A *seed* is a piece of data fed to the PRNG to get it going. Given a single, known seed at startup, the PRNG should produce a predictable set of outputs. That is, if you seed the PRNG and ask for three random numbers, reseed with the same value, and then ask for three more random numbers, the first three numbers and the second three numbers should be identical.

The seed itself must be a random number, but it can't just be a cryptographically random number. It must be truly unguessable to keep the PRNG outputs unguessable. *Entropy* is a measurement of how much unguessable information actually exists in data from the point of view of an attacker who might be able to make reasonable guesses about the state of the machine on which the number is stored. If a single bit is just as likely to be a 0 as a 1, then it is one bit of entropy. If you have 128 bits of data, it can have up to 128 bits of entropy. However, it may have as little as 0 bits of entropy—as would be the case if the data's value is public knowledge. The work an attacker must do to guess a piece of data is directly related to how much entropy there is in the data. If the data has 4 bits of entropy, then the attacker has a 1 in 2^4 chance (1 in 16) chance of guessing right the first time. Additionally, within 16 guesses, the attacker will have tried the right value (On average, he will find the right value in 8 guesses). If the data has 128 bits of entropy in it, then the attacker will need, on average 2^{127} guesses to find the seed, which is such a large number as to be infeasible for all practical purposes. In practice, if you're using 128-bit keys, it's desirable to use a seed with 128 bits of entropy or more. Anything less than 64 bits of entropy can probably be broken quickly by an organization with a modest hardware budget.

To illustrate, in 1996, Ian Goldberg and David Wagner found a problem with the way Netscape was seeding its PRNG in its implementation of SSLv2. Netscape was using three inputs hashed with the MD5 message digest algorithm, the time of day, the process ID, and the parent process ID. None of these values is particularly random. At most, their PRNG seed could have had 47 bits of entropy. A clever attacker could decrease that substantially. Indeed, in practice, Goldberg and Wagner were able to compromise real SSL sessions within 25 seconds.

If you try to use OpenSSL without bothering to seed the random number generator, the library will complain. However, the library has no real way to know whether the seed you give it contains enough entropy. Therefore, you must have some idea how to get entropy. There are certainly hardware devices that do a good job of collecting it, including most of the cryptographic accelerator cards. However, in many cases hardware is impractical, because your software will be deployed across a large number of clients, most of whom will have no access to such devices.

Many software tricks are commonly employed for collecting entropy on a machine. They tend to work by indirectly measuring random information in external events that affect the machine. You should never need to worry about those actual techniques. Instead, use a package that harvests entropy for you. Many Unix-based operating systems now come with a random device, which provides entropy harvested by the operating system. On other Unix systems, you can use tools such as EGADS (*http://www.securesw.com/egads/*), which is a portable entropy collection system.* EGADS also works on Windows systems.

If you're interested in the entropy harvesting techniques behind random devices and tools like EGADS, see Chapter 10 of the book *Building Secure Software* by John Viega and Gary McGraw (Addison-Wesley).

Insecure Cryptography

While Version 3 of the SSL protocol and TLS are believed to be reasonably secure if used properly,† SSLv2 (Version 2) had fundamental design problems that led to wide-ranging changes in subsequent versions (Version 1 was never publicly deployed). For this reason, you should not support Version 2 of the protocol, just to ensure that an attacker does not launch a network attack that causes the client and server to settle upon the insecure version of the protocol. All you need to do is intercept the connection request and send a response that makes it look like a v3 server does not exist. The client will then try to connect using Version 2 of the protocol.

---

* We realize that Linux isn't technically a Unix operating system, since it is not derived from the original Unix code base. However, we feel the common usage of the term Unix extends to any Unix-like operating system, and that's how we use this term throughout the book.

† While a Netscape engineer designed previous versions of SSL, Paul Kocher, a well-regarded cryptographer, designed Version 3 of the protocol, and it has subsequently seen significant review, especially during the standardization process that led to TLS.

Unfortunately, people commonly configure their clients and servers to handle both versions of the protocol. Don't do that. Support only SSLv3 and TLS, to whatever degree possible. Note that clients can't really support TLS only, because TLS implementations are supposed to be able to speak SSLv3. If you wish to use only TLS in a client, you must connect then terminate the connection if the server chooses SSLv3.

As we mentioned when discussing different types of cryptographic algorithms, you should also avoid small key lengths and, to a lesser degree, algorithms that aren't well regarded. 40-bit keys are never secure and neither is 56-bit DES. Nonetheless, it's common to see servers that support only these weak keys, due to old U.S. export regulations that no longer apply.

As for individual algorithm choices in SSL, RC4 and 3DES are both excellent solutions. RC4 is much faster, and 3DES is more conservative. Soon, TLS will be standardizing on AES, at which time this will be widely regarded as a good choice.

Note that the server generally picks a cipher based on a list of supported ciphers that the client presents. We recommend supporting only strong ciphers in the server, where feasible. In other cases, make sure to prefer the strongest cipher the client offers. We discuss cipher selection in detail in Chapter 5.

What SSL Doesn't Do Well

SSL is a great general-purpose algorithm for securing network connections. So far, we've seen the important risks with SSL that you must avoid. Here, we'll look at those things people would like SSL to do, even though it doesn't really do them well (or at all).

Other Transport Layer Protocols

SSL works well with TCP/IP. However, it doesn't work at all with transport layer protocols that are not connection-oriented, such as UDP and IPX. There's not really a way to make it work for such protocols, either. Secure encryption of protocols in which order and reliability are not ensured is a challenge, and is outside the scope of SSL. We do outline solutions for encrypting UDP traffic in Chapter 6.

Non-Repudiation

Let's say that Alice and Bob are communicating over SSL. Alice may receive a message from Bob that she would like to show to Charlie, and she would like to prove that she received the message from Bob. If that was possible, the message would be *non-repudiated*, meaning that Bob cannot deny that he sent the message. For example, Alice may receive a receipt for a product, and wish to demonstrate that she purchased the product for tax purposes.

SSL has no support for non-repudiation. However, it is simple to add on top of SSL, if both Alice and Bob have well-established certificates. In such a case, they can sign each message before SSL-encrypting it. Of course, in such a situation, if Bob wishes to have a message he can repudiate, he just attaches an invalid signature. In such a case, Alice should refuse further communications.

In Chapter 10, we discuss how to sign encrypted messages using S/MIME. This same technique can be used for sending messages over SSL by signing the data before sending it. Alternatively, S/MIME messages could simply be sent over an SSL connection to achieve the same result.

Protection Against Software Flaws

Sometimes SSL fails to secure an application because of a fundamental security flaw in the application itself, not because of any actual problem in SSL's design. That is, SSL doesn't protect against buffer overflows, race conditions, protocol errors, or any other design or implementation flaws in the application that uses SSL.

Even though there are many common risks when deploying SSL, those risks are often minor compared to the gaping holes in software design and implementation. Attackers will tend to target the weakest link, and SSL is often not the weakest link.

Developers should thoroughly educate themselves on building secure software. For administrators deploying other people's software, try to use well-regarded software if you have any option whatsoever.

General-Purpose Data Security

SSL can protect data in transit on a live connection, but it provides no facilities for protecting data before it is sent, or after it arrives at its destination. Additionally, if there is no active connection, SSL can do nothing. For any other data security needs, other solutions are necessary.

OpenSSL Basics

Now that you have a good understanding of cryptography basics, and have seen the SSL protocol at a high level (warts and all), it's time to look specifically at the OpenSSL library. OpenSSL is a derived work from SSLeay. SSLeay was originally written by Eric A. Young and Tim J. Hudson beginning in 1995. In December 1998, development of SSLeay ceased, and the first version of OpenSSL was released as 0.9.1c, using SSLeay 0.9.1b (which was never actually released) as its starting point. OpenSSL is essentially two tools in one: a cryptography library and an SSL toolkit.

The SSL library provides an implementation of all versions of the SSL protocol, including TLSv1. The cryptography library provides the most popular algorithms for symmetric key and public key cryptography, hash algorithms, and message digests. It also provides a pseudorandom number generator, and support for manipulating common certificate formats and managing key material. There are also general-purpose helper libraries for buffer manipulation and manipulation of arbitrary precision numbers. Additionally, OpenSSL supports most common cryptographic acceleration hardware (prior to Version 0.9.7, forthcoming as of this writing, hardware support is available only by downloading the separate "engine" release).

OpenSSL is the only free, full-featured SSL implementation currently available for use with the C and C++ programming languages. It works across every major platform, including all Unix OSs and all common versions of Microsoft Windows.

OpenSSL is available for download in source form from *http://www.openssl.org/*. Detailed installation instructions for a variety of platforms, including Unix, Windows, Mac OS (versions prior to Mac OS X), and OpenVMS are included in the source distribution. If you're installing on Mac OS X, you should follow the Unix instructions.* The instructions for Mac OS and OpenVMS are very specific for their respective platforms, so we'll not discuss them here. Instead, we recommend that you read and follow the instructions included with the source distribution carefully.

Installations on Unix and Windows have similar requirements; they both require Perl and a C compiler. On Windows systems, Borland C++, Visual C++, and the GNU C compilers are supported. If you want to use the assembly language optimizations on Windows, you'll also need either MASM or NASM. The details of how to build on Windows vary depending on which compiler you're using and whether you're using the assembly language optimizations. We recommend that you refer to the included installation instructions for full details.

The process of building OpenSSL on Unix and Windows systems involves first running a configuration script that is included in the distribution. The configuration script examines the environment on which it's running in to determine what libraries and options are available. Using that information, it builds the make scripts. On Unix systems, the configuration script is named *config*; it figures some Unix-specific parameters and then runs the *Configure* script, which is written in Perl. On Windows systems, *Configure* is run directly. Example 1-1 shows the basic steps necessary to build on a Unix system.

Example 1-1. Building and installing OpenSSL on a Unix system

```
$ ./config
$ make
$ make test # This step is optional.
$ su  # You need to be root to "make install"
# make install
```

---

* OS X comes with the OpenSSL library preinstalled, but it is usually not the most current version. Additionally, if you are a developer, the OpenSSL header files are most likely not installed.

Once the configuration script has been run, the source is ready to be compiled. This is normally achieved by running the make program. If you're building on Windows with Visual C++, you'll need to use the nmake program. On Unix systems, once the build is complete, some optional tests can be run to ensure that the library was built properly. This is done by running make test, as shown in Example 1-1.

When the library is finally built and optionally tested, it's ready to be installed. On Unix systems, this is done by running make again and specifying a target of install. On Windows systems, there is no install process, per se. You'll need to create directories for the header files, import libraries, dynamic load libraries, and the command-line tool. You can place the files anywhere you like, but you should make sure that you put the DLLs and command-line tool into a directory that is in your path.

Securing Third-Party Software

While much of this book focuses on how to use the OpenSSL API to add security to your own applications, you'll often want to use OpenSSL to secure other people's applications. Many applications are already built to support OpenSSL. For example, OpenSSH uses the OpenSSL cryptography foundation extensively, and requires the library to be present before it can compile. In this particular case, the normal process of installing the software will take care of all the details, as long as you have a version of OpenSSL installed in a well-known place on the system. Otherwise, you can explicitly specify the location of OpenSSL when configuring the software.

OpenSSH is special, because it requires OpenSSL to function. However, many other software packages can support OpenSSL as an option. MySQL is a great example. Simply configure the package with two options, --with-openssl and --with-vio, and the package will build with SSL support.*

Sometimes it would be nice to use SSL for encrypting arbitrary protocols without actually modifying the source code implementing the protocol. For example, you may have a preferred POP3 implementation that does not support SSL. You'd like to make an SSL-enabled version available, but you have no desire to hack OpenSSL into the code.

In most cases, you can use Stunnel (*http://www.stunnel.org/*) to SSL-enable arbitrary protocols, which it does by proxying. Stunnel in and of itself is not a complete tool—it requires OpenSSL to run.

You can use Stunnel to protect HTTP traffic. However, it's generally better to use the web server's preferred SSL solution. For example, Apache's mod_ssl (see *http://www. modssl.org*) is a far better solution for Apache users than Stunnel, because it is far

---

* By default, MySQL connections are not encrypted, even after compiling with SSL. You have to explicitly state that a particular user connects with SSL. See the MySQL GRANT documentation for details.

more configurable. And, under the hood, mod_ssl also uses the OpenSSL library. The details of mod_ssl are beyond the scope of this book. For more information on this topic, refer to the mod_ssl web site or the book *Apache: The Definitive Guide*, by Ben Laurie and Peter Laurie (O'Reilly).

Server-Side Proxies

Let's say that we want to run SSL-enabled POP3 on the standard port for this (995). If we already have the unencrypted POP3 server running on port 110, we simply put Stunnel on port 995, and tell it to forward connections to port 110 on the loopback interface (so that unencrypted data isn't sent over your local network, just to come back onto the current machine). When SSL-enabled POP3 clients connect to port 995, Stunnel will negotiate the connection, connect itself to the POP3 port, then start decrypting data. When it has data to pass on to the POP3 server, it does so. Similarly, when the POP3 server responds to a client request, it talks with the Stunnel proxy, which encrypts the response, and passes it on to the client. See Figure 1-5 for a graphical overview of the process.

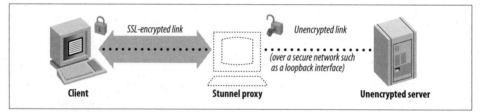

Figure 1-5. Stunnel proxies

To use Stunnel on the server side, you must install a valid server certificate and private key. An appropriate Certification Authority should sign the certificate. You can generate your own credentials using OpenSSL. That process is covered in Chapter 3.

These server credentials will need to be made available to Stunnel. Often, the correct location of these credentials will be hardcoded into the Stunnel binary. If not, you can specify their location on the command line.

Assuming the POP3 server is already running, here is how you would run Stunnel from the command line to implement the above scenario (assuming that you're running as root, which is necessary for binding to low ports on Unix machines):

```
# stunnel -d 995 -r 127.0.0.1:110
```

The -d flag specifies that Stunnel should run as a proxy in daemon mode on the specified port (you can also specify the IP address on which to bind; the default is all IPs on the machine). The -r flag specifies the location of the service to which Stunnel will proxy. In this case, we specifically mention the loopback address to avoid exposing unencrypted traffic to other hosts on the same local network. Optionally, we could hide the port from external eyes using a firewall.

The location of the certificate file can be specified with the -p flag, if necessary. If your machine's services file contains entries for the POP3 and the Secure POP3 protocol, you can also run Stunnel like this:

```
# stunnel -d pop3s -r 127.0.0.1:pop3
```

You can also run Stunnel from inetd. However, this is generally not desirable, because you forego the efficiency benefits of session caching. If you're running on Windows, Stunnel is available as a precompiled binary, and can be easily launched from a DOS-style batch file. See the Stunnel FAQ (*http://www.stunnel.org/faq*) for more details.

Unfortunately, Stunnel can't protect all the services you might want to run. First, it can protect only TCP connections, not UDP connections. Second, it can't really protect protocols like FTP that use out-of-band connections. The FTP daemon can bind to arbitrary ports, and there's no good way to have Stunnel detect it. Also, note that some clients that support SSL-enabled versions of a protocol will expect to negotiate SSL as an option. In such cases, the client won't be able to communicate with the Stunnel proxy, unless it goes through an SSL proxy on the client end as well.

Since Stunnel will proxy to whatever address you tell it to use, you can certainly proxy to services running on other machines. You can use this ability to offload the cost of establishing SSL connections to a machine by itself, providing a cost-effective way of accelerating SSL. In such a scenario, the unencrypted server should be connected only to the SSL proxy by a crossover cable, and should be connected to no other machines. That way, the unencrypted data won't be visible to other machines on your network, even if they are compromised. If you have a load balancer, you can handle even more SSL connections by installing additional proxies (see Figure 1-6). For most applications, a single server is sufficient to handle the unencrypted load.

The biggest problem with using Stunnel as a proxy is that IP header information that would normally be available to the server isn't. In particular, the server may log IP addresses with each transaction. Since the server is actually talking to the proxy, from the server's point of view, every single connection will appear to come from the proxy's IP address. Stunnel provides a limited solution to this problem. If the secure port is on a Linux machine, then the Stunnel process can be configured to rewrite the IP headers, thus providing transparent proxying. Simply adding the -T flag to the command line does this. For transparent proxying to work this way, the client's default route to the unencrypted server must go through the proxy machine, and the route cannot go through the loopback interface.

Stunnel can be configured to log connections to a file by specifying the -o flag and a filename. That at least allows you to get information about connecting IP addresses (which should never be used for security purposes anyway, since they are easy to forge), even when transparent proxying is not an option.

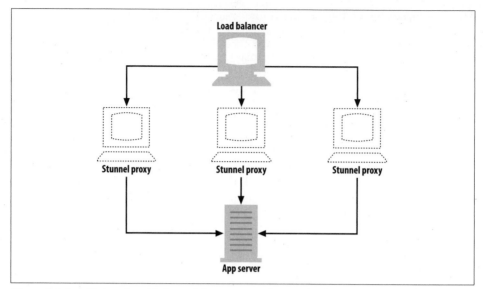

Figure 1-6. Load balancing with Stunnel for cryptographic acceleration

Client-Side Proxies

Stunnel can also be used to connect clients that are SSL-unaware with servers that do speak the protocol. Setting up a client-side proxy is a bit more work than setting up a server-side proxy because, while clients are usually authenticated using some sort of password mechanism, servers are authenticated primarily using cryptographic certificates. You can set up the client not to authenticate, but if you do so, be warned that man-in-the-middle attacks will be easy to perform. Unauthenticating client proxies only buys you security against the most naïve eavesdropping attacks, but is still better than no protection at all.

Let's start with a case in which we are not yet validating certificates. Let's say that we'd like to connect to Amazon.com's SSL-enabled web server, running on port 443 on *www.amazon.com*. First, we can interactively test the connection by running Stunnel in client mode (specified by the -c flag):

```
$ stunnel -c -r www.amazon.com:443
```

Stunnel silently connects. We type in an HTTP request, and get back the appropriate response. For example:

```
GET /
<!DOCTYPE HTML PUBLIC "-//IETF//DTD HTML 2.0//EN">
<HTML><HEAD>
<TITLE>302 Found</TITLE>
</HEAD><BODY>
<H1>Found</H1>
The document has moved <A HREF="http://www.amazon.com/">here</A>.<P>
</BODY></HTML>
```

After sending its response, the server closes the connection.

As you can see, we can talk with the SSL-enabled web server running on Amazon.com, yet the SSL handling is completely transparent from our point of view.

Running Stunnel in interactive mode is useful for the purposes of debugging. However, interactive mode is not practical for use with arbitrary clients. Let's say we wish to point an SSL-unaware POP3 client at an SSL-enabled POP3 server running on *mail.example.com*. On the machine running the client, we would like to set up a proxy that only accepts connections from the local machine, and then makes connections on behalf of the local machine to the SSL-enabled server. We can easily do that with the following command:

```
# stunnel -c -r mail.example.com:pop3s -d 127.0.0.1:pop3
```

This command sets up a proxy on the local machine that does what we want it to. Now we can simply point our mail client to our loopback interface, and we will magically connect to the intended SSL-enabled POP3 server (assuming no man-in-the-middle attacks).

Note that the above command will work only if you have permission to bind to the POP3 port locally. If that is an issue, and your POP client can connect to servers on arbitrary ports, the problem is easy to fix. Otherwise, you'll need to grant the proxy process root privileges, or find a new client. Root privileges pose a big risk, because there may be an obscure security bug in Stunnel that would allow data passing through the proxy to gain root privileges. If you do choose to grant the proxy root privileges, on most operating systems you should probably run the proxy as root, and then use the -s flag to specify a username to switch to after the port is bound. You might consider making the binary setuid—but you shouldn't, because you would then let any user bind to privileged ports as long as he can run the Stunnel binary.

As we mentioned previously, you should always have client proxies perform certificate validation. To use certificate validation, you must specify where on the client machine valid CA certificates live, and you must specify the level of validation you want. We recommend maximum validation (level 3), and we think you should completely stay away from level 1, since it offers no real validation. Here's an extension of the above example that takes into account certificate validation:

```
# stunnel -c -r mail.example.com:pop3s -d 127.0.0.1:pop3 -A /etc/ca_certs -v 2
```

The file */etc/ca_certs* stores a list of trusted CA certificates (see Chapter 3 for more information on obtaining such certificates). Unfortunately, Stunnel doesn't support validation based on domain-name matching. If you wish to restrict valid servers to a small set (usually a very good idea), you can use validation level 3 (the maximum), and place the known certificates in a directory of their own. The certificate's filename must be the hash value of the certificate's subjected (see the -hash option to the x509 command in Chapter 2 to find out how to generate this value), with a ".0" file extension. Additionally, you use the -a flag to specify where valid server certificates live. For example:

```
# stunnel -c -r mail.example.com:pop3s -d 127.0.0.1:pop3 -A /etc/ca_certs -a
/etc/server_certs -v 3
```

Again, we talk more about certificate formats in Chapter 3.

As with server-side SSL proxies, there are some situations in which client-side use of Stunnel isn't appropriate. Once again, it doesn't make sense to use Stunnel in a UDP-based environment or with a protocol that makes out-of-band connections. Additionally, some servers that support SSL expect to negotiate whether or not to use it. These servers won't understand a connection that is encrypted with SSL from start to finish. Such negotiation is especially popular with SSL-enabled SMTP servers.

Stunnel has support for negotiating some of the more common protocols. To use that support, invoke Stunnel in the same way as in the previous client-side example, but add the -n argument, which takes a single argument (the name of the protocol). Currently, SSL supports SMTP, POP3, and NNTP. For example, to connect to a secure SMTP server over SSL, use the command:

```
# stunnel -c -r mail.example.com:smtp -d 127.0.0.1:smtp -A /etc/ca_certs -a /etc/
server_certs -v 3 -n smtp
```

Unfortunately, as of this writing, Stunnel doesn't support any other protocols for which SSL is a negotiated option, most notably SSL-TELNET.

## CHAPTER 2

Command-Line Interface

OpenSSL is primarily a library that is used by developers to include support for strong cryptography in their programs, but it is also a tool that provides access to much of its functionality from the command line. The command-line tool makes it easy to perform common operations, such as computing the MD5 hash of a file's contents. What's more, the command-line tool provides the ability to access much of OpenSSL's higher-level functionality from shell scripts on Unix or batch files on Windows. It also provides a simple interface for languages that do not have native SSL bindings, but can run shell commands.

There's no question that the command-line tool can seem quite complex to the uninitiated. It sports a large set of commands, and even larger sets of options that can be used to further refine and control those commands. OpenSSL does come with some documentation that covers most of the available commands and options supported by the command-line tool, but even that documentation can seem intimidating. Indeed, when you're trying to discover the magical incantation to create a self-signed certificate, the documentation provided with OpenSSL does not provide an intuitive way to go about finding that information, even though it is in fact buried in there.

This chapter contains an overview of the command-line tool, providing some basic background information that will help make some sense of how the tool's command structure is organized. We'll also provide a high-level overview of how to accomplish many common tasks, including using message digests, symmetric ciphers, and public key cryptography. The Appendix contains a reference for the commands that the command-line tool supports.

We will refer to the command-line tool throughout this book, and, in some instances, we also provide examples that are more complex than what we've included in this chapter. In particular, Chapter 3 makes extensive use of the command-line tool.

The Basics

The command-line tool executable is aptly named *openssl* on Unix, and *openssl.exe* on Windows. It has two modes of operation: interactive and batch. When the program is started without any options, it will enter interactive mode. When operating in interactive mode, a prompt is displayed indicating that it is ready to process your command. After each command is completed, the prompt is redisplayed, and it's once again ready to process another command. The program can be exited by simply issuing the quit command. Commands entered in interactive mode are handled in precisely the same manner as if you'd entered them from the command line in batch mode; the only difference is that you don't need to type "openssl" before each command. We'll normally operate the tool in batch mode in our examples, but if you feel more comfortable using the interactive mode, that's fine.

The first part of a command is the name of the command itself. It's followed by any options that you wish to specify, each one separated by a space. Options normally begin with a hyphen and often require a parameter of their own, in which case the parameter is placed after a space.

Unless indicated otherwise, the order in which you specify options is not significant. There are only a small number of cases in which the order is significant, usually because a specific option must appear on the command line as the last option specified.

Configuration Files

The command-line tool provides a large number of options for each of its many commands. Remembering the option names, their defaults if they're not specified, and even to include them with a command to obtain the desired result can be difficult, if not downright frustrating at times. The task of managing options is made considerably simpler using configuration files.

OpenSSL includes a default configuration file that is normally used unless an alternate one is specified. The settings in the default configuration are all quite reasonable, but it can often be useful to replace them with settings that are better tailored to your own needs. The location of the default configuration file varies greatly, depending on the operating system that you're using and how OpenSSL was built and installed. So, unfortunately, we can't point you to any one specific location to find it. Although it is not at all intuitive, the command-line tool will tell you where the default configuration file is located if you issue the ca command without any options. Any errors that are issued due to the lack of options may be safely ignored.

Unfortunately, only three of the many commands supported by the command-line tool make any use of the configuration file. On the bright side, the three commands that do use it are perhaps the most complex of all of the supported commands, and accept the greatest number of options to control their behavior. The commands that do support the configuration file are ca, req, and x509 (we discuss these commands below).

An OpenSSL configuration file is organized in sections. Each section contains a set of keys, and each key has an associated value. Sections and keys are both named and case-sensitive. A configuration file is parsed from top to bottom with sections delimited by a line containing the name of the section surrounded by square brackets. The other lines contain key and value pairs that belong to the most recently parsed section delimiter. In addition, an optional global section that is unnamed occurs before the first named section in the file. Keys are separated from their associated value by an equals sign (=).

For the most part, whitespace is insignificant. Comments may begin anywhere on a line with a hash mark (#), and they end at the end of the line on which they begin. Key and section names may not contain whitespace, but they may be surrounded by it. Leading and trailing whitespace is stripped from a value, but any whitespace in the middle is significant. Example 2-1 shows an excerpt from the default OpenSSL configuration file.

Example 2-1. An excerpt from the default OpenSSL configuration file

```
[ ca ]
default_ca      = CA_default           # The default ca section


####################################################################
[ CA_default ]

dir             = ./demoCA             # Where everything is kept
certs           = $dir/certs           # Where the issued certs are kept
crl_dir         = $dir/crl             # Where the issued crl are kept
database        = $dir/index.txt       # database index file
new_certs_dir   = $dir/newcerts        # default place for new certs

certificate     = $dir/cacert.pem      # The CA certificate
serial          = $dir/serial          # The current serial number
crl             = $dir/crl.pem         # The current CRL
private_key     = $dir/private/cakey.pem# The private key
RANDFILE        = $dir/private/.rand    # private random number file

x509_extensions = usr_cert             # The extentions to add to the cert

# Extensions to add to a CRL. Note: Netscape communicator chokes on V2 CRLs
# so this is commented out by default to leave a V1 CRL.
# crl_extensions        = crl_ext

default_days    = 365                  # how long to certify for
default_crl_days= 30                   # how long before next CRL
default_md      = md5                  # which md to use
preserve        = no                   # keep passed DN ordering

# A few difference way of specifying how similar the request should look
# For type CA, the listed attributes must be the same, and the optional
# and supplied fields are just that :-)
policy          = policy_match
```

In the example, you'll notice the use of $dir. Used in a value, a key name preceded by a dollar sign is known as a macro, and is replaced with the value for that key. Only macros using keys that are defined within the same section or in the global section will be expanded. Additionally, the key must be defined before you use it as a macro in a value, because the macro is expanded as the configuration file parses rather than when the value is used. Macros are particularly useful when you have a number of values referencing the same path in a filename.

Although only a few commands currently make any use of a configuration file, other commands may be modified in the future to take advantage of them. Each command that currently uses the configuration file reads its base configuration information from a section that shares the name of the command. Other sections that are not named after a command may exist, and quite frequently, they do. Many keys' values are interpreted as the name of a section to use for finding more keys. We'll see frequent examples of this as we examine the commands that do use the configuration file in detail.

Message Digest Algorithms

In Chapter 1, we introduced cryptographic hash functions, better known as message digest algorithms, which can be used for computing a checksum of a block of data. OpenSSL includes support for MD2, MD4, MD5, MDC2, SHA1 (sometimes called DSS1), and RIPEMD-160. SHA1 and RIPEMD-160 produce 160-bit hashes, and the others all produce 128-bit hashes. Unless you have a need for compatibility, we recommend that you use only SHA1 or RIPEMD-160. Both SHA1 and RIPEMD-160 provide excellent security for general-purpose use, but SHA1 is significantly more common. MD5 is a very popular message digest algorithm, but it does not have a good security margin for all applications. We discuss message digests in detail in Chapter 7.

OpenSSL handles SHA1 oddly. There are places where you must refer to it as DSS1 (the dgst command, described later), and there are places where you cannot refer to it as DSS1 (everywhere else). This is a limitation of the implementation. Use SHA1 as the name, unless we specifically mention that you need to use DSS1.

The command-line tool provides commands for using most of the supported algorithms. The dgst command is the main command for accessing message digests, but most of the algorithms can be accessed using a command of the same name as the algorithm. The exception is RIPEMD-160, which is named rmd160.

When using the dgst command, the algorithm is specified using an option with the name of the algorithm, with the exception of RIPEMD-160, which also uses the name rmd160 for this interface. Regardless of the algorithm or form of the command, each of the algorithms accepts the same options to control how the command will function.

The default operation performed with any of the message digest commands is computing a hash for a block of data. That block of data can be read from stdin, or it can be one or more files. When more than one file is used, a separate hash is computed for each file. By default, the computed hash or hashes are written in hexadecimal format to stdout, unless an alternate output file is specified.

In addition to computing hashes, the message digest commands can also be used for signing and verifying signatures. When signing or verifying a signature, only one file should be used at a time; otherwise, the signatures will run together and end up being difficult to separate into a usable form. When signing, a signature is generated for the hash of the file to be signed. A private key is required to sign, and either RSA or DSA may be used. When you use a DSA private key, you must use the DSS1 message digest (even though it is the same as the SHA1 algorithm). You may use any algorithm other than DSS1 with an RSA private key. Verifying a signature is simply the reverse of signing. Normally, a public key is required to verify a signature, but a private key will work, too, because a public key can be derived from the private key, but not vice versa! When verifying a signature with an RSA key, public or private, you'll also need to know which message digest algorithm was used to generate the signature.

Examples

The following examples illustrate the use of the message digest commands:

```
$ openssl dgst -sha1 file.txt
```
Computes an SHA1 hash for the file named *file.txt* and write it to stdout in hexadecimal form.

```
$ openssl sha1 -out digest.txt file.txt
```
Computes an SHA1 hash for the file named *file.txt* and write it in hexadecimal form to the file named *digest.txt*.

```
$ openssl dgst -dss1 -sign dsakey.pem -out dsasign.bin file.txt
```
Signs the SHA1 (DSS1) hash of the file named *file.txt* using the DSA private key in the file *dsakey.pem* and write the signature out to the file *dsasign.bin*. The PEM file format is a widely used format for storing cryptographic objects such as private keys, certificates, and so on. The "bin" extension indicates that the output is raw binary.

```
$ openssl dgst -dss1 -prverify dsakey.pem -signature dsasign.bin file.txt
```
Verifies the signature of the file named *file.txt* that is contained in the file *dsasign.bin* using the SHA1 (DSS1) message digest algorithm and the DSA private key from the file *dsakey.pem*.

```
$ openssl sha1 -sign rsaprivate.pem -out rsasign.bin file.txt
```
Signs the SHA1 hash of the file named *file.txt* using the RSA private key in the file *rsaprivate.pem* and write the signature out to the file *rsasign.bin*.

```
$ openssl sha1 -verify rsapublic.pem -signature rsasign.bin file.txt
```
Verifies the signature of the file named *file.txt* that is contained in the file *rsasign.bin* using the SHA1 message digest algorithm and the RSA public key from the file *rsapublic.pem*.

Symmetric Ciphers

OpenSSL supports a wide variety of symmetric ciphers. Of course, these ciphers are also available for use with the command-line tool. Many of the large number of ciphers are variations of a base cipher. The basic ciphers supported by the command-line tool are Blowfish, CAST5, DES, 3DES (Triple DES), IDEA, RC2, RC4, and RC5. Version 0.9.7 of OpenSSL adds support for AES. Most of the supported symmetric ciphers support a variety of different modes, including CBC, CFB, ECB, and OFB. For each cipher, the default mode is always CBC if a mode is not explicitly specified. Each of the supported symmetric ciphers and their various modes of operation are discussed in detail in Chapter 6. In particular, it is important to mention that you should generally never use ECB, because it is incredibly difficult to use securely.

The enc command is the main command for accessing symmetric ciphers, but each cipher can also be accessed using a command of the same name as the cipher. With the enc command, the cipher is specified using an option with the name of the cipher. Regardless of the cipher or form of the command that is used, each of the ciphers accepts the same options to control how the command will function. In addition to providing encryption and decryption of data with symmetric ciphers, the base64 command or option to the enc command can also be used for encoding and decoding of data in base64.

The default operation to be performed with any of the cipher commands is to encrypt or base64 encode the data. Normally, data is read from stdin and written to stdout, but input and output files may be specified. Only a single file can be encrypted, decrypted, base64 encoded, or base64 decoded at a time. When encrypting or decrypting, an option can be specified to perform base64 encoding after encryption or base64 decoding before decryption.

Each of the ciphers requires a key when encryption or decryption is performed. Recall from the brief discussion of symmetric ciphers in Chapter 1 that the key is what provides the security of a symmetric cipher. In contrast with traditional cryptographic techniques, modern cipher algorithms are widely available to be scrutinized by anyone that has the time and interest. The key used to encrypt data must be known only to you and the intended recipient or recipients of the encrypted data.

A password is often used to derive a key and initialization vector that will encrypt or decrypt the data. It is also possible to specify the key and initialization vector to be used explicitly, but supplying that information on your own is often prone to error. In addition, different ciphers have different key requirements, so supplying your own key requires in-depth knowledge of the particular cipher. The password can be specified with the pass option, according to the general guidelines for passwords and passphrases outlined later in this chapter. If no password or key information is specified, the tool will present a prompt to obtain it.

If you specify a password or passphrase to derive the key and initialization vector, the command-line tool uses a standard OpenSSL function to perform the task. Essentially, the password or passphrase that you specify is combined with a *salt*. The salt that is used in this case is simply eight random bytes. The MD5 hash of the combined salt and password or passphrase is then computed and broken into two parts, which are then used as the key and initialization vector.

Examples

The following examples illustrate the use of the symmetric cipher commands:

```
$ openssl enc -des3 -salt -in plaintext.doc -out ciphertext.bin
```
Encrypts the contents of the file *plaintext.doc* using DES3 in CBC mode and places the resulting ciphertext into *ciphertext.bin*. Since no password or key parameters were specified, a prompt for a password from which a key can be derived will be presented.

```
$ openssl enc -des3-ede-ofb -d -in ciphertext.bin -out plaintext.doc -pass
pass:trousers
```
Decrypts the contents of the file *ciphertext.bin* using DES3 operating in OFB mode and places the resulting plaintext into *plaintext.doc*. The password "trousers" will be used to decrypt the file. Note that this example will not successfully decrypt the file from the previous example, since we used a different mode of encryption (CBC instead of OFB).

```
$ openssl bf-cfb -salt -in plaintext.doc -out ciphertext.bin -pass env:PASSWORD
```
Encrypts the contents of the file *plaintext.doc* using the Blowfish cipher in CFB mode and places the resulting ciphertext into *ciphertext.bin*. The contents of the environment variable PASSWORD will be used for the password to generate the key.

```
$ openssl base64 -in ciphertext.bin -out base64.txt
```
Encodes the contents of the file *ciphertext.bin* in base64 and writes the result to the file *base64.txt*.

```
$ openssl rc5 -in plaintext.doc -out ciphertext.bin -S C62CB1D49F158ADC -iv
E9EDACA1BD7090C6 -K 89D4B1678D604FAA3DBFFD030A314B29
```
Encrypts the contents of the file *plaintext.doc* using the RC5 cipher in CBC mode and places the resulting ciphertext into *ciphertext.bin*. The specified salt, key, and initialization vector will be used to encrypt the plaintext. Keys are specified by their hexadecimal representation.

The Appendix gives a complete list of algorithms used to perform symmetric encryption.

Public Key Cryptography

The SSL protocol relies heavily on a variety of different cryptographic algorithms, including message digest algorithms, symmetric ciphers, and public key cryptography.

Its use of most of these algorithms is generally done without the need for any human intervention. A common exception, though, is its use of public key cryptography. For example, in order for a server to employ the SSL protocol, it requires a private key and a *certificate*. The certificate contains the public key that matches the server's private key. These keys must be created as part of the process for configuring the server to use SSL, and they are frequently not created automatically. Instead, they must be created by whoever is configuring the server.

SSL isn't the only protocol that makes use of public key cryptography. Most modern software that supports encrypted communications uses it, too. Some of the more popular examples include SSH, PGP (Pretty Good Privacy), and S/MIME. All of these examples use public key cryptography in some form, and we're overlooking many other applications as well. We discuss OpenSSL's support for public key cryptography in detail in Chapter 8.

Diffie-Hellman

Diffie-Hellman is used for *key agreement*. In simple terms, key agreement is the exchange of information over an insecure medium that allows each of the two parties in a conversation to compute a value that is typically used as the key for a symmetric cipher. By itself, Diffie-Hellman cannot be used for encryption or authentication; it only provides secrecy. Because the exchange of information takes place over an insecure medium, it should never be used by itself. Some means of authenticating the parties in the conversation should also be used.

Diffie-Hellman works by first creating a set of parameters that are agreed upon by both parties in the conversation. The parameters, consisting of a randomly chosen prime number and a *generator* value that is typically specified as either 2 or 5, are public and can be either agreed upon before the conversation begins or exchanged as part of the conversation. Using the agreed-upon parameters, each party computes a public and private key. As its name implies, the private key is never shared with anyone. The parties exchange their public keys, and then each party can compute the shared secret using their private key and the peer's public key.

The command-line tool provides a command for generating Diffie-Hellman parameters, but the only method for generating keys is deprecated, and should not be used. OpenSSL 0.9.5 added the dhparam command, and in doing so, deprecated the two commands dh and gendh, which were capable of generating Diffie-Hellman parameters and keys, respectively. As of this writing, the two deprecated commands are still accessible in OpenSSL 0.9.7, but because they're deprecated, we'll pretend that they do not exist, because they're likely to be completely removed from the next release of OpenSSL. Unfortunately, the new dhparam command does not support the generation of Diffie-Hellman keys, but it is likely that future versions will add support for it.

Examples

The following examples illustrate the use of the Diffie-Hellman commands:

```
$ openssl dhparam -out dhparam.pem -2 1024
```
Generates a new set of Diffie-Hellman parameters using a generator of 2 and a random 1,024-bit prime, and writes the parameters in PEM format to the file *dhparam.pem*.

```
$ openssl dhparam -in dhparam.pem -noout -C
```
Reads a set of Diffie-Hellman parameters from the file *dhparam.pem* and writes a C code representation of the parameters to `stdout`.

Digital Signature Algorithm

As its name implies, the Digital Signature Algorithm (DSA) is used for creating and verifying digital signatures. It provides authentication, but cannot be used for encryption or secrecy. DSA is frequently used in combination with Diffie-Hellman. Two parties in a conversation can exchange DSA public keys before the conversation begins (or during the conversation using certificates, as we'll explain in Chapter 3) and use the DSA keys to authenticate the communication of Diffie-Hellman parameters and keys. Combining Diffie-Hellman with DSA provides authentication and secrecy, and by using the shared secret resulting from the Diffie-Hellman exchange as a key, a symmetric cipher can then be used for encryption.

Just like Diffie-Hellman, DSA also requires parameters from which keys are generated. There is no harm in making the parameters used to generate a key pair public, but there's equally no compelling reason to do so. Only the private key that is generated must be kept private, as is implied by its name. The public key is the only thing that really needs to be shared with any party that wishes to verify the authenticity of anything signed with a private key.

Three commands are provided by the command-line tool for generating DSA parameters and keys, as well as for examining and manipulating them. The dsaparam command is used to generate and examine DSA parameters. Its function and options are not unlike those of the dhparam command. One major difference between the two is that the dsaparam command also provides an option to generate a private DSA key. The private key resulting from the dsaparam command will be unencrypted, which means that neither a password nor a passphrase will be required to decrypt and make use of it.

The gendsa command is used for generating private keys from a set of DSA parameters. By default, the generated private key will not be encrypted, but options are available that allow the key to be encrypted using any one of the DES, 3DES, or IDEA ciphers. No options are provided for specifying the password or passphrase to use for encryption on the command line, so encrypted DSA private key generation cannot be easily automated.

Both the `dsaparam` and `gendsa` commands are capable of generating private keys, either encrypted or not, but neither of them has the capability for generating a public key, which is required in order for DSA to provide any utility. The `dsa` command provides the means by which a public key can be generated from a private key. It also allows changes to be made to the encryption on a private key. For private keys that are not encrypted, encryption can be added, and for private keys that are already encrypted, the password or passphrase can be changed, as well as the encryption cipher that's used to encrypt it. It's also possible to remove the encryption on a private key with this command.

Examples

The following examples illustrate the use of the DSA commands:

```
$ openssl dsaparam -out dsaparam.pem 1024
```
Generates a new set of DSA parameters and writes them to the file *dsaparam.pem*. The length of the prime and generator parameters will be 1,024 bits.

```
$ openssl gendsa -out dsaprivatekey.pem -des3 dsaparam.pem
```
Generates a new DSA private key using the parameters from the file *dsaparam.pem*, encrypts the newly generated private key with the 3DES cipher, and writes the result out to the file *dsaprivatekey.pem*.

```
$ openssl dsa -in dsaprivatekey.pem -pubout -out dsapublickey.pem
```
Computes the public key that corresponds to the private key contained in the file *dsaprivatekey.pem* and writes the public key out to the file *dsapublickey.pem*.

```
$ openssl dsa -in dsaprivatekey.pem -out dsaprivatekey.pem -des3 -passin
pass:oldpword -passout pass:newpword
```
Reads a private key from the file *dsaprivatekey.pem*, decrypts it using the password "oldpword", re-encrypts it using the password "newpword", and writes the newly encrypted private key back out to the file *dsaprivatekey.pem*.

RSA

RSA is the most popular public key algorithm currently in use, despite the fact that it was encumbered by patent restrictions until the patent expired in September of 2000. It is named after its creators, Ron Rivest, Adi Shamir, and Leonard Adleman. One of the reasons that it is so popular is because it provides secrecy, authentication, and encryption all in one neat little package.

Unlike Diffie-Hellman and DSA, the RSA algorithm does not require parameters to be generated before keys can be generated, which simplifies the amount of work that is necessary to generate keys, and authenticate and encrypt communications. The command-line tool provides three commands for generating, examining, manipulating, and using RSA keys.

OpenSSL's genrsa command is used to generate a new RSA private key. Generation of an RSA private key involves finding two large prime numbers, each approximately half the length of the key. A typical key size for RSA is 1,024. We don't recommend that you use smaller key lengths or key lengths greater than 2,048 bits. By default, the generated private key will be unencrypted, but the command does have the ability to encrypt the resultant key using DES, 3DES, or IDEA.

The rsa command is used to manipulate and examine RSA keys and is the RSA version of the dsa command for DSA keys. It is capable of adding, modifying, and removing the encryption protecting an RSA private key. It is also capable of producing an RSA public key from a private key. The command can also be used to display information about a public or private key.

The rsautl command provides the ability to use an RSA key pair for encryption and signatures. Options are provided for encrypting and decrypting data, as well as for signing and verifying signatures. Remember that signing is normally performed on hashes, so this command is not useful for signing large amounts of data, or even more than 160 bits of data. In general, we do not recommend that you use this command at all for encrypting data. You should use the enc command instead. Additionally, encryption and decryption using RSA is slow, and for that reason, it should not be used on its own. Instead, it is commonly used to encrypt a key for a symmetric cipher. This is discussed in more detail in Chapter 8.

Examples

The following examples illustrate the use of the RSA commands:

```
$ openssl genrsa -out rsaprivatekey.pem -passout pass:trousers -des3 1024
```
Generates a 1,024-bit RSA private key, encrypts it using 3DES and a password of "trousers", and writes the result to the file *rsaprivatekey.pem*.

```
$ openssl rsa -in rsaprivatekey.pem -passin pass:trousers -pubout -out
rsapublickey.pem
```
Reads an RSA private key from the file *rsaprivatekey.pem*, decrypts it using the password "trousers", and writes the corresponding public key to the file *rsapublickey.pem*.

```
$ openssl rsautl -encrypt -pubin -inkey rsapublickey.pem -in plain.txt -out
cipher.txt
```
Using the RSA public key from the file *rsapublickey.pem*, the contents of the file *plain.txt* are encrypted and written to the file *cipher.txt*.

```
$ openssl rsautl -decrypt -inkey rsaprivatekey.pem -in cipher.txt -out plain.txt
```
Using the RSA private key from the file *rsaprivatekey.pem*, the contents of the file *cipher.txt* are decrypted and written to the file *plain.txt*.

```
$ openssl rsautl -sign -inkey rsaprivatekey.pem -in plain.txt -out signature.bin
```
Using the RSA private key from the file *rsaprivatekey.pem*, the contents of the file *plain.txt* are signed, and the signature is written to the file *signature.bin*.

```
$ openssl rsautl -verify -pubin -inkey rsapublickey.pem -in signature.bin -out
plain.txt
```
Using the RSA public key from the file *rsapublickey.pem*, the signature in the file *signature.bin* is verified, and the original unsigned data is written out to the file *plain.txt*.

S/MIME

S/MIME is a competing standard to PGP (Pretty Good Privacy) for the secure exchange of email. It provides authentication and encryption of email messages using public key cryptography, as does PGP. One of the primary differences in the two standards is that S/MIME uses a *public key infrastructure* to establish trust, whereas PGP does not. Trust is established when there is some means of proving that someone with a public key is actually that person, and that the key belongs to that person.

PGP was written and released in 1991 by Phil Zimmermann. It quickly became the de facto standard for the secure exchange of information throughout the world. Today, PGP has become an open standard known as OpenPGP, and is documented in RFC 2440. Because PGP does not rely on a public key infrastructure to establish trust, it is easy to set up and use. Today, one of the most common methods of establishing trust is obtaining someone's public key either from a key server or directly from that person, and manually verifying the key's fingerprint by comparing it with the fingerprint information obtained directly from the key's owner over some trusted medium, such as the telephone or paper mail. It is also possible to sign a public key, so if Alice trusts Bob's key, and Bob has used his key to sign Charlie's key, Alice knows that she can trust Charlie's key if the signature matches Bob's. PGP works for small groups of people, but it does not scale well.

S/MIME stands for *Secure Multipurpose Internet Mail Exchange*. RSA Security developed the initial version in 1995 in cooperation with several other software companies; the IETF developed Version 3. Like PGP, S/MIME also provides encryption and authentication services. A public key infrastructure is used as a means of establishing trust, which means that S/MIME is capable of scaling to support large groups of people. The downside is that it requires the use of a public key infrastructure, which means that it is slightly more difficult to set up than PGP because a certificate must be obtained from a Certification Authority that is trusted by anyone using the certificate to encrypt or verify communications. Public keys are exchanged in the form of X.509 certificates, which require a Certification Authority to issue certificates that can be used. Because a Certification Authority is involved in the exchange of public keys, trust can be established if the certificate that issued a certificate is trusted. Public key infrastructure is discussed in detail in Chapter 3.

S/MIME messages may have multiple recipients. For an encrypted message, the body of the message is encrypted using a symmetric cipher, and the key for the symmetric cipher is encrypted using the recipient's public key. When multiple recipients are involved, the same symmetric key is used, but the key is encrypted using each recipient's public key. For example, if Alice sends the same message to Bob and Charlie, two encrypted copies of the key for the symmetric cipher are included in the message. One copy is encrypted using Bob's public key, and the other is encrypted using Charlie's public key. To decrypt a message, the recipient's certificate is required to determine which encrypted key to decrypt.

The command-line tool provides the smime command, which supports encryption, decryption, signing, and verifying S/MIME v2 messages (support for S/MIME v3 is limited and is not likely to work). Email applications that do not natively support S/MIME can often be made to support it by using the command-line tool's smime command to process incoming and outgoing messages. The smime command does have some limitations, and it is not recommended in any kind of production environment. However, it provides a good foundation for building a more powerful and fully featured S/MIME implementation.

Examples

The following examples illustrate the use of the S/MIME commands:

```
$ openssl smime -encrypt -in mail.txt -des3 -out mail.enc cert.pem
```
Obtains a public key from the X.509 certificate in the file *cert.pem* and encrypts the contents of the file *mail.txt* using that key and 3DES. The resulting encrypted S/MIME message is written to the file *mail.enc*.

```
$ openssl smime -decrypt -in mail.enc -recip cert.pem -inkey key.pem -out
mail.txt
```
Obtains the recipient's public key from the X.509 certificate in the file *cert.pem* and decrypts the S/MIME message from the file *mail.enc* using the private key from the file *key.pem*. The decrypted message is written to the file *mail.txt*.

```
$ openssl smime -sign -in mail.txt -signer cert.pem -inkey key.pem -out mail.sgn
```
The signer's X.509 certificate is obtained from the file *cert.pem*, and the contents of the file *mail.txt* are signed using the private key from the file *key.pem*. The certificate is included in the S/MIME message that is written to the file *mail.sgn*.

```
$ openssl smime -verify -in mail.sgn -out mail.txt
```
Verifies the signature on the S/MIME message contained in the file *mail.sgn* and writes the result to the file *mail.txt*. The signer's certificate is expected to be included as part of the S/MIME message.

Passwords and Passphrases

Many commands (particularly those that involve a private key) require a password or passphrase to complete successfully, usually to decrypt a key that is stored securely on a disk. Normally, the command-line tool will prompt you to enter a password or passphrase when appropriate, even if you're not running the tool in interactive mode. The need for a password or passphrase to be physically entered by someone using the keyboard at the computer when it's needed makes using the tool for automated processes difficult, to say the least.

Fortunately, there's a solution. Many of the commands accept options that allow you to specify the necessary password or passphrase. Unfortunately, the options are not consistently named, so you need to use the right option with the right command. In general, the options `passin` and `passout` are used. No matter what the option is named, it requires a parameter that specifies how the password or passphrase will be obtained. A variety of sources may be specified, some of them not very secure at all. None of them provides the level of security that someone sitting at the computer and typing in the password or passphrase does, but you need to determine for yourself what you consider to be an acceptable risk.

stdin

> This method for reading a password is distinctly different from the default method. The default method reads passwords from the actual terminal device (TTY), thus explicitly avoiding input redirection from the command line. The `stdin` method for providing passwords allows for such input redirection.

pass:<password>

> This method can be used to supply the password or passphrase directly on the command line itself. If your password or passphrase contains spaces, you typically need to enclose the whole of the parameter in quotes, but the precise method of handling such a situation may differ on the platform that you're using.

> We strongly recommend that you do not use this method, for two reasons. First, if you're using batch mode, the command line for a process is readily accessible to any other process that is running on the system. In fact, on such systems there are commands specifically designed for this purpose, such as the `ps` command on Unix systems. Second, if you're using this as part of a script, it usually means the password or passphrase will be contained in your script, which also means that the password or passphrase can be easily compromised.

env:<variable>

> This method obtains the password or passphrase from an environment variable. We recommend against using this method, although not as strongly as we do against specifying the password or passphrase directly on the command line. This method is slightly more secure, but a process's environment is still available to other processes on some operating systems under the right circumstances.

---

file:<filename>

This method obtains the password or passphrase by reading it from the named file. The file containing the password or passphrase should be well protected, denying read access to any user on the system other than the owner of the file. Additionally, on Unix systems steps should be taken to ensure that each directory that parents the file does not allow access to a user other than the owner.

fd:<number>

This method obtains the password or passphrase by reading it from the specified file descriptor. This method is really useful only when the tool is launched from another process and not directly from the command line because the tool's process must have inherited the file descriptor from its parent in order for it to gain access.

Seeding the Pseudorandom Number Generator

In Chapter 1, we briefly discussed the need for cryptographic randomness. We'll expand on this discussion in Chapter 4. For now, we'll just deal with how to seed the OpenSSL PRNG properly from the command line. Because many of the cryptographic commands depend on random numbers, it is important that the PRNG be seeded properly.

The command-line tool will attempt to seed the PRNG on its own, but it may not always be able to do so. When the PRNG is not properly seeded, the tool will emit a warning message indicating that the random numbers it generates will be predictable. Additionally, you may wish to use a more conservative seeding mechanism than the one used by default.

On Windows systems, a variety of sources will be used to seed the PRNG, including the contents of the screen. None of these sources is particularly entropic, and depending on the version of Windows that you're using, the entropy sources vary. Unix systems that have a device named */dev/urandom* will use that device to obtain entropy for seeding the PRNG. Most modern versions of Unix provide support for this device, which we'll discuss in detail in Chapter 4. In addition, beginning with Version 0.9.7, OpenSSL will also attempt to seed the PRNG by connecting to an EGD socket to obtain entropy. By default, OpenSSL is built with four well-known names for sockets that it will attempt a connection with.

In addition to the base entropy sources, the command-line tool will also look for a file to obtain seed data from. If the RANDFILE environment variable is set, its value will be used as the name of the file to use for seeding the PRNG. If it is not set, a default filename of *.rnd* will be used, and the value of the HOME environment variable will be used to specify the location of that file. If the HOME environment variable is not set, as is often the case on non-Unix systems, the current directory will be used to find the file. Once the name of the file has been determined, the contents of that file will be loaded and used to seed the PRNG if it exists.

Many of OpenSSL's commands require that its PRNG be properly seeded so that the random numbers it generates are unpredictable. In particular, any of the commands that generate key pairs always require unpredictable random numbers in order for them to be effective. When the tool is unable to seed the PRNG on its own, the tool provides an option named rand that can be used to provide additional entropy sources.

The rand option requires a parameter that contains a list of files to be used as entropy sources. The list may be as short as a single file, or as long as the number of filenames you can fit on the command line. Each file in the list is separated by a platform-dependent separator character rather than a space. The separator character is a semi-colon (;) on Windows, a comma (,) on OpenVMS, and a colon (:) on all other platforms. On Unix systems, each filename in the list is first checked to see if it is an Entropy Gathering Daemon (EGD) socket. If it is, entropy will be gathered from an EGD server; otherwise, seed data will be read from the contents of the named file.

EGD is an entropy-gathering daemon written in Perl that is intended for use in the absence of */dev/random* or */dev/urandom*. It is available from *http://egd.sourceforge.net/* and runs on any Unix-based system that has Perl installed. It doesn't work on Windows, but other entropy-gathering solutions are available for Windows. In particular, we recommend EGADS (Entropy Gathering And Distribution System), a C-based infrastructure that supports both Unix and Windows. This is a preferable solution even on Unix machines because it is far more conservative in its entropy collection and estimation. It is even a good solution on systems with a */dev/random*. In such cases, it uses */dev/random* as a single source of entropy. EGADS is available from *http://www.securesw.com/egads/*. It can be used anywhere an EGD socket is expected.

If Perl is installed on your system, EGD is easy to set up and run. Perl has become ubiquitous in the Unix world, so it's unlikely that a modern system does not have it installed. Because EGD uses Perl, it's very portable, even though it was originally written for Linux systems. On the other hand, EGD works by gathering its entropy from the output of running processes, a number of which produce a questionable amount of unpredictable data. Perhaps its biggest limitation is that it works only on Unix systems.

EGADS can be a bit more difficult to get up and running, but will usually compile straight from the distribution with a minimal amount of effort. On systems that do not have */dev/random*, EGADS also gathers its entropy from the output of running processes. These processes are not as widely varied as EGD's list. EGADS provides an EGD-compatible interface on Unix systems. Because EGADS provides an EGD interface and will use */dev/random* to gather entropy, it provides a simplified interface for gathering entropy to clients such as those built with OpenSSL. It also supports Windows NT 4.0 and higher, which have no built-in entropy gathering services. It does not work on Windows 95, 98, or ME. Finally, EGADS also contains a cryptographically secure PRNG.

## CHAPTER 3

Public Key Infrastructure (PKI)

In Chapter 1, we described a scenario known as a man-in-the-middle attack, in which an attacker could intercept and even manipulate communications secured with public key cryptography. The attack is possible because public key cryptography provides no means of establishing trust when used on its own. *Public Key Infrastructure* (PKI) provides the means to establish trust by binding public keys and identities, thus giving reasonable assurance that we're communicating securely with who we think we are.

Using public key cryptography, we can be sure that only the encrypted data can be decrypted with the corresponding private key. If we combine this with the use of a message digest algorithm to compute a signature, we can be sure that the encrypted data has not been tampered with. What's missing is some means of ensuring that the party we're communicating with is actually who they say they are. In other words, trust has not been established. This is where PKI fits in.

In the real world, we often have no way of knowing firsthand who a public key belongs to, and that's a big problem. Unfortunately, there is no sure-fire way to know that we're communicating with who we think we are. The best we can do is extend our trust to a third party to certify that a public key belongs to the party that is claiming ownership of it.

Our intention in this chapter is to give you a basis for understanding how PKI fits into the big picture. PKI is important to using public key cryptography effectively, and is essential to understanding and using the SSL protocol. A comprehensive discussion of PKI is beyond the scope of this book. For much more in-depth discussion, we recommend the book *Planning for PKI: Best Practices Guide for Deploying Public Key Infrastructure* by Russ Housley and Tim Polk (John Wiley & Sons).

In this chapter, we'll look at how PKI functions. We start by examining the various components that comprise such an infrastructure. Then we demonstrate how to become a part of a public infrastructure so that others wishing to communicate securely with us can do so. Finally, we look at how to use the OpenSSL command-line tool to set up our own private infrastructure.

Certificates

At the heart of PKI is something called a *certificate*. In simple terms, a certificate binds a public key with a *distinguished name*. A distinguished name is simply the name of the person or entity that owns the public key to which it's bound. Perhaps a certificate can be best compared to a passport, which binds a picture with a name, thus solidifying a person's identity. A passport is issued by a trusted third party (the government) and contains information about the person to whom it has been issued (the subject) as well as information about the government that issued it (the issuer). Similarly, a certificate is also issued by a trusted third party, contains information about the subject, and contains information about the third party that issued it.

Not unlike a passport, which contains a watermark used to verify its authenticity, a certificate also contains safeguards intended to allow the authenticity of the certificate to be verified, and aid in the detection of forgery or tampering. Also similar to a passport, a certificate is valid only for a defined period. Once it has expired, a new certificate must be issued, and the old one should no longer be trusted.

A certificate is signed with the issuer's private key, and it contains almost all of the information necessary to verify its validity. It contains information about the subject, the issuer, and the period for which it is valid. The key component that is missing is the issuer's certificate. The issuer's certificate is the key component for verifying the validity of a certificate because it contains the issuer's public key, which is necessary for verifying the signature on the subject's certificate.

By signing a certificate with the issuer's private key, anyone that has the issuer's public key can verify its authenticity. The signature serves as a safeguard to prevent tampering. By signing the subject's certificate, the issuer asserts that it has verified the authenticity of the public key that the certificate contains and states that it may be trusted. As long as the issuer is trusted, the certificates that it issues can also be trusted.

It's important to note that the issuer's certificate or public key may be contained in an issued certificate. It's more important to note that this information cannot be trusted to authenticate the certificate. If it was trusted, the element of trust established from a third party is effectively eliminated. Anyone could create another key pair to use in signing a certificate and place that public key in the certificate.

Certificates are also created with a serial number embedded in them. The serial number is unique only to the issuer of the certificate. No two certificates issued by the same issuer should ever be assigned the same serial number. The certificate's serial number is often used to identify a certificate quickly.

Certification Authorities

A Certification Authority (CA) is an organization or company that issues certificates. By its very nature, a CA has a huge responsibility to ensure that the certificates it issues are legitimate. That is, the CA must ensure beyond all reasonable doubt that every certificate it issues contains a public key that was issued by the party that claims to have issued it. It must be able to produce acceptable proof for any certificate that it issues on demand. Otherwise, how can the CA itself be trusted?

There are two basic types of CAs. A private CA has the responsibility of issuing certificates only for members of its own organization, and is likewise trusted only by members of its own organization. A public CA, such as VeriSign or Thawte, has the responsibility of issuing certificates for any member of the public, and must be trusted by the public. The burden of proof varies depending on the type of CA that has issued a certificate and the type of certificate that is issued.

A CA must be trusted, and so for that trust to be extended, its certificate containing its public key must be widely distributed. For public CAs, their certificates are generally published so that anyone can obtain them. More commonly, the software that makes use of them, such as a web browser, is shipped containing them. Most often, the software allows certificates from other CAs to be added to its list of trusted certificates, thus facilitating the use of private CAs with off-the-shelf software.

Private Certification Authorities

A private CA is often ideal for use in a corporate setting. For example, a company could set up its own CA for email, using S/MIME as the standard for encrypting and authenticating email messages. The company's CA would issue certificates to each employee, and each employee would configure their S/MIME-capable email clients to recognize the company's CA as being trusted.

For a private CA, verifying the identity of a subject is often a reasonably simple and straightforward matter. When used in a corporate environment, for example, employees are known, and their identities can be easily identified using information obtained from the company's human resources department. In such a scenario, the human resources department is said to be acting as a *Registration Authority* (RA).

Public Certification Authorities

A public CA commonly issues certificates for public web sites requiring encryption and/or authentication, often for e-commerce in which customer information must be transmitted securely to place an order. For such operations, it's essential that the customers transmit their information to the site that is supposed to be receiving it without worrying about someone else obtaining the information.

For a public CA, verifying the identity of a subject[*] is considerably more difficult than it is for a private CA. The information required from the subject to prove its

---

[*] As we mentioned in Chapter 1, this is technically the job of an RA instead of a CA, but the CA generally deals with the RA transparently.

identity to the CA varies depending on whether the subject is an individual or a business. For an individual, the proof required could be as simple as a photocopy of a government-issued ID, such a driver's license or passport. For a business or other organization, similar government documentation proving your right to use the name will also likely be required.

It's important to note that most public CAs provide their services to make money, and not to simply benefit the public. They still have a responsibility to verify a subject's identity, but not actually guarantee anything—the liability is too great to provide an absolute guarantee. Certainly, it is in the CA's best interests to verify a subject's identity to the best of its ability, however. If a CA gains the reputation of issuing certificates to anyone who asks (and pays them enough money), they're not going to remain in business for very long because nobody will trust them.

Certificate Hierarchies

A certificate that is issued by a CA can be used to issue and sign another certificate, if the issued certificate is created with the appropriate permissions to do so. In this way, certificates can be chained. At the root of the chain is the root CA's certificate. Because it is at the root of the chain and there is no other authority to sign its certificate, the root CA signs its own certificate. Such a certificate is known as a *self-signed certificate*.

There is no way to digitally verify the authenticity of a self-signed certificate because the issuer and the subject are the same, which is why it has become a common practice to provide them with the software that uses them. When they're included with an application, they are generally obtained by the software author through some physical means. For example, Thawte provides its root certificates on its web site, free and clear, but strongly advises anyone making use of them to confirm the certificate fingerprints with Thawte via telephone before using or distributing them.

To verify the authenticity and validity of a given certificate, each certificate in the chain must also be verified, from the certificate in question's issuer all the way up to the root certificate. If any certificate in the chain is invalid, each certificate below it in the chain must also be considered invalid. Invalid certificates typically have either expired or been revoked (perhaps due to certificate theft). A certificate is also considered invalid if it has been tampered with and the signatures on the certificate don't match with the ones that should have been used to sign it.

The decision whether to employ a certificate hierarchy more complex than a single root CA depends on many factors. These factors and their trade-offs are well beyond the scope of this book. Entire books have been devoted to PKI, and we strongly recommend that you consult one or more of them to assist you in making an informed decision. Again, we strongly recommend *Planning for PKI* by Russ Housley and Tim Polk.

Certificate Extensions

The most widely accepted format for certificates is the X.509 format, first introduced in 1988. There are three versions of the format, known as X.509v1, X.509v2, and X.509v3. The most recent revision of the standard was introduced in 1996, and most, if not all, modern software now supports it. A large number of changes were made between X.509v1 and X.509v3, but perhaps one of the most significant features introduced in the X.509v3 standard is its support of extensions.

Version 3 extensions allow a certificate to contain additional fields beyond those defined by previous versions of the X.509 standard. The additional fields may be standard in X.509v3, such as the basicConstraints or keyUsage fields, or they may be completely nonstandard, perhaps recognized only by a single application. Each extension has a name for its field, a designation indicating whether the extension is *critical*, and a value to be associated with the extension field. When an extension is designated as critical, software that does not recognize the extension must reject the certificate as being invalid. If the extension is noncritical, it may be ignored.

The X.509v3 standard defines 14 extensions in an effort to consolidate the most common extensions implemented by third parties. One example is the permissible uses for a certificate—for instance, whether a certificate is allowed to sign another certificate, or is usable in an SSL Server. If each application were to create its own disparate extensions, the information in those extensions would be either unusable by other applications or significantly complicate the process of validating a certificate because it would need to recognize a virtually unlimited number of different extensions that all essentially mean the same thing.

Of the 14 standard extensions defined by X.509v3, only 4 are well-supported and in widespread use. Only one of them must be designated critical according to the standard, while the other three may or may not be. Since the majority of the standard extensions are not well supported, we won't discuss them here. Later in this chapter, when we setup our own CA, we'll be making use of some of the better-supported extensions, as appropriate.

The basicConstraints extension is a *sequence* that may contain two possible components: cA and pathLenConstraint. Without getting into the technical details of an X.509 certificate, a sequence can best be thought of as a container, which contains other components; it has no value of its own. The cA component is a boolean indicating whether the certificate may be used as a CA's certificate. If the cA component is absent, OpenSSL will check the keyUsage extension to determine whether to allow the certificate to be used as a CA certificate. If the keyUsage extension is present and the keyCertSign bit is not set, the certificate may not be used as a CA certificate. The optional pathLenConstraint component is an integer that specifies the maximum number of certificates in the chain that may be used below this certificate. If the value is less than the number of certificates in the chain that have already been validated, this certificate must be rejected.

The keyUsage extension is a bit string that defines how a certificate can be used, and may or may not be designated critical. If the extension is present in the certificate, it should be marked critical. If it is designated critical, the information that it contains will always be used to determine valid usage. If the extension is absent or designated noncritical, the certificate should be treated as though all bits are set. Rather than individually explain what each bit means, it's more useful to show which bits should be set for each of the common uses for a certificate, which we do in Table 3-1.

Table 3-1. Common bit settings for the keyUsage extension

Purpose of certificate	Bit settings to use
Certification Authority Certificate	keyCertSign and cRLSign
Certificate Signing	keyCertSign
Object Signing	digitalSignature
S/MIME Encryption	keyEncipherment
S/MIME Signing	digitalSignature
SSL Client	digitalSignature
SSL Server	keyEncipherment

The extKeyUsage extension is a sequence of object identifiers that further defines which uses of the certificate are permissible, and may or may not be designated critical. As with the keyUsage extension, if this extension is present, it should be designated critical. If it is designated critical, the certificate must be used for one of the purposes defined by the extension. If it is designated noncritical, the information is advisory only and may be ignored. There are eight possible purposes defined for use with this extension, as summarized in Table 3-2.

Table 3-2. Purposes defined for the extKeyUsage extension

Purpose of certificate	Object identifier (OID)
Server Authentication	1.3.6.1.5.5.7.3.1
Client Authentication	1.3.6.1.5.5.7.3.2
Code Signing	1.3.6.1.5.5.7.3.3
Email	1.3.6.1.5.5.7.3.4
IPSec End System	1.3.6.1.5.5.7.3.5
IPSec Tunnel	1.3.6.1.5.5.7.3.6
IPSec User	1.3.6.1.5.5.7.3.7
Timestamping	1.3.6.1.5.5.7.3.8

It's worth noting that neither the keyUsage nor the extKeyUsage extension is well-defined, and as such, their usage is subject to wide interpretation. In particular, how to treat the critical flag on either extension is not well-defined, but it would seem that in many existing software products, the extensions are largely ignored. In addition, various profiles (guidelines that dictate what certificates should contain) specify their usage differently. For instance, PKIX (the IETF Public Key Infrastructure working group) has obsoleted the three IPSec-related OIDs that may be present in an extKeyUsage sequence. Additionally, they are not implemented consistently across vendors. As a result of these problems, these two extensions are mostly useless. If you do use them, be sure that you are using them in a consistent manner with any existing software with which you'll be interoperating.

The cRLDistributionPoints extension is a sequence that is used to communicate how the CA that issued the certificate makes its CRLs available. The standard indicates that this extension should be designated noncritical; however, it does advise CAs to include the information. Providing the location of the CRL that would contain this certificate's serial number if it is revoked inside the certificate itself is perhaps the best possible way for software validating a certificate to obtain the information.

Certificate Revocation Lists

Once a certificate has been issued, it is generally put into production, where it will be distributed to many clients. If an attacker compromises the associated private key, he now has the ability to use the certificate even though it doesn't belong to him. Assuming the proper owner is aware of the compromise, a new certificate with a new key pair should be obtained and put into use. In this situation there are two certificates for the same entity—both are technically valid, but one should not be trusted. The compromised certificate will eventually expire, but in the meantime, how will the world at large know not to trust it?

The answer lies in something called a *certificate revocation list* (CRL). A CRL contains a list of all of the revoked certificates a CA has issued that have yet to expire. When a certificate is revoked, the CA declares that the certificate should no longer be trusted.

Bandwidth is a significant concern when distributing CRLs, since clients need to have reasonably current revocation information in order to properly validate a certificate. In an ideal world, the client would get up-to-date revocation information as soon as the CA gets the information. Unfortunately, many CAs distribute CRLs only as a huge list. Downloading a huge list before validating each certificate could easily add unacceptable latency and place an undue load on the server when there are a lot of clients. As a result, CAs tend to update their CRLs regularly, but not immediately after they learn about key compromises. Included in the revocation list is the date and time that the next update will be published, so once an application has downloaded the list, it doesn't need to do so again until the one it has expires. Clients are encouraged to cache the information (which can be infeasible if the client has limited storage space).

This scheme leaves a window of vulnerability in which the CA knows about a revoked certificate, yet the client does not find out about it immediately. If a CA publishes the list too frequently, it will require massive amounts of bandwidth in order to sustain the frequent demand for the list. On the other hand, if a CA publishes the list too infrequently, certificates that need to be revoked will still be considered valid until the next list is published. Each CA needs to strike a balance with the community that it's serving to determine how frequently to publish its list.

One solution to this problem is for the CA to break up its CRLs into segments. To do this, the CA specifies ranges of certificate serial numbers that each CRL contains. For example, the CA could create a different CRL for each 1,000 serial numbers. Therefore, the first CRL would be for serial numbers 1 through 1,000; the second would be for serial numbers 1,001 through 2,000, and so on. This solution does require forethought and planning on the part of the CA, but it reduces the size of the CRLs that the CA issues. Another option is to use "delta CRLs," where a CA periodically publishes incremental changes to its CRL list. Delta CRLs still require the client to cache CRL information or download everything anew each time a certificate needs to be validated.

Another problem with CRLs is that while there is a standard means to publish them formally, specified in RFC 2459, that mechanism is optional, and many of the more common public CAs, such as VeriSign, do not distribute their CRLs this way. There are also other standard methods for distributing CRLs, but the overall problem is that there isn't just one, and so many software applications do not actually make use of CRLs. Of the various methods of distribution, LDAP is most commonly used as a repository for CRLs. Additionally, multiple applications on the same machine, or even on the local network, could be interested in the same data and require that it be queried from the CA multiple times within a short period.

The problems with the distribution of CRLs currently make them difficult to manage, and what's worse, few applications even make the attempt. This essentially makes CRLs useless and leaves no way for a CA to revoke a certificate effectively once it's been issued. Ideally, CAs need to standardize a method for CRL distribution, and both CAs and applications need to start making use of it.

Another potentially serious problem that has not been addressed is what happens when a root CA's certificate needs to be revoked. A CRL is not suited to handle this, and neither are applications. The reason for this is that CRLs are issued by a parent (a CA) for its children, but a root CA has no parent. It is possible for a CA to revoke its own certificate as long as it still has its private key. For the purposes of signing a CRL containing its own certificate, the CA's compromised key can still be trusted. Unfortunately, given the poor state of CRL handling in existing software in general, it's not likely that this situation is handled very well, if at all.

A classic example demonstrating that CRLs are poorly supported is what happened in early 2001 when VeriSign issued two class 3 code-signing certificates to Microsoft Corporation. The problem was that Microsoft never requested these certificates—someone claiming to represent Microsoft did. VeriSign handled the situation in the appropriate manner and published the serial numbers of the certificates in a new

CRL. What really demonstrated the flaws with CRLs was how Microsoft handled the situation. It quickly became clear that Microsoft's software, while distributing Veri-Sign's root certificates and using their services, did not check VeriSign's CRLs. Microsoft issued a patch to deal with the problem of the revoked certificates, but the patch did nothing to fix the problem of their software not utilizing the CRLs at all. Had Microsoft's software made proper use (or, arguably, any use at all) of CRLs, no patch would have been necessary, and the problem would have ended with Veri-Sign's publication of its CRL (minus the inherent window of vulnerability).

It could be argued that if a major software company like Microsoft can't handle CRLs properly, how can smaller software companies and individual software developers be expected to handle them properly? While the argument may very well be faulty in a number of respects, it is still a question worth asking, and in truth, the answer, at least for right now, is not one that we would all like to hear. PKI is still relatively imma-ture, and much work needs to be done to remedy not only the issues that we've dis-cussed here, but others that we leave as an exercise for the reader to explore as well. While CRLs may not be the ultimate answer to revoking a certificate, for the time being, they are the most widely implemented means by which to do so. It's worth tak-ing the time to ensure that your software is capable of dealing with the technology and provides for a reasonably safe and pleasant experience for your users.

To complicate matters more, the standard CRL specification has changed over time, and both the old format (Version 1) and the new format (Version 2) are actively used. OpenSSL supports both Version 1 and Version 2 CRLs, but there is much soft-ware still in common use that does not yet support Version 2, and certainly old leg-acy applications that are no longer being developed or supported never will, even though they continue to be used. The major addition that Version 2 offers is exten-sions. The standard defines four extensions that are used primarily to indicate when a certificate was revoked, why a certificate was revoked, and how to handle a certifi-cate that has been revoked.

The fourth standard extension is used in indirect CRLs. An indirect CRL is one that is not necessarily issued by a CA, but instead by a third party. Such a CRL can con-tain certificates from multiple CAs. The extension, then, is used to indicate which CA issued the certificate that has been revoked. Currently, indirect CRLs are not very common, because CRLs in Version 2 format are not widely supported.

Online Certificate Status Protocol

The *Online Certificate Status Protocol* (OCSP), formally specified in RFC 2560, is a relatively new addition to PKI. Its primary aim is to address some of the distribution problems that have traditionally plagued CRLs.

Using OCSP, an application makes a connection to an OCSP responder and requests the status of a certificate by passing the certificate's serial number. The responder replies "good," "revoked," or "unknown." A "good" response indicates that the certificate is valid, so far as the responder knows. This does not necessarily mean that the certificate was ever issued, just that is hasn't been revoked. A "revoked" response indicates that the certificate has been issued and that it has indeed been revoked. An "unknown" response indicates that the responder doesn't know anything about the certificate. A typical reason for this response could be that the certificate was issued by a CA that is unknown to the responder.

An OCSP responder is typically operated by a CA or by a trusted third party that is authorized by the CAs for which it provides information. The client must trust the OCSP responder in a manner similar to a root CA. More importantly, there is only one way to revoke an OCSP's trusted status, and it's not pretty. If an OCSP responder is compromised, every client that makes use of that responder must be reconfigured manually either not to trust it or to use a new certificate that can be trusted.

A client's request includes information about the issuer of the certificate it is requesting status information for, so it is possible for a single OCSP responder to provide certificate revocation information for more than a single CA. Unfortunately, one of the problems of OCSP responders when run by a third party is that the information they're serving can become stale. At the very least, a delay often occurs between the time when a CA revokes a certificate and when the responder receives the information from the CA, particularly if the responder is relying on CRLs published by its serviceable CAs to supply its information.

Currently, OCSP is not nearly as widely recognized or implemented as CRLs are, so unless you know that all your users will have an OCSP server available, it is generally best to use the technology to supplement CRLs rather than replace them completely.

Three of the more significant problems that OCSP introduces are the potential for denial of service, replay, and man-in-the-middle attacks. Most servers are vulnerable to denial of service attacks to some extent, but the nature of the service, the amount of information transferred, and the way requests are handled help determine just how vulnerable a given server is to such an attack. The details of denial of service attacks are beyond the scope of this book; however, OCSP responders are typically more susceptible to them than other common services such as HTTP.

The OCSP Version 1 specification allows responders to pre-produce signed responses in an effort to reduce the load on the responder required by signing definitive responses. Allowing for pre-produced signed responses opens the door for replay attacks. Man-in-the-middle attacks are possible because error responses are not signed, although this type of attack could more accurately be considered a denial of service attack. Perhaps what's most disturbing about the aforementioned vulnerabilities is the fact that each one is noted in the RFC, yet nothing was done when formalizing the standard to prevent them.

There are only a handful of public OCSP responders available at the time of this writing, as listed by *OpenValidation.org*. The small number of responders is a clear indication that OCSP is not widely deployed. While OCSP is an attempt at resolving the problems of CRLs, we feel that the additional problems it creates, at least in its current state, outweigh the problems that it solves. Certainly, it cannot be reasonably considered as a replacement for CRLs. In its defense, there was an IETF draft submitted in March of 2001 for Version 2 of the protocol, which addresses some of the issues, but this has not yet completed the standards process.

Obtaining a Certificate

Before obtaining a certificate, you first need to determine what purpose the certificate will serve. There are many different types of certificates offered by a variety of CAs, both public and private. For the purposes of this discussion, we will investigate what is necessary to obtain three different types of certificates from a public CA. While it is certainly not the only public CA, we've chosen VeriSign as the CA that we'll obtain a certificate from because it is perhaps the most established public CA and offers the widest variety of certificates for a variety of uses.

As we mentioned, there are many different types of certificates, each used for different purposes. VeriSign's offerings range from personal certificates for use with S/MIME to enterprise solutions that are more sophisticated. We'll find out how to get a personal certificate for S/MIME, a code-signing certificate for signing your software so that users can verify that it came from you, and a certificate for securing your web site for applications such as e-commerce.

Personal Certificates

S/MIME email relies on personal certificates (as opposed to certificates granted to an organization), which VeriSign calls a *Class 1 Digital ID*. It is the easiest kind of certificate to obtain, and is available for a modest price, but it is limited to email security only. You can get a Class 1 Digital ID that works with Netscape Messenger, or you can get one intended to work with Microsoft Outlook express. If you use a different application to read and write your email, you should consult with that application's vendor to find out whether it interoperates with either of these certificate types.

The first step in obtaining a personal certificate is to visit VeriSign's web site at *http://www.verisign.com/* and follow the links from the main page to "Secure E-Mail", which is listed under "Home & Home Office" products, to the Digital ID enrollment form. We won't outline all of the links here, not only because they're subject to change, but because there's a wealth of information on the site that is well worth reading, including information on how to make use of the certificate once it has been issued. Once you have filled out and submitted the enrollment form, VeriSign will send an automated email to the address you provided with instructions on how to "pick up" the certificate.

The first set of questions on the enrollment form is self-explanatory. The first and last name that you enter will be how your Digital ID is listed in VeriSign's directory service. The email address that you enter should be the one that you will be using with the Digital ID. It becomes the certificate's distinguished name. It is also listed alongside your first and last name in the directory. VeriSign will also use the address to verify its validity by sending an automated email to that address with instructions on how to retrieve the certificate that has been issued.

Next, VeriSign will request a challenge phrase, which will be used to protect the certificate. The phrase will be available to you and VeriSign. You should not share it with anyone else! VeriSign will use the phrase to verify that you are the owner of the certificate when you request that it be revoked, renewed, or replaced. Be sure to choose a phrase that you'll be able to remember, but one that will not be easily guessed by someone that knows you well.

VeriSign chooses a default key length for the certificate and issues it to you based upon the information from your browser. You shouldn't need to change the key length that is selected for you unless you're using something other than Netscape or Microsoft products to access your email, in which case the documentation for your email software or the vendor of the software should have advised you on the proper setting to choose.

If you're using Microsoft Internet Explorer, your private key will be unprotected by default. That is, once you install it in your email software, you will not be required to enter any password or passphrase to gain access to it. If you opt to keep your certificate unprotected in this manner, you must make every assurance that the private key for your certificate is not compromised. It is generally not a good idea to leave your private key unprotected, so VeriSign offers two methods of protecting it. One step up from the default of low security is medium security, which requires your approval each time the private key is accessed. With medium security, you still are not required to enter a password or passphrase to unlock the private key. High security requires you to enter a password or passphrase to unlock the key each time it is accessed.

Remember that anybody gaining access to your private key will be able to use your certificate to masquerade as you. When an email is signed with your private key, people are going to trust it, and this can have disastrous effects if your key is compromised. Anyone with access to your private key will also be able to decrypt email that has been encrypted with your public key. Sure, your certificate can be revoked, but as we discussed earlier, revoking a certificate doesn't have any effect if its revocation status is not being checked. With this in mind, particularly for mobile users, we strongly recommend that you choose high security.

Finally, you must read and accept VeriSign's subscriber agreement and privacy policy. If you're using Microsoft Internet Explorer and you checked the checkbox for securing your certificate, a dialog will be presented to you to select the security level that you wish to apply to the certificate. Within an hour or so, you will receive an email from VeriSign at the address that you entered into the enrollment form containing instructions on how to "pick up" your certificate from VeriSign. Included in the email are a URL and a PIN, both of which will be required to get the certificate from VeriSign. You should use the same machine and browser to retrieve the certificate as you did to request it.

That's all there is to it! Once you've retrieved your certificate from VeriSign, follow the directions presented on VeriSign's site to use the certificate in either Netscape or Microsoft Internet Explorer. Again, if you're using other software to access your email, follow the vender's directions to enable the certificate. Now you're ready to start sending and receiving secure email!

Code-Signing Certificates

VeriSign offers code-signing certificates for use by software developers and software vendors. The purpose of such a certificate is to sign code that users download off the Internet. By signing your code, users can be assured that the code has not been tampered with or corrupted since it was digitally signed with your private key. In the online world where people are not only becoming increasingly aware of security issues, but also worry about viruses and worms, signing your code provides a certain assurance to your users that they are getting the software that they're expecting to get.

Obtaining a code-signing certificate is not nearly as quick and easy as obtaining a personal certificate. They are also considerably more expensive, but then again, they're not really intended for everyday individual users. At the time that this text was written, VeriSign offered six different types of code-signing certificates for various types of programs. You must be sure to get the proper certificate for the code that you wish to sign because the different types of certificates may not work properly with other types of code. For example, Microsoft Authenticode certificates only work for Microsoft's Internet Explorer browser. For Netscape browsers, you need to get a Netscape Object Signing certificate. The available types of code-signing certificates are listed as part of the process of obtaining a code-signing certificate. Choosing a type is the first step in obtaining a code-signing certificate.

The type of code-signing certificate determines the specific requirements for making the request to VeriSign to obtain it. For a Microsoft Authenticode Digital ID, for example, much of the work is automated through Microsoft's Internet Explorer, while a Sun Java Signing Digital ID requires you to generate a certificate request using Sun's Java tools to be submitted along with the request. For each type of certificate, VeriSign supplies full instructions on what code-signing-certificate–dependent information is needed and how to go about obtaining and supplying it to VeriSign.

While each type of code-signing certificate has its own specific requirements for making the request, there are common requirements that must be met as well. Most of the requirements are self-explanatory, such as contact and payment information. Each certificate must also have information about who owns the certificate. Such information includes the name of the company or organization and the location from which it does business. For example, a company doing business from the United States would be required to supply the city and state in which it is located.

There is, of course, also the very important need for the CA, VeriSign in this case, to verify that they'd be issuing the certificate to someone who should legitimately have it. The quickest and easiest way for VeriSign to verify this information is with a Dun & Bradstreet D-U-N-S number. Supplying this information is optional, but the alternatives require more time and effort both on your part and VeriSign's. If you do not have or do not want to use a D-U-N-S number, you can optionally mail or fax copies of your business license, articles of incorporation, or partnership papers along with your request for a code-signing certificate.

Once your request, including any appropriate documentation, has been submitted, VeriSign takes it under review. If everything is in order, a code-signing certificate is issued and instructions on how to retrieve the certificate so that you may distribute and use it are provided. Unlike a personal certificate, the request for a code-signing certificate is reviewed and verified by an actual living human being, and so is not made immediately available. Depending on VeriSign's workload, it may take several days for the certificate to be issued, although VeriSign expedites requests for an additional fee.

Web Site Certificates

The process of obtaining a certificate for use in securing a web site, which VeriSign calls a *secure server certificate*, is similar to the process for obtaining a certificate for a code-signing certificate. Much of the same information is required, although there are some differences worth noting. Obviously, one of the primary differences is in the types of certificates offered. While code-signing certificates differ based on the type of code that will be signed (Netscape plug-ins versus Java applets, for example), secure server certificates are one of either 40-bit or 128-bit SSL certificates. That is, web site certificates explicitly restrict the size of the symmetric keys that should be used with the certificate. We recommend you stick with 128-bit certificates, since 40-bit symmetric keys are widely regarded as unacceptably weak.

No matter which server software you plan to use, you must follow its instructions on how to generate a *Certificate Signing Request* (CSR). Due to the wide variety of servers available today, it is not practical for us to provide instructions on how to do this here. VeriSign has instructions for many of the more popular servers available on its web site. The CSR you generate will also generate a key pair. While you must submit the CSR to VeriSign to have the certificate issued, you should keep the private key to yourself. It should not be sent to VeriSign or to anybody else.

As with code-signing certificates, you must also provide acceptable proof to VeriSign that you have a right to the certificate you are requesting. The options for providing this proof are the same—provide either a D-U-N-S number or a copy of one of the aforementioned acceptable documents. Additionally, a secure server certificate is bound to a domain name. VeriSign will issue certificates only to the registered owner of a domain. This means that if the domain is owned by a corporate entity, you must be an employee of that company.

Once your request, including any appropriate documentation, has been submitted, VeriSign takes it under review. If everything is in order, a secure server certificate is issued and the certificate is emailed to the technical contact that was provided when the request was submitted. As with code-signing certificates, an actual living human being reviews the information, so it may take several days for the certificate to be issued, depending on VeriSign's workload. Expedited processing is also available for an additional fee.

Setting Up a Certification Authority

Setting up a CA can seem like a daunting task, but it doesn't have to be. There are a number of free and commercial CA packages available. The OpenSSL command-line tool even provides all of the functionality required to set up a minimal CA that can be used in a small organization. The OpenSSL command-line tool's CA functionality was originally intended as an example only, but two of the more popular freely available CA packages, OpenCA and pyCA, use it as their foundation. As of this writing, these tools are still fairly immature, and offer very little that the OpenSSL command-line tool doesn't have (LDAP storage is the notable exception).

In this section, we'll go through the necessary steps to set up a CA using OpenSSL's command-line tools. We'll show you how to create a self-signed root certificate for use by your CA, how to build a configuration file that OpenSSL can use for your CA, and how to issue certificates and CRLs with your CA. Since OpenSSL's command-line CA functionality was intended primarily as an example of how to use OpenSSL to build a CA, we don't recommend that you attempt to use it in a large production environment. Instead, it should be used primarily as a tool to learn how PKI works and as a starting point for building a real CA with tools designed specifically for use in a production environment.

Creating an Environment for Your Certification Authority

The first step in setting up a CA with the OpenSSL command-line tool is creating an environment for it to run in. Several files and directories must be created. The easiest way to set everything up is from the command line, using your favorite text editor to create the necessary files. For our example CA, we'll be using the bash shell on a Unix system. Whether the system is Linux or FreeBSD or some other variety of Unix doesn't matter; the instructions will be the same. There will be some variation for Windows-based systems.

First, we must choose a location for all of our CA's files to reside. For our example, we use *lopt/exampleca* as the root directory for our CA, but you may choose any location you like on your system. All of our CA's files, including issued certificates and CRLs, will be contained within this directory. Keeping the files together makes it easier to find any of the files used by our CA and to set up multiple CAs.

Within the CA's root directory, we need to create two subdirectories. We'll name them *certs* and *private*. The subdirectory *certs* will be used to keep copies of all of the certificates that we issue with our CA. The subdirectory *private* will be used to keep a copy of the CA certificate's private key. For the most part, the majority of the files that the CA uses are visible to anyone on the system. In fact, many of the files are supposed to be distributed to the public, or at least to anyone who makes any use of the certificates issued by our CA. The one notable exception is the CA certificate's private key. The private key should never be disclosed to anyone not authorized to issue a certificate or CRL from our CA.

A good CA needs to protect its private key as best it can. 2,048 bits are the bare minimum length for a CA key. The private key should be stored in hardware, or at least on a machine that is never put on a network (CSRs would arrive via the sneaker net).

Besides key generation, we will create three files that our CA infrastructure will need. The first file is used to keep track of the last serial number that was used to issue a certificate. It's important that no two certificates ever be issued with the same serial number from the same CA. We'll call this file *serial* and initialize it to contain the number 1. OpenSSL is somewhat quirky about how it handles this file. It expects the value to be in hex, and it must contain at least two digits, so we must pad the value by prepending a zero to it. The second file is a database of sorts that keeps track of the certificates that have been issued by the CA. Since no certificates have been issued at this point and OpenSSL requires that the file exist, we'll simply create an empty file. We'll call this file *index.txt* (see Example 3-1).

Example 3-1. Creating the CA's environment

```
# mkdir /opt/exampleca
# cd /opt/exampleca
# mkdir certs private
# chmod g-rwx,o-rwx private
# echo '01' > serial
# touch index.txt
```

Building an OpenSSL Configuration File

One more file still needs to be created, but it is significantly more complex than the first two files that we've already created. It is a configuration file that will be used by the OpenSSL command-line tool to obtain information about how to issue certificates. We could conceivably skip creating this file and use the OpenSSL defaults, which are actually quite sane, but by using a configuration file, we save ourselves some work in issuing commands to OpenSSL. We briefly discussed configuration files and their use with the command-line tool in the Chapter 2. Now it's time to actually create a configuration file of our own and put it to use.

The OpenSSL command for the CA functions is aptly named ca, and so the first section that we're interested in is named ca. For our purposes, this section is quite simple, containing only a single key: default_ca. The value is the name of a section containing the configuration for the default CA. OpenSSL allows for multiple CA configurations in the same configuration file. If the name of a configuration to use is not specified, OpenSSL uses the name paired with the default_ca key. The default can be overridden on the command line with the name option.

Example 3-2 shows the configuration file for our CA. We've already explained what the files and directories we've created are for, so the first set of keys in the example should be clear; we're simply telling OpenSSL where we've decided to place the files and directories that it needs to use. The three keys, default_crl_days, default_days, and default_md, correspond to the command-line crldays, days, and md options, and may be overridden by using them.

The default_crl_days key specifies the number of days between CRLs. You may wish to use default_crl_hours instead if you plan to publish CRLs more than once a day. This setting computes the nextUpdate field of the CRL when it is generated. The default_days key specifies the number of days an issued certificate will be valid. The default_md specifies the message digest algorithm that will be used to sign issued certificates and CRLs. Possible legal values for this key include md5, sha1, and mdc2.

The policy key specifies the name of a section that will be used for the default policy. It may be overridden on the command line with the policy option. A policy definition is a set of keys with the same name as the fields in a certificate's distinguished name. For each key or field, there are three legal values: match, supplied, or optional. A value of match means that the field by that name in a certificate request must match the same field in the CA's certificate. A value of supplied means that the certificate request must contain the field. A value of optional means that the field is not required in the certificate request.

By default, when a certificate is issued, OpenSSL orders the DN (distinguished name) fields in the same order as they appear in the policy definition being used. Any fields that are present in the certificate request but not present in the policy definition are omitted from the issued certificate. This behavior can be changed by using the preserveDN option or by setting the preserve key to yes in the CA definition section. When this option is set, all of the fields in the certificate request are included in the issued certificate, and they remain in the same order as they were in the certificate request. Ordinarily, you should not need to enable this option unless you're dealing with older versions of Microsoft Internet Explorer, which require the fields in the issued certificate to match the certificate request. If you're dealing with very old versions of Microsoft Internet Explorer, you may also need to enable the "MSIE hack" either by using the msie_hack option or by setting the msie_hack key to yes in the CA definition section.

The x509_extensions key specifies the name of a section that will contain the extensions to be added to each certificate issued by our CA. If this key is absent, OpenSSL creates an X.509v1 certificate, but if it is present, even if it is empty, an X.509v3 certificate is created. The only extension that we've included in our example is the basicConstraints extension, and we've set its cA component to false so that the certificates issued by our CA, in turn, may not be used as CA certificates. The certificate chain stops with certificates that we issue. Example 3-2 shows the configuration file.

Example 3-2. A simple CA configuration definition

```
[ ca ]
default_ca = exampleca

[ exampleca ]
dir               = /opt/exampleca
certificate       = $dir/cacert.pem
database          = $dir/index.txt
new_certs_dir     = $dir/certs
private_key       = $dir/private/cakey.pem
serial            = $dir/serial

default_crl_days = 7
default_days     = 365
default_md       = md5

policy            = exampleca_policy
x509_extensions = certificate_extensions

[ exampleca_policy ]
commonName             = supplied
stateOrProvinceName    = supplied
countryName            = supplied
emailAddress           = supplied
organizationName       = supplied
organizationalUnitName = optional

[ certificate_extensions ]
basicConstraints = CA:false
```

Now that we've created a configuration file, we need to tell OpenSSL where to find it. By default, OpenSSL uses a system-wide configuration file. Its location is determined by your particular installation, but common locations are */usr/local/ssl/lib/openssl.cnf* or */usr/share/ssl/openssl.cnf*. Since we've created our own configuration file solely for the use of our CA, we do not want to use the system-wide configuration file. There are two ways to tell OpenSSL where to find our configuration file:

---

using the environment variable OPENSSL_CONF, or specifying the filename with the config option on the command line. Since we will issue a sizable number of commands that should make use of our configuration file, the easiest way for us to tell OpenSSL about it is through the environment (see Example 3-3).

Example 3-3. Telling OpenSSL where to find our configuration file

```
# OPENSSL_CONF=/opt/exampleca/openssl.cnf
# export OPENSSL_CONF
```

Creating a Self-Signed Root Certificate

Before we can begin issuing certificates with our CA, it needs a certificate of its own with which to sign the certificates that it issues. This certificate will also be used to sign any CRLs that are published. Any certificate that has the authority to sign certificates and CRLs will do. By this definition, a certificate from another CA or a self-signed root certificate will work. For our purposes, we should create our own self-signed root certificate to do the job.

The first thing that we need to do is add some more information to our configuration file. Example 3-4 shows the newly added information. Note that we'll be using the command-line tool's req command, so we'll start by adding a new section by the same name. Since we will use only this configuration file for our CA, and since we will use only the command-line tool's req command this one time, we'll put all of the necessary information that OpenSSL allows in the configuration file rather than typing it out on the command line. It's a little more work to do it this way, but it is the only way to specify X.509v3 extensions, and it also allows us to keep a record of how the self-signed root certificate was created.

Example 3-4. Configuration file additions for generating a self-signed root certificate

```
 [ req ]
default_bits        = 2048
default_keyfile     = /opt/exampleca/private/cakey.pem
default_md          = md5

prompt              = no
distinguished_name  = root_ca_distinguished_name

x509_extensions     = root_ca_extensions

 [ root_ca_distinguished_name ]
commonName          = Example CA
stateOrProvinceName = Virginia
countryName         = US
emailAddress        = ca@exampleca.org
organizationName    = Root Certification Authority

 [ root_ca_extensions ]
basicConstraints = CA:true
```

The `default_bits` key in the `req` section tells OpenSSL to generate a private key for the certificate with a length of 2,048 bits. If we don't specify this, the default is to use 512 bits. A key length of 2,048 bits provides significantly more protection than 512, and for a self-signed root certificate, it's best to use all of the protection afforded to us. With the vast computing power that is affordable today, the speed penalty for using a 2,048-bit key over a 512-bit key is well worth the trade-off in protection, since the security of this one key directly impacts the security of all keys issued by our CA.

The `default_keyfile` key in the `req` section tells OpenSSL where to write the newly generated private key. Note that we're specifying the same directory for output as we specified earlier in the `ca` section as the location of the private key for the certificate. We can't use the `$dir` "macro" here because the `dir` key is private to the `ca` section, so we need to type out the full path again.

The `default_md` key in the `req` section tells OpenSSL which message digest algorithm to use to sign the key. Since we specified MD5 as the algorithm to use when signing new certificates and CRLs, we'll use the same algorithm here for consistency. The SHA1 algorithm is actually a stronger algorithm and would be preferable, but for the sake of this example, we've chosen MD5 because it is more widely used and all but guaranteed to be supported by any software that could possibly be using our certificates. If you will be using only software that you know supports SHA1 with your certificates, we recommend that you use SHA1 instead of MD5.

The `prompt` and `distinguished_name` keys determine how OpenSSL gets the information it needs to fill in the certificate's distinguished name. By setting `prompt` to `no`, we're telling OpenSSL that it should get the information from the section named by the `distinguished_name` key. The default is to prompt for the information, so we must explicitly turn prompting off here. The keys in the `distinguished_name` section that we've defined by the name of `root_ca_distinguished_name` are the names of the fields making up the distinguished name, and the values are the values that we want placed in the certificate for each field. We've included only the distinguished name fields that we previously configured as required and omitted the one optional field.

Finally, the `x509_extensions` key specifies the name of a section that contains the extensions that we want included in the certificate. The keys in the section we've named `root_ca_extensions` are the names of the extension fields that we want filled in, and the values are the values we want them filled in with. We discussed the `basicConstraints` key earlier in this chapter. We've set the `cA` component of the extension to `true`, indicating that this certificate is permitted to act as a CA to sign both certificates and CRLs.

Now that we have the configuration set up for generating our self-signed root certificate, it's time to actually create the certificate and generate a new key pair to go along with it. The options required on the command line are minimal because we've specified most of the options that we want in the configuration file. From the root directory of the CA, */opt/exampleca*, or whatever you've used on your system, execute the following command. Make sure that you've set the `OPENSSL_CONF` environment variable first so that OpenSSL can find your configuration file!

```
# openssl req -x509 -newkey rsa -out cacert.pem -outform PEM
```

When you run the command, OpenSSL prompts you twice to enter a passphrase to encrypt your private key. Remember that this private key is a very important key, so choose your passphrase accordingly. If this key is compromised, the integrity of your CA is compromised, which essentially means that any certificates issued, whether they were issued before the key was compromised or after, can no longer be trusted. The key will be encrypted with 3DES, using a key derived from your passphrase. Example 3-5 shows the results of the command we just generated followed by a textual dump of the resulting certificate. Although your certificate will be different because your public and private key will be different from ours, your output should look similar.

Example 3-5. Output from generating a self-signed root certificate

```
# openssl req -x509 -newkey rsa -out cacert.pem -outform PEM

Using configuration from /opt/exampleca/openssl.cnf
Generating a 2048 bit RSA private key
...............................................++++++
.........++++++
writing new private key to '/opt/exampleca/private/cakey.pem'
Enter PEM pass phrase:
Verifying password - Enter PEM pass phrase:
-----
# openssl x509 -in cacert.pem -text -noout
Certificate:
    Data:
        Version: 3 (0x2)
        Serial Number: 0 (0x0)
        Signature Algorithm: md5WithRSAEncryption
        Issuer: CN=Example CA, ST=Virginia, C=US/Email=ca@exampleca.org, O=Root
Certificate Authority
        Validity
            Not Before: Jan 13 10:24:19 2002 GMT
            Not After : Jan 13 10:24:19 2003 GMT
        Subject: CN=Example CA, ST=Virginia, C=US/Email=ca@exampleca.org, O=Root
Certificate Authority
        Subject Public Key Info:
            Public Key Algorithm: rsaEncryption
            RSA Public Key: (1024 bit)
                Modulus (1024 bit):
                    00:cb:4f:55:6c:a4:2c:8a:f4:21:44:ec:fc:ca:9f:
                    ca:c7:43:2f:14:7d:07:1a:05:e7:3f:08:6c:ee:88:
                    30:ef:5b:24:6c:90:59:a2:81:af:99:bc:f6:94:96:
                    ab:48:53:98:b3:13:b2:42:aa:01:31:7d:59:0d:9a:
                    99:dc:95:b8:c2:0a:fc:b5:d0:d1:7a:5c:db:87:a3:
                    e0:db:8a:3f:c3:10:40:b5:d5:e9:5f:58:8d:fd:f1:
```

```
                    06:65:e2:73:7a:17:7f:98:ac:6f:b5:be:56:e1:5f:
                    16:2b:43:02:60:d8:80:b7:7e:0e:d4:48:3e:6a:c9:
                    2d:a6:02:3d:b0:e1:ac:fc:3d
                Exponent: 65537 (0x10001)
        X509v3 extensions:
            X509v3 Basic Constraints:
                CA:TRUE
    Signature Algorithm: md5WithRSAEncryption
        2e:54:2c:cf:d8:1a:d0:bc:bb:9d:eb:3e:2f:fa:8b:7b:21:ef:
        4f:30:0e:93:6c:85:26:8d:c2:62:69:49:7b:55:26:09:6a:ea:
        00:bc:a0:03:ab:5b:45:8a:71:eb:39:46:6c:50:29:4b:00:ff:
        19:a1:e8:a2:4a:75:07:79:50:f0:38:6d:d2:20:09:63:48:75:
        67:6b:59:41:74:ae:63:69:13:4e:27:6b:5d:7e:55:6a:7b:3c:
        86:c8:b2:c5:15:01:e3:68:08:ec:3c:8a:00:68:43:ce:43:f0:
        76:e2:e2:97:ad:88:08:bf:87:ec:ba:d1:db:fa:c4:91:fb:b6:
        33:95
```

You'll notice in Example 3-5's output that when OpenSSL displays a DN in a shortened form, it uses a nonstandard representation that can be somewhat confusing. In this example, we see C=US/Email=ca@exampleca.org as an example of this representation. What's confusing here is the slash separating the two fields. The reason for this is that the Email and O fields are nonstandard in a DN. OpenSSL lists the standard fields first and the nonstandard fields second, separating them with a slash.

Issuing Certificates

Everything is now set up for our CA, and it's time to take it out for a test drive by issuing a certificate. To do that, we need a certificate request. It's also a good idea to know how to create a certificate request that your CA will be able to use. Unless you plan to create both the certificate requests and certificates for anybody you'll be issuing a certificate to, you'll probably need to be able to tell someone how to give you a certificate request that you can use. Either way, you'll still need to know how to do it yourself.

To create a certificate request, start with a clean shell without the OPENSSL_CONF environment variable set so that the default configuration file is used. We don't want to use our custom configuration file to do this, as that configuration file is intended for use only by the CA, and generating a certificate request is not at all a function of a CA.

The command to generate a certificate request is similar to the command we used to create our self-signed root certificate. We use the command-line tool's req command, but we'll need to specify some extra parameters. The operation will be much more interactive, prompting for information to fill in the certificate request's distinguished name. Example 3-6 shows the output from generating a certificate request.

Example 3-6. Generating a certificate request

```
# openssl req -newkey rsa:1024 -keyout testkey.pem -keyform PEM -out testreq.pem
-outform PEM
Using configuration from /usr/share/ssl/openssl.cnf
```

Example 3-6. Generating a certificate request (continued)

```
Generating a 1024 bit RSA private key
.........++++++
.........++++++
writing new private key to 'testkey.pem'
Enter PEM pass phrase:
Verifying password - Enter PEM pass phrase:
-----
You are about to be asked to enter information that will be incorporated
into your certificate request.
What you are about to enter is what is called a Distinguished Name or a DN.
There are quite a few fields but you can leave some blank
For some fields there will be a default value,
If you enter '.', the field will be left blank.
-----
Country Name (2 letter code) [AU]:US
State or Province Name (full name) [Some-State]:Virginia
Locality Name (eg, city) []:Manassas
Organization Name (eg, company) [Internet Widgits Pty Ltd]:Test Request
Organizational Unit Name (eg, section) []:
Common Name (eg, your name or your server's hostname) []:www.exampleca.org
Email Address []:ca@exampleca.org

Please enter the following 'extra' attributes
to be sent with your certificate request
A challenge password []:cloud noon sundry presto madrid baker
An optional company name []:Examples-R-Us, Inc.
```

The result of this command is the creation of two files: *testreq.pem* and *testkey.pem*. The former, *testreq.pem*, contains the certificate request as shown in Example 3-7, and *testkey.pem* contains the private key that matches the public key embedded in the certificate request. As part of the process to generate a certificate request, a new key pair was also generated. The first passphrase that is prompted for is the passphrase used to encrypt the private key. The challenge phrase is stored in the certificate request, and is otherwise ignored by OpenSSL. Some CAs may make use of it, however.

Example 3-7. The resulting certificate request

```
# openssl req -in testreq.pem -text -noout
Using configuration from /usr/share/ssl/openssl.cnf
Certificate Request:
    Data:
        Version: 0 (0x0)
        Subject: C=US, ST=Virginia, L=Manassas, O=Test Request, CN=www.exampleca.org/
Email=ca@exampleca.org
        Subject Public Key Info:
            Public Key Algorithm: rsaEncryption
            RSA Public Key: (1024 bit)
                Modulus (1024 bit):
                    00:d8:a5:1b:c6:b6:e4:75:bf:f3:e3:ce:29:1d:ab:
                    e2:5b:0d:bb:2e:94:de:52:a1:20:51:b1:77:d9:42:
                    a3:6c:26:1f:c3:3e:58:8f:91:b1:b3:ed:bd:7c:62:
```

Example 3-7. The resulting certificate request (continued)

```
                    1c:71:05:3b:47:ff:1a:de:98:f3:b4:a6:91:fd:91:
                    26:db:41:76:85:b5:10:3f:c2:10:04:26:4f:bc:03:
                    39:ff:b9:42:d0:d3:2a:89:db:91:8e:75:6d:f5:71:
                    ec:96:e8:d6:03:29:8e:fe:20:3f:5d:d8:cb:14:5e:
                    e5:64:fc:be:fa:d1:27:42:b6:72:eb:b4:16:16:71:
                    77:d3:0e:8c:cc:87:16:fc:41
                Exponent: 65537 (0x10001)
        Attributes:
            unstructuredName          :drowssap egnellahc
            challengePassword         :drowssap egnellahc
    Signature Algorithm: md5WithRSAEncryption
        25:aa:ca:78:64:fa:29:46:cf:dc:df:d9:95:dd:48:24:bf:4f:
        7b:7e:f4:09:76:96:c4:c5:b1:10:9b:64:95:19:30:8d:cd:d0:
        da:ac:b2:21:5e:34:e6:be:7b:41:52:2c:b3:e7:d4:dc:99:e5:
        a0:c2:46:12:9f:ef:99:0e:03:89:c1:f9:db:0d:0d:21:1b:e2:
        da:4e:23:ef:c1:aa:1b:24:b5:ce:53:a1:05:08:6e:4a:85:78:
        6e:71:ef:bc:36:48:5c:3e:ee:b1:bb:28:f4:31:df:23:a9:89:
        96:35:1b:b4:01:f9:63:4d:46:b4:ed:5d:be:1d:28:50:1c:86:
        43:5e
```

With a certificate request now in hand, we can use our CA to issue a certificate. For the sake of convenience in this example, the certificate request that we'll be using, *testreq.pem*, which we just created, should be in the CA's root directory. Make sure that the OPENSSL_CONF variable is set to the CA's configuration file, and issue the command to generate a certificate, as shown in Example 3-8.

Example 3-8. Issuing a certificate from a certificate request

```
# openssl ca -in testreq.pem
Using configuration from /opt/exampleca/openssl.cnf
Enter PEM pass phrase:
Check that the request matches the signature
Signature ok
The Subjects Distinguished Name is as follows
countryName           :PRINTABLE:'US'
stateOrProvinceName   :PRINTABLE:'Virginia'
localityName          :PRINTABLE:'Manassas'
organizationName      :PRINTABLE:'Test Request'
commonName            :PRINTABLE:'www.exampleca.org'
emailAddress          :IA5STRING:'ca@exampleca.org'
Certificate is to be certified until Jan 14 04:31:25 2003 GMT (365 days)
Sign the certificate? [y/n]:y

1 out of 1 certificate requests certified, commit? [y/n]y
Write out database with 1 new entries
Certificate:
    Data:
        Version: 3 (0x2)
        Serial Number: 1 (0x1)
        Signature Algorithm: md5WithRSAEncryption
        Issuer: CN=Example CA, ST=Virginia, C=US/Email=ca@exampleca.org, O=Root
```

Example 3-8. Issuing a certificate from a certificate request (continued)

```
Certificate Authority
        Validity
            Not Before: Jan 14 04:58:29 2002 GMT
            Not After : Jan 14 04:58:29 2003 GMT
        Subject: CN=www.exampleca.org, ST=Virginia, C=US/Email=ca@exampleca.org,
O=Test Request
        Subject Public Key Info:
            Public Key Algorithm: rsaEncryption
            RSA Public Key: (1024 bit)
                Modulus (1024 bit):
                    00:d8:a5:1b:c6:b6:e4:75:bf:f3:e3:ce:29:1d:ab:
                    e2:5b:0d:bb:2e:94:de:52:a1:20:51:b1:77:d9:42:
                    a3:6c:26:1f:c3:3e:58:8f:91:b1:b3:ed:bd:7c:62:
                    1c:71:05:3b:47:ff:1a:de:98:f3:b4:a6:91:fd:91:
                    26:db:41:76:85:b5:10:3f:c2:10:04:26:4f:bc:03:
                    39:ff:b9:42:d0:d3:2a:89:db:91:8e:75:6d:f5:71:
                    ec:96:e8:d6:03:29:8e:fe:20:3f:5d:d8:cb:14:5e:
                    e5:64:fc:be:fa:d1:27:42:b6:72:eb:b4:16:16:71:
                    77:d3:0e:8c:cc:87:16:fc:41
                Exponent: 65537 (0x10001)
        X509v3 extensions:
            X509v3 Basic Constraints:
                CA:FALSE
    Signature Algorithm: md5WithRSAEncryption
        13:33:75:8e:a4:05:9b:76:de:0b:d0:98:b8:86:2a:95:5a:13:
        0b:14:c7:48:83:f3:95:0e:3e:bf:76:04:f7:ab:ae:cc:cd:76:
        ae:32:77:ea:8c:96:60:28:52:4e:89:c5:ed:85:68:47:68:95:
        74:53:9f:dc:64:95:62:1a:b0:21:09:76:75:14:25:d4:fd:17:
        de:f9:87:7f:d5:dc:e4:41:1e:ad:f6:7b:2d:bf:a6:8a:cd:65:
        60:3b:71:74:bc:4d:0d:94:5a:22:c4:35:de:b0:19:46:f3:c1:
        bb:c5:e0:d4:f7:a2:92:65:ec:40:4c:cc:d4:b7:a3:84:bd:a9:
        b0:86
-----BEGIN CERTIFICATE-----
MIICcjCCAdugAwIBAgIBATANBgkqhkiG9w0BAQQFADB7MRMwEQYDVQQDEwpFeGFt
cGxlIENBMREwDwYDVQQIEwhWaXJnaW5pYTELMAkGA1UEBhMCVVMxHzAdBgkqhkiG
9w0BCQEWEGNhQGV4YW1wbGVjYS5vcmcxIzAhBgNVBAoTGlJvb3QgQ2VydGlmaWNh
dGUgQXV0aG9yaXR5MB4XDTAyMDExNDA0NTgyOVoXDTAzMDExNDA0NTgyOVowdDEa
MBgGA1UEAxMRd3d3LmV4YW1wbGVjYS5vcmcxETAPBgNVBAgTCFZpcmdpbmlhMQsw
CQYDVQQGEwJVUzEfMB0GCSqGSIb3DQEJARYQY2FAZXhhbXBsZWNhLm9yZzEVMBMG
A1UEChMMVGVzdCBSZXF1ZXN0MIGfMA0GCSqGSIb3DQEBAQUAA4GNADCBiQKBgQDY
pRvGtuR1v/Pjzikdq+JbDbsulN5SoSBRsXfZQqNsJh/DPliPkbGz7b18YhxxBTtH
/xremPOoppH9kSbbQXaFtRA/whAEJk+8Azn/uULQOyqJ25GOdW31ceyW6NYDKY7+
ID9d2MsUXuVk/L760SdCtnLrtBYWcXfTDozMhxb8QQIDAQABowOwCzAJBgNVHRME
AjAAMA0GCSqGSIb3DQEBBAUAA4GBABMzdY6kBZt23gvQmLiGKpVaEwsUxOiD85UO
Pr92BPerrszNdq4yd+qMlmAoUk6Jxe2FaEdolXRTn9xklWIasCEJdnUUJdT9F975
h3/V3ORBHq32ey2/porNZWA7cXS8TQ2UWiLENd6wGUbzwbvF4NT3opJl7EBMzNS3
o4S9qbCG
-----END CERTIFICATE-----
Data Base Updated
```

The first thing that happens is OpenSSL asks for a passphrase. The passphrase that it is looking for is not the passphrase for the certificate request, but the passphrase for the CA's private key. The private key will be used to sign the new certificate. After displaying the subject's distinguished name, OpenSSL prompts you for confirmation to sign the certificate. Since certificate requests are likely to come from people needing certificates from you, you should check to be sure that the information they've provided in their certificate requests is correct before issuing the certificate. The next and final prompt is to confirm whether the certificates should be committed to the CA's database. Finally, the new certificate will be written to stdout, and the command is finished.

The confirmation prompts that are issued can be suppressed and automatically answered in the affirmative by adding the batch option. This is useful if you're building a wrapper around the OpenSSL command-line tool, or if you've already manually verified the information in the request and you don't want to be prompted. It's also possible to issue multiple certificates for multiple certificate requests all with one command. For example, suppose you have three certificate requests that need to have certificates issued. The infiles option can be used instead of the in option; the list of files to be processed follows immediately after it. If you use the infiles option, be aware that it must be the last option specified; everything after it is treated as an input filename.

The resulting certificate is also written to the directory that we specified in our configuration file with the new_certs_dir key. It's written out in PEM format and given a filename composed of the certificate's serial number and an extension of *.pem*. The output of the certificate to stdout when it is created can be suppressed by using the notext option. Using the out option, the name of a file to write the certificate to can be specified. We recommend that you also use the notext option if you use the out option. The result will be a file containing a certificate that is identical to the one written to the new_certs_dir directory, */opt/exampleca/certs* in our example. If you use the out option, it'll save you having to search through all of the certificates that you've issued and pick the highest numbered among them to pass on to their owners.

After the command has completed and the certificate has been issued, you should see a new file in the subdirectory *certs* that we created. This file is the certificate that was issued. You should also be able to see that information was added to the file *index.txt*, OpenSSL's CA database. Finally, you should be able to see that the serial number in the file *serial* was incremented. When you look at the text dump of the certificate that was created, you'll notice that it was assigned a serial number of "1", the number that we used to seed the serial number file.

Revoking Certificates

The first certificate that we issued with our CA was simply a test certificate to make sure that the CA is working properly. We can see that the certificate was issued properly, but it's a certificate that we don't actually want anybody to be able to use, so we will need to revoke the certificate. This provides us with an excellent opportunity to find out how certificate revocation works using OpenSSL's CA command.

Revoking a certificate is a simple process. All you need is a copy of the certificate to be revoked. Even if you don't keep a copy of all of the certificates that you've issued, the CA infrastructure we created does. We can obtain a copy of the certificate that way, but it's much easier to keep a copy of your own and name the file something meaningful since the CA simply names the file containing the certificates it issues with each certificate's serial number. Using the command in the example from the last section to create the test certificate, we didn't keep a copy for ourselves, but we issued only a single certificate, so it's quite easy to get a copy of the certificate file. We'll make a copy of that certificate file in the CA's root directory and call it *testcert. pem*. Then we'll use that file as the certificate required by the revoke option to the ca command (see Example 3-9).

Example 3-9. Revoking a certificate

```
# cp certs/01.pem testcert.pem
# openssl ca -revoke testcert.pem
Using configuration from /opt/exampleca/openssl.cnf
Enter PEM pass phrase:
Revoking Certificate 01.
Data Base Updated
```

Once again, the command-line tool prompts us for a passphrase. The passphrase it is looking for is the passphrase that protects the CA's private key. Although the key is not actually used for any signing as part of the certificate revocation process, it is required to validate the certificate as the CA's own and as a security measure to ensure that only someone authorized to use the CA can revoke a certificate that it has issued.

No change is made to the certificate at all. In fact, the only noticeable change is to the CA's database to indicate that the certificate has been revoked. Remember that once a certificate has been issued, it cannot be modified. It's presumably out in the wild and there's no way to ensure that every copy of the certificate in existence can be updated. This is where CRLs become relevant. We've revoked the first certificate that we issued with our CA, but the only entity that is aware of the revocation is the CA itself. By itself, this doesn't do anybody any good. Anybody that might be using the certificate also needs to know that the certificate has been revoked, so we need to issue a CRL.

When we issue our first CRL, we set the initial policy for how frequently we'll be issuing CRLs. In our configuration, we've indicated that we'll issue them once a week. When a CRL is made available, it contains a field that indicates the next time a new one will be published. In other words, each CRL is given an expiration date, and a new one must be obtained once the current one expires. Whether there are any new certificate revocations, a new CRL should be generated when the old one expires.

While CRLs should be published on a regularly scheduled periodic basis, it is also possible to generate and publish CRLs when a new one is needed. In fact, it's good practice to do so. Consider that not all software may cache the CRLs that it retrieves, particularly if they're retrieved automatically. It's also possible that the current CRL was most likely not retrieved by everyone that may be using certificates issued by your CA. Therefore, it's best to make the information as current as possible rather than waiting until the current CRL expires, especially if the period between issuance is large.

Issuing a CRL before a new one is due means there are possibly two or more CRLs from your CA in distribution, but that's fine. CRLs usually have only data added to them, and any time data is removed, it's because the revoked certificate has expired, and thus its revocation status is irrelevant. Some CAs may opt to keep even expired certificates in their CRLs. While this may not be a bad idea for a short period of time after a certificate expires, it's generally not a good idea to keep the information indefinitely; otherwise, the CRL could grow to be quite large and make distribution of it more costly in terms of both time and bandwidth.

Without any further ado, let's issue our first CRL. This is done by issuing a simple ca command using the gencrl option, along with an out option to specify the name of the file to write the resultant CRL to (see Example 3-10). OpenSSL prompts us for the passphrase protecting the CA's private key, which it will use to sign the CRL that it generates.

The command completes without writing anything to stdout indicating success, but if there is a problem, an appropriate error message will be written. We can see that the command completed successfully by noting that the file we specified with the -out option has been written. With that file, we can use the command-line tool's crl command to investigate the details of the CRL that we just generated.

Example 3-10. A certificate revocation list

```
# openssl ca -gencrl -out exampleca.crl
Using configuration from /opt/exampleca/openssl.cnf
Enter PEM pass phrase:
# openssl crl -in exampleca.crl -text -noout
Certificate Revocation List (CRL):
        Version 1 (0x0)
        Signature Algorithm: md5WithRSAEncryption
        Issuer: /CN=Example CA/ST=Virginia/C=US/Email=ca@exampleca.org/O=Root Ce
rtificate Authority
        Last Update: Jan 14 05:42:08 2002 GMT
        Next Update: Jan 21 05:42:08 2002 GMT
Revoked Certificates:
    Serial Number: 01
        Revocation Date: Jan 14 05:16:43 2002 GMT
    Signature Algorithm: md5WithRSAEncryption
        32:73:3b:e5:b4:f6:2d:57:58:15:e8:87:05:23:27:c3:5d:e5:
        10:a0:5d:1d:09:68:27:b8:8c:70:5c:5d:4a:0d:07:ff:63:09:
        2d:df:61:13:7b:ea:5a:49:74:3b:0a:e9:2b:2d:92:3e:4d:c6:
```

Example 3-10. A certificate revocation list (continued)

```
        f4:4f:18:fa:c9:9e:f7:bb:92:b5:ed:46:14:a1:c2:25:5d:3f:
        9d:5a:b4:c9:63:5f:06:fc:04:22:0b:80:aa:fd:77:a5:16:9d:
        36:47:f7:e9:5b:95:16:ff:bb:e6:db:98:3c:2a:aa:bd:4f:91:
        eb:20:86:44:09:7f:ef:62:69:ef:db:1e:79:7e:24:70:72:34:
        cf:1e
# openssl crl -in exampleca.crl -noout -CAfile cacert.pem
verify OK
```

When we get a text dump of the CRL, we can see the algorithm that was used to sign it, the CA that issued it, when it was issued, when the next list will be issued, and a list of all of the certificates that it contains. We can also use the crl command to verify the signature on the CRL. Doing so requires us to have a copy of the certificate that was used to sign it.

We can see in Example 3-10 that the version of the CRL that was generated was Version 1. By default, this is what OpenSSL will produce unless the crl_extensions key is specified in the configuration file in the ca section. We strongly recommend that you produce only Version 1 CRLs, unless you can be sure all of the software you're using with your certificates supports Version 2. If it's important that the software that supports Version 2 CRLs get them, you can produce both Version 1 and Version 2 lists.

Note that you are essentially on your own when it comes to publishing CRLs. One reasonable solution is to make CRLs available to all via secure HTTP.

CHAPTER 4

Support Infrastructure

The OpenSSL library is composed of many different packages. Some of the lower-level packages can be used independently, while the higher-level ones may make use of several of the lower-level ones. To use the OpenSSL library effectively, it is important to understand the fundamental concepts of cryptography that we've already introduced, and to gain familiarity with the more important supplemental package offerings.

In this chapter, we concentrate on the lower-level APIs that are most useful with the higher-level APIs that we discuss through the rest of this book. We'll start by demonstrating what is necessary when using the OpenSSL library in a multithreaded environment by developing a small "drop-in" library for Windows and Unix platforms that use POSIX threads. We'll also examine OpenSSL's error handling and its input/output interface, which are both quite different from how most other development libraries deal with the same things. OpenSSL also provides packages for arbitrary precision math and secure random number generation, as we already mentioned. These packages are both fundamental to strong crypto, and we'll cover them as well.

For all of the packages that we examine in this chapter, we'll discuss how to use them and provide examples. Additionally, we'll discuss some of the common pitfalls that developers often encounter.

Note that if some of the material in this chapter doesn't seem immediately relevant and interesting, it is safe to skip it, and come back to this chapter when necessary.

Multithread Support

Most modern operating systems provide support for multithreaded applications, and it is becoming increasingly more common for applications to take advantage of that support. OpenSSL can certainly be used in a multithreaded environment; however, it requires that the developer do some work in order to make a program thread-safe. A common mistake that many developers make with OpenSSL is that they assume the library is thread-safe without requiring anything special to be done in the application.

This is most certainly an incorrect assumption, and failing to set up OpenSSL for use in a multithreaded environment can result in unpredictable behavior and seemingly random crashes that are very difficult to debug.

OpenSSL uses many data structures on which operations must be atomic. That is, it must be guaranteed that only one thread will access them at a time. If two or more threads are allowed to modify the same structure concurrently, there is no way to predict which one's changes will be realized. What's worse, the operations could end up mixed—part of the first thread's changes could be made, while part of the second thread's changes could also be made. In either case, the results are unpredictable, so steps must be taken to make the structures thread-safe.

OpenSSL provides for the thread safety of its data structures by requiring each thread to acquire a mutually exclusive lock known as a *mutex* that protects the structure before allowing it to be accessed. When the thread is finished with the data structure, it releases the mutex, allowing another thread to acquire the lock and access the data structure. Because OpenSSL is designed for use on multiple platforms that differ in their implementation of threading, OpenSSL doesn't make direct calls to create, destroy, acquire, and release mutexes: it requires the application programmer to perform these operations in a manner appropriate for the platform it's running on by making callbacks to functions that the application registers with OpenSSL for this purpose.

There are two different sets of callbacks that an application is expected to provide to safely operate in a multithreaded environment. *Static locks* provide a fixed number of mutexes available for OpenSSL's use. *Dynamic locks* allow OpenSSL to create mutexes as it needs them. OpenSSL does not currently make use of dynamic locks, but reserves the right to do so in the future. If you want your applications to continue working with a minimal amount of effort in the future, we recommend that you implement both static and dynamic locks now.

Static Locking Callbacks

The static locking mechanism requires the application to provde two callback functions. In addition to providing an implementation for the functions, the application must tell OpenSSL about them so that it knows to call them when appropriate. The first callback function is used either to acquire or release a lock, and is defined like this:

```
void locking_function(int mode, int n, const char *file, int line);
```

mode

> Determines the action that the locking function should take. When the CRYPTO_LOCK flag is set, the lock should be acquired; otherwise, it should be released.

n

> The number of the lock that should be acquired or released. The number is zero-based, meaning that the first lock is identified by 0. The value will never be greater than or equal to the return from the CRYPTO_num_locks function.

file

> The name of the source file requesting the locking operation to take place. It is intended to aid in debugging and is usually supplied by the `__FILE__` preprocessor macro.

line

> The source line number requesting the locking operation to take place. Like the file argument, it is also intended to aid in debugging, and it is usually supplied by the `__LINE__` preprocessor macro.

The next callback function is used to get a unique identifier for the calling thread. For example, `GetCurrentThreadId` on Windows will do just that. For reasons that will soon become clear, it is important the value returned from this function be consistent across calls for the same thread, but different for each thread within the same process. The return value from the function should be the unique identifier. The function is defined like this:

```
unsigned long id_function(void);
```

Example 4-1 introduces two new OpenSSL library functions: `CRYPTO_set_id_callback` and `CRYPTO_set_locking_callback`. These two functions are used to tell OpenSSL about the callbacks that we've implemented for the static locking mechanism. We can either pass a pointer to a function to install a callback or `NULL` to remove a callback.

Example 4-1. Static locking callbacks for WIN32 and POSIX threads systems

```
int THREAD_setup(void);
int THREAD_cleanup(void);

#if defined(WIN32)
    #define MUTEX_TYPE HANDLE
    #define MUTEX_SETUP(x)   (x) = CreateMutex(NULL, FALSE, NULL)
    #define MUTEX_CLEANUP(x) CloseHandle(x)
    #define MUTEX_LOCK(x)    WaitForSingleObject((x), INFINITE)
    #define MUTEX_UNLOCK(x)  ReleaseMutex(x)
    #define THREAD_ID        GetCurrentThreadId( )
#elif defined(_POSIX_THREADS)
    /* _POSIX_THREADS is normally defined in unistd.h if pthreads are available
       on your platform. */
    #define MUTEX_TYPE       pthread_mutex_t
    #define MUTEX_SETUP(x)   pthread_mutex_init(&(x), NULL)
    #define MUTEX_CLEANUP(x) pthread_mutex_destroy(&(x))
    #define MUTEX_LOCK(x)    pthread_mutex_lock(&(x))
    #define MUTEX_UNLOCK(x)  pthread_mutex_unlock(&(x))
    #define THREAD_ID        pthread_self( )
#else
    #error You must define mutex operations appropriate for your platform!
#endif

/* This array will store all of the mutexes available to OpenSSL. */
static MUTEX_TYPE *mutex_buf = NULL;
```

```
static void locking_function(int mode, int n, const char * file, int line)
{
    if (mode & CRYPTO_LOCK)
        MUTEX_LOCK(mutex_buf[n]);
    else
        MUTEX_UNLOCK(mutex_buf[n]);
}

static unsigned long id_function(void)
{
    return ((unsigned long)THREAD_ID);
}

int THREAD_setup(void)
{
    int i;

    mutex_buf = (MUTEX_TYPE *)malloc(CRYPTO_num_locks( ) * sizeof(MUTEX_TYPE));
    if (!mutex_buf)
        return 0;
    for (i = 0;  i < CRYPTO_num_locks( );  i++)
        MUTEX_SETUP(mutex_buf[i]);
    CRYPTO_set_id_callback(id_function);
    CRYPTO_set_locking_callback(locking_function);
    return 1;
}

int THREAD_cleanup(void)
{
    int i;

    if (!mutex_buf)
        return 0;
    CRYPTO_set_id_callback(NULL);
    CRYPTO_set_locking_callback(NULL);
    for (i = 0;  i < CRYPTO_num_locks( );  i++)
        MUTEX_CLEANUP(mutex_buf[i]);
    free(mutex_buf);
    mutex_buf = NULL;
    return 1;
}
```

To use these static locking functions, we need to make one function call before our program starts threads or calls OpenSSL functions, and we must call THREAD_setup, which returns 1 normally and 0 if it is unable to allocate the memory required to hold the mutexes. In our example code, we do make a potentially unsafe assumption that the initialization of each individual mutex will succeed. You may wish to add additional error handling code to your programs. Once we've called THREAD_setup and it returns successfully, we can safely make calls into OpenSSL from multiple threads. After our program's threads are finished, or if we are done using OpenSSL, we should call THREAD_cleanup to reclaim any memory used for the mutex structures.

Dynamic Locking Callbacks

The dynamic locking mechanism requires a data structure (CRYPTO_dynlock_value) and three callback functions. The structure is meant to hold the data necessary for the mutex, and the three functions correspond to the operations for creation, locking/unlocking, and destruction. As with the static locking mechanism, we must also tell OpenSSL about the callback functions so that it knows to call them when appropriate.

The first thing that we must do is define the CRYPTO_dynlock_value structure. We'll be building on the static locking support that we built in Example 4-1, so we can use the same platform-dependent macros that we defined already. For our purposes, this structure will be quite simple, containing only one member:

```
struct CRYPTO_dynlock_value
{
    MUTEX_TYPE mutex;
};
```

The first callback function that we need to define is used to create a new mutex that OpenSSL will be able to use to protect a data structure. Memory must be allocated for the structure, and the structure should have any necessary initialization performed on it. The newly created and initialized mutex should be returned in a released state from the function. The callback is defined like this:

```
struct CRYPTO_dynlock_value *dyn_create_function(const char *file, int line);
```

file

> The name of the source file requesting that the mutex be created. It is intended to aid in debugging and is usually supplied by the __FILE__ preprocessor macro.

line

> The source line number requesting that the mutex be created. Like the file argument, it is also intended to aid in debugging, and it is usually supplied by the __LINE__ preprocessor macro.

The next callback function is used for acquiring or releasing a mutex. It behaves almost identically to the corresponding static locking mechanism's callback, which performs the same operation. It is defined like this:

```
void dyn_lock_function(int mode, struct CRYPTO_dynlock_value
                       *mutex, const char *file, int line);
```

mode

> Determines the action that the locking function should take. When the CRYPTO_LOCK flag is set, the lock should be acquired; otherwise, it should be released.

mutex

> The mutex that should be either acquired or released. It will never be NULL and will always be created and initialized by the mutex creation callback first.

---

file

> The name of the source file requesting that the locking operation take place. It is intended to aid in debugging and is usually supplied by the __FILE__ preprocessor macro.

line

> The source line number requesting that the locking operation take place. Like the file argument, it is also intended to aid in debugging, and it is usually supplied by the __LINE__ preprocessor macro.

The third and final callback function is used to destroy a mutex that OpenSSL no longer requires. It should perform any platform-dependent destruction of the mutex and free any memory that was allocated for the CRYPTO_dynlock_value structure. It is defined like this:

```
void dyn_destroy_function(struct CRYPTO_dynlock_value *mutex,
                          const char *file, int line);
```

mutex

> The mutex that should be destroyed. It will never be NULL and will always have first been created and initialized by the mutex creation callback.

file

> The name of the source file requesting that the mutex be destroyed. It is intended to aid in debugging and is usually supplied by the __FILE__ preprocessor macro.

line

> The source line number requesting that the mutex be destroyed. Like the file argument, it is also intended to aid in debugging, and it is usually supplied by the __LINE__ preprocessor macro.

Using the static locking mechanism's code from Example 4-1, we can easily build a dynamic locking mechanism implementation. Example 4-2 shows an implementation of the three dynamic locking callback functions. It also includes new versions of the THREAD_setup and THREAD_cleanup functions extended to support the dynamic locking mechanism in addition to the static locking mechanism. The modifications to these two functions are simply to make the appropriate OpenSSL library calls to install and remove the dynamic locking callback functions.

Example 4-2. Extensions to the library to support the dynamic locking mechanism

```
struct CRYPTO_dynlock_value
{
    MUTEX_TYPE mutex;
};

static struct CRYPTO_dynlock_value * dyn_create_function(const char *file,
                                                         int line)
{
    struct CRYPTO_dynlock_value *value;
```

```
    value = (struct CRYPTO_dynlock_value *)malloc(sizeof(
                                        struct CRYPTO_dynlock_value));
    if (!value)
        return NULL;
    MUTEX_SETUP(value->mutex);
    return value;
}

static void dyn_lock_function(int mode, struct CRYPTO_dynlock_value *l,
                        const char *file, int line)
{
    if (mode & CRYPTO_LOCK)
        MUTEX_LOCK(l->mutex);
    else
        MUTEX_UNLOCK(l->mutex);
}

static void dyn_destroy_function(struct CRYPTO_dynlock_value *l,
                        const char *file, int line)
{
    MUTEX_CLEANUP(l->mutex);
    free(l);
}

int THREAD_setup(void)
{
    int i;

    mutex_buf = (MUTEX_TYPE *)malloc(CRYPTO_num_locks() * sizeof(MUTEX_TYPE));
    if (!mutex_buf)
        return 0;
    for (i = 0;  i < CRYPTO_num_locks();  i++)
        MUTEX_SETUP(mutex_buf[i]);
    CRYPTO_set_id_callback(id_function);
    CRYPTO_set_locking_callback(locking_function);

    /* The following three CRYPTO_... functions are the OpenSSL functions
       for registering the callbacks we implemented above */
    CRYPTO_set_dynlock_create_callback(dyn_create_function);
    CRYPTO_set_dynlock_lock_callback(dyn_lock_function);
    CRYPTO_set_dynlock_destroy_callback(dyn_destroy_function);

    return 1;
}

int THREAD_cleanup(void)
{
    int i;

    if (!mutex_buf)
        return 0;
    CRYPTO_set_id_callback(NULL);
```

```
    CRYPTO_set_locking_callback(NULL);
    CRYPTO_set_dynlock_create_callback(NULL);
    CRYPTO_set_dynlock_lock_callback(NULL);
    CRYPTO_set_dynlock_destroy_callback(NULL);
    for (i = 0;  i < CRYPTO_num_locks();  i++)
        MUTEX_CLEANUP(mutex_buf[i]);
    free(mutex_buf);
    mutex_buf = NULL;
    return 1;
}
```

Internal Error Handling

OpenSSL has a package, known as the ERR package, devoted to the handling and processing of errors. When an OpenSSL function encounters an error, it creates an error report and logs the information to an error queue. Because the information is logged to a queue, if multiple errors occur, information can be gathered for each of them. It is our responsibility as developers to check the error queue to obtain detailed information when a function returns an error so that we can handle error conditions appropriately. The OpenSSL error handling mechanism is more complex than most other libraries of similar stature, but that also means more information is available to help resolve the error condition.

Let's suppose for a moment that OpenSSL didn't log errors onto a queue. Consider, for example, a rather common case in which an application calling into a high-level OpenSSL library function causes OpenSSL to make several successive calls into various lower-level packages that make up OpenSSL. If an error were to occur at a low level, that error would be propagated back up the call stack to the application. The problem is that by the time the application gets the information, it's likely to have changed to something less detailed than the initial error as each function in the chain causes a new error to be generated all because of the initial low-level error.

Manipulating Error Queues

When an error occurs in the OpenSSL library, a significant amount of information is logged. Some of the information can be useful in attempting to recover from an error automatically, but much of it is for debugging and reporting the error to a user.

The ERR package provides six basic functions that are useful for obtaining information from the error queue. Each function always retrieves the oldest information from the queue so that errors are returned in the order that they were generated. The most basic piece of information that is logged is an error code, which describes the error that occurred. The error code is a 32-bit integer that has meaning only to OpenSSL. That is, OpenSSL defines its own unique error codes for any error condition that it could possibly encounter. It does not rely on error codes defined by any other library, including the standard C runtime. For each of the six basic functions, this error code is the return value from the function. If there is no error in the queue, the return from any of them will be 0, which also tells us that 0 is never a valid error code.

This first function retrieves only the error code from the error queue. It also removes that error report from the queue, so the next call will retrieve the next error that occurred or possibly 0 if there are no more errors in the queue:

```
unsigned long ERR_get_error(void);
```

The second function also retrieves only the error code from the error queue, but it does not remove the error report from the queue, so the next call will retrieve the same error:

```
unsigned long ERR_peek_error(void);
```

The third function builds on the information returned by ERR_get_error and ERR_peek_error. In addition to returning the error code, it also returns the name of the source file and source line number that generated the error. Like ERR_get_error, it also removes the error report from the queue:

```
unsigned long ERR_get_error_line(const char **file, int *line);
```

> file
>
> > Receives the name of the source file that generated the error. It is usually supplied to the error handler from the __FILE__ preprocessor macro.
>
> line
>
> > Receives the source line number that generated the error. It is usually supplied to the error handler from the __LINE__ preprocessor macro.

The fourth function returns the same information as ERR_get_error_line, but like ERR_peek_error, it does not remove the error report from the queue. Its arguments and their meanings are identical to ERR_get_error_line:

```
unsigned long ERR_peek_error_line(const char **file, int *line);
```

The fifth function builds on the information returned by ERR_get_error_line and ERR_peek_error_line. In addition to returning the error code, source filename, and line number, it also returns extra data and a set of flags that indicate how that data should be treated. The extra data and flags are supplied when the error is generated. Like ERR_get_error and ERR_get_error_line, this function also removes the error report from the queue:

```
unsigned long ERR_get_error_line_data(const char **file, int *line,
                                      const char **data, int *flags);
```

> file
>
> > Receives the name of the source file that generated the error. It is usually supplied to the error handler from the __FILE__ preprocessor macro.
>
> line
>
> > Receives the source line number that generated the error. It is usually supplied to the error handler from the __LINE__ preprocessor macro.

data

> Receives a pointer to the extra data that was included with the error report. The pointer that is returned is not a copy, and so it should not be modified or freed. See below.

flags

> Receives a set of flags that define the attributes of the extra data.

The sixth function returns the same information as ERR_get_error_line_data, but like ERR_peek_error and ERR_peek_error_line, it does not remove the error report from the queue. Its arguments and their meanings are identical to ERR_get_error_line_data:

```
unsigned long ERR_peek_error_line_data(const char **file, int *line,
                const char **data, int *flags);
```

ERR_get_error_line_data and ERR_peek_error_line_data both retrieve the optional piece of data that can be associated with an error report. This optional piece of data can be anything, but most frequently, it's a string. Stored along with the data is a bit mask of flags that describe the data so that it can be dealt with appropriately by the error handling package. If the flag ERR_TXT_MALLOCED is set, the memory for the data will be freed by a call to OpenSSL's OPENSSL_free function. If the flag ERR_TXT_STRING is set, the data is safe to be interpreted as a C-style string.

Note that the file and data information that can be obtained from the queue is returned as a pointer to the information on the queue. It is not a copy, so you should not attempt to modify the data. In the case of the file information, it is usually a constant string from the _ _FILE_ _ preprocessor macro. For the data information, if you need to store the information for any reason, you should make a copy and not store the pointer that is returned. When you use the "get" family of functions to obtain this data, the data remains valid for a short period, but you should be sure to make a copy before any other error handler function is called if you need to preserve it. Example 4-3 demonstrates how to print out the error information that is in the calling thread's error queue.

Example 4-3. Accessing error information on the error queue

```
void print_errors(void)
{
    int          flags, line;
    char         *data, *file;
    unsigned long code;

    code = ERR_get_error_line_data(&file, &line, &data, &flags);
    while (code)
    {
        printf("error code: %lu in %s line %d.\n", code, file, line);
        if (data && (flags & ERR_TXT_STRING))
            printf("error data: %s\n", data);
        code = ERR_get_error_line_data(&file, &line, &data, &flags);
    }
}
```

There is one last queue-manipulation function that we'll discuss here: the function for clearing the error queue. It will delete all errors currently in the queue. In general, there is no need to call this function unless we are trying to reset the error status for the current thread and don't care about any other errors that are on the queue. There is no way to recover the previous errors once it's been called, so use it judiciously:

```
void ERR_clear_error(void);
```

Human-Readable Error Messages

In some cases, the most appropriate way to handle an error condition is to display or log the error so that the user of your application can take the necessary steps to resolve the error. To do that, it's best to display a human-readable error message rather than an error code. The error handling package provides standard error messages for its error codes for just this purpose, but before they can be used, they must be loaded.

There are two sets of error messages: one for the errors generated by libcrypto, and one for the errors generated by libssl. The function ERR_load_crypto_strings loads the errors generated by libcrypto, and the function ERR_load_SSL_strings loads the errors generated by libssl. There is an additional function, SSL_load_error_strings, which will load both sets of error messages.

Once the error strings are loaded, ERR_error_string and ERR_error_string_n can be used to translate an error code into an error message that is more meaningful to humans. Particularly in a multithreaded application, ERR_error_string should never be used. It is always best to use ERR_error_string_n. Both functions always return a pointer to the start of the buffer into which the translated error message was written.

```
char *ERR_error_string(unsigned long e, char *buf);
```

e
>   The error code that will be translated.

buf
>   The buffer into which the error message is written. The buffer must be at least 256 bytes in size, or it can be specified as NULL, in which case an internal buffer will be used. Use of this buffer is never thread-safe.

```
char *ERR_error_string_n(unsigned long e, char *buf, size_t len);
```

e
>   The error code that will be translated.

buf
>   The buffer into which the error message is written. It must never be NULL.

len
>   The size of the buf argument in bytes. It should include space for the NULL terminating character.

The resultant error message is formatted into a colon-separated list of fields. The first field is always the word "error", and the second field is always the error code represented in hexadecimal. The third field is the name of the package that generated the error, such as "BIO routines" or "bignum routines". The fourth field is the name of the function that generated the error, and the fifth field is the reason why the error was generated. The function name is taken from an internal table that is actually rather small, and may very likely be represented as func(<code>), in which code is a number representing the function.

To get information about an error, ERR_get_error_line_data and ERR_error_string should be used. Armed with all of the information from these two functions, we can emit rather detailed error information. The OpenSSL library provides us with two functions that ease this process for us, however. ERR_print_errors will produce an error listing and write it to a BIO. ERR_print_errors_fp will produce an error listing and write it to a standard C runtime FILE object. The error listings are produced by iterating through each error report in the error queue and removing them as it goes. For each error report, ERR_get_error_line_data and ERR_error_string are used to obtain the information necessary to produce the listing:

```
void ERR_print_errors(BIO *bp);
```

> bp
>> The BIO that the error listing should be written to.

```
void ERR_print_errors_fp(FILE *fp);
```

> fp
>> The FILE object that the error listing should be written to.

Threading and Practical Applications

A common concern of developers is the handling of errors produced by a library when using threaded code, and rightly so. With a few exceptions that can be easily avoided, OpenSSL's error handling is completely thread-safe. Each thread is assigned its own error queue, which is one of the reasons why the id_function callback that we described earlier in the chapter must return a different identifier for each thread. Each error queue will contain only errors that were caused by that thread. This is convenient for threaded applications because the programmer doesn't need to do anything special to handle errors correctly.

By creating a separate error queue for each thread, it would seem that all the bases are covered for error handling, but that's not entirely true. OpenSSL does not use *thread-local storage* for the error queues, and so there is no way for each queue to be automatically destroyed when a thread terminates. Thread-local storage is a great feature to have in a multithreaded environment, but unfortunately, it is not supported on all platforms. The bottom line is that the application is responsible for destroying a thread's error queue when a thread terminates because OpenSSL has no way of knowing on its own when a thread has terminated.

OpenSSL provides a function to destroy a thread's error queue called ERR_remove_state. It should be called by a thread just before it terminates, or it may be called by another thread within the process after the thread has terminated. The function requires a single argument that is the identifier of the thread as it would be returned by the id_function callback that we described earlier in the chapter.

Until now, we have overlooked the implications of loading the strings for error processing. These strings do take up memory, and it isn't always appropriate to load them. It should be mentioned that all of the error handling routines work properly without the strings loaded. The translated error messages will merely have internal OpenSSL codes inserted instead of the more meaningful strings. If we do choose to load the error strings, we should also be sure to free them when they're no longer needed by calling ERR_free_strings. For most applications, this should happen after the program is done making calls into the OpenSSL library.

Abstract Input/Output

The BIO package provides a powerful abstraction for handling input and output. Many different types of BIO objects are available for use, but they all fall into one of two basic categories: source/sink and filter, both of which will be described in detail in upcoming sections. BIOs can be attached together in chains, allowing the data to flow through multiple BIO objects for processing as it is read or written. For example, a BIO chain can be created that causes data to be base64-encoded as it is written out to a file and decoded as it is read from a file. This feature of BIOs makes them very flexible and powerful. A single function with a BIO parameter can be written to read or write some data, and just by setting up a BIO chain, it is possible for that one function to deal with all kinds of different types of data encoding.

The OpenSSL library provides a variety of functions for creating and destroying BIOs, chaining them together, and reading or writing data. It's important to note that the BIO package is a low-level package, and as such, you must exercise care in using it. Many of the functions will allow you to perform operations that could later lead to unpredictable behavior and even crashes.

BIO_new function is used to create a new BIO. It requires a BIO_METHOD object to be specified, which defines the type of BIO the new object will be. We'll discuss the available BIO_METHOD objects in the next two sections. If the BIO is created successfully, it will be returned. If an error occurred in creating the BIO, NULL will be returned.

```
The BIO *BIO_new(BIO_METHOD *type);
```

Once a BIO is created, its `BIO_METHOD` can be changed to some other type using the `BIO_set` function, which will return 0 if an error occurs; otherwise, the return will be nonzero to indicate success. You should take care in using `BIO_set`, particularly if the BIO is part of a chain because the call will improperly break the chain.

```
int BIO_set(BIO *bio, BIO_METHOD *type);
```

When a BIO is no longer needed, it should be destroyed. The function `BIO_free` will destroy a single BIO and return nonzero if it was successfully destroyed; otherwise, it will return 0.

```
int BIO_free(BIO *bio);
```

The `BIO_vfree` function is identical to `BIO_free` except that it does not return a value.

```
void BIO_vfree(BIO *bio);
```

The `BIO_free_all` function can be used to free an entire chain of BIOs. When using `BIO_free_all`, you must ensure that you specify the BIO that is the head of the chain, which is usually a filter BIO. If the BIO that you wish to destroy is part of a chain, you must first remove it from the chain before calling `BIO_free` or `BIO_vfree`; otherwise, the chain will end up with a dangling pointer to the BIO that you've destroyed.

```
void BIO_free_all(BIO *bio);
```

The `BIO_push` and `BIO_pop` functions are poorly named because they imply that a stack is being operated on, but in fact, there is no stack.

The `BIO_push` function will append a BIO to a BIO, either creating or lengthening a BIO chain. The returned BIO will always be the BIO that was initially specified as the head of the chain. In other words, the return value will be the same as the first argument, `bio`.

```
BIO *BIO_push(BIO *bio, BIO *append);
```

bio
> The BIO that should have another BIO, typically a filter BIO, appended to its chain.

append
> The BIO that should be appended to the chain.

The `BIO_pop` function will remove the specified BIO from the chain that it is part of and return the next BIO in the chain or `NULL` if there is no next BIO.

```
BIO *BIO_pop(BIO *bio);
```

bio
> The BIO that should be removed from the chain of which it is a part.

`BIO_read` behaves almost identically to the C runtime function read. The primary difference between the two is in how the return value is interpreted. For both functions, a return value that is greater than zero is the number of bytes that were successfully read. A return value of 0 indicates that no data is currently available to be read. For the C read function, a return value of −1 indicates that an error occurred. Often, this is the case with BIO_read as well, but it doesn't necessarily mean that an error has occurred. We'll talk more about this in a moment.

```
int BIO_read(BIO *bio, void *buf, int len);
```

bio

> The first BIO in a chain that will be used for reading data. If there is no chain, this is a source BIO; otherwise, it should be a filter BIO.

buf

> The buffer that will receive the data that is read.

len

> The number of bytes to read. It may be less than the actual buffer size, but it should never be larger.

Another function that is provided for reading data from a source BIO is BIO_gets, which usually behaves almost identically to its C runtime counterpart, fgets. In general, you should probably avoid using this function if you can, because it is not supported by all types of BIOs, and some types of BIOs may behave differently than you might expect. Normally, though, it will read data until it finds an end-of-line character or the maximum number of bytes are read, whichever happens first. If an end-of-line character is read, it will be included in the buffer. The return value from this function is the same as for BIO_read.

```
int BIO_gets(BIO *bio, char *buf, int len);
```

bio

> The first BIO in a chain that will be used for reading data. If there is no chain, this is a source BIO; otherwise, it should be a filter BIO.

buf

> The buffer that will receive the data that is read.

len

> The maximum number of bytes to read. This length should include space for the NULL terminating character, and of course, should never exceed the size of the buffer that will receive the data.

Corresponding to BIO_read for reading from a source BIO is BIO_write, which writes data to a sink BIO. It behaves almost identically to the C runtime function write. The primary difference between the two is in how the return value is interpreted, as is true for BIO_read, as we just described. The return value is interpreted in much the same way as it is for BIO_read and BIO_gets, with the difference being that a positive value indicates the number of bytes that were successfully written.

```
int BIO_write(BIO *bio, const void *buf, int len);
```

bio

> The first BIO in a chain that will be used for writing data. If there is no chain, this is a sink BIO; otherwise, it should be a filter BIO.

buf

> The buffer that contains the data to be written.

len

> The number of bytes from the buffer that should be written. It may be less than the actual buffer size, but it should never be larger.

BIO_puts interprets the specified buffer as a C-style string and attempts to write it out in its entirety. The buffer must contain a NULL terminating character, but it will not be written out with the rest of the data. The return value from this function is interpreted the same as it is for BIO_write.

```
int BIO_puts(BIO *bio, const char *buf);
```

bio

> The first BIO in a chain that will be used for writing data. If there is no chain, this is a sink BIO; otherwise, it should be a filter BIO.

buf

> The buffer that contains the data to be written.

We mentioned that for each of the four reading and writing functions, a 0 or −1 return value may or may not necessarily indicate that an error has occurred. A suite of functions is provided that allows us to determine whether an error really did occur, and whether we should retry the operation.

If BIO_should_retry returns a nonzero value, the call that caused the condition should be retried later. If it returns 0, the actual error condition is determined by the type of BIO. For example, if BIO_read and BIO_should_retry both return 0 and the type of BIO is a socket, the socket has been closed.

```
int BIO_should_retry(BIO *bio);
```

If BIO_should_read returns nonzero, the BIO needs to read data. As an example, this condition could occur when a filter BIO is decrypting a block cipher, and a complete block has not been read from the source. In such a case, the block would need to be completely read in order for the data to be successfully decrypted.

```
int BIO_should_read(BIO *bio);
```

If BIO_should_write returns nonzero, the BIO needs to write data. This condition could possibly occur when more data is required to satisfy a block cipher's need to fill a buffer before it can be encrypted.

```
int BIO_should_write(BIO *bio);
```

If BIO_should_io_special returns nonzero, an exceptional condition has occurred, and the meaning is entirely dependent on the type of BIO that caused the condition. For example, with a socket BIO, this could mean that out-of-band data has been received.

```
int BIO_should_io_special(BIO *bio);
```

The function `BIO_retry_type` returns a bit mask that describes the condition. Possible bit fields include `BIO_FLAGS_READ`, `BIO_FLAGS_WRITE`, and `BIO_FLAGS_IO_SPECIAL`. It is conceivable that more than one bit could be set, but with the types of BIOs that are currently included as part of OpenSSL, only one will ever be set. The functions `BIO_should_read`, `BIO_should_write`, and `BIO_should_io_special` are implemented as macros that test the three bits corresponding to their names.

```
int BIO_retry_type(BIO *bio);
```

The function `BIO_get_retry_BIO` will return a pointer to the BIO in the BIO chain that caused the retry condition. If its second argument, reason, is not `NULL`, it will be loaded with the reason code for the retry condition. The retry condition doesn't necessarily have to be caused by a source/sink BIO, but can be caused by a filter BIO as well.

```
BIO *BIO_get_retry_BIO(BIO *bio, int *reason);
```

The function `BIO_get_retry_reason` returns the reason code for the retry operation. The retry condition must be a special condition, and the BIO passed must be the BIO that caused the condition. In most cases, the BIO passed to `BIO_get_retry_reason` should be the BIO that is returned by `BIO_get_retry_BIO`.

```
int BIO_get_retry_reason(BIO *bio);
```

In many cases, `BIO_flush` will do nothing, but in cases in which buffered I/O is involved, it will force any buffered data to be written. For example, with a buffered file sink, it's effectively the same as calling `fflush` on the `FILE` object attached to the BIO.

```
int BIO_flush(BIO *bio);
```

Source/Sink BIOs

A BIO that is used for reading is known as a source BIO, and a sink BIO is one that is used for writing. A source/sink BIO is attached to a concrete input/output medium such as a file, a socket, or memory. Only a single source/sink BIO may exist in a chain. It is possible to conceive of situations in which it might be useful to have more than one, particularly for writing, but the source/sink types of BIOs provided by OpenSSL do not currently allow for more than one source/sink BIO to exist in a chain.

OpenSSL provides nine source/sink types of BIOs that can be used with `BIO_new` and `BIO_set`. A function is provided for each that simply returns a `BIO_METHOD` object suitable for passing to `BIO_new` or `BIO_set`. Most of the source/sink types of BIOs require additional setup work beyond just creating a BIO with the appropriate `BIO_METHOD`. We'll cover only the four most commonly used types in any detail here due to space limitations and the huge number of individual functions that are available to operate on them in various ways.

Memory sources/sinks

A memory BIO treats a memory segment the same as a file or socket, and can be created by using BIO_s_mem to obtain a BIO_METHOD object suitable for use with BIO_new and BIO_set. As an alternative, the function BIO_new_mem_buf can be used to create a read-only memory BIO, which requires a pointer to an existing memory segment for reading as well as the size of the buffer. If the size of the buffer is specified as −1, the buffer is assumed to be a C-style string, and the size of the buffer is computed to be the length of the string, not including the NULL terminating character.

When a memory BIO is created using BIO_new and BIO_s_mem, a new memory segment is created, and resized as necessary. The memory segment is owned by the BIO in this case and is destroyed when the BIO is destroyed unless BIO_set_close prevents it. BIO_get_mem_data or BIO_get_mem_ptr can be used to obtain a pointer to the memory segment. A memory BIO created with BIO_new_mem_buf will never destroy the memory segment attached to the BIO, regardless of whether BIO_set_close is used to enable it. Example 4-4 demonstrates how to create a memory BIO.

Example 4-4. Creating a memory BIO

```
/* Create a read/write BIO */
bio = BIO_new(BIO_s_mem());

/* Create a read-only BIO using an allocated buffer */
buffer = malloc(4096);
bio = BIO_new_mem_buf(buffer, 4096);

/* Create a read-only BIO using a C-style string */
bio = BIO_new_mem_buf("This is a read-only buffer.", -1);

/* Get a pointer to a memory BIO's memory segment */
BIO_get_mem_ptr(bio, &buffer);

/* Prevent a memory BIO from destroying its memory segment when it is destroyed
 */
BIO_set_close(bio, BIO_NOCLOSE);
```

File sources/sinks

Two types of file BIOs are available: buffered and unbuffered. A buffered file BIO is a wrapper around the standard C runtime FILE object and its related functions. An unbuffered file BIO is a wrapper around a file descriptor and its related functions. With the exception of how the two different types of file BIOs are created, the interface for using them is essentially the same.

A buffered file BIO can be created by using BIO_s_file to obtain a BIO_METHOD object suitable for use with BIO_new and BIO_set. Alternatively, BIO_new_file can be used the same way as the standard C runtime function, fopen, is used, or BIO_new_fp can be used to create a BIO around an already existing FILE object. Using BIO_new_fp, you must specify the FILE object to use and a flag indicating whether the FILE object should be closed when the BIO is destroyed.

An unbuffered file BIO can be created by using BIO_s_fd to obtain a BIO_METHOD object suitable for use with BIO_new and BIO_set. Alternatively, BIO_new_fd can be used in the same way that BIO_new_fp cis used for buffered BIOs. The difference is that a file descriptor rather than a FILE object must be specified.

For either a buffered or an unbuffered file BIO created with BIO_new or BIO_set, additional work must be done to make the BIO usable. Initially, no underlying file object is attached to the BIO, and any read or write operations performed on the BIO always fail. Unbuffered file types of BIOs require that BIO_set_fd be used to attach a file descriptor to the BIO. Buffered file types of BIOs require that BIO_set_file be used to attach a FILE object to the BIO, or one of BIO_read_filename, BIO_write_filename, BIO_append_filename, or BIO_rw_filename be used to create an underlying FILE object with the appropriate mode for the BIO. Example 4-5 shows how to create a file BIO.

Example 4-5. Creating a file BIO

```
/* Create a buffered file BIO with an existing FILE object that will be closed
   when the BIO is destroyed. */
file = fopen("filename.ext", "r+");
bio = BIO_new(BIO_s_file());
BIO_set_file(bio, file, BIO_CLOSE);

/* Create an unbuffered file BIO with an existing file descriptor that will not
   be closed when the BIO is destroyed. */
fd = open("filename.ext", O_RDWR);
bio = BIO_new(BIO_s_fd());
BIO_set_fd(bio, fd, BIO_NOCLOSE);

/* Create a buffered file BIO with a new FILE object owned by the BIO */
bio = BIO_new_file("filename.ext", "w");

/* Create an unbuffered file BIO with an existing file descriptor that will be
   closed when the BIO is destroyed. */
fd = open("filename.ext", O_RDONLY);
bio = BIO_new_fd(fd, BIO_CLOSE);
```

Socket sources/sinks

There are three types of socket BIOs. The simplest is a socket BIO that must have an already existing socket descriptor attached to it. Such a BIO can be created using BIO_s_socket to obtain a BIO_METHOD object suitable for use with BIO_new and BIO_set. The socket descriptor can then be attached to the BIO using BIO_set_fd. This type of BIO works almost like an unbuffered file BIO. Alternatively, BIO_new_socket can be used in the same way that BIO_new_fd works for unbuffered file BIOs.

The second type of BIO socket is a connection socket. This type of BIO creates a new socket that is initially unconnected. The IP address and port to connect to must be set, and the connection established before data can be read from or written to the BIO. `BIO_s_connect` is used to obtain a `BIO_METHOD` object suitable for use with `BIO_new` and `BIO_set`. To set the address, either `BIO_set_conn_hostname` can be used to set the hostname or `BIO_set_conn_ip` can be used to set the IP address in dotted decimal form. Both functions take the connection address as a C-style string. The port to connect to is set using `BIO_set_conn_port` or `BIO_set_conn_int_port`. The difference between the two is that `BIO_set_conn_port` takes the port number as a string, which can be either a port number or a service name such as "http" or "https", and `BIO_set_conn_int_port` takes the port number as an integer. Once the address and port are set for making a connection, an attempt to establish a connection can be made via `BIO_do_connect`. Once a connection is successfully established, the BIO can be used just as if it was a plain socket BIO.

The third type of BIO socket is an accept socket. This type of BIO creates a new socket that will listen for incoming connections and accept them. When a connection is established, a new BIO object is created that is bound to the accepted socket. The new BIO object is chained to the original BIO and should be disconnected from the chain before use. Data can be read or written with the new BIO object. The original BIO object can then be used to accept more connections.

In order to create an accept socket type of socket BIO, use `BIO_s_accept` to obtain a `BIO_METHOD` object suitable for use with `BIO_new` and `BIO_set`. The port used to listen for connections must be set before the BIO can be placed into listening mode. This can be done using `BIO_set_accept_port`, which accepts the port as a string. The port can be either a number or the name of a service, just like with `BIO_set_conn_port`. Once the port is set, `BIO_do_accept` will place the BIO's socket into listening mode. Successive calls to `BIO_do_accept` will block until a new connection is established. Example 4-6 demonstrates.

Example 4-6. Creating a socket BIO

```
/* Create a socket BIO attached to an already existing socket descriptor.  The
   socket descriptor will not be closed when the BIO is destroyed. */
bio = BIO_new(BIO_s_socket());
BIO_set_fd(bio, sd, BIO_NOCLOSE);

/* Create a socket BIO attached to an already existing socket descriptor.  The
   socket descriptor will be closed when the BIO is destroyed. */
bio = BIO_new_socket(sd, BIO_CLOSE);

/* Create a socket BIO to establish a connection to a remote host. */
bio = BIO_new(BIO_s_connect());
BIO_set_conn_hostname(bio, "www.ora.com");
BIO_set_conn_port(bio, "http");
BIO_do_connect(bio);

/* Create a socket BIO to listen for an incoming connection. */
bio = BIO_new(BIO_s_accept());
```

Example 4-6. Creating a socket BIO (continued)

```
BIO_set_accept_port(bio, "https");
BIO_do_accept(bio); /* place the underlying socket into listening mode */
for (;;)
{
    BIO_do_accept(bio); /* wait for a new connection */
    new_bio = BIO_pop(bio);
    /* new_bio now behaves like a BIO_s_socket() BIO */
}
```

BIO pairs

The final type of source/sink BIO that we'll discuss is a BIO pair. A BIO pair is similar to an anonymous pipe,* but does have one important difference. In a BIO pair, two source/sink BIOs are bound together as peers so that anything written to one can be read from the other. Similarly, an anonymous pipe creates two endpoints, but only one can be written to, and the other is read from. Both endpoints of a BIO pair can be read to and written from.

A BIO pair can be formed by joining two already existing BIO objects, or two new BIO objects can be created in a joined state. The function BIO_make_bio_pair will join two existing BIO objects created using the BIO_METHOD object returned from the BIO_s_bio function. It accepts two parameters, each one a BIO that will be an endpoint in the resultant pair. When a BIO is created using BIO_s_bio to obtain a BIO_METHOD suitable for use with BIO_new, it must be assigned a buffer with a call to BIO_set_write_buf_size, which accepts two parameters. The first is the BIO to assign the buffer to, and the second is the size in bytes of the buffer to be assigned.

New BIO objects can be created already joined with the convenience function BIO_new_bio_pair, which accepts four parameters. The first and third parameters are pointers to BIO objects that will receive a pointer to each newly created BIO object. The second and fourth parameters are the sizes of the buffers to be assigned to each half of the BIO pair. If an error occurs, such as an out of memory condition, the function will return zero; otherwise, it will return nonzero.

The function BIO_destroy_bio_pair will sever the pairing of the two endpoints in a BIO pair. This function is useful when you want to break up a pair and reassign one or both of the endpoints to other potential endpoints. The function accepts one parameter, which is one of the endpoints in a pair. It should only be called on one half of a pair, not both. Calling BIO_free will also cleanly sever a pair, but will only free the one endpoint of the pair that is passed to it.

---

* An anonymous pipe is a common operating system construct in which two file descriptors are created, but no file is created or socket opened. The two descriptors are connected to each other where one can be written to and the other read from. The data written to one half of the pipe can be read from the other half of the pipe.

One of the useful features of BIO pairs is their ability to use the SSL engine (which requires the use of BIO objects) while maintaining control over the low-level IO primitives. For example, you could provide an endpoint of a BIO pair to the SSL engine for reading and writing, and then use the other end of the endpoint to read and write the data however you wish. In other words, if the SSL engine writes to the BIO, you can read that data from the other endpoint and do what you wish with it. Likewise, when the SSL engine needs to read data, you write to the other endpoint, and the SSL engine will read it. Included in the OpenSSL distribution is a test application (the source file is *ssl/ssltest.c*) that is a good example of how to use BIO pairs. It implements a client and a server in the same application. The client and the server talk to each other within the same application without requiring sockets or some other low-level communication mechanism. Example 4-7 demonstrates how BIO pairs can be created, detached, and reattached.

Example 4-7. Creating BIO pairs

```
a = BIO_new(BIO_s_bio());
BIO_set_write_buf_size(a, 4096);
b = BIO_new(BIO_s_bio());
BIO_set_write_buf_size(b, 4096);
BIO_make_bio_pair(a, b);

BIO_new_bio_pair(&a, 8192, &b, 8192);

c = BIO_new(BIO_s_bio());
BIO_set_write_buf_size(c, 1024);
BIO_destroy_bio_pair(a); /* disconnect a from b */
BIO_make_bio_pair(a, c);
```

Filter BIOs

A filter BIO by itself provides no utility. It must be chained with a source/sink BIO and possibly other filter BIOs to be useful. The ability to chain filters with other BIOs is perhaps the most powerful feature of OpenSSL's BIO package, and it provides a great deal of flexibility. A filter BIO often performs some kind of translation of data before writing to or after reading from a concrete medium, such as a file or socket.

Creating BIO chains is reasonably simple and straightforward; however, care must be taken to keep track of the BIO that is at the end of the chain so that the chain can be manipulated and destroyed safely. If you destroy a BIO that is in the middle of a chain without first removing it from the chain, it's a safe bet that your program will crash shortly thereafter. As we mentioned earlier, the BIO package is one of OpenSSL's lower-level packages, and as such, little error checking is done. This places the burden on the programmer to be sure that any operations performed on a BIO chain are both legal and error-free.

When creating a chain, you must also ensure that you create the chain in the proper order. For example, if you use filters that perform base64 conversion and encryption, you would probably want to perform base64 encoding *after* encryption, not before. It's also important to ensure that your source/sink BIO is at the end of the chain. If it's not, none of the filters in the chain will be used.

The interface for creating a filter BIO is similar to creating source/sink BIO. BIO_new is used to create a new BIO with the appropriate BIO_METHOD object. Filter BIOs are provided by OpenSSL for performing encryption and decryption, base64 encoding and decoding, computing message digests, and buffering. There are a handful of others as well, but they are of limited use, since they are either platform-specific or meant for testing the BIO package.

The function shown in Example 4-8 can be used to write data to a file using the BIO package. What's interesting about the function is that it creates a chain of four BIOs. The result is that the data written to the file is encrypted and base64 encoded with the base64 encoding performed after the data is encrypted. The data is first encrypted using outer triple CBC DES and the specified key. The encrypted data is then base64-encoded before it is written to the file through an in-memory buffer. The in-memory buffer is used because triple CBC DES is a block cipher, and the two filters cooperate to ensure that the cipher's blocks are filled and padded properly. Chapter 6 discusses symmetric ciphers in detail.

Example 4-8. Assembling and using a BIO chain

```
int write_data(const char *filename, char *out, int len, unsigned char *key)
{
    int total, written;
    BIO *cipher, *b64, *buffer, *file;

    /* Create a buffered file BIO for writing */
    file = BIO_new_file(filename, "w");
    if (!file)
        return 0;

    /* Create a buffering filter BIO to buffer writes to the file */
    buffer = BIO_new(BIO_f_buffer());

    /* Create a base64 encoding filter BIO */
    b64 = BIO_new(BIO_f_base64());

    /* Create the cipher filter BIO and set the key.  The last parameter of
       BIO_set_cipher is 1 for encryption and 0 for decryption */
    cipher = BIO_new(BIO_f_cipher());
    BIO_set_cipher(cipher, EVP_des_ede3_cbc(), key, NULL, 1);

    /* Assemble the BIO chain to be in the order cipher-b64-buffer-file */
    BIO_push(cipher, b64);
    BIO_push(b64, buffer);
    BIO_push(buffer, file);
```

Example 4-8. Assembling and using a BIO chain (continued)

```
    /* This loop writes the data to the file.  It checks for errors as if the
       underlying file were non-blocking */
    for (total = 0;  total < len;  total += written)
    {
        if ((written = BIO_write(cipher, out + total, len - total)) <= 0)
        {
            if (BIO_should_retry(cipher))
            {
                written = 0;
                continue;
            }
            break;
        }
    }

    /* Ensure all of our data is pushed all the way to the file */
    BIO_flush(cipher);

    /* We now need to free the BIO chain. A call to BIO_free_all(cipher) would
       accomplish this, but we'll first remove b64 from the chain for
       demonstration purposes. */
    BIO_pop(b64);

    /* At this point the b64 BIO is isolated and the chain is cipher-buffer-file.
       The following frees all of that memory */
    BIO_free(b64);
    BIO_free_all(cipher);
}
```

Random Number Generation

Many functions throughout the OpenSSL library require the availability of random numbers. For example, creating session keys and generating public/private key pairs both require random numbers. To meet this requirement, the RAND package provides a cryptographically strong *pseudorandom number generator* (PRNG). This means that the "random" data it produces isn't truly random, but it is computationally difficult to predict.

Cryptographically secure PRNGs, including those of the RAND package, require a *seed*. A seed is essentially a secret, unpredictable piece of data that we use to set the initial state of the PRNG. The security of this seed is the basis for the unpredictability of the output. Using the seed value, the generator can use mathematical and cryptographic transforms to ensure that its output cannot be determined. Ideally, the seed should be high in *entropy*. Entropy is a measurement of how random data is. To illustrate, let's consider generating a bit of data by flipping a fair coin. The resulting bit would have a 50% chance of being 0, and a 50% chance of being 1. The output can be said to have one bit of entropy. We can also say that the value of the bit is truly random. If the coin flip was not fair, then we would have less than a bit of entropy, indicating that the resulting output isn't truly random.

It is difficult for a deterministic machine like a computer to produce true entropy. Often, entropy is collected in small bits from all sorts of unpredictable events such as the low-order bits of the time between keystrokes, thread exits, and hard-disk interrupts. It's hard to determine how much entropy actually exists in a piece of data, though. It's fairly common to overestimate how much entropy is available.

In general, entropy is unpredictable data, whereas pseudorandom numbers generated by a PRNG are not unpredictable at all if both the algorithm and the seed are known. Aside from using entropic data to seed the PRNG, it's also a good idea to use pure entropy for generating important keys. If we generate a 256-bit key using a pseudorandom number generator that has a 128-bit seed, then our key does not contain 256-bits of strength, despite its length. At most, it has 128 bits. Similarly, if multiple keys are generated using the same seed, there will be correlations between the keys that are undesirable. The security of the keys should be independent.

For all other random number requirements, pseudorandom numbers generated by the PRNG are suitable for use.

Seeding the PRNG

A common security pitfall is the incorrect seeding of the OpenSSL PRNG. There are functions that seed the generator easily enough, but the problems occur when a developer uses some predictable data for the seed. While the internal routines can quantify the amount of "seed" data, they can do nothing to determine the quality of that data (i.e., how much entropy the data contains). We've stated that the seed is an important value, but we haven't explicitly looked at why this is so. For example, when using a session key to secure a connection, the basis for security is both the encryption algorithm used to encrypt the messages and the inability of the attacker to simply guess the session key. If an insecure seed is used, the PRNG output is predictable. If the output is predictable, the keys generated are predictable; thus the security of even a correctly designed application will be compromised. Clearly, a lot depends on the PRNG's output and as such, OpenSSL provides several functions for manipulating it. It's important to understand how to use these functions so that security can be assured.

The function RAND_add seeds the PRNG with the specified data, considering only the specified number of bytes to be entropic. For example, suppose the buffer contained a pointer to the current time as returned by the standard C runtime function, time. The buffer size would be four bytes, but only a single byte of that could be reasonably considered entropic because the high bytes don't change frequently and are extremely predictable. The current time by itself is never a good source of entropy; we've only used it here for clarity.

```
void RAND_add(const void *buf, int num, double entropy);
```
> buf
>> The buffer that contains the data to be used as the seed for the PRNG.

> num
>> The number of bytes contained in the buffer.

> entropy
>> An estimate of the quantity of entropy contained in the buffer.

Like `RAND_add`, the function `RAND_seed` seeds the PRNG with the specified data, but considers it to contain pure entropy. In fact, the default implementation of `RAND_seed` is simply to call `RAND_add` using the number of bytes in the buffer as the amount of entropy contained in the buffer's data.

```
void RAND_seed(const void *buf, int num);
```
> buf
>> The buffer that contains the data to be used as the seed for the PRNG.

> num
>> The number of bytes contained in the buffer.

Two additional functions are provided for use on Windows systems. They're not the best sources of entropy, but lacking a better source, they're better than what most programmers would typically use or devise on their own. In general, it's a good idea to avoid using either of these two functions unless there is no other entropy source available, especially if your application is running on a machine that ordinarily has no user interaction, such as a server. They're intended to be a last resort, and you should treat them as such.

```
int  RAND_event(UINT iMsg, WPARAM wParam, LPARAM lParam);
```

`RAND_event` should be called from message handling functions and pass each message's identifier and parameters. The current implementation uses only the `WM_KEYDOWN` and `WM_MOUSEMOVE` messages for gathering entropy.

```
void RAND_screen(void);
```

`RAND_screen` can be called periodically to gather entropy as well. The function will take a snapshot of the contents of the screen, generate a hash for each scan-line, and use the hash value as entropy. This function should not be called too frequently for a couple of reasons. One reason is that the screen won't change much, which can lead to predictability. The other reason is that the function is not particularly fast.

A common misuse of the PRNG seeding functions is to use a static string as the seed buffer. Most often, this is done for no reason other than to silence OpenSSL because it will generate warning messages whenever the PRNG is not seeded and an attempt to use it is made. Another bad idea is to use an uninitialized memory segment, assuming its contents will be unpredictable enough. There are plenty of other examples of how not to seed the PRNG, but rather than enumerate them all here, we'll concentrate on the right way. A good rule of thumb to determine whether you're seeding the PRNG correctly is this: if you're not seeding it with data from a service whose explicit purpose is to gather entropy, you're not seeding the PRNG correctly.

On many Unix systems, */dev/random* is available as an entropy-gathering service. On systems that provide such a device, there is usually another device, */dev/urandom*. The reason for this is that the */dev/random* device will block if there is not enough entropy available to produce the output requested. The */dev/urandom* device, on the other hand, will use a cryptographic PRNG to assure that it never blocks. It's actually most accurate to say that */dev/random* produces entropy and that */dev/urandom* produces pseudorandom numbers.

The OpenSSL package provides a function, RAND_load_file, which will seed the PRNG with the contents of a file up to the number of bytes specified, or its entirety if the limit is specified as −1. It is expected that the file read will contain pure entropy. Since OpenSSL has no way of knowing whether the file actually does contain pure entropy, it assumes that the file does; OpenSSL leaves it to the programmer. Example 4-9 shows some example uses of this function and its counterpart, RAND_write_file. On systems that do have */dev/random* available, seeding the PRNG with RAND_load_file from */dev/random* is the best thing to do. Be sure to limit the number of bytes read from */dev/random* to some reasonable value, though! If you specify −1 to read the entire file, RAND_load_file will read data forever and never return.

The RAND_write_file function will write 1,024 bytes of random bytes obtained from the PRNG to the specified file. The bytes written are not purely entropic, but they can be safely used to seed an unseeded PRNG in the absence of a better entropy source. This can be particularly useful for a server that starts running immediately when a system boots up because */dev/random* will not have much entropy available when the system first boots. Example 4-9 demonstrates various methods of employing RAND_load_file and RAND_write_file.

Example 4-9. Using RAND_load_file() and RAND_write_file()

```
int RAND_load_file(const char *filename, long bytes);
int RAND_write_file(const char *filename);

/* Read 1024 bytes from /dev/random and seed the PRNG with it */
RAND_load_file("/dev/random", 1024);

/* Write a seed file */
RAND_write_file("prngseed.dat");

/* Read the seed file in its entirety and print the number of bytes obtained */
nb = RAND_load_file("prngseed.dat", -1);
printf("Seeded the PRNG with %d byte(s) of data from prngseed.dat.\n", nb);
```

When you write seed data to a file with RAND_write_file, you must be sure that you're writing the file to a secure location. On a Unix system, this means the file should be owned by the user ID of the application, and all access to group members and other users should be disallowed. Additionally, the directory in which the file resides and all parent directories should have only write access enabled for the directory owner. On a Windows system, the file should be owned by the Administrator and allow no permissions to any other users

One final point worth mentioning is that OpenSSL will try to seed the PRNG transparently with */dev/urandom* on systems that have it available. While this is better than nothing, it's a good idea to go ahead and read better entropy from */dev/random*, unless there is a compelling reason not to. On systems that don't have */dev/urandom*, the PRNG will not be seeded at all, and you must make sure that you seed it properly before you attempt to use the PRNG or any other part of OpenSSL that utilizes the PRNG. For systems that have */dev/random*, Example 4-10 demonstrates how to use it to seed the OpenSSL PRNG.

Example 4-10. Seeding OpenSSL's PRNG with /dev/random

```
int seed_prng(int bytes)
{
    if (!RAND_load_file("/dev/random", bytes))
        return 0;
    return 1;
}
```

Using an Alternate Entropy Source

We've discussed */dev/random* and */dev/urandom* as entropy sources at some length, but what about systems that don't have these services available? Many operating systems do not provide them, including Windows. Obtaining entropy on such systems can be problematic, but luckily, there is a solution. Several third-party packages are available for various platforms that perform entropy-gathering services. One of the more full-featured and portable solutions available is EGADS (Entropy Gathering and Distribution System). It's licensed under the BSD license, which means that it's free and the source code is available. You can obtain a copy of EGADS from *http://www.securesw.com/egads/*.

As we mentioned, there are other entropy solutions available in addition to EGADS. EGD is an entropy-gathering daemon that is written in Perl by Brian Warner and is available from *http://egd.sourceforge.net/*. Because it is written in Perl, it requires a Perl interpreter to be installed. It provides a Unix domain socket interface for clients to obtain entropy. It does not support Windows at all. PRNGD is another popular entropy-gathering daemon written by Lutz Jänicke. It provides an EGD-compatible interface for clients to obtain entropy from it; like EGD itself, Windows is not supported. Because neither EGD nor PRNGD support Windows, we'll concentrate primarily on EGADS, which does support Windows. Where appropriate, we will also discuss EGD and PRNGD together, because all three use the same interface.

Before we can use EGADS to obtain entropy, we must first initialize it. This is done with a simple call to egads_init. Once the library is initialized, we can use the function egads_entropy to obtain entropy. Like *dev/random* on systems that make it available, egads_entropy will block until enough entropy is available to satisfy the request. Example 4-11 shows how to use EGADS to seed OpenSSL's PRNG.

Example 4-11. Seeding OpenSSL's PRNG with EGADS

```
int seed_prng(int bytes)
{
    int        error;
    char       *buf;
    prngctx_t ctx;

    egads_init(&ctx, NULL, NULL, &error);
    if (error)
        return 0;

    buf = (char *)malloc(bytes);
    egads_entropy(&ctx, buf, bytes, &error);
    if (!error)
        RAND_seed(buf, bytes);
    free(buf);

    egads_destroy(&ctx);
    return (!error);
}
```

EGADS, EGD, and PRNGD all provide a Unix domain socket that allows clients to obtain entropy. EGD defines a simple protocol for clients to communicate with that both EGADS and PRNGD have mimicked. Many cryptographic applications, such as GnuPG and OpenSSH, provide support for obtaining entropy from a daemon using the EGD protocol. OpenSSL also provides support for seeding its PRNG using the EGD protocol.

OpenSSL provides two functions for communicating with a server that speaks the EGD protocol. Version 0.9.7 of OpenSSL adds a third. In addition, Version 0.9.7 will attempt to automatically connect to four different commonly used names for EGD sockets in the following order: */var/run/egd-pool*, */dev/egd-pool*, */etc/egd-pool*, and */etc/entropy*.

RAND_egd attempts to connect to the specified Unix domain socket. If the connection is successful, 255 bytes of entropy will be requested from the server. The data returned will be passed in a call to RAND_add to seed the PRNG. RAND_egd is actually a wrapper around the next function, RAND_egd_bytes.

```
int RAND_egd(const char *path);
```

RAND_egd_bytes will attempt to connect to the specified Unix domain socket. If the connection is successful, the specified number of bytes of entropy will be requested from the server. The data returned will be passed in a call to RAND_add to seed the

PRNG. Both RAND_egd and RAND_egd_bytes will return the number of bytes obtained from the EGD server if they're successful. If an error occurred connecting to the daemon, they'll both return −1.

```
int RAND_egd_bytes(const char *path, int bytes);
```

Version 0.9.7 of OpenSSL adds the function RAND_query_egd_bytes to make a query for data from an EGD server without automatically feeding the returned data into OpenSSL's PRNG via RAND_add. It attempts to connect to the specified Unix domain socket and obtain the specified number of bytes. The data that is returned from the EGD server is copied into the specified buffer. If the buffer is specified as NULL, the function works just like RAND_egd_bytes and passes the returned data to RAND_add to seed the PRNG. It returns the number of bytes received on success; otherwise, it returns −1 if an error occurs.

```
int RAND_query_egd_bytes(const char *path, unsigned char *buf, int bytes);
```

Example 4-12 demonstrates how to use the RAND functions to access an EGD socket and seed the PRNG with the entropy that is obtained from a running entropy-gathering server, whether it's EGADS, EGD, PRNGD, or another server that provides an EGD socket interface.

Example 4-12. Seeding OpenSSL's PRNG via an EGD socket

```
#ifndef DEVRANDOM_EGD
#define DEVRANDOM_EGD "/var/run/egd-pool", "/dev/egd-pool", "/etc/egd-pool", \
                      "/etc/entropy"
#endif

int seed_prng(int bytes)
{
    int  i;
    char *names[] = { DEVRANDOM_EGD, NULL };

    for (i = 0;  names[i];  i++)
        if (RAND_egd(names[i]) != -1)  /* RAND_egd_bytes(names[i], 255) */
            return 1;
    return 0;
}
```

Arbitrary Precision Math

To implement many public key encryption algorithms, the library must have support for mathematical operations on large integers. Use of standard C or C++ data types is not adequate in these situations. To alleviate this problem, OpenSSL provides the BN package. This package declares routines on the aggregate type BIGNUM, which have virtually no limits on the upper bounds of numbers. More specifically, the size of the number that a BIGNUM-typed variable can hold is limited only by available memory.

It's likely that direct exposure to the BN package in developing an SSL-enabled application will be limited since it is a very low-level package, and the higher-level packages generally hide the details. However, because the package is so widely used and integral to public key cryptography, we've briefly covered it here.

The Basics

To use the BIGNUM package in your programs, you'll need to include the header file *openssl/bn.h*. Before we can use a BIGNUM, we must first initialize it. The BN package provides support for both statically allocated and dynamically allocated BIGNUMs. The function BN_new will allocate a new BIGNUM and initialize it for use. The function BN_init will initialize a statically allocated BIGNUM. When you're done using a BIGNUM, you should always be sure to destroy it, even if it is allocated on the stack, because internally, a BIGNUM dynamically allocates memory. The function BN_free will destroy a BIGNUM. Example 4-13 shows some examples of how these three functions are used.

Example 4-13. Creating, initializing, and destroying BIGNUMs

```
BIGNUM static_bn, *dynamic_bn;

/* Initialize a statically allocated BIGNUM */
BN_init(&static_bn);

/* Allocate an initialize a new BIGNUM */
dynamic_bn = BN_new( );

/* Destroy the two BIGNUMs that we just created */
BN_free(dynamic_bn);
BN_free(&static_bn);
```

A BIGNUM is implemented as an opaque structure that contains dynamically allocated memory. The functions provided to operate on a BIGNUM allow the programmer to remain blissfully unaware of what's going on for the most part, but it is important that the programmer does understand that there is much more going on internally. One such instance is when the value of one BIGNUM needs to be assigned to another BIGNUM. The natural inclination is to perform a shallow copy of the structure, but this should never be done! Deep copies must be performed, and the BN package provides functions for doing just that. Example 4-14 demonstrates the right way and the wrong way to make a copy of a BIGNUM.

Example 4-14. The wrong way and the right way to copy a BIGNUM

```
BIGNUM a, b *c;

/* First, the wrong way to copy a BIGNUM */
a = b;
*c = b;
```

```
/* Now the right way to copy a BIGNUM */
BN_copy(&a,&b);    /* Copies b to a */
c = BN_dup(&b);    /* Creates c and initializes it to the same value as b */
```

It is important that we copy BIGNUMs properly. If we don't, we're likely to experience unpredictable behavior or crashes. When programming with BIGNUMs, there will likely be situations in which you'll need to make copies, so it's best to learn this lesson early.

Another operation that is similar in nature is the comparison of two BIGNUMs. We cannot simply compare two BIGNUMs using normal C comparison operators like =, <, or >. Instead, we must use the BN_cmp function to compare two BIGNUMs. This function will compare the two values, a and b, and return −1 if a is less than b, 0 if they are equal, and 1 if a is greater than b. The function BN_ucmp will perform the same type of comparison on the absolute values of a and b.

It may be useful to convert a BIGNUM into a flat binary representation for the purpose of storing it in a file or sending it over a socket connection to a peer. Since a BIGNUM contains pointers to internal, dynamically allocated memory, it is not a flat structure, so we must convert it to one before we can send it anywhere. Conversely, we must be able to convert a flat representation of a BIGNUM back into a BIGNUM structure that the BN package can use. Two functions are provided for performing these respective operations. The first, BN_bn2bin, will convert a BIGNUM to a flat binary representation in big-endian form. The second, BN_bin2bn, performs the inverse operation, converting a flat binary representation of a big-endian number into a BIGNUM.

Before converting a BIGNUM into a flat binary representation, we need to know the number of bytes of memory that will be required to hold the converted data. It's also important to know how big the binary representation is before converting it back into a BIGNUM. The number of bytes required to represent a BIGNUM in flat binary form can be discovered using the BN_num_bytes function. Example 4-15 demonstrates converting between BIGNUM and flat binary representations.

Example 4-15. Converting between BIGNUM and binary representations

```
/* Converting from BIGNUM to binary */
len = BN_num_bytes(num);
buf = (unsigned char *)malloc(len);
len = BN_bn2bin(num, buf);

/* Converting from binary to BIGNUM */
BN_bin2bn(buf, len, num);
num = BN_bin2bn(buf, len, NULL);
```

When BN_bn2bin performs its conversion, it will return the number of bytes that were written out into the supplied buffer. If an error occurs in the conversion, the return will be 0. When BN_bin2bn performs its conversion, the result is placed into the BIGNUM specified as the third argument, overwriting any value that it may have previously held. If the third argument is specified as NULL, a new BIGNUM is created and initialized with the value from the binary representation. In either case, the BN_bin2bn will always return a pointer to the BIGNUM that received the value or NULL if an error occurred during the conversion.

Binary-encoded numbers are fine when we want to transfer the data over a medium that supports it—for example, a binary file or a socket. However, for circumstances in which we need a text-based representation, such as printing the number on the screen, it is inadequate. We can always base64-encode the data before emitting it, but the BN package provides more intuitive methods.

The function BN_bn2hex converts a BIGNUM into a hexadecimal representation stored in a C-style string. The C-style string is allocated dynamically using OPENSSL_malloc, which must then be freed by the caller using OPENSSL_free.

```
char *BN_bn2hex(const BIGNUM *num);
```

The function BN_bn2dec converts a BIGNUM into a decimal representation stored in a C-style string. The C-style string is allocated dynamically using OPENSSL_malloc, which must then be freed by the caller using OPENSSL_free.

```
char *BN_bn2dec(const BIGNUM *num);
```

The function BN_hex2bn converts a hexadecimal representation of a number stored in a C-style string to a BIGNUM. The resulting value is stored in the supplied BIGNUM, or a new BIGNUM is created with BN_new if the BIGNUM is supplied as NULL.

```
int BN_hex2bn(BIGNUM **num, const char *str);
```

The function BN_dec2bn converts a decimal representation of a number stored in a C-style string to a BIGNUM. The resulting value is stored in the supplied BIGNUM, or a new BIGNUM is created with BN_new if the BIGNUM is supplied as NULL.

```
int BN_dec2bn(BIGNUM **num, const char *str);
```

Mathematical Operations

With few exceptions, the majority of the remainder of the functions that make up the BN package all perform mathematical operations such as addition and multiplication. Most of the functions require at least two BIGNUM operands and store their result in a third BIGNUM. It is often safe to use one of the operands to store the result, but it isn't always, so you should exercise care in doing so. Consult Table 4-1, which lists the most common arithmetic functions, if you're not sure. Unless otherwise noted in the table, the BIGNUM that will receive the result of the operation may not be the same as any of the operands. Each of the functions returns nonzero or zero, indicating success or failure, respectively.

Many of the functions in Table 4-1 are shown as accepting an argument labeled "ctx". This argument is a pointer to a BN_CTX structure. This argument may not be specified as NULL, but instead should be a context structure returned by BN_CTX_new.

The purpose of the context structure is to store temporary values used by many of the arithmetic operations. Storing the temporary values in a context increases the performance of the various functions. When a context structure is no longer needed, it should be destroyed using BN_CTX_free.

Table 4-1. Arithmetic functions for BIGNUMs

Function	Comments
BN_add(r, a, b)	(r = a + b) r may be the same as a or b.
BN_sub(r, a, b)	(r = a − b)
BN_mul(r, a, b, ctx)	(r = a × b) r may be the same as a or b.
BN_sqr(r, a, ctx)	(r = pow(a, 2)) r may be the same as a. This function is faster than BN_mul(r, a, a).
BN_div(d, r, a, b, ctx)	(d = a / b, r = a % b) Neither d nor r may be the same as either a or b. Either d or r may be NULL.
BN_mod(r, a, b, ctx)	(r = a % b)
BN_nnmod(r, a, b, ctx)	(r = abs(a % b))
BN_mod_add(r, a, b, m, ctx)	(r = abs((a + b) % m))
BN_mod_sub(r, a, b, m, ctx)	(r = abs((a − b) % m))
BN_mod_mul(r, a, b, m, ctx)	(r = abs((a × b) % m)) r may be the same as a or b.
BN_mod_sqr(r, a, m, ctx)	(r = abs(pow(a, 2) % m))
BN_exp(r, a, p, ctx)	(r = pow(a, p))
BN_mod_exp(r, a, p, m, ctx)	(r = pow(a, 2) % m)
BN_gcd(r, a, b, ctx)	Finds the greatest common divisor of a and b. r may be the same as a or b.

Generating Prime Numbers

One of the functions provided by the BN package that is most import to public key cryptography is BN_generate_prime. As its name implies, the function generates prime numbers, but more importantly, it generates pseudorandom primes. In other words, it repeatedly chooses numbers at random until one of the choices it makes is a prime number. Such a function can be quite useful for other applications as well, which is one of the reasons why we've chosen to pay so much attention to it in this chapter. Another reason is because its parameter list is rather large and complex, which can make using the function seem to be a daunting task.

```
BIGNUM *BN_generate_prime(BIGNUM *ret, int bits, int safe, BIGNUM *add,
            BIGNUM *rem, void (*callback)(int, int, void *), void *cb_arg);
```

ret

> Used to receive the prime number that is generated. If it is specified as NULL, a new BIGNUM will be created, initialized with BN_new, and returned.

bits

> The number of bits that should be used to represent the generated prime.

safe

> Either zero or nonzero, indicating whether the generated prime should be safe or not. A safe prime is defined as a prime, p, in which $(p-1)/2$ is also prime.

add

> Used to specify additional properties that the generated prime should have. If it is specified as NULL, no additional properties will be required. Otherwise, the generated prime must satisfy the condition that when divided by this value, the remainder is one.

rem

> Used to specify additional properties that the generated prime should have. If it is specified as NULL, no additional properties will be required. Otherwise, the generated prime must satisfy the condition that when divided by add, the remainder must be this value. If add is specified as NULL, this argument is ignored.

callback

> A function that is called during the generation of the prime to report the status of the operation. Generating a prime can often be a rather time-consuming task, so this provides some means of advising a user that work is being done and that the program hasn't crashed or hung.

cb_arg

> A value that is used only to pass to the callback function if one is specified. OpenSSL does not use this argument for anything else and will never attempt to interpret its value or meaning.

If one is used, the callback function should accept three arguments and return no value. The third argument to the callback function is always the cb_arg argument to BN_generate_prime. The first argument passed to the callback function is a status code indicating which phase of the prime generation has just completed. The status code will always be 0, 1, or 2. The meaning of the second argument depends on the status code. When the status code is 0, it indicates that a potential prime has been found, but it has not yet been tested to ensure that it conforms to the criteria specified in the call to BN_generate_prime. The callback can be called with a status code of 0 many times, and each time the second argument will contain a counter of the number of primes that have been found so far, not including the current one. When the status code is 1, the second argument indicates the number of Miller-Rabin probabilistic primality tests that have been completed. Finally, when the status code is 2, a conforming prime has been found, and the second argument indicates the number of candidates that were tested before it. Example 4-16 demonstrates how to use the BN_generate_prime function with a callback for displaying the status of the process.

Example 4-16. Generating a pseudorandom prime number with BN_generate_prime()

```
static void prime_status(int code, int arg, void *cb_arg)
{
    if (code == 0)
        printf("\n  * Found potential prime #%d ...", (arg + 1));
    else if (code == 1 && arg && !(arg % 10))
        printf(".");
    else
        printf("\n Got one!\n");
}

BIGNUM *generate_prime(int bits, int safe)
{
    char   *str;
    BIGNUM *prime;

    printf("Searching for a %sprime %d bits in size ...", (safe ? "safe " : ""),
           bits);

    prime = BN_generate_prime(NULL, bits, safe, NULL, NULL, prime_status, NULL);
    if (!prime)
        return NULL;

    str = BN_bn2dec(prime);
    if (str)
    {
        printf("Found prime: %s\n", str);
        OPENSSL_free(str);
    }

    return prime;
}
```

Using Engines

OpenSSL has built-in support for cryptographic acceleration. Using the ENGINE object type, an application can get a reference to a changeable, underlying representation, most often a hardware device. This support was built in the 0.9.6 versions of OpenSSL that included the name *engine*; it will be incorporated into the main branch of OpenSSL beginning with Version 0.9.7. While 0.9.7 will have a much more robust feature specification for the ENGINE package, 0.9.6-engine contains some simple functions to set up an ENGINE object. These functions do not appear to have changed at the time of writing. If they do, we'll update our web site with the relevant information.

The general idea is simple: we retrieve an object representing the type of hardware we wish to utilize, then we tell OpenSSL to use the device we chose. Example 4-17 shows a small code example of how we would perform this operation.

Example 4-17. Enabling use of a hardware engine

```
ENGINE *e;

if (!(e = ENGINE_by_id("cswift")))
    fprintf(stderr, "Error finding specified ENGINE\n");
else if (!ENGINE_set_default(e, ENGINE_METHOD_ALL))
    fprintf(stderr, "Error using ENGINE\n");
else
    fprintf(stderr, "Engine successfully enabled\n");
```

The function call ENGINE_by_id will look up an implementation from the built-in methods available and return an ENGINE object. The single argument to this function should be the string identifier of the underlying implementation we wish to use. Table 4-2 shows the available methods for supported cryptographic hardware and software.

Table 4-2. Supported hardware and software engines

ID string	Description
openssl	The engine uses the normal built-in functions for cryptographic operations. This is the default.
openbsd_dev_crypto	On the OpenBSD operating system, this engine will use the kernel level cryptography built into the operating system.
cswift	Used for CryptoSwift acceleration hardware.
chil	Used for nCipher CHIL acceleration hardware.
atalla	Used for Compaq Atalla acceleration hardware.
nuron	Used for Nuron acceleration hardware.
ubsec	Used for Broadcom uBSec acceleration hardware.
aep	Used for Aep acceleration hardware.
sureware	Used for SureWare acceleration hardware.

The ENGINE object that we receive from the lookup should be used in the call to ENGINE_set_default to allow cryptographic functions to utilize the capabilities of the specific ENGINE. The second parameter allows us to specify constraints on what we allow the engine to implement. For example, if we had an engine that implemented only RSA, making a call like the one in Example 4-17 would allow RSA to be handled by the engine. On the other hand, if we called ENGINE_set_default with our RSA engine and ENGINE_METHOD_DSA, OpenSSL would not use the engine for any cryptographic calls, since this flag allows the engine to work only on DSA functions. Table 4-3 provides a complete list of the restraints we can use. They can be combined with the logical OR operation.

Table 4-3. Flags for ENGINE_set_default

Flag	Description
ENGINE_METHOD_RSA	Limit engine usage to only RSA operations.
ENGINE_METHOD_DSA	Limit engine usage to only DSA operations.

Table 4-3. Flags for ENGINE_set_default (continued)

Flag	Description
ENGINE_METHOD_DH	Limit engine usage to only DH operations.
ENGINE_METHOD_RAND	Limit engine usage to only random number operation.
ENGINE_METHOD_CIPHERS	Limit engine usage to only symmetric ciphers operations.
ENGINE_METHOD_DIGESTS	Limit engine usage to only digest operations.
ENGINE_METHOD_ALL	Allow OpenSSL to use any of the above implementations.

Aside from setting the default engine, ENGINE objects are typically used in several other places in OpenSSL Version 0.9.7. For instance, the function EVP_EncryptInit has been deprecated and replaced by EVP_EncryptInit_ex. This "ex" function takes one additional parameter: the ENGINE object. In general, these replacement functions can be passed a NULL argument for the ENGINE, which will cause OpenSSL to use the default engine. Recall that the default engine is changed when a call to ENGINE_set_default is made; if no such call is made, the built-in software implementation is used.

The purpose of these new "ex" functions is to allow a more fine-grained control over which underlying cryptographic device is used for each call. This is particularly useful for circumstances in which we have multiple cryptographic accelerators, and we wish to utilize them differently depending on application code.

CHAPTER 5
SSL/TLS Programming

The main feature of the OpenSSL library is its implementations of the Secure Sockets Layer (SSL) and Transport Layer Security (TLS) protocols. Originally developed by Netscape for secure web transactions, the protocol has grown into a general solution for secure stream-based communications. Netscape's first public version of SSL is what we now call SSL Version 2. From that point, security experts began working to improve upon some of the flaws in SSLv2, and that gave birth to SSL Version 3. Development of a standard for transport layer security based on SSL was being done concurrently, which resulted in TLS Version 1. Because of the security flaws with SSLv2, modern applications should not support it. In this chapter, we'll discuss only programming with the SSLv3 and TLSv1 protocols in OpenSSL. Unless otherwise noted, when we refer to SSL, we refer to both SSLv3 and TLSv1.

From a design perspective, we need to know more than just that we want to use SSL in our application. The correct implementation of an SSL-enabled program can be difficult due to complexities in protocol setup, the large size of the API, and developer inexperience with the library. OpenSSL's SSL support was originally designed to mimic the Unix socket interface; however, the likenesses quickly fade as we get into the subtleties of the API. In order to make the process of becoming acquainted with the massive library easier, we take a small example client and server through a step-by-step process of making it SSL-enabled and secure. To aid understanding, we start with some simplifying assumptions that may not be practical for real-world applications.

From that point, we'll bridge the gap to the more advanced OpenSSL features. The goal of this chapter is to compartmentalize the features of the library into smaller groups to establish a sense of process. We hope that this process will serve as a template for developers when it comes to implementing SSL in their own applications. In adding SSL to an application, the application's unique requirements must be considered, and the best decision must be made for both security and functionality.

Programming with SSL

OpenSSL's API for SSL is large and can be daunting to inexperienced programmers. Additionally, as discussed in Chapter 1, SSL can be ineffective at accomplishing its security goals if implemented incorrectly. These factors compound to leave the developer with a difficult task. In hopes of disentangling the mystery of implementing secure programs, we attack the problem in three steps. At each step, the developer must provide some application-specific knowledge to make sure SSL does its job. For example, the choices made by a developer of a highly compatible web browser will be different from those made by a developer of a highly secure server application.

The steps below provide a template for developers to follow when implementing an SSL client or server. We will start with a small example and build upon it. This example will not be secure to our satisfaction until all of the steps have been thought through. In each step, we will introduce a small dose of the API; after all the steps, the developer should be able to think through the design of an SSL-enabled application much more clearly. Completing these steps is not the end of the road, however. In order to address the requirements of many applications, we need to go further and look into the advanced features of the API.

The Application(s) to Secure

We will be using two very simple applications: a client and server in which the server simply echoes data from the client to the console. Our goal is to augment our two applications so that they can perform their tasks in a hostile environment. In other words, we'll implement each program to strictly authenticate connecting peers. As we walk the path to creating SSL-enabled versions of our programs, we discuss the choices that a developer must make at each stage.

Before moving forward, let's look at our sample applications. There a total of four files: *common.h*, *common.c*, *client.c*, and *server.c*. The code for each is presented in Example 5-1 through Example 5-4. Also, we use the code presented in Example 4-2 so we can use multiple threads. For Unix systems, we'll continue to use POSIX threads.

Starting with *common.h* in Example 5-1, Lines 1–5 include relevant headers from OpenSSL. Right now, we don't make use of anything from a few of these headers, but we soon will, so they are included. Lines 22–24 define the strings for the client and server machines as well as the server's listening port. In addition, the header contains some definitions for convenient error handling and for threading in a platform-independent manner similar to the definitions set forth in Chapter 4's threading examples.

Example 5-1. common.h

```
1  #include <openssl/bio.h>
2  #include <openssl/err.h>
3  #include <openssl/rand.h>
4  #include <openssl/ssl.h>
```

Example 5-1. common.h (continued)

```
 5  #include <openssl/x509v3.h>
 6
 7  #ifndef WIN32
 8  #include <pthread.h>
 9  #define THREAD_CC
10  #define THREAD_TYPE                        pthread_t
11  #define THREAD_CREATE(tid, entry, arg) pthread_create(&(tid), NULL, \
12                                                         (entry), (arg))
13  #else
14  #include <windows.h>
15  #define THREAD_CC                          __cdecl
16  #define THREAD_TYPE                        DWORD
17  #define THREAD_CREATE(tid, entry, arg) do { _beginthread((entry), 0, (arg));\
18                                              (tid) = GetCurrentThreadId( );   \
19                                              } while (0)
20  #endif
21
22  #define PORT          "6001"
23  #define SERVER        "splat.zork.org"
24  #define CLIENT        "shell.zork.org"
25
26  #define int_error(msg)  handle_error(__FILE__, __LINE__, msg)
27  void handle_error(const char *file, int lineno, const char *msg);
28
29  void init_OpenSSL(void);
```

Example 5-2, the file *common.c*, defines our error reporting function handle_error. The error handling in our example applications is a bit draconian, and you'll most likely want to handle errors in your own applications in a much more user-friendly manner. In general, it's not appropriate to handle all possible errors by bringing the application to such an abrupt halt.

The file *common.c* also defines a function that will perform common initialization such as setting up OpenSSL for multithreading, initializing the library, and loading error strings. The call to SSL_load_error_strings loads the associated data for error codes so that when errors occur and we print the error stack, we get human-readable information about what went wrong. Since loading these diagnostic strings does take memory, there are circumstances in which we would not want to make this call, such as when we're developing applications for embedded systems or other machines with limited memory. Generally, it's a good idea to load the strings since it makes the job of decoding error messages much easier.

As we build in SSL support, the file *common.c* will hold the implementations of functions used by both our client and server, and *common.h* will receive the prototypes.

Example 5-2. common.c

```
1  #include "common.h"
2
3  void handle_error(const char *file, int lineno, const char *msg)
```

Example 5-2. common.c (continued)

```
 4  {
 5      fprintf(stderr, "** %s:%i %s\n", file, lineno, msg);
 6      ERR_print_errors_fp(stderr);
 7      exit(-1);
 8  }
 9
10  void init_OpenSSL(void)
11  {
12      if (!THREAD_setup() || !SSL_init_library())
13      {
14          fprintf(stderr, "** OpenSSL initialization failed!\n");
15          exit(-1);
16      }
17      SSL_load_error_strings();
18  }
```

The bulk of our client application is in Example 5-3, *client.c*. At a high level, it creates a connection to the server on port 6001, as specified in *common.h*. Once a connection is established, it reads data from stdin until EOF is reached. As data is read and an internal buffer is filled, the data is sent over the connection to the server. Note that at this point, although we're using OpenSSL for socket communications, we have not yet enabled the use of the SSL protocol.

Lines 27–29 create a new BIO object with a BIO_METHOD returned from BIO_s_connect; the call to BIO_new_connect is a simplified function to accomplish this task. As long as no error occurs, lines 31–32 do the work of actually making the TCP connection and checking for errors. When a connection is successfully established, do_client_loop is called, which continually reads data from stdin and writes that data out to the socket. If an error while writing occurs or an EOF is received while reading from the console, the function exits and the program terminates.

Example 5-3. client.c

```
 1  #include "common.h"
 2
 3  void do_client_loop(BIO *conn)
 4  {
 5      int  err, nwritten;
 6      char buf[80];
 7
 8      for (;;)
 9      {
10          if (!fgets(buf, sizeof(buf), stdin))
11              break;
12          for (nwritten = 0;  nwritten < sizeof(buf);  nwritten += err)
13          {
14              err = BIO_write(conn, buf + nwritten, strlen(buf) - nwritten);
15              if (err <= 0)
16                  return;
17          }
18      }
```

Example 5-3. client.c (continued)

```
19  }
20
21  int main(int argc, char *argv[])
22  {
23      BIO  *conn;
24
25      init_OpenSSL();
26
27      conn = BIO_new_connect(SERVER ":" PORT);
28      if (!conn)
29          int_error("Error creating connection BIO");
30
31      if (BIO_do_connect(conn) <= 0)
32          int_error("Error connecting to remote machine");
33
34      fprintf(stderr, "Connection opened\n");
35      do_client_loop(conn);
36      fprintf(stderr, "Connection closed\n");
37
38      BIO_free(conn);
39      return 0;
40  }
```

The server application in Example 5-4, *server.c*, differs from the client program in a few ways. After making the call to our common initialization function (line 44), it creates a different kind of BIO, one based on the BIO_METHOD returned from BIO_s_accept. This type of BIO creates a server socket that can accept remote connections. In lines 50–51, a call to BIO_do_accept binds the socket to port 6001; subsequent calls to BIO_do_accept will block and wait for a remote connection. The loop in lines 53–60 blocks until a connection is made. When a connection is made, a new thread to handle the new connection is spawned, which then calls do_server_loop with the connected socket's BIO. The function do_server_loop simply reads data from the socket and writes it back out to stdout. If any errors occur here, the function returns and the thread is terminated. As a note, we call ERR_remove_state on line 33 to make sure any memory used by the error queue for the thread is freed.

Example 5-4. The server application

```
1   #include "common.h"
2
3   void do_server_loop(BIO *conn)
4   {
5       int err, nread;
6       char buf[80];
7
8       do
9       {
10          for (nread = 0;  nread < sizeof(buf);  nread += err)
11          {
12              err = BIO_read(conn, buf + nread, sizeof(buf) - nread);
```

Example 5-4. The server application (continued)

```
13                  if (err <= 0)
14                      break;
15          }
16          fwrite(buf, 1, nread, stdout);
17      }
18      while (err > 0);
19  }
20
21  void THREAD_CC server_thread(void *arg)
22  {
23      BIO *client = (BIO *)arg;
24
25  #ifndef WIN32
26      pthread_detach(pthread_self());
27  #endif
28      fprintf(stderr, "Connection opened.\n");
29      do_server_loop(client);
30      fprintf(stderr, "Connection closed.\n");
31
32      BIO_free(client);
33      ERR_remove_state(0);
34  #ifdef WIN32
35      _endthread();
36  #endif
37  }
38
39  int main(int argc, char *argv[])
40  {
41      BIO          *acc, *client;
42      THREAD_TYPE tid;
43
44      init_OpenSSL();
45
46      acc = BIO_new_accept(PORT);
47      if (!acc)
48          int_error("Error creating server socket");
49
50      if (BIO_do_accept(acc) <= 0)
51          int_error("Error binding server socket");
52
53      for (;;)
54      {
55          if (BIO_do_accept(acc) <= 0)
56              int_error("Error accepting connection");
57
58          client = BIO_pop(acc);
59          THREAD_CREATE(tid, server_thread, client);
60      }
61
62      BIO_free(acc);
63      return 0;
64  }
```

Now that we understand the sample application, we're ready to take the steps necessary to secure the communications with SSL.

Step 1: SSL Version Selection and Certificate Preparation

In order for SSL connections to be secure, we must select a secure version of the protocol and provide accurate certificate information for the peer to validate. Since this is our first introduction to the SSL API, we will cover the background information about the structures and functions we need to accomplish our task.

Background

We need to examine three relevant object types: SSL_METHOD, SSL_CTX, and SSL. An SSL_METHOD represents an implementation of SSL functionality. In other words, it specifies a protocol version. OpenSSL provides populated SSL_METHOD objects and some accessor methods for them. They are listed in Table 5-1. The extent of our interaction with this type of object will be to select the protocol version we wish to support by making a function call from the table.

Table 5-1. Functions to retrieve pointers to SSL_METHOD objects

Function	Comments
SSLv2_method	Returns a pointer to SSL_METHOD for generic SSL Version 2
SSLv2_client_method	Returns a pointer to SSL_METHOD for an SSL Version 2 client
SSLv2_server_method	Returns a pointer to SSL_METHOD for an SSL Version 2 server
SSLv3_method	Returns a pointer to SSL_METHOD for generic SSL Version 3
SSLv3_client_method	Returns a pointer to SSL_METHOD for an SSL Version 3 client
SSLv3_server_method	Returns a pointer to SSL_METHOD for an SSL Version 3 server
TLSv1_method	Returns a pointer to SSL_METHOD for generic TLS Version 1
TLSv1_client_method	Returns a pointer to SSL_METHOD for a TLS Version 1 client
TLSv1_server_method	Returns a pointer to SSL_METHOD for a TLS Version 1 server
SSLv23_method	Returns a pointer to SSL_METHOD for generic SSL/TLS
SSLv23_client_method	Returns a pointer to SSL_METHOD for an SSL/TLS client
SSLv23_server_method	Returns a pointer to SSL_METHOD for an SSL/TLS server

OpenSSL provides implementations for SSL Version 2, SSL Version 3, and TLS Version 1. Also, some SSLv23 functions don't indicate a specific protocol version but rather a compatibility mode. In such a mode, a connection will report that it can handle any of the three SSL/TLS protocol versions. To reiterate, applications should not use SSLv2, since this protocol is known to have security flaws. Using an SSL_METHOD object retrieved by one of the functions in Table 5-1, we create an SSL_CTX object.

How would we create an application that supports both SSLv3 and TLSv1? If we are to create a server that needs to communicate with both SSLv3 and TLSv1 clients, using either SSLv3_method or TLSv1_method will prevent one kind of client from connecting properly. Since we do not want to use SSL Version 2 (it is insecure), it would seem that the compatibility implementation SSLv23_method is also not an option. This isn't actually true. We can use the compatibility mode and set an option in the SSL_CTX object to have it remove SSLv2 from the acceptable protocols. The function to do this is SSL_CTX_set_options, and the relevant details for doing this are in Step 3.

An SSL_CTX object will be a factory for producing SSL connection objects. This context allows us to set connection configuration parameters before the connection is made, such as protocol version, certificate information, and verification requirements. It is easiest to think of SSL_CTX objects as the containers for default values for the SSL connections to be made by a program. Objects of this type are created with the function SSL_CTX_new. This function takes only one argument, generally supplied from the return value of one of the functions in Table 5-1.

In general, an application will create just one SSL_CTX object for all of the connections it makes. From this SSL_CTX object, an SSL type object can be created with the SSL_new function. This function causes the newly created SSL object to inherit all of the parameters set forth in the context. Even though most of the settings are copied to the SSL object on invocation of SSL_new, the order in which calls are made to OpenSSL functions can cause unexpected behavior if we're not careful.

Applications should set up an SSL_CTX completely, with all connection invariant settings, before creating SSL objects from it. In other words, after calling SSL_new with a particular context object, no more calls operating on that SSL_CTX object should be made until all produced SSL objects are no longer in use. The reason is simple. Modifying a context can sometimes affect the SSL connections that have already been created (i.e.., a function we examine later, SSL_CTX_set_default_passwd_cb, changes the callback in the context and in all connections that were already created from this context). To avoid any unpredictability, never modify the context after connection creation has begun. If there are any connection-specific parameters that we do need to set, most SSL_CTX functions have SSL counterparts that act on SSL-type objects.

Certificate preparation

The SSL protocol usually requires the server to present a certificate. The certificate contains credentials that the client may look at to determine if the server is authentic and can be trusted. As we know, a peer validates a certificate through verification of its chain of signers. Thus, to implement an SSL server correctly, we must provide certificate and chain information to the peer. The SSL protocol also allows the client to optionally present certificate information so that the server may authenticate it.

There are, in fact, ways of using SSL to create anonymous connections in which neither the server nor client presents a certificate. These are done by using the Diffie-Hellman key-agreement protocol and setting the SSL cipher suite to include the anonymous DH algorithm. This is discussed further in the section "Cipher suite selection" below.

In general, server applications should always provide certificates to peers, and clients can do so optionally. The purpose and the desired security of the application should dictate whether client certificates are used. For instance, a server may request a client certificate, and if our client does not have one to present, we may not be able to establish a secure connection. Thus, it's a good idea to implement client certificates if it makes sense to do so. On the other hand, server certificates are usually required, and, unless our goal is to create a completely nonauthenticated connection, we should implement them.

OpenSSL presents the client certificate to the server during handshakes, as long as we assign a certificate to the client and the server asks for it. This is actually a small violation of the TLS protocol. The protocol calls for the server to present a list of valid CAs, and the client should send a certificate only if it matches. In practice, this infraction of the standard should not affect anything, but the behavior may be fixed in future versions of OpenSSL.

The SSL API has several ways to incorporate certificate information into an SSL_CTX object. The function to use is SSL_CTX_use_certificate_chain_file. It loads the chain of certificates from the filename specified by the second argument. The file should contain the certificate chain in order, starting with the certificate for the application and ending with the root CA certificate. Each of these entries must be in PEM format.

In addition to loading the certificate chain, the SSL_CTX object must have the application's private key. This key must correspond to the public key embedded within the certificate. The easiest way that we can supply this key to the context is through the SSL_CTX_use_PrivateKey_file function. The second argument specifies the filename, and the third specifies the type of encoding. The type is specified by using a defined name—either SSL_FILETYPE_PEM or SSL_FILETYPE_ASN1. It bears mentioning that this private key must be kept secret for the application to remain secure. Therefore, using an encrypted PEM format for on-disk storage is recommended; using triple DES in CBC mode is a good choice. The SSL_CTX will fail to incorporate an encrypted private key correctly unless the correct passphrase is supplied.

OpenSSL collects passphrases through a callback function. The default callback prompts the user on the terminal. For some applications, the default will not be acceptable. The function SSL_CTX_set_default_passwd_cb allows us to set the callback to something more appropriate for the application. The assigned function is invoked during the call to SSL_CTX_use_PrivateKey_file if the indicated file contains an encrypted key. Therefore, the callback should be set before making that call. In fact, the certificates in our chain could be encrypted even though there is nothing secret about them, and our callback function would be invoked to gather the pass-phrase. More accurately, we could state that the passphrase function is called any time a piece of encrypted information is loaded as a parameter to the SSL_CTX.

The callback function's obligation is to copy the passphrase into the buffer that is supplied to it when it is called. The callback function is called with four arguments.

```
int passwd_cb(char * buf, int size, int flag, void *userdata);
```

buf
> The buffer that the passphrase should be copied into. The buffer must be NULL terminated.

size
> The size of the buffer in bytes; includes space for the NULL terminating character.

flag
> Passed as either zero or nonzero. When the flag is nonzero, this passphrase will be used to perform encryption; otherwise, it will be used to perform decryption.

userdata
> Application-specific data; SSL_CTX_set_default_passwd_cb_userdata is used to set this data. Whatever data is set by the application is passed to the call-back function untouched by OpenSSL.

There are two approaches to implementing the passphrase callback. The first method is simply to have the callback prompt the user, copy the collected passphrase to the buffer, and return. This method is viable for applications that need to decrypt a key only once, commonly on application startup. The second way to implement the call-back is for the application to prompt the user for a passphrase on startup and store the collected information in a buffer. The passphrase can be added to the SSL_CTX as user data via the function SSL_CTX_set_default_passwd_cb_userdata. With this method, the callback itself only needs to copy the data from the fourth parameter to the first. This method is viable for applications that need to decrypt keys during normal operation in which constant user prompting is a nuisance.

An unlimited number of PEM-encoded items can be stored in a file, but only one DER item may be stored in a file. Also, different types of PEM items may be stored within a single file. As a result, if the pri-vate key is kept in PEM encoding, it can be appended to the certifi-cate chain file, and the same filename can be used for the calls to SSL_CTX_use_certificate_chain_file and SSL_CTX_use_PrivateKey_file. This trick is used in Example 5-5. PEM and DER encodings are dis-cussed in Chapter 8.

At this stage, we will limit our discussion to the process of providing certificate infor-mation to the peer, rather than discussing the processes of validation. The validation problem will be discussed in Step 2.

Our example extended

Using the same example applications that we've already provided, let's modify them with what we've learned about making SSL connections. Keep in mind that this example is not yet secure. It does not validate anything about the peer to which it connects; it merely provides the authentication information. The new version of our client in *client1.c* is shown in Example 5-5. The bold lines are those that we have added or changed.

Example 5-5. client1.c

```
1  #include "common.h"
2
3  #define CERTFILE "client.pem"
4  SSL_CTX *setup_client_ctx(void)
5  {
6      SSL_CTX *ctx;
7
8      ctx = SSL_CTX_new(SSLv23_method( ));
9      if (SSL_CTX_use_certificate_chain_file(ctx, CERTFILE) != 1)
10         int_error("Error loading certificate from file");
11     if (SSL_CTX_use_PrivateKey_file(ctx, CERTFILE, SSL_FILETYPE_PEM) != 1)
12         int_error("Error loading private key from file");
13     return ctx;
14 }
15
16 int do_client_loop(SSL *ssl)
17 {
18     int  err, nwritten;
19     char buf[80];
20
21     for (;;)
22     {
23         if (!fgets(buf, sizeof(buf), stdin))
24             break;
25         for (nwritten = 0;  nwritten < sizeof(buf);  nwritten += err)
26         {
27             err = SSL_write(ssl, buf + nwritten, strlen(buf) - nwritten);
28             if (err <= 0)
29                 return 0;
30         }
31     }
32     return 1;
33 }
34
35 int main(int argc, char *argv[])
36 {
37     BIO     *conn;
38     SSL     *ssl;
39     SSL_CTX *ctx;
40
41     init_OpenSSL( );
```

Example 5-5. client1.c (continued)

```
42        seed_prng( );
43
44        ctx = setup_client_ctx( );
45
46        conn = BIO_new_connect(SERVER ":" PORT);
47        if (!conn)
48            int_error("Error creating connection BIO");
49
50        if (BIO_do_connect(conn) <= 0)
51            int_error("Error connecting to remote machine");
52
53        if (!(ssl = SSL_new(ctx)))
54            int_error("Error creating an SSL context");
55        SSL_set_bio(ssl, conn, conn);
56        if (SSL_connect(ssl) <= 0)
57            int_error("Error connecting SSL object");
58
59        fprintf(stderr, "SSL Connection opened\n");
60        if (do_client_loop(ssl))
61            SSL_shutdown(ssl);
62        else
63            SSL_clear(ssl);
64        fprintf(stderr, "SSL Connection closed\n");
65
66        SSL_free(ssl);
67        SSL_CTX_free(ctx);
68        return 0;
69    }
```

In this example, we make a call to the function seed_prng. As its name suggests, this function seeds the OpenSSL PRNG. Its implementation is left out; see Chapter 4 for details on an appropriate implementation. It is very important to maintaining the security of SSL for the PRNG to be properly seeded, so this function should never be left out in real-world applications.

The function setup_client_ctx performs the actions as discussed earlier to provide certificate data to the server properly. In this setup process, we leave out any calls to SSL_CTX_set_default_passwd_cb since the default OpenSSL passphrase callback is acceptable for our purposes. The only other point of interest is the error checking performed. This example prints errors and exits if anything goes wrong; a more robust error handling technique was left out for clarity. The sidebar contains more information about the contents of the file *client.pem*.

Lines 54–58 create the SSL object and connect it. There are some functions used here that we have not yet discussed. The call to SSL_new creates our SSL object and copies the settings we've already placed in the SSL_CTX to the newly created object. At this point, the SSL object is still in a generic state. In other words, it could play the role of the server or the client in an SSL handshake.

Generating the Files Needed by the Examples

Our example programs refer to several filenames that contain PEM-encoded certificates and keys. In this sidebar, we'll describe the process of creating each of them. There are two certificates used, the files *server.pem* and *client.pem*. In addition, we have a trusted root certificate in the file *root.pem*. As the example develops, we will also require two other files that will contain DH parameters (*dh512.pem* and *dh1024.pem*). All of the files were generated using the command-line tool described in Chapter 2.

Before moving into the details of the commands themselves, we should first describe our certificate hierarchy. As we've stated, there is just one trusted certificate: the root CA's. This certificate is self-signed, as are all root CA certificates. This root CA represents the CA for a company. The qualifications for peer certificate validation for both our example client and server will be simply to verify that the other has been signed by the root CA. To demonstrate how a chain can grow and still be verifiable, we will create a server CA. This CA will be signed by the root CA and it, in turn, will be used to sign all server identity certificates. The client certificates, on the other hand, will be signed directly by the root CA. Nothing prevents us from making the hierarchy arbitrarily complex, but we've left just one intermediate CA to demonstrate how to do it. Creating more intermediates would follow the same pattern, as we'll see.

The first command shown in each example below generates a certificate signing request. In creating the request, the command-line utility will prompt the user for the contents of the data fields that will be put in the request. The values we typed in are printed when the last command in each example runs. The values that aren't seen are those of the subjectAltName field. We embed the server and client fully qualified domain name (FQDN) in the respective certificate's commonName field, and also in the dNSName field of the subjectAltName. The latter is done by changing the configuration file to include "subjectAltName = DNS:*FQDN*" under the certificate extensions section (the "usr_cert" section); the configuration file is the default aside from this change.

To create the root CA:

```
$ openssl req -newkey rsa:1024 -sha1 -keyout rootkey.pem -out rootreq.pem
$ openssl x509 -req -in rootreq.pem -sha1 -extfile myopenssl.cnf \
> -extensions v3_ca -signkey rootkey.pem -out rootcert.pem
$ cat rootcert.pem rootkey.pem > root.pem
$ openssl x509 -subject -issuer -noout -in root.pem
subject= /C=US/ST=VA/L=Fairfax/O=Zork.org/CN=Root CA
issuer= /C=US/ST=VA/L=Fairfax/O=Zork.org/CN=Root CA
```

To create the server CA and sign it with the root CA:

```
$ openssl req -newkey rsa:1024 -sha1 -keyout serverCAkey.pem -out \
> serverCAreq.pem
$ openssl x509 -req -in serverCAreq.pem -sha1 -extfile \
> myopenssl.cnf -extensions v3_ca -CA root.pem -CAkey root.pem \
> -CAcreateserial -out serverCAcert.pem
```

—continued—

```
$ cat serverCAcert.pem serverCAkey.pem rootcert.pem > serverCA.pem
$ openssl x509 -subject -issuer -noout -in serverCA.pem
subject= /C=US/ST=VA/L=Fairfax/O=Zork.org/OU=Server Division/CN=Server CA
issuer= /C=US/ST=VA/L=Fairfax/O=Zork.org/CN=Root CA
```

To create the server's certificate and sign it with the Server CA:

```
$ openssl req -newkey rsa:1024 -sha1 -keyout serverkey.pem -out \
>  serverreq.pem
$ openssl x509 -req -in serverreq.pem -sha1 -extfile myopenssl.cnf \
>  -extensions usr_cert -CA serverCA.pem -CAkey serverCA.pem \
>  -CAcreateserial -out servercert.pem
$ cat servercert.pem serverkey.pem serverCAcert.pem rootcert.pem > \
>  server.pem
$ openssl x509 -subject -issuer -noout -in server.pem
subject= /C=US/ST=VA/L=Fairfax/O=Zork.org/CN=splat.zork.org
issuer= /C=US/ST=VA/L=Fairfax/O=Zork.org/OU=Server Division/CN=Server CA
```

To create the client certificate and sign it with the Root CA

```
$ openssl req -newkey rsa:1024 -sha1 -keyout clientkey.pem -out \
>  clientreq.pem
$ openssl x509 -req -in clientreq.pem -sha1 -extfile myopenssl.cnf \
>  -extensions usr_cert -CA root.pem -CAkey root.pem \
>  -CAcreateserial -out clientcert.pem
$ cat clientcert.pem clientkey.pem rootcert.pem > client.pem
$ openssl x509 -subject -issuer -noout -in client.pem
subject= /C=US/ST=VA/L=Fairfax/O=Zork.org/CN=shell.zork.org
issuer= /C=US/ST=VA/L=Fairfax/O=Zork.org/CN=Root CA
```

To create *dh512.pem* and *dh1024.pem*:

```
$ openssl dhparam -check -text -5 512 -out dh512.pem
$ openssl dhparam -check -text -5 1024 -out dh1024.pem
```

Another factor left unspecified is the path of communications for the SSL object. Since SSL objects are flexible in the sense that they can perform SSL functions on top of many different types of I/O methods, we must specify a BIO for our object to use. Line 56 does this through a call to SSL_set_bio. This function is passed our connection BIO twice since SSL objects are robust enough to operate on two one-way I/O types instead of requiring a single full-duplex I/O method. Basically, we must specify the BIO to use for writing separately from the BIO used for reading. In this case, they are the same object, since sockets allow two-way communication.

The last unfamiliar function used here is SSL_connect. This function causes the SSL object to initiate the protocol using the underlying I/O. In other words, it begins the SSL handshake with the application on the other end of the underlying BIO. This function will return an error for problems such as incompatible protocol versions.

The do_client_loop function is almost identical to that of our non-SSL client. We've simply changed the parameter to an SSL object instead of a BIO, and the BIO_write becomes an SSL_write. In addition, we've added a return value to this function. If no errors occur, we can call SSL_shutdown to stop the SSL connection; otherwise, we call SSL_clear. This is done to force OpenSSL to remove any session with errors from the session cache. We will look at session caching in more detail later in this chapter, but for now, it is worth noting that session caching is effectively disabled in the examples we've provided so far.

The last point to make about this example is that we removed the call to BIO_free. This is done because SSL_free automatically frees the SSL object's underlying BIOs for us.

Example 5-6 has the contents of *server1.c*, the file containing the implementation of our SSL-enabled server. Again, it isn't yet secure since it validates nothing about the peer; it simply provides its certificate information to the client.

Example 5-6. server1.c

```
 1  #include "common.h"
 2
 3  #define CERTFILE "server.pem"
 4  SSL_CTX *setup_server_ctx(void)
 5  {
 6      SSL_CTX *ctx;
 7
 8      ctx = SSL_CTX_new(SSLv23_method( ));
 9      if (SSL_CTX_use_certificate_chain_file(ctx, CERTFILE) != 1)
10          int_error("Error loading certificate from file");
11      if (SSL_CTX_use_PrivateKey_file(ctx, CERTFILE, SSL_FILETYPE_PEM) != 1)
12          int_error("Error loading private key from file");
13      return ctx;
14  }
15
16  int do_server_loop(SSL *ssl)
17  {
18      int  err, nread;
19      char buf[80];
20
21      do
22      {
23          for (nread = 0;  nread < sizeof(buf);  nread += err)
24          {
25              err = SSL_read(ssl, buf + nread, sizeof(buf) - nread);
26              if (err <= 0)
27                  break;
28          }
29          fwrite(buf, 1, nread, stdout);
30      }
31      while (err > 0);
32      return (SSL_get_shutdown(ssl) & SSL_RECEIVED_SHUTDOWN) ? 1 : 0;
33  }
34
35  void THREAD_CC server_thread(void *arg)
36  {
37      SSL *ssl = (SSL *)arg;
38
```

Example 5-6. server1.c (continued)

```
39  #ifndef WIN32
40      pthread_detach(pthread_self( ));
41  #endif
42      if (SSL_accept(ssl) <= 0)
43          int_error("Error accepting SSL connection");
44      fprintf(stderr, "SSL Connection opened\n");
45      if (do_server_loop(ssl))
46          SSL_shutdown(ssl);
47      else
48          SSL_clear(ssl);
49      fprintf(stderr, "SSL Connection closed\n");
50      SSL_free(ssl);
51
52  ERR_remove_state(0);
53
54  #ifdef WIN32
55      _endthread( );
56  #endif
57  }
58
59  int main(int argc, char *argv[])
60  {
61      BIO         *acc, *client;
62      SSL         *ssl;
63      SSL_CTX     *ctx;
64      THREAD_TYPE tid;
65
66      init_OpenSSL( );
67      seed_prng( );
68
69      ctx = setup_server_ctx( );
70
71      acc = BIO_new_accept(PORT);
72      if (!acc)
73          int_error("Error creating server socket");
74
75      if (BIO_do_accept(acc) <= 0)
76          int_error("Error binding server socket");
77
78      for (;;)
79      {
80          if (BIO_do_accept(acc) <= 0)
81              int_error("Error accepting connection");
82
83          client = BIO_pop(acc);
84          if (!(ssl = SSL_new(ctx)))
85              int_error("Error creating SSL context");
86
87          SSL_set_bio(ssl, client, client);
88          THREAD_CREATE(tid, server_thread, ssl);
89      }
90
```

Example 5-6. server1.c (continued)

```
91      SSL_CTX_free(ctx);
92      BIO_free(acc);
93      return 0;
94  }
```

After looking at the new client program, the modifications to the server should be clear. Since this is the server side of the SSL negotiation, a different function call is made: SSL_accept. The SSL_accept function initiates communication on the underlying I/O layer to perform the SSL handshake.

In the do_server_loop function, we use a call to SSL_get_shutdown to check into the error status of the SSL object. This essentially allows us to differentiate normal client terminations from actual errors. If the SSL_RECEIVED_SHUTDOWN flag is set, we know the session hasn't had an error and it's safe to cache. In other words, we can call SSL_shutdown rather than simply clear the connection. The remainder of the modifications to the server program parallel those made to the client.

In summary, we've taken our applications and built them to the point of creating the objects necessary for SSL connections. Each application does provide its certificate data to the peers to which it connects, but they do not verify the certificates they receive. We will build further in the next step and learn how to validate peer certificates.

Step 2: Peer Authentication

The security of an SSL-enabled program is compromised by failure to verify peer certificates properly. In this step, we'll look into the various API calls that deal with trusted certificates, certificate chain verification, CRL usage, and post-connection verification.

Background

Certificate verification can often be confusing, so we'll discuss the theory before delving into the details. As we already know, a certificate is a set of credentials that has been cryptographically signed by a CA. Each certificate, including a CA certificate, contains a public key with a private key counterpart held in secret by the certificate owner. Moving forward, the process of signing a certificate involves using the private key of a CA to sign the public key in the new certificate. Thus, it should be clear that the process of verification will involve using the public key in a CA certificate to verify the signature on a certificate.

Aside from using a CA to create an entity certificate, a CA may also sign a certificate and give it permissions, via X.509v3 extensions, to act as a CA itself. Generally, this procedure allows for a CA to permit another certificate to act as a CA for a specialized purpose. Through this mechanism, we become aware of certificate hierarchies, i.e., a certificate tree. Understanding this, we can see that a single entity certificate may have a list of signing certificates leading up to the original, self-signed root certificate. This list of certificates, each signed by the next, is called a *certificate chain*.

Jumping back to a simple example of a root CA signing a single entity certificate, any party may verify the entity certificate by checking the signature on it, presuming it trusts the root CA. The process of validating an entity certificate is that simple. Extending this to a certificate chain, we must validate each subsequent signature in the list until we reach a trusted CA certificate or until we reach the end of the list. If we hit a CA we trust and the signatures are all valid, our entity certificate is verified; if we find an invalid signature or reach the end of the chain without reaching a trusted certificate, the entity certificate is not verified.

Incorporating trusted certificates

As we previously discussed, verifying a certificate's authenticity requires that the verifying agent have a list of CAs that it trusts. Therefore, we must provide our application with such a list in order for it to verify the peer. We will start our discussion of peer verification by first concentrating on accomplishing this task.

Loading trusted CA certificates into our application is manifested as additional setup to the SSL_CTX object. The function SSL_CTX_load_verify_locations performs this task. This function will load certificates from files, directories, or both.

```
int SSL_CTX_load_verify_locations(SSL_CTX *ctx, const char *CAfile,
                                  const char *CApath);
```

ctx
> The SSL context object that trusted CA certificates will be loaded into.

CAfile
> The name of a file containing CA certificates in PEM format. More than one CA certificate may be present in the file.

CApath
> The name of a directory containing CA certificates. Each file in the directory must contain only a single CA certificate, and the files must be named by the subject name's hash and an extension of ".0".

We can call SSL_CTX_load_verify_locations with either the second or the third arguments specified as NULL, but not both. The behavior of this function is to perform the loading for the non-NULL arguments. An important difference between file and directory storage is the time when the certificates get loaded. With a flat file, the file is parsed and certificates loaded during the call to SSL_CTX_load_verify_locations. However, with a directory, certificates are read only when needed, i.e., during the verification phase that occurs during the SSL handshake.

OpenSSL also has default CA certificate locations. When building the library, these paths are hardcoded into the library based on the parameters that are used to build it.

In general, there is an OpenSSL directory (commonly */usr/local/openssl* on Unix systems). The default certificate file is named *cert.pem*, and it lives in this OpenSSL directory. Likewise, the default certificate directory is named *certs*, and it too lives in the OpenSSL directory. These default locations provide a convenient place to store system-wide CA certificates that all of the OpenSSL-based applications running on the machine require. Using the default files, we will not need to keep separate copies of common certificates for each application. The function SSL_CTX_set_default_verify_paths loads these default locations into our SSL_CTX object. For calls to this function, the same rules for determining when the CA certificates actually get loaded apply as with a call to SSL_CTX_load_verify_locations.

> When we load a certificate location into an SSL_CTX object, we are making the statement that we trust those certificates. It is important to understand that if our application runs on a multiuser system, any user with permissions to write to the certificate locations that we load can subvert the security of our application. This is especially important when electing to load the default verify locations. For instance, if our application loads these defaults, a user with the correct permissions could slip in a new CA certificate, thus connecting our application with peers presenting certificates signed by this rogue CA certificate.

Using these two functions, we can load trusted CA certificates into our SSL_CTX. Even though they are loaded, the certificates are still not used to verify the peer. We will explore the details of enabling this in the next section.

Certificate verification

Certificate verification entails checking the cryptographic signatures on a certificate to be sure an entity we trust has signed that certificate. It also involves checking the certificate's notBefore and notAfter dates, trust settings, purpose, and revocation status. Verification of a certificate takes place during the SSL handshake (during the call to SSL_connect or SSL_accept, depending on whether the SSL object is a client or a server).

Once we've properly loaded trusted certificates into the SSL_CTX object, OpenSSL has a built-in function to verify the peer's certificate chain automatically. The routine used to verify the certificate chain could be changed from the default via a call to SSL_CTX_set_cert_verify_callback, but under almost all circumstances, this is undesirable since the default routine for signature verification is amply complete and robust. Instead, the developer can specify a different callback that filters the return status of the default verification and returns the new verification status. The function to perform this task is SSL_CTX_set_verify.

Aside from assigning a filter verify callback, this function's primary purpose is to assign the type of verification our SSL_CTX object's connections will perform. More accurately, we can use it to control how certificates and requests are handled during a handshake. The second argument to this function is a set of flags that determine this. Four flags are defined with names that can be combined with a logical OR operation. Depending on whether the context is being used in client mode or server mode, these flags can have different meanings.

SSL_VERIFY_NONE

When the context is being used in server mode, no request for a certificate will be sent to the client, and the client should not send a certificate. When the context is being used in client mode, any certificate received from the server will be verified, but failure will not terminate the handshake. Do not combine this flag with any others; the others will take precedence over this one. This flag should only be used by itself.

SSL_VERIFY_PEER

When the context is being used in server mode, a request for a certificate will be sent to the client. The client may opt to ignore the request, but if a certificate is sent back, it will be verified. If the verification fails, the handshake will be terminated immediately.

When the context is being used in client mode, if the server sends a certificate, it will be verified. If the verification fails, the handshake will be terminated immediately. The only time that a server would not send a certificate is when an anonymous cipher is in use. Anonymous ciphers are disabled by default. Any other flags combined with this one in client mode are ignored.

SSL_VERIFY_FAIL_IF_NO_PEER_CERT

If the context is not being used in server mode or if SSL_VERIFY_PEER is not set, this flag is ignored. Use of this flag will cause the handshake to terminate immediately if no certificate is provided by the client.

SSL_VERIFY_CLIENT_ONCE

If the context is not being used in server mode or if SSL_VERIFY_PEER is not set, this flag is ignored. Use of this flag will prevent the server from requesting a certificate from the client in the case of a renegotiation. A certificate will still be requested during the initial handshake.

The third argument to SSL_CTX_set_verify is a pointer to the verification filter callback. Since the internal verification routine is called for each level of the peer certificate chain, our filter routine will be called just after each step. This function's first argument is nonzero if the verification succeeded, and zero otherwise. The second argument is an X509_STORE_CTX object. This type of object contains the information necessary to verify a certificate. The object holds the current certificate being verified and the verification result. The return value from the function should be either zero or nonzero to indicate whether the certificate should be considered valid or not.

As in most of the callbacks used with OpenSSL, there is a default supplied that simply returns the value of the first argument. When implementing our own version of this function, we need to maintain this behavior. If we return nonzero when the first parameter is actually zero, an unverified client certificate will be accepted as a verified one. Likewise, the reverse would cause a valid certificate to fail verification. At this point, it may seem as if there is no real purpose to implementing our own version, but this isn't accurate. The reason we should supply our own is so that more detailed information about the results of verification can be obtained, especially when verification fails. For instance, if a peer presents an expired certificate and we do not implement a verify callback to check status, then we find out only that the call to SSL_connect or SSL_accept failed because of "handshake failure." Example 5-7 shows an implementation for this callback that we will use in our example applications. To use it in our examples, it should be implemented in *common.c* and prototyped in *common.h*.

Example 5-7. A verify callback (implemented in common.c and prototyped in common.h)

```
int verify_callback(int ok, X509_STORE_CTX *store)
{
    char data[256];

    if (!ok)
    {
        X509 *cert = X509_STORE_CTX_get_current_cert(store);
        int  depth = X509_STORE_CTX_get_error_depth(store);
        int  err = X509_STORE_CTX_get_error(store);

        fprintf(stderr, "-Error with certificate at depth: %i\n", depth);
        X509_NAME_oneline(X509_get_issuer_name(cert), data, 256);
        fprintf(stderr, " issuer   = %s\n", data);
        X509_NAME_oneline(X509_get_subject_name(cert), data, 256);
        fprintf(stderr, " subject  = %s\n", data);
        fprintf(stderr, " err %i:%s\n", err, X509_verify_cert_error_string(err));
    }

    return ok;
}
```

This callback employs several functions from the X509 family of functions to report the detailed error information.

The call to SSL_CTX_set_verify is done before any SSL objects are created from the context. We should also make a call to SSL_CTX_set_verify_depth. This function sets the maximum allowable depth for peer certificates. In other words, it limits the number of certificates that we are willing to verify in order to ensure the chain is trusted. For example, if the depth was set to four and six certificates are present in the chain to reach the trusted certificate, the verification would fail because the required depth would be too great. For nearly all applications, the default depth of nine is more than high enough to ensure that the peer certificate will not fail due to too large of a certificate chain. On the other hand, if we know that our application will be used only with peers presenting certificates of some smaller chain length, it is a good idea to set the value to exclude certificates composed of longer chains from being verified successfully. Setting the depth to zero allows chains of unlimited length to be used.

 There is a known security vulnerability in SSL_CTX_set_verify_depth in versions of OpenSSL prior to 0.9.6. The problem stemmed from the fact that the internal verification routine did not properly check extensions on peer certificate chains; it approved certificate chains that contained non-CA certificates as long as they led to a trusted root CA. Thus, using any verification depth greater than one left the application susceptible to attack from anyone signed by the trusted root CA. Since this problem has been fixed in newer versions of OpenSSL by checking the X509v3 fields regarding CA authorization, this vulnerability should be of only academic interest.

Incorporating certificate revocation lists

A large problem with SSL security is the availability and usage of certificate revocation lists. Since certificates can be revoked by the issuing CA, we must somehow account for this in our SSL implementation. To do this, an application must load CRL files in order for the internal verification process to ensure each certificate it verifies is not revoked. Unfortunately, OpenSSL's CRL functionality is incomplete in Version 0.9.6. The features necessary to utilize CRL information will be complete in new versions starting with 0.9.7.

Because this functionality is not available at the time of writing, CRL usage will not be incorporated in this example. However, we can tell you what you will need to do once newer releases are made. Remember, it is paramount to include CRL checking when verifying certificates. If any new version of OpenSSL is used when building applications, this step is required for security.

The SSL interface itself does not support CRL incorporation directly; instead, we must use the underlying X509 interface.

The function SSL_CTX_get_cert_store retrieves the internal X509_STORE object from the SSL_CTX object. Operations on this store object allow us to perform a variety of tweaks on the verification process. In fact, the functions SSL_CTX_load_verify_locations and SSL_CTX_set_default_paths call functions against this same X509_STORE object to perform their respective operations.

```
X509_STORE *SSL_CTX_get_cert_store(SSL_CTX *ctx);
```

All of the details for interacting with certificate stores to set further verification parameters or incorporate CRL data are discussed in Chapter 10 with the verification of certificate chains. We strongly recommend that developers implementing applications consult the verification process in Chapter 10 that uses X509_STORE objects to learn the proper method of SSL certificate verification against CRLs. The process involves adding the CRL files to the X509_STORE via a file lookup method and then setting the store's flags to check certificates against the CRLs.

Post-connection assertions

Essentially, `SSL_CTX_set_verify` and `SSL_CTX_set_verify_depth` are all we need to use in order for OpenSSL to verify the peer certificate chain upon connection. There is more, however. After connecting the `SSL` object, we need to assert that some assumed properties about the connection are indeed true. OpenSSL provides several functions that allow us to create a post-connection verification routine to make sure that we haven't been fooled by a malicious peer. This post-connection verification routine is very important because it allows for much finer grained control over the certificate that is presented by the peer, beyond the certificate verification that is required by the SSL protocol proper.

The function `SSL_get_peer_certificate` will return a pointer to an X509 object that contains the peer's certificate. While the handshake is complete and, presumably, the verification completed correctly, we must still use this function. Consider the case in which the peer presents no certificate when one is requested but not required. The certificate verification routines—both the built-in and the filter—will not return errors since there was nothing wrong with the NULL certificate. Thus, to prevent this condition, we must call this function and check that the return value is not NULL. If this function returns a non-NULL value, the reference count of the return object is increased. In order to prevent memory leaks, we must call `X509_free` to decrement the count after we're done using the object.

Our application will be vulnerable if we do not check the peer certificate beyond verification of the chain. For example, let's say that we're making a web browsing application. To keep it simple, we'll allow just one trusted CA. When we do this, any SSL peer with a certificate signed by the same CA will be verified correctly. This isn't secure. Nothing prevents an attacker from getting his own certificate signed by the CA and then hijacking all your sessions. We thwart this kind of masquerade by tying the certificate to some piece of information unique to the machine. For purposes of SSL, this piece of information is the entity's *fully qualified domain name* (FQDN), also called the DNS name.

The common practice with X.509v1 certificates was to put the FQDN in the certificate's `commonName` field of the `subjectName` field. This practice is no longer recommended for new applications since X.509v3 allows certificate extensions to hold the FQDN as well as other identifying information, such as IP address. The proper place for the FQDN is in the `dNSName` field of the `subjectAltName` extension.

We use the function `post_connection_check` to perform these checks for us. We recommend always checking for the `dNSName` field first, and if it isn't present, we can check the `commonName` field. Checking the `commonName` field is strictly for backward compatibility, so if this isn't a concern, it can safely be omitted. Our example function will check for the extension first and then fall back to the `commonName`. One feature our example does omit is the optional wildcard expansion. RFC 2818 specifies a paradigm for allowing FQDNs in certificates to contain wildcards. Implementing this functionality is simply a text-processing issue and is thus omitted for clarity.

SSL_get_verify_result is another API function that we will employ in our post-connection check. This function returns the error code last generated by the verification routines. If no error has occurred, X509_V_OK is returned. We should call this function and make sure the returned value equals X509_V_OK. When browsing the example application, it is obvious that robust error handling has been left out for clarity. For example, the programs simply exit when an error occurs. In most cases, we will want to do something better to handle errors in some application-specific way. Checking the verify result is always a good idea. It makes an assertion that no matter what error handling occurred up to this point, if the result isn't OK now, we should disconnect.

Example 5-8 shows a function that performs the checks that we've just described. In the example, we'll check to be sure that the certificate contains the FQDN of the peer to which we expect to be connecting. For the client, we'll want to make sure that the server presents a certificate that contains the FQDN of the server's address. Likewise, for the server, we'll want to make sure that the client presents a certificate that contains the FQDN of the client's address. In this case, our checking of the client certificate will be very strict because we'll be expecting the client to be using a specific FQDN, and we'll allow only that one. For the purposes of our example client and server, this function should appear in *common.c* and be prototyped in *common.h*.

Example 5-8. A function to do post-connection assertions (implemented in common.c and prototyped in common.h)

```
long post_connection_check(SSL *ssl, char *host)
{
    X509        *cert;
    X509_NAME *subj;
    char        data[256];
    int         extcount;
    int         ok = 0;

    /* Checking the return from SSL_get_peer_certificate here is not strictly
     * necessary.  With our example programs, it is not possible for it to return
     * NULL.  However, it is good form to check the return since it can return NULL
     * if the examples are modified to enable anonymous ciphers or for the server
     * to not require a client certificate.
     */
    if (!(cert = SSL_get_peer_certificate(ssl)) || !host)
        goto err_occured;
    if ((extcount = X509_get_ext_count(cert)) > 0)
    {
        int i;

        for (i = 0;  i < extcount;  i++)
        {
            char                *extstr;
```

Example 5-8. A function to do post-connection assertions (implemented in common.c and prototyped in common.h) (continued)

```
            X509_EXTENSION      *ext;

            ext = X509_get_ext(cert, i);
            extstr = OBJ_nid2sn(OBJ_obj2nid(X509_EXTENSION_get_object(ext)));

            if (!strcmp(extstr, "subjectAltName"))
            {
                int                 j;
                unsigned char       *data;
                STACK_OF(CONF_VALUE) *val;
                CONF_VALUE          *nval;
                X509V3_EXT_METHOD   *meth;

                if (!(meth = X509V3_EXT_get(ext)))
                    break;
                data = ext->value->data;

                val = meth->i2v(meth,
                            meth->d2i(NULL, &data, ext->value->length),
                            NULL);
                for (j = 0;  j < sk_CONF_VALUE_num(val);  j++)
                {
                    nval = sk_CONF_VALUE_value(val, j);
                    if (!strcmp(nval->name, "DNS") && !strcmp(nval->value, host))
                    {
                        ok = 1;
                        break;
                    }
                }
            }
            if (ok)
                break;
        }
    }

    if (!ok && (subj = X509_get_subject_name(cert)) &&
        X509_NAME_get_text_by_NID(subj, NID_commonName, data, 256) > 0)
    {
        data[255] = 0;
        if (strcasecmp(data, host) != 0)
            goto err_occured;
    }

    X509_free(cert);
    return SSL_get_verify_result(ssl);

err_occured:
    if (cert)
        X509_free(cert);
    return X509_V_ERR_APPLICATION_VERIFICATION;
}
```

At a high level, the function post_connection_check is implemented as a wrapper around SSL_get_verify_result, which performs our extra peer certificate checks. It uses the reserved error code X509_V_ERR_APPLICATION_VERIFICATION to indicate errors where there is no peer certificate present or the certificate presented does not match the expected FQDN. This function will return an error in the following circumstances:

- If no peer certificate is found
- If it is called with a NULL second argument, i.e., if no FQDN is specified to compare against
- If the dNSName fields found (if any) do not match the host argument and the commonName also doesn't match the host argument (if found)
- Any time the SSL_get_verify_result routine returns an error

As long as none of the above errors occurs, the value X509_V_OK will be returned. Our example programs are further extended below to employ this function.

Unfortunately, the code to check the dNSName is not very clear. We use the X509 functions to access the extensions. We then iterate through the extensions and use the extension-specific parsing routines to find all extensions that are subjectAltName fields. Since a subjectAltName field may itself contain several fields, we must then iterate through those fields to find any dNSName fields (they are tagged with the short name DNS). Since it is rather confusing, we will step through this function to explain its behavior. Having a stronger understanding of some of the more advanced programming techniques presented in Chapter 10 will help demystify the implementation of this function.

At the onset, we simply get the peer certificate from the SSL object. If the function X509_get_ext_count returns a positive number, we know there are some X.509v3 extensions present in the peer's certificate. Given this, we iterate over the extensions to look for a subjectAltName. The function X509_get_ext will retrieve an extension for us based on the counter. We also use the variable extstr to hold the extracted short name of the extension. Unfortunately, we must use three functions to perform this task: the innermost extracts the ASN1_OBJECT, the next fetches the NID, and the outermost function gets the short name as a const char * from the NID.

Next, we check if the extension is what we're looking for by comparing the short name against the string constant subjectAltName. Once we're sure it's the right extension, we need to extract the X509V3_EXT_METHOD object from the extension. This object is a container of extension-specific functions for manipulating the data within the extension. We access the data we wish to manipulate directly through the value member of the X509_EXTENSION structure. The d2i and i2v functions serve the purpose of converting the raw data in the subjectAltName to a stack of CONF_VALUE objects. This is necessary to make it simple to iterate over the several kinds of fields in the subjectAltName so that we may find the dNSName field(s). We check each member of this CONF_VALUE stack to see if we have a match for the host string in a dNSName field. Keep in mind that the dNSName field is named DNS in the extension itself, since it's referenced by its short name. As soon as we find a match, we stop the iterations over all the extensions.

We only pursue checking the commonName of the certificate if no match is found in a dNSName field. If we fail to find an FQDN that matches the host argument in either the dNSName field or the commonName, we return the code for an application-specific error. In most real-world cases, matching one specific FQDN is not desirable. Most often, a server would have a list (known as a whitelist) that contains all of the acceptable FQDNs for connecting clients. If the client's certificate contains an FQDN that appears on this list, the certificate is accepted; otherwise, it is rejected.

Further extension of the examples

Employing what we know about verifying the authenticity of the peer, we can extend our example applications to make them one step closer to being secure. For these examples, we've added the functions verify_callback and post_connection_check to *common.c* and their prototypes to *common.h*.

The code for our revised client application, *client2.c*, is provided in Example 5-9. The lines that differ from *client1.c* are marked. Line 3 defines the file we use to store trusted certificates. We define CADIR to be NULL on line 4 since we will use a flat file instead. Nothing prevents us from specifying both a file and a directory; but in this case, we do not need a directory.

Example 5-9. client2.c

```
 1  #include "common.h"
 2
 3  #define CAFILE "root.pem"
 4  #define CADIR NULL
 5  #define CERTFILE "client.pem"
 6  SSL_CTX *setup_client_ctx(void)
 7  {
 8      SSL_CTX *ctx;
 9
10      ctx = SSL_CTX_new(SSLv23_method());
11      if (SSL_CTX_load_verify_locations(ctx, CAFILE, CADIR) != 1)
12          int_error("Error loading CA file and/or directory");
13      if (SSL_CTX_set_default_verify_paths(ctx) != 1)
14          int_error("Error loading default CA file and/or directory");
15      if (SSL_CTX_use_certificate_chain_file(ctx, CERTFILE) != 1)
16          int_error("Error loading certificate from file");
17      if (SSL_CTX_use_PrivateKey_file(ctx, CERTFILE, SSL_FILETYPE_PEM) != 1)
18          int_error("Error loading private key from file");
19      SSL_CTX_set_verify(ctx, SSL_VERIFY_PEER, verify_callback);
20      SSL_CTX_set_verify_depth(ctx, 4);
21      return ctx;
22  }
23
```

Example 5-9. client2.c (continued)

```c
24  int do_client_loop(SSL *ssl)
25  {
26      int  err, nwritten;
27      char buf[80];
28
29      for (;;)
30      {
31          if (!fgets(buf, sizeof(buf), stdin))
32              break;
33          for (nwritten = 0;  nwritten < sizeof(buf);  nwritten += err)
34          {
35              err = SSL_write(ssl, buf + nwritten, strlen(buf) - nwritten);
36              if (err <= 0)
37                  return 0;
38          }
39      }
40      return 1;
41  }
42
43  int main(int argc, char *argv[])
44  {
45      BIO     *conn;
46      SSL     *ssl;
47      SSL_CTX *ctx;
48      long    err;
49
50      init_OpenSSL();
51      seed_prng();
52
53      ctx = setup_client_ctx();
54
55      conn = BIO_new_connect(SERVER ":" PORT);
56      if (!conn)
57          int_error("Error creating connection BIO");
58
59      if (BIO_do_connect(conn) <= 0)
60          int_error("Error connecting to remote machine");
61
62      ssl = SSL_new(ctx);
63      SSL_set_bio(ssl, conn, conn);
64      if (SSL_connect(ssl) <= 0)
65          int_error("Error connecting SSL object");
66      if ((err = post_connection_check(ssl, SERVER)) != X509_V_OK)
67      {
68          fprintf(stderr, "-Error: peer certificate: %s\n",
69                  X509_verify_cert_error_string(err));
70          int_error("Error checking SSL object after connection");
71      }
72      fprintf(stderr, "SSL Connection opened\n");
73      if (do_client_loop(ssl))
74          SSL_shutdown(ssl);
75      else
```

Example 5-9. client2.c (continued)

```
76          SSL_clear(ssl);
77      fprintf(stderr, "SSL Connection closed\n");
78
79      SSL_free(ssl);
80      SSL_CTX_free(ctx);
81      return 0;
82  }
```

To load the trusted certificates from *root.pem*, we call SSL_CTX_load_verify_locations on line 11 and check for errors. Since we trust the users of the system on which this client will run, we also call SSL_CTX_set_default_verify_paths to load the built-in certificate stores. Our example does not explicitly require the loading of the default locations; it is included for illustration. It is good design practice to load these defaults only when the application will run on a trusted system and when the application itself needs to incorporate these extra certificates.

After loading the trusted certificates, we set the verification mode to SSL_VERIFY_PEER and assign the callback (line 19). When implementing SSL clients, the verification mode should always include SSL_VERIFY_PEER. Without this, we could never tell if the server we connect with is properly authenticated. As we discussed in the section above, the verify_callback function simply reports errors in more detail and does not change the behavior of the internal verification process. The following line, line 20, sets the maximum depth for verification to four. For this client example, four levels of verification ought to be plenty because our certificate hierarchy is not too complex. Given the details from the previous sidebar describing our example PKI, the minimum depth we can assign to our client is two, since the server's certificate is signed by the server CA, which, in turn, is signed by the root CA that we trust.

The last major change to this version of the client is in lines 66–71. These lines use the post_connection_check function that we developed in Example 5-8. This call asserts that the server we are connected with did present a certificate and the certificate it provided has "splat.zork.org" as the FQDN. If any errors occur, we can call X509_verify_cert_error_string to convert our error code into a string to print to the console.

Example 5-10 shows the contents of *server2.c*, our example server program. The changes made to it are congruent with the changes made to the client application.

Example 5-10. server2.c

```
1   #include "common.h"
2
3   #define CAFILE "root.pem"
4   #define CADIR NULL
5   #define CERTFILE "server.pem"
6   SSL_CTX *setup_server_ctx(void)
7   {
8       SSL_CTX *ctx;
9
```

Example 5-10. server2.c (continued)

```
10      ctx = SSL_CTX_new(SSLv23_method( ));
11      if (SSL_CTX_load_verify_locations(ctx, CAFILE, CADIR) != 1)
12          int_error("Error loading CA file and/or directory");
13      if (SSL_CTX_set_default_verify_paths(ctx) != 1)
14          int_error("Error loading default CA file and/or directory");
15      if (SSL_CTX_use_certificate_chain_file(ctx, CERTFILE) != 1)
16          int_error("Error loading certificate from file");
17      if (SSL_CTX_use_PrivateKey_file(ctx, CERTFILE, SSL_FILETYPE_PEM) != 1)
18          int_error("Error loading private key from file");
19      SSL_CTX_set_verify(ctx, SSL_VERIFY_PEER|SSL_VERIFY_FAIL_IF_NO_PEER_CERT,
20                          verify_callback);
21      SSL_CTX_set_verify_depth(ctx, 4);
22      return ctx;
23  }
24
25  int do_server_loop(SSL *ssl)
26  {
27      int  err, nread;
28      char buf[80];
29
30      for (;;)
31      {
32          for (nread = 0;  nread < sizeof(buf);  nread += err)
33          {
34              err = SSL_read(ssl, buf + nread, sizeof(buf) - nread);
35              if (err <= 0)
36                  break;
37          }
38          fwrite(buf, 1, nread, stdout);
39      }
40      return (SSL_get_shutdown(ssl) & SSL_RECEIVED_SHUTDOWN) ? 1 : 0;
41  }
42
43  void THREAD_CC server_thread(void *arg)
44  {
45      SSL *ssl = (SSL *)arg;
46  long err;
47
48  #ifndef WIN32
49      pthread_detach(pthread_self( ));
50  #endif
51      if (SSL_accept(ssl) <= 0)
52          int_error("Error accepting SSL connection");
53      if ((err = post_connection_check(ssl, CLIENT)) != X509_V_OK)
54      {
55          fprintf(stderr, "-Error: peer certificate: %s\n",
56                  X509_verify_cert_error_string(err));
57          int_error("Error checking SSL object after connection");
58      }
59      fprintf(stderr, "SSL Connection opened\n");
60      if (do_server_loop(ssl))
61          SSL_shutdown(ssl);
```

Example 5-10. server2.c (continued)

```
62      else
63          SSL_clear(ssl);
64      fprintf(stderr, "SSL Connection closed\n");
65      SSL_free(ssl);
66  ERR_remove_state(0)
67  #ifdef WIN32
68      _endthread( );
69  #endif
70  }
71
72  int main(int argc, char *argv[])
73  {
74      BIO     *acc, *client;
75      SSL     *ssl;
76      SSL_CTX *ctx;
77      THREAD_TYPE tid;
78
79      init_OpenSSL( );
80      seed_prng( );
81
82      ctx = setup_server_ctx( );
83
84      acc = BIO_new_accept(PORT);
85      if (!acc)
86          int_error("Error creating server socket");
87
88      if (BIO_do_accept(acc) <= 0)
89          int_error("Error binding server socket");
90
91      for (;;)
92      {
93          if (BIO_do_accept(acc) <= 0)
94              int_error("Error accepting connection");
95
96          client = BIO_pop(acc);
97          if (!(ssl = SSL_new(ctx)))
98          int_error("Error creating SSL context");
99          SSL_set_accept_state(ssl);
100         SSL_set_bio(ssl, client, client);
101         THREAD_create(tid, server_thread, ssl);
102     }
103
104     SSL_CTX_free(ctx);
105     BIO_free(acc);
106     return 0;
107 }
```

One way the changes to the server stray from the changes to the client is in the verification mode. In server applications, the behavior of SSL_VERIFY_PEER is slightly different; it causes the server to solicit a certificate from the client. The other verification flag used is SSL_VERIFY_FAIL_IF_NO_PEER_CERT. This flag instructs the server to fail on the handshake if the client presents no certificate.

The choice of whether to require a client to supply a certificate depends on the type of server application you're building. In many cases, requiring a client certificate may not be strictly necessary, but it's generally a bad idea to request a certificate without requiring one because it may often cause a client to present the user with a prompt to select the certificate to use. Particularly in a web-based environment, this is not desirable. If you need to require a certificate only for specific commands or options, it's better to force a renegotiation instead.

The client's usage of the SERVER-defined value and the server's usage of CLIENT is an oversimplification. In many cases, especially with that of a server, the string containing the peer's FQDN will not be so readily available. Instead, we may need to look at the IP address to which we are connected and use it to discover the FQDN. For purposes of clarity, this process was omitted, and the names were hardcoded. Additionally, when verifying peer certificates, the owner will often not be a machine with a FQDN but rather a person, organization, etc. For these cases, it's important to change the post_connection_check routine accordingly to allow for successful connections.

Using the tricks we learned in this step, we have now developed a viable framework for verifying a peer and assuring authentication is done properly. The majority of the battle to SSL-enable our application is over; however, we still have one more step.

Step 3: SSL Options and Cipher Suites

We have not yet discussed a few important points about SSL connections. For instance, we mentioned that SSLv2 shouldn't be used, yet our example was created with the SSLv23_method that still allows for this insecure protocol version. Beyond protocol limitation, OpenSSL provides for many workarounds for known bugs in other SSL implementations. While these bugs don't affect security, our application may lose interoperability if we do not account for them.

Additionally, we need to delve into the selection of *cipher suites*. A cipher suite is a combination of lower-level algorithms that an SSL connection uses to do authentication, key exchange, and stream encryption. Suite selection is important because OpenSSL supports some algorithms for compatibility that we want to exclude for security reasons. Similarly, some of the cipher suites that are secure require an application to provide callbacks in order to be utilized. Learning how to do these things properly and extending our example for this final step will be the topic of this section.

Setting SSL options

The SSL_CTX_set_options function provides the developer with finer-grained control over the SSL connections spawned from the context. Using this function, we can enable the bug workarounds built into the OpenSSL library. For instance, a particular version of a Netscape product (Netscape-Commerce 1.12) will truncate the material used for key generation. In order for our SSL programs to establish a connection to a peer with such a bug, we need to enable the workaround. These fixes are useful only to programs that will communicate with a peer known to have bugs, but enabling the workarounds does not hurt anything as a rule. These bug fixes can be enabled individually, but instead we should set the SSL_OP_ALL flag, which will enable all of the workaround code.

Like the function SSL_CTX_set_verify, the second parameter to this function is a set of flags. Again, the flags can be combined with the logical OR operation. An important fact about this call is that once an option is set, it can't be cleared: this function only adds the options presented by the second argument to the options set contained in the SSL_CTX object. The new set of options is returned by this function.

In addition to the workarounds for buggy SSL peers, this function allows us to tighten the security of our SSL connections. By setting the option SSL_OP_NO_SSLv2, we prevent the SSLv2 protocol from being used. As we noted in Step 1, this is a very useful feature. Using this option, we can create an SSL_CTX object based on the compatibility method, SSLv23_method, and the context will not allow SSLv2 peers. This is useful since electing to base our context upon either SSLv3_method or TLSv1_method would prevent the other from connecting correctly.

Two server-side-only options that bear consideration are SSL_OP_EPHEMERAL_RSA and SSL_OP_SINGLE_DH_USE. The former causes our context object to attempt to use a temporary RSA key for the key exchange. The details of this process are discussed below, but generally, this option should never be used, since it violates the SSL/TLS protocol specification. We discuss the SSL_OP_SINGLE_DH_USE flag in the next section.

Ephemeral keying

In our examples thus far, both the server and the client certificates have been based on RSA key pairs. Because the RSA algorithm can be used for most signing and encrypting, SSL uses it to perform the key agreement necessary to create the shared key under which the data in the stream is encrypted. This technique, such as when the key exchange is conducted through a persistent key, is called *static keying*. Building on this definition, *ephemeral keying* is defined as key exchange through a temporary key. At first, it may seem that temporary keys may not allow for proper authentication—not true. Generally, with ephemeral keying, the authentication is accomplished through signature verification with persistent keys, and the temporary keys are used only for key agreement. There are two main advantages of ephemeral keying over static keying from a security perspective.

We've said that our example uses RSA keys in the certificates, but consider a case in which the certificates are based upon DSA keys. The DSA algorithm provides a mechanism for signing but not for encrypting. Thus, having only DSA keys on either side of an SSL connection leaves the protocol unable to perform key exchange. It follows that static keying is not even an option for DSA-based certificates; we must supplement them with ephemeral keys.

The second advantage of using temporary keys is that they provide *forward secrecy*. At a high level, forward secrecy means that if the private key is obtained by a third party, that third party will not be able to decode previous sessions conducted with that key or even future sessions conducted by someone else with the compromised key. This is due to the ephemeral keys used for the secrecy of the sessions. When using static keys, there is no forward secrecy since the secrecy of the key exchange, and hence the following transmission stream, is based on the private key. With an ephemeral key, the data on which the key exchange was performed no longer exists after the key exchange, and thus the session remains private regardless of private key compromise. Thus, forward secrecy means that private key compromise will only allow an attacker to masquerade as the key owner, but not access the key owner's private data.

These two points make the benefits of using ephemeral keying clear. In the case of DSA certificates, it's necessary for the protocol to succeed, and in the case of RSA certificates, it affords us forward secrecy. In terms of SSL, using ephemeral keys essentially mandates that the keys embedded in the certificates shall be used only for signatures and not for encryption. Understanding this, it seems as though we've left a hole in the protocol since we do not have a method for key exchange. OpenSSL provides two options: temporary RSA keys or Diffie-Hellman (DH) key agreement. Of these two choices, DH is better because temporary RSA keys violate the SSL/TLS protocols. The RSA keying was originally implemented to make sure export restrictions on cryptography were not violated.[*] Today, this issue is not a primary concern; thus, ephemeral RSA keys tend not to be used. Additionally, generation of these temporary RSA keys is much slower than using DH, presuming the DH parameters are pre-generated.

In order to allow OpenSSL to use ephemeral Diffie-Hellman (EDH), we must set up the server-side SSL_CTX object properly. Providing DH parameters directly or, alternatively, a callback that returns the DH parameters accomplishes this goal. The function SSL_CTX_set_tmp_dh sets the DH parameters for a context, while the function SSL_CTX_set_tmp_dh_callback sets the callback. Since the callback mechanism subsumes the functionality of the former method, applications should provide only the callback. The callback function has the following signature:

```
DH *tmp_dh_callback(SSL *ssl, int is_export, int keylength);
```

The first argument to the callback is the SSL object representing the connection on which the parameters will be used. The second argument indicates whether an export-restricted cipher is being used; the argument value is nonzero, and zero otherwise. The main advantage of the callback is its ability to provide different functionality based on the third parameter, the key size. The DH parameters returned should have a key size equal to the last argument's value. Below, our server application is extended with a fully functional callback. The server application in its final form shows an implementation of this callback.

---

[*] Export restrictions once required weak RSA keys for encryption, but stronger keys were acceptable for signing.

We've deferred discussion of the SSL option SSL_OP_SINGLE_DH_USE to this point. Some of the details from Chapter 8 will be helpful in understanding the impact of this option. Essentially, DH parameters are public information. A private key is generated and used for the key exchange from these parameters. Setting this option causes the server to generate a new private key for each new connection. In the end, setting this option provides better security at the cost of more computational power to make new connections. Unless there are special processor usage considerations, we should enable this option.

Cipher suite selection

A cipher suite is a set of algorithms that SSL uses to secure a connection. In order to make a suite, we need to provide algorithms for four functions: signing/authentication, key exchange, cryptographic hashing, and encrypting/decrypting. Keep in mind that some algorithms can serve multiple purposes. For example, RSA can be used for signing and for key exchange.

OpenSSL implements a variety of algorithms and cipher suites when it comes to SSL connections. When designing secure applications, it is essential that algorithms having known security vulnerabilities not be allowed.

The SSL_CTX_set_cipher_list function allows us to set the list of cipher suites that we authorize our SSL objects to use. The list of ciphers is specified by a specially formatted string. This string is a colon-delimited list of algorithms. Given the number of possible combinations, specifying all the acceptable ones explicitly would be quite cumbersome. OpenSSL allows for several keywords in the list, which are shortcuts for sets of ciphers. For instance, "ALL" is a shortcut for every available combination. Additionally, we can precede a keyword with the "!" operator to remove all ciphers associated with the keyword from the list. Using this, we will create a string to define our custom cipher list. There are other operators such as "+" or "-", but they are not essential for specifying a secure list. For applications that need a custom definition, the ciphers manpage is a good reference on string formation.

SSL allows the use of *anonymous ciphers*. Anonymous ciphers allow the SSL connection to succeed without proper authentication of the peer by using the DH algorithm. In almost all circumstances, we want to block these ciphers; they are identified by the "ADH" keyword. In addition to suites that do not allow us to authenticate properly, we want to block low-security algorithms. The "LOW" keyword refers to ciphers that use a key of 64 bits or 56 bits without export crippling. Accordingly, the "EXP" keyword marks the ciphers that are export-crippled to 56 or 40 bits. Finally, we should block algorithms that have known weaknesses, e.g., "MD5".

We can also use the special keyword "@STRENGTH". Using this indicates that the list of cipher suites should be sorted by their strength (their key size) in order of highest to lowest. Employing this keyword causes our SSL connections to attempt to select the most secure suite possible, and if necessary, back off to the next most secure, and so on down the list. This keyword should be specified last on the list.

The final product

Using our knowledge of SSL options, ephemeral keying, and cipher suite selection, we will implement the last step necessary to make our examples fully SSL-enabled, secure applications. After looking at the code for the client and server, we will discuss some of the simplifications that our applications employ.

Example 5-11 contains the code for *client3.c*, the final client application. Because the only changes we're making are to the setup_client_ctx function, we truncated the example to only the contents of the source file up to and including that function.

Example 5-11. client3.c

```
1   include "common.h"
2
3   #define CIPHER_LIST "ALL:!ADH:!LOW:!EXP:!MD5:@STRENGTH"
4   #define CAFILE "root.pem"
5   #define CADIR NULL
6   #define CERTFILE "client.pem"
7   SSL_CTX *setup_client_ctx(void)
8   {
9       SSL_CTX *ctx;
10
11      ctx = SSL_CTX_new(SSLv23_method( ));
12      if (SSL_CTX_load_verify_locations(ctx, CAFILE, CADIR) != 1)
13          int_error("Error loading CA file and/or directory");
14      if (SSL_CTX_set_default_verify_paths(ctx) != 1)
15          int_error("Error loading default CA file and/or directory");
16      if (SSL_CTX_use_certificate_chain_file(ctx, CERTFILE) != 1)
17          int_error("Error loading certificate from file");
18      if (SSL_CTX_use_PrivateKey_file(ctx, CERTFILE, SSL_FILETYPE_PEM) != 1)
19          int_error("Error loading private key from file");
20      SSL_CTX_set_verify(ctx, SSL_VERIFY_PEER, verify_callback);
21      SSL_CTX_set_verify_depth(ctx, 4);
22      SSL_CTX_set_options(ctx, SSL_OP_ALL|SSL_OP_NO_SSLv2);
23      if (SSL_CTX_set_cipher_list(ctx, CIPHER_LIST) != 1)
24          int_error("Error setting cipher list (no valid ciphers)");
25      return ctx;
26  }
```

Line 3 contains a definition of the cipher list we discussed in the previous section. Translated to plain terms, the list is composed of all cipher suites in order of strength except those containing anonymous DH ciphers, low bit-size ciphers, export-crippled ciphers, or the MD5 hash algorithm.

As discussed at the beginning of this step, we enable all bug workarounds and disable SSL Version 2 with the call on line 22. Finally, lines 23–24 actually load our cipher list into the SSL_CTX object.

The server application appears in Example 5-12. We've made significantly more changes than in the client, but most of our changes are the addition of new functions that are used only by the SSL context setup function. We've similarly truncated the source listing for the server example.

Example 5-12. server3.c

```
1   #include "common.h"
2
3   DH *dh512 = NULL;
4   DH *dh1024 = NULL;
5
6   void init_dhparams(void)
7   {
8       BIO *bio;
9
10      bio = BIO_new_file("dh512.pem", "r");
11      if (!bio)
12          int_error("Error opening file dh512.pem");
13      dh512 = PEM_read_bio_DHparams(bio, NULL, NULL, NULL);
14      if (!dh512)
15          int_error("Error reading DH parameters from dh512.pem");
16      BIO_free(bio);
17
18      bio = BIO_new_file("dh1024.pem", "r");
19      if (!bio)
20          int_error("Error opening file dh1024.pem");
21      dh1024 = PEM_read_bio_DHparams(bio, NULL, NULL, NULL);
22      if (!dh1024)
23          int_error("Error reading DH parameters from dh1024.pem");
24      BIO_free(bio);
25  }
26
27  DH *tmp_dh_callback(SSL *ssl, int is_export, int keylength)
28  {
29      DH *ret;
30
31      if (!dh512 || !dh1024)
32          init_dhparams();
33
34      switch (keylength)
35      {
36          case 512:
37              ret = dh512;
38              break;
39          case 1024:
40          default: /* generating DH params is too costly to do on the fly */
41              ret = dh1024;
42              break;
43      }
44      return ret;
45  }
46
47  #define CIPHER_LIST "ALL:!ADH:!LOW:!EXP:!MD5:@STRENGTH"
48  #define CAFILE "root.pem"
49  #define CADIR NULL
50  #define CERTFILE "server.pem"
51  SSL_CTX *setup_server_ctx(void)
52  {
```

Example 5-12. server3.c (continued)

```
53      SSL_CTX *ctx;
54
55      ctx = SSL_CTX_new(SSLv23_method());
56      if (SSL_CTX_load_verify_locations(ctx, CAFILE, CADIR) != 1)
57          int_error("Error loading CA file and/or directory");
58      if (SSL_CTX_set_default_verify_paths(ctx) != 1)
59          int_error("Error loading default CA file and/or directory");
60      if (SSL_CTX_use_certificate_chain_file(ctx, CERTFILE) != 1)
61          int_error("Error loading certificate from file");
62      if (SSL_CTX_use_PrivateKey_file(ctx, CERTFILE, SSL_FILETYPE_PEM) != 1)
63          int_error("Error loading private key from file");
64      SSL_CTX_set_verify(ctx, SSL_VERIFY_PEER|SSL_VERIFY_FAIL_IF_NO_PEER_CERT,
65                          verify_callback);
66      SSL_CTX_set_verify_depth(ctx, 4);
67      SSL_CTX_set_options(ctx, SSL_OP_ALL | SSL_OP_NO_SSLv2 |
68                          SSL_OP_SINGLE_DH_USE);
69      SSL_CTX_set_tmp_dh_callback(ctx, tmp_dh_callback);
70      if (SSL_CTX_set_cipher_list(ctx, CIPHER_LIST) != 1)
71          int_error("Error setting cipher list (no valid ciphers)");
72      return ctx;
73  }
```

The most obvious change to this file is the addition of the functions init_dhparams and tmp_dh_callback. The initializing function reads the DH parameters from the files *dh512.pem* and *dh1024.pem* and loads them into the global parameters. The callback function simply switches on the required key size and returns either a 512-bit DH parameter set or a 1,024-bit set. This function intentionally does not try to perform any on-the-fly generation of parameters because it is simply too computationally expensive to be worthwhile.

The only other changes to the server not done to the client, aside from the call on line 60 to set the callback, is the inclusion of the SSL option SSL_OP_SINGLE_DH_USE. As discussed earlier, this causes the private part of the DH key exchange to be recomputed for each client connecting.

Beyond the example

For purposes of clarity in the example code, we have avoided several serious considerations for real applications. The most obvious is error handling. Our examples simply exit if errors of any kind occur. For most applications, extension of the example to more robustly handle errors is application-specific. While specific functions may return different error codes, OpenSSL functions and macros will generally return 1 on success; thus, implementing better error handling should be straightforward.

In addition, the examples we've built do two-way authentication. When making a new client and server application, this should always be done. However, when making applications that are meant to connect with other SSL peers, such as a web server, we should take into account that the stringent security requirements of our example are not always desirable. For instance, to entirely remove client authentication from a server, we simply need to remove the calls that load the verify locations, the call to set the verify mode, and the call to the post-connection verification routine. This isn't the best approach, though. When making such compatibility-first applications, we need to try to incorporate as much security as possible. For instance, instead of removing all of the verification calls, we could still load the verification locations and request a peer certificate with the SSL option SSL_VERIFY_PEER. We can, however, omit the SSL_VERIFY_FAIL_IF_NO_PEER_CERT option and modify the post-connection verification so that if the client does present a certificate, we go on with high security. If the client does not present the server with a certificate, the condition and associated information can be logged so that we can keep track of unauthenticated connections.

Another point we avoided was the password callback for the encrypted private key for the certificate. For most server applications, common practice is to leave the private key in a file that isn't encrypted so that the application can start up and stop without user input. This convention, born of simplicity of implementation, can easily be subverted. When doing something like this, it is essential that we make sure users on the machine do not have read permission on the private key file; ideally, the file will also be owned by the root or administrator user so that the likelihood of compromise is further reduced. For most client applications, tying the encryption passphrase to the user should not be a problem.

DSA parameters can be converted to DH parameters. This method is often utilized since the computational power necessary to generate the DSA parameters is smaller. Often, parameters generated in this fashion are used for ephemeral DH parameters. Without having to get into the mathematics behind the algorithms, the SSL option SSL_OP_SINGLE_DH_USE should always be used in these cases. Without it, applications are susceptible to a subtle attack.

A large flaw of our example programs is their handling of I/O on SSL connections. The examples rely on blocking I/O operations. For most real applications, this is unacceptable. In the following section, we broach the important topic of non-blocking I/O on SSL connections. We have also neglected to consider renegotiations (requesting that a handshake be performed during an already established connection) on SSL connections and their impact on I/O. While this should occur automatically when the peer requests it, the I/O routines must be robust enough to handle its subtle impacts. In the next section, we begin by addressing server efficiency with respect to session caching and then move into a more in-depth look at I/O paradigms.

Advanced Programming with SSL

OpenSSL provides many more routines than those we've discussed up to this point. In fact, most of the SSL_CTX routines have SSL counterparts that perform the same function except on an SSL object instead of the context that creates it. Aside from this small point, we will discuss techniques for caching SSL sessions, using renegotiations, and properly reading and writing on SSL connections—including during renegotiation.

SSL Session Caching

An SSL *session* is different from an SSL connection. A session refers to the set of parameters and encryption keys created by performing a handshake, whereas a connection is an active conversation that uses a session. In other words, the connection refers to the process of communication, and the session refers to the parameters by which that communication was set up. Understanding this, we can delve into some of the OpenSSL routines that provide for SSL session caching.

Since the majority of the computational expense associated with an SSL server is in setting up connections with clients and not in maintaining them, session caching can be a lifesaver when it comes to server load reduction. OpenSSL implements sessions as SSL_SESSION objects. While the majority of the work in implementing session caching falls on the server side, the client must also keep its previous sessions in order for the efficiency benefit to be realized.

From the server's perspective, once it has established a connection, it merely needs to label the data and cache the session. This label, called the *session ID context*, is described in the section "Server-side SSL sessions." After establishing a session, the server assigns a timeout value to it, which is simply a time after which the session will be discarded and another will need to be negotiated. The default behavior of a session caching server is to flush expired sessions automatically. From the client side, an SSL_SESSION object is received from the server. The client can then save this session and reuse it if it needs to make another connection. For instance, a web browser may need to make several connections to display all of the information presented from an SSL-enabled web server. By keeping this session information around, the client connects quickly, and the load on the server is reduced, since it need not negotiate a new session for each connection.

As we've said, the server determines the valid session ID context. When a client attempts to connect to a caching server, it has only one attempt at presenting the correct value. If incorrect, a normal handshake occurs, and a new session is created. If the client saves this newly created session, it will then have the correct session ID context for future connections.

The details associated with sessions, such as enabling a client and server, dealing with timeouts, and flushing old sessions, are discussed in the following sections. In addition, we will also outline a mechanism for server-side, on-disk storage of sessions.

Client-side SSL sessions

When a connection is established, the function SSL_get_session returns the SSL_SESSION object representing the parameters used on the SSL connection. This function returns

NULL if there is no session established on the SSL connection; otherwise, it returns the object. Actually, this function is called as either SSL_get0_session or SSL_get1_session. These two variants are used to ensure that the reference counting on the SSL_SESSION object is updated correctly. The former does not change the reference count, and the latter increments it. In general, we want to use the latter function since SSL_SESSION objects can timeout asynchronously. If this occurs, our object disappears and we are holding an invalid reference to it. Using SSL_get1_session requires that we call SSL_SESSION_free on the object when we're done using it, in order to prevent memory leaks.

After saving a reference to the SSL_SESSION object, we can close down the SSL connection and its underlying transport (normally a socket). For most clients, there will not be a large number of SSL sessions established at one time, so caching them in memory is adequate. If this isn't the case, we can always write the sessions out to disk using PEM_write_bio_SSL_SESSION or PEM_write_SSL_SESSION, and reread them later using PEM_read_bio_SSL_SESSION or PEM_read_SSL_SESSION. The syntax of these functions is the same as the functions used for reading and writing public-key objects. They are discussed in Chapter 8 in the section "Writing and Reading PEM-Encoded Objects."

To reuse a saved session, we need to call SSL_set_session before calling SSL_connect. The reference count of the SSL_SESSION object will be incremented automatically so we should follow the call with SSL_SESSION_free. After reusing a session, it is a good idea to call SSL_get1_session before disconnecting to replace the SSL_SESSION object that we've cached. The reason is that renegotiations may occur during the connection. Renegotiations cause the creation of a new SSL_SESSION, so we should keep only the most recent (renegotiation is discussed in more detail later).

Now that we understand the basics of enabling session caching, we'll take a brief look at incorporating it into a client application. Example 5-13 shows pseudocode for our client-side session caching. Now that we've established an implementation for a client, we'll elaborate upon some of the details of session caching as we explore the implementation necessary for server-side caching.

Example 5-13. Pseudocode for client-side caching

```
ssl = SSL_new(ctx)
... setup underlying communications layer for ssl ...
... connect to host:port ...
if (saved session for host:port in cache)
  SSL_set_session(ssl, saved session)
  SSL_SESSION_free(saved session)
SSL_connect(ssl)
call post_connection_check(ssl, host) and check return value
... normal application code here ...
saved session = SSL_get1_session(ssl)
if (saved session != NULL)
  enter saved session into cache under host:port
SSL_shutdown(ssl)
SSL_free(ssl)
```

Server-side SSL sessions

All sessions must have a session ID context. For the server, session caching is disabled by default unless a call to SSL_CTX_set_session_id_context is made. The purpose of the session ID context is to make sure the session is being reused for the same purpose for which it was created. For instance, a session created for an SSL web server should not be automatically allowed for an SSL FTP server. Along the same lines, we can use session ID contexts to exercise a finer-grained control over sessions within our application. For example, authenticated clients could have a different session ID context than unauthenticated ones. The context itself can be any data we choose. We set the context through a call to the above function, passing in our context data as the second argument and its length as the third.

After setting the session ID context, session caching is enabled on the server side; however, it isn't configured completely yet. Sessions have a limited lifetime. The default value for session timeout with OpenSSL is 300 seconds. If we want to change this lifetime, a call to SSL_CTX_set_timeout is necessary. Although the default server automatically flushes expired sessions, we may still want to call SSL_CTX_flush_sessions manually, e.g., when we disable automatic session flushing.

One important function that allows us to tweak the behavior of a server with respect to caching is SSL_CTX_set_session_cache_mode. Like several other mode-setting calls in OpenSSL, the mode is set using flags that are joined by a logical OR operation. One such flag is SSL_SESS_CACHE_NO_AUTO_CLEAR. This disables the automatic flushing of expired sessions. It is useful for servers with tighter processor usage constraints. The automatic behavior can cause unexpected delays; thus, disabling it and manually calling the flush routine when free cycles are available can improve performance. Another flag that can be set is SSL_SESS_CACHE_NO_INTERNAL_LOOKUP. Up to this point, we've relied solely on the internal lookup, but in the next section, we'll outline an on-disk caching method that can replace the internal lookup methods.

Session caching adds subtleties when we also use connection renegotiations. Before implementing a caching server, we should be aware of the potential pitfalls. The section below on renegotiation explores some of these problems after explaining a little more about what renegotiation entails.

An on-disk, session caching framework

OpenSSL's session caching features include API calls to set three callbacks for synchronization of sessions with external caches. Like other OpenSSL callbacks, three functions are used to set a pointer to the callback function. For each one, the first argument is an SSL_CTX object, and the second argument is a pointer to the callback function.

The callback set by SSL_CTX_sess_set_new_cb is invoked whenever a new SSL_SESSION is created by the SSL_CTX object. This callback enables us to add the new session to our external container. If the callback returns zero, the session object will not be cached. A nonzero return allows the session to be cached.

```
int new_session_cb(SSL *ctx, SSL_SESSION *session);
```

ctx
> The SSL connection's connection object.

session
> A newly created session object.

The callback set by `SSL_CTX_sess_set_remove_cb` is invoked whenever an `SSL_SESSION` is destroyed. It is called just before the session object is destroyed because it is invalid or has expired.

```
void remove_session_cb(SSL_CTX *ctx, SSL_SESSION *session);
```

ctx
> The SSL_CTX object that is destroying the session.

session
> The session object that is about to be destroyed because it's invalid or expiring.

The `SSL_CTX_sess_set_get_cb` function is used to set a cache retrieval callback. The assigned function is called whenever the internal cache cannot find a hit for the requested session resumption. In other words, this callback should query our external cache in hopes of finding a match.

```
SSL_SESSION *get_session_cb(SSL *ctx, unsigned char *id, int len, int *ref);
```

ctx
> The SSL connection's connection object.

id
> The session ID that's being requested by the peer. It should be noted that the session ID is distinctly different from the session ID context. The context is an application specific classification on session groups, whereas the session ID is an identifier for a peer.

len
> The length of the session ID. Since the session ID can be any arbitrary string of characters, it may not necessarily be NULL terminated. Thus, the length of the session ID must also be specified.

ref
> An output from the callback. It is used to allow the callback to specify whether the reference count on the returned session object should be incremented or not. It returns as nonzero if the object's reference count should be incremented; otherwise, zero is returned.

Some of the features required by the caching mechanism in Example 5-14 are easily implemented. Since we are using files to store the sessions, we can use the filesystem's built-in locking mechanisms. In order to write the keys to disk, we can use the macro PEM_write_bio_SSL_SESSION, but it doesn't allow for encryption. Remember, SSL_SESSION objects hold the shared secrets that were negotiated; thus, their contents shoud be protected when serialized. Instead, we can call the underlying function PEM_ASN1_write_bio directly. Alternatively, it may be sufficient for some applications to simply use a secure directory and write the sessions unencrypted. In general, it is far safer to use encryption with an in-memory key.

Example 5-14. A framework for external session caching

```
new_session_cb()
{
  acquire a lock for the file named according to the session id
  open file named according to session id
  encrypt and write the SSL_SESSION object to the file
  release the lock
}

remove_session_cb()
{
  acquire a lock for the file named according to the session id
  remove the file named according to the session id
  release the lock
}

get_session_cb()
{
  acquire a lock for the file named according to the session id in the 2nd arg
  read and decrypt contents of file and create a new SSL_SESSION object
  release the lock
  set the integer referenced by the fourth parameter to 0
  return the new session object
}
```

This framework, when implemented, provides a powerful mechanism for session caching. By using the filesystem, the cache isn't constrained by memory restrictions. Additionally, it is easier to use than an in-memory caching scheme since the on-disk scheme allows multiple processes to access the session cache.

I/O on SSL Connections

The motivation behind creating an SSL connection is to transfer data back and forth securely. Thus far, we've concentrated on making this connection very secure, but we've avoided the details on how data is transferred. In the earlier examples, we cheated on the I/O processing, since the client only writes to the SSL connection, and the server only reads from it. Most real-world applications do not operate on such a simple model. Since the calls we used to perform the reading and writing (SSL_read and SSL_write) closely mirror the system calls read and write, it seems as though I/O would not be significantly different from I/O in non-SSL applications. Unfortunately, this is far from the truth.

There are many subtleties in performing I/O correctly with OpenSSL. We will first look at SSL_read and SSL_write in more detail. Once we understand them, we will get into the detail of the differences between performing blocking and non-blocking I/O on SSL connections. By the end of this chapter, we will have built up our knowledge of the pitfalls with I/O in OpenSSL. This will enable us to avoid them when implementing real-world applications that require I/O paradigms that are more complex than the ones provided in our examples.

Reading and writing functions

In the examples, we used the I/O functions SSL_read and SSL_write for SSL connections, but we didn't discuss them in any detail. The arguments for these calls are similar to the system calls read and write. The way these calls differ from their system call counterparts is in their return values. Table 5-2 provides the details of the possible return values.

Table 5-2. Return values of SSL_read and SSL_write

Return value	Description
> 0	Success. The data requested was read or written, and the return value is the number of bytes.
0	Failure. Either an error with the SSL connection occurred or the call failed because the underlying I/O could not perform the operation at the time of calling.
< 0	Failure. Either an error with the SSL connection occurred or the application is required to perform a different function before retrying the failed call.

Knowing these return values helps, but we still can't tell if an error actually occured without some more information. OpenSSL provides the function SSL_get_error, which accepts the return value of an SSL I/O function and returns different values based on what actually happened.

This function inspects the I/O routine's return value, the SSL object, and the current thread's error queue to determine what the effect of the call was. Because the internal errors for OpenSSL are stored on a per-thread basis, the call to check the errors must be made from the same thread as the I/O call. Robust applications should always check the detailed error status of all I/O operations with SSL_get_error. Remember that functions like SSL_connect and SSL_accept are also I/O operations.

The return value of SSL_get_error can be many different values. Our application needs to be able to handle a subset of these conditions and provide a reasonable default behavior of shutting down the SSL connection. Table 5-3 provides the descriptions of the values we should always be able to handle.

Table 5-3. Some common return values of SSL_get_error

Return value	Description
SSL_ERROR_NONE	No error occurred with the I/O call.
SSL_ERROR_ZERO_RETURN	The operation failed due to the SSL session being closed. The underlying connection medium may still be open.

Table 5-3. Some common return values of SSL_get_error (continued)

Return value	Description
SSL_ERROR_WANT_READ	The operation couldn't be completed. The underlying medium could not fulfill the read requested. This error code means the call should be retried.
SSL_ERROR_WANT_WRITE	The operation couldn't be completed. The underlying medium could not fulfill the write requested. This error code means the call should be retried.

The handling of the first error code in the table, SSL_ERROR_NONE, is straightforward. SSL_ERROR_ZERO_RETURN should be handled in an application-specific way, knowing that the SSL connection has been closed. In order to handle SSL_ERROR_WANT_READ and SSL_ERROR_WANT_WRITE, we need to retry the I/O operation; this is discussed in more detail below. Any of the other possible return values of SSL_get_error should be considered errors.

In order to implement a call to an I/O function correctly, we should check for these different return values. A sample piece of code is given in Example 5-15. The handlers for SSL_ERROR_WANT_READ and SSL_ERROR_WANT_WRITE have been omitted; the details on handling them properly are discussed below, since the correct actions vary based on whether the application is using blocking or non-blocking I/O. This example's purpose is to provide a template of what a robust I/O call should look like. Using the switch statement, we handle all the conditions for which we have interest and error on any others. As stated above, there are other return values possible, and we may wish to handle them with specific error messages, for instance.

Example 5-15. A sample I/O call template

```
code = SSL_read(ssl, buf + offset, size - offset);
switch (SSL_get_error(ssl, code))
{
    case SSL_ERROR_NONE:
        /* update the offset value */
        offset += code;
        break;
    case SSL_ERROR_ZERO_RETURN:
        /* react to the SSL connection being closed */
        do_cleanup(ssl);
        break;
    case SSL_ERROR_WANT_READ:
        /* handle this in an application specific way to retry the SSL_read */
        break;
    case SSL_ERROR_WANT_WRITE:
        /* handle this in an application specific way to retry the SSL_read */
        break;
    default:
        /* an error occurred. shutdown the connection */
        shutdown_connection(ssl);
}
```

Typically, using blocking I/O alleviates the complications of retrying failed calls. With SSL, this is not the case. There are times when a call to SSL_read or SSL_write on a blocking connection requires a retry.

Blocking I/O

Blocking I/O means that an operation will wait until it can be completed or until an error occurs. Thus, with blocking I/O in general, we shouldn't have to retry an I/O call, since a single call's failure indicates an error with the communication channel, such that the channel is no longer usable; with blocking I/O using OpenSSL, this is not true. The SSL connection is based upon an underlying I/O layer that handles the actual transfer of data from one side to the other. The blocking property of an SSL connection is based solely on the underlying communication layer. For instance, if we create an SSL connection from a socket, the SSL connection will be blocking if and only if the socket is blocking. It is also possible to change this property in a connection we've already established; we change the property on the underlying layer and then handle all SSL I/O functions appropriate for the new paradigm.

Conceptually, SSL_read and SSL_write read and write data from the peer. Actually, a call to SSL_read may write data to the underlying I/O layer, and a call to SSL_write may read. This usually occurs during a renegotiation. Since a renegotiation may occur at any time, this behavior can cause unexpected results when using a blocking I/O layer; namely, an I/O call may require a retry. Thus, our implementation must handle this.

In order to handle a blocking call correctly, we need to retry the SSL I/O operation if we receive SSL_ERROR_WANT_READ or SSL_ERROR_WANT_WRITE. Don't let the names of these errors confuse you. Even though they tell us the SSL connection needs to wait until we can read or write, respectively, we just need to retry whatever operation caused the condition. For instance, if an SSL_read caused the SSL_ERROR_WANT_WRITE error, we must retry the SSL_read rather than making the call to SSL_write. It is worth taking a moment to understand the potential errors for a single I/O call. Though nonintuitive, a call to SSL_read may indeed return the error SSL_ERROR_WANT_WRITE due to the possibility of renegotiations at any point.

In many ways, implementing a blocking call is similar to implementing a non-blocking one. It's similar in the sense that we must loop for retries, but it differs in that we don't need to check for I/O availability on the underlying layer, as with poll or select. In the end, we will not show an example of looping to accomplish the blocking call; there is an easier way.

Using the SSL_CTX_set_mode function or its counterpart for SSL objects, SSL_set_mode, we can set some I/O behaviors of SSL connections. The second parameter is a set of defined properties joined with the logical OR operator. SSL_MODE_AUTO_RETRY is one such mode. Setting this on a blocking SSL object (or on the context that will create a object) will cause all I/O operations to automatically retry all reads and complete all negotiations before returning.

Using this option allows us to implement I/O as simply as normal blocking I/O with the system calls read and write. In general, we should set this option on the SSL_CTX object before creating the SSL object. We can set the option later on the SSL object itself, but it's best to do so before any calls to I/O routines on that object.

If we elect not to use this option and instead implement our blocking I/O with our own loops, we might fall into a few traps. This is due to some special requirements for function call retries, which are detailed with our discussion of non-blocking I/O.

Non-blocking I/O

This paradigm causes all of our I/O calls never to block. If the underlying layer is unable to handle a request, it reports its requirement immediately, without waiting. As we've hinted, this adds complexity to our I/O routines.

A non-blocking SSL I/O call returns the reason of failure, but only the application can check to see if that status has been cleared. This is the source of the complexity in implementation. For instance, a call to SSL_read may return SSL_ERROR_WANT_READ, which tells the application that once the underlying I/O layer is ready to fulfill a read request, the SSL call may be retried. Generally, the application's I/O loop will need to serve both read and write requests, however. The problem we need to solve in the I/O loop is that once we've made a call to an SSL I/O function, and it requires a retry, we should not call other I/O functions until the original call has succeeded.

Since the logic for correctly implementing I/O routines for the application can have several subtleties, especially with multiple input and output sources, we'll look at a detailed example. Example 5-16 provides the code for the function data_transfer. This function takes two SSL objects as parameters, which are expected to have connections to two different peers. The data_transfer function will read data from one connection (A) and write it to the other (B) and at the same time read data from B and write it to A.

Example 5-16. A sample non-blocking I/O loop

```
 1  #include <openssl/ssl.h>
 2  #include <openssl/err.h>
 3  #include <string.h>
 4
 5  #define BUF_SIZE 80
 6
 7  void data_transfer(SSL *A, SSL *B)
 8  {
 9      /* the buffers and the size variables */
10      unsigned char A2B[BUF_SIZE];
11      unsigned char B2A[BUF_SIZE];
12      unsigned int A2B_len = 0;
13      unsigned int B2A_len = 0;
```

Example 5-16. A sample non-blocking I/O loop (continued)

```
14      /* flags to mark that we have some data to write */
15      unsigned int have_data_A2B = 0;
16      unsigned int have_data_B2A = 0;
17      /* flags set by check_availability() that poll for I/O status */
18      unsigned int can_read_A = 0;
19      unsigned int can_read_B = 0;
20      unsigned int can_write_A = 0;
21      unsigned int can_write_B = 0;
22      /* flags to mark all the combinations of why we're blocking */
23      unsigned int read_waiton_write_A = 0;
24      unsigned int read_waiton_write_B = 0;
25      unsigned int read_waiton_read_A = 0;
26      unsigned int read_waiton_read_B = 0;
27      unsigned int write_waiton_write_A = 0;
28      unsigned int write_waiton_write_B = 0;
29      unsigned int write_waiton_read_A = 0;
30      unsigned int write_waiton_read_B = 0;
31      /* variable to hold return value of an I/O operation */
32      int code;
33
34      /* make the underlying I/O layer behind each SSL object non-blocking */
35      set_nonblocking(A);
36      set_nonblocking(B);
37      SSL_set_mode(A, SSL_MODE_ENABLE_PARTIAL_WRITE|
38                     SSL_MODE_ACCEPT_MOVING_WRITE_BUFFER);
39      SSL_set_mode(B, SSL_MODE_ENABLE_PARTIAL_WRITE|
40                     SSL_MODE_ACCEPT_MOVING_WRITE_BUFFER);
41
42      for (;;)
43      {
44          /* check I/O availability and set flags */
45          check_availability(A, &can_read_A, &can_write_A,
46                             B, &can_read_B, &can_write_B);
47
48          /* this "if" statement reads data from A. it will only be entered if
49           * the following conditions are all true:
50           * 1. we're not in the middle of a write on A
51           * 2. there's space left in the A to B buffer
52           * 3. either we need to write to complete a previously blocked read
53           *    and now A is available to write, or we can read from A
54           *    regardless of whether we're blocking for availability to read.
55           */
56          if (!(write_waiton_read_A || write_waiton_write_A) &&
57              (A2B_len != BUF_SIZE) &&
58              (can_read_A || (can_write_A && read_waiton_write_A)))
59          {
60              /* clear the flags since we'll set them based on the I/O call's
61               * return
62               */
63              read_waiton_read_A = 0;
64              read_waiton_write_A = 0;
65
```

Example 5-16. A sample non-blocking I/O loop (continued)

```
66                  /* read into the buffer after the current position */
67                  code = SSL_read(A, A2B + A2B_len, BUF_SIZE - A2B_len);
68                  switch (SSL_get_error(A, code))
69                  {
70                      case SSL_ERROR_NONE:
71                          /* no errors occured.  update the new length and make
72                           * sure the "have data" flag is set.
73                           */
74                          A2B_len += code;
75                          have_data_A2B = 1;
76                          break;
77                      case SSL_ERROR_ZERO_RETURN:
78                          /* connection closed */
79                          goto end;
80                      case SSL_ERROR_WANT_READ:
81                          /* we need to retry the read after A is available for
82                           * reading
83                           */
84                          read_waiton_read_A = 1;
85                          break;
86                      case SSL_ERROR_WANT_WRITE:
87                          /* we need to retry the read after A is available for
88                           * writing
89                           */
90                          read_waiton_write_A = 1;
91                          break;
92                      default:
93                          /* ERROR */
94                          goto err;
95                  }
96          }
97
98          /* this "if" statement is roughly the same as the previous "if"
99           * statement with A and B switched
100          */
101         if (!(write_waiton_read_B || write_waiton_write_B) &&
102             (B2A_len != BUF_SIZE) &&
103             (can_read_B || (can_write_B && read_waiton_write_B)))
104         {
105             read_waiton_read_B = 0;
106             read_waiton_write_B = 0;
107
108             code = SSL_read(B, B2A + B2A_len, BUF_SIZE - B2A_len);
109             switch (SSL_get_error(B, code))
110             {
111                 case SSL_ERROR_NONE:
112                     B2A_len += code;
113                     have_data_B2A = 1;
114                     break;
115                 case SSL_ERROR_ZERO_RETURN:
116                     goto end;
117                 case SSL_ERROR_WANT_READ:
```

Example 5-16. A sample non-blocking I/O loop (continued)

```
118                    read_waiton_read_B = 1;
119                    break;
120                case SSL_ERROR_WANT_WRITE:
121                    read_waiton_write_B = 1;
122                    break;
123                default:
124                    goto err;
125            }
126        }
127
128        /* this "if" statement writes data to A. it will only be entered if
129         * the following conditions are all true:
130         * 1. we're not in the middle of a read on A
131         * 2. there's data in the A to B buffer
132         * 3. either we need to read to complete a previously blocked write
133         *    and now A is available to read, or we can write to A
134         *    regardless of whether we're blocking for availability to write
135         */
136        if (!(read_waiton_write_A || read_waiton_read_A) &&
137            have_data_B2A &&
138            (can_write_A || (can_read_A && write_waiton_read_A)))
139        {
140            /* clear the flags */
141            write_waiton_read_A = 0;
142            write_waiton_write_A = 0;
143
144            /* perform the write from the start of the buffer */
145            code = SSL_write(A, B2A, B2A_len);
146            switch (SSL_get_error(A, code))
147            {
148                case SSL_ERROR_NONE:
149                    /* no error occured. adjust the length of the B to A
150                     * buffer to be smaller by the number bytes written.  If
151                     * the buffer is empty, set the "have data" flags to 0,
152                     * or else, move the data from the middle of the buffer
153                     * to the front.
154                     */
155                    B2A_len -= code;
156                    if (!B2A_len)
157                        have_data_B2A = 0;
158                    else
159                        memmove(B2A, B2A + code, B2A_len);
160                    break;
161                case SSL_ERROR_ZERO_RETURN:
162                    /* connection closed */
163                    goto end;
164                case SSL_ERROR_WANT_READ:
165                    /* we need to retry the write after A is available for
166                     * reading
167                     */
168                    write_waiton_read_A = 1;
169                    break;
```

Example 5-16. A sample non-blocking I/O loop (continued)

```
170                  case SSL_ERROR_WANT_WRITE:
171                      /* we need to retry the write after A is available for
172                       * writing
173                       */
174                      write_waiton_write_A = 1;
175                      break;
176                  default:
177                      /* ERROR */
178                      goto err;
179              }
180          }
181
182          /* this "if" statement is roughly the same as the previous "if"
183           * statement with A and B switched
184           */
185          if (!(read_waiton_write_B || read_waiton_read_B) &&
186              have_data_A2B &&
187              (can_write_B || (can_read_B && write_waiton_read_B)))
188          {
189              write_waiton_read_B = 0;
190              write_waiton_write_B = 0;
191
192              code = SSL_write(B, A2B, A2B_len);
193              switch (SSL_get_error(B, code))
194              {
195                  case SSL_ERROR_NONE:
196                      A2B_len -= code;
197                      if (!A2B_len)
198                          have_data_A2B = 0;
199                      else
200                          memmove(A2B, A2B + code, A2B_len);
201                      break;
202                  case SSL_ERROR_ZERO_RETURN:
203                      /* connection closed */
204                      goto end;
205                  case SSL_ERROR_WANT_READ:
206                      write_waiton_read_B = 1;
207                      break;
208                  case SSL_ERROR_WANT_WRITE:
209                      write_waiton_write_B = 1;
210                      break;
211                  default:
212                      /* ERROR */
213                      goto err;
214              }
215          }
216      }
217
218  err:
219      /* if we errored, print then before exiting */
220      fprintf(stderr, "Error(s) occured\n");
221      ERR_print_errors_fp(stderr);
```

Example 5-16. A sample non-blocking I/O loop (continued)

```
222  end:
223       /* close down the connections. set them back to blocking to simplify. */
224       set_blocking(A);
225       set_blocking(B);
226       SSL_shutdown(A);
227       SSL_shutdown(B);
228  }
```

Since the code sample is rather large, we'll dissect it and explain the reasons behind the implementation decisions. We use two buffers, A2B and B2A, to hold the data read from A to be written to B, and the data read from B to be written to A, respectively. The length variables corresponding to each buffer (A2B_len and B2A_len) are initialized to zero; throughout our function, they will hold the number of bytes of data in their counterpart buffer. An important observation to make at this point is that we do not use an offset variable for pointing into our buffer; the data we want to write will always be at the front of our buffers.

We also declare three sets of flags. The first set (have_data_A2B and have_data_B2A) indicates whether there is any data in our buffers. We could have left these two variables out, since throughout the function they will be zero only if the corresponding buffer length's variable is also zero. We opted to use them for code readability. The next set of variables is *availability* flags, which are of the form can_read_A, can_write_B, etc. These flags are set to indicate that the named operation on the named object can be performed, i.e., the connection is available to perform the operation without needing to block. The last set of flags is the *blocking* flags. When one of these is set, it tells us that a particular kind of I/O operation requires the availability of the connection to perform another kind of I/O operation. For instance, if write_waiton_read_B is set, it means that the last write operation performed on B must be retried after B is available to read.

We use three functions in this example that are not explicitly defined. The first is set_nonblocking. This function takes an SSL object as its only argument and must be implemented in a platform-specific way to set the underlying I/O layer of the SSL object to be non-blocking. Likewise, set_blocking needs to set the connection to a blocking state. The last platform-specific function is check_availability. This function's obligation is to check the I/O status of the underlying layers of both A and B and set the variables appropriately. Additionally, this function should wait until at least one variable is set before returning. We cannot perform any I/O operations if nothing is available for either connection. These omitted functions can be implemented easily. For instance, on a Unix system with SSL objects based on sockets, set_nonblocking and set_blocking can be implemented using the fcntl system call, and the check_availability function can use fd_set data structures along with the select system call.

The calls to SSL_set_mode set two mode variables we've not discussed. Normally, a call to SSL_write will not return success until all of the data in the buffer has been written, even with non-blocking I/O. Thus, a call that requests a large amount of data to be written can return many retry requests before succeeding. This behavior is undesirable in our function because we wish to interlace the reading routines with those that write, and to do this effectively, we cannot retry a single call for too long because it will prevent us from reading more data from that connection. To alleviate this problem, the SSL_MODE_ENABLE_PARTIAL_WRITE mode flag instructs the library to allow partially complete writes to count as successes. This allows our function to perform several write operations successfully, and between those calls, we can read more data. Because the SSL protocol is built around sending complete messages on the channel, sometimes we'll be required to retry a call because only a part of the requested data was actually sent. As a result, all retried operations must be called with the exact same arguments as the original call that caused the error. This behavior can be cumbersome since it does not allow us to add to the write buffer after making a call to SSL_write that needed a retry. To change this property partially, we use the SSL_MODE_ACCEPT_MOVING_WRITE_BUFFER flag. This flags allows us to retry the write operation with different parameters, i.e., a different buffer and size, so long as the original data is still contained in the new buffer. In our example, we use the same buffer, but enable this mode so that we can keep reading into the end of the buffer without causing errors on attempts to retry writes.

The function has one main loop, beginning on line 42 and ending on line 216. In this loop, we have four separated subsections, lines 56–96, lines 101–126, lines 136–180 and lines 185–215. Each of these conditional blocks corresponds respectively to reading data from A, reading data from B, writing data to A, and writing data to B. Looking carefully, we can see that the first and second section mirror each other just as the third and fourth do.

We must be sure it is safe to read. The entry conditions on the if statements do this. They assert we are not in the middle of a read operation by checking the write blocking flags for the connection (!(write_waiton_read_... || write_waiton_write_...)). Additionally, it needs to be sure there is space in the buffers (..._len != BUF_SIZE). In addition to these conditions, we must be sure this is the right time to call the read function, i.e., either we're waiting to retry a failed read because it was waiting for the connection to be available for writing (can_write_... && read_waiton_write_...), or we simply have data to read (can_read_...). If all of these conditions are met, we can attempt a read. Before we do, though, we reset the blocking flags for the read operation, and then perform the I/O call and check the error code. The I/O call itself instructs the SSL library to write the data into the buffer offset by the number of bytes already stored within it. If the call succeeds, we'll update the length counter and make sure that the have_data_... flag is set. If we are instructed to retry through either SSL_ERROR_WANT_READ or SSL_ERROR_WANT_WRITE, we will set the appropriate blocking flag and carry on. If an error occurs, or the end of the SSL connection is detected, we will break out of the I/O loop.

As with read operations, write operations are protected by an `if` statement to assure entry conditions. These statements ensure that we are not in the middle of a read operation (`!(read_waiton_write_... || read_waiton_read_...)`). Additionally, there must be data in the buffer (`have_data_...`). Lastly, the write operation must make sure that writing is possible, i.e., either we've been waiting for read availability to retry a write operation (`can_read_... && write_waiton_read_...`), or there is write availability (`can_write_...`). Before attempting the write, we must zero the blocking flags. The write operation always tries to write from the beginning of the buffer. If we are successful, we move the data in the buffer forward so that data already written is pushed out. If the buffer is empty after writing, we zero the `have_data_...` flag. As with the read operation, if we are instructed to retry, we set the corresponding blocking flag and continue. If errors occur, or if the SSL connection has been closed, we break out of the I/O loop.

These paradigms for performing reading and writing enable us to do effective non-blocking communication when combined in the loop. For instance, if B cannot be written to, we will continue to buffer data from A until the buffers fill and we are forced to wait for writing on B. We can extend the general form presented in this function to allow for many different non-blocking I/O needs that applications may have.

SSL Renegotiations

An SSL *renegotiation* is essentially an SSL handshake during a connection. This causes client credentials to be reevaluated and a new session to be created. We've discussed the effects of renegotiation on the I/O and other aspects of a program's implementation, but haven't talked about why renegotiations are important.

Since renegotiations cause the creation of a new session, the session key is replaced. For long-lasting SSL connections or for those that transfer a high quantity of data, it is a good idea to replace the session key periodically. In general, the longer a session key exists, the more the likelihood of key compromise increases. Using renegotiations, we can replace the session key so that we don't encrypt too much data with just one key.

SSL renegotiations can occur during normal application data transfer. When the new handshake is completed, both parties switch to using the new key. The function to request renegotiation on an SSL connection is `SSL_renegotiate`.

This function does not actually perform the new handshake when called; however, it sets a flag that causes a renegotiation request to be sent to the peer. The request is sent out on the next call to an I/O function on the SSL connection. An important point to consider is that the peer has the option of not renegotiating the connection. If the peer chooses not to respond to the request and to continue transferring data instead, no renegotiation will occur; unless the requestor checks for negotiation success, it may not have happened. This is especially important when making applications that will connect with other non-OpenSSL SSL implementations.

A renegotiation can also be done explicitly. In other words, we will send a request and not send or receive application data until the new handshake has completed successfully. While this will sometimes be the appropriate way to refresh session keys for long-term connections, it serves another important purpose. It allows us to upgrade client authentication from the server side. For instance, our example server above requires a valid client certificate to be presented in order for the initial connection to take place. This is overly restrictive since at connection time, we do not know the client's intentions.

As an example, consider a simple protocol that allows clients to connect via SSL and send commands to the server. A subset of these commands will be reserved for administrators. Our goal is to allow anyone to connect to the server to run the general commands and allow only administrators to run reserved commands. If we require all users to present a certificate at connection time, we must issue a certificate to every possible client and special certificates to administrators. This can become cumbersome rather quickly. Alternatively, we can run two servers, one for normal users and another for administrators. This is also a suboptimal solution since it requires extra consumption of resources.

We can use renegotiations to make our job simpler. First, we will allow anyone to connect without a certificate. When a client connects, it sends its command. If it's a reserved command, we require a renegotiation with the more stringent requirements on the client in place. If the client renegotiates successfully, we can accept the command, or otherwise discard it. Thus, we need to issue certificates only to administrators. This option is clearly better than the previous two since it allows us to determine what the client is attempting before putting stronger authentication requirements in place.

Implementing renegotiations

As we've said before, to do a passive renegotiation (i.e., one in which the handshake occurs during application I/O) we need to call only SSL_renegotiate. In general, applications can get away with having the handshake occur during application I/O, but making sure that it did indeed happen is important. Unfortunately, this isn't easy to do with OpenSSL Version 0.9.6. In fact, many aspects of renegotiations don't work cleanly in this version. However, the forthcoming Version 0.9.7 promises to improve this considerably. These changes are described in the next section.

With Version 0.9.6, we should always use explicit renegotiation since there is no way to determine if a renegotiation request was ignored by the peer. This is the same problem we find in renegotiating client credentials; we will focus on determining if a request was ignored, since it is far more common. Renegotiating for session key refreshment is a subset of this problem. Example 5-17 shows an incomplete code fragment to force a renegotiation from a server.

Example 5-17. Code fragment to force a renegotiation from a server

```
/* assume ssl is connected and error free up to here */
set_blocking(ssl); /* this is unnecessary if it is already blocking */
SSL_renegotiate(ssl);
SSL_do_handshake(ssl);
if (ssl->state != SSL_ST_OK)
    int_error("Failed to send renegotiation request");
ssl->state |= SSL_ST_ACCEPT;
SSL_do_handshake(ssl);
if (ssl->state != SSL_ST_OK)
    int_error("Failed to complete renegotiation");
/* our renegotiation is complete */
```

This example uses some functions we've seen before. To avoid extra complication, we ensure the SSL object is blocking so we don't need to retry failed I/O calls. The call to SSL_renegotiate sends out the request to the peer. The function SSL_do_handshake is a generic routine that calls the accept function for server objects or the connect function for client objects. This first call to SSL_do_handshake sends out our request and returns. After doing this, we need to check that the SSL connection hasn't received any errors. We do this by making sure its state is SSL_ST_OK. At this point, if we call the handshake function again, it will just return if the peer chose not to renegotiate. This occurs because the SSL/TLS protocols allow requests to be ignored. Since we have a reason for renegotiating, and we need it to complete before continuing, we must manually set the SSL_ST_ACCEPT state of the server object. This will cause the subsequent call to SSL_do_handshake, which will force a handshake to occur before continuing.

Obviously, this method of renegotiation isn't very clean because it requires us to set internal variables of the SSL object manually. Unfortunately, it is the only way to accomplish a forced renegotiation. This code fragment is not complete, though. Consider session caching, which allows a client to skip the handshake by resuming a previously created session. This can be extremely bad when our purpose is to collect stronger client credentials since the client has already obtained a valid session with weak credentials. When we attempt to renegotiate a connection from a server that does session caching, we must take extra precautions that the client doesn't simply present the previously negotiated session and bypass the handshake. To make this discrepancy between the sessions, we need to change the session ID context. Recall that the session ID context's function is to discern sessions established with clients for different purposes. To change its value, we use the function SSL_set_session_id_context. It behaves exactly as the SSL_CTX version discussed above, except that it operates on SSL objects. The change to the session ID context must be made before the renegotiation is started.

We haven't discussed the minor detail of setting stronger requirements for verification of the client during renegotiation. To do this, we use the function SSL_set_verify and pass it our new verify flags. Example 5-18 shows the code fragment that must be built around the fragment shown in Example 5-17 in order for the renegotiation to be effective. This fragment is for a caching server that wishes to upgrade client authentication; if our server isn't caching, we can omit the calls to set the session ID context.

Example 5-18. Code to cause forced renegotiation in order to request stronger client authentication and distinguish the sessions

```
/* assume ctx is an SSL_CTX object that is setup to not have any verify
   options. */
int normal_user = 1;
int admin_user = 2;
SSL_CTX_set_session_id_context(ctx, &normal_user, sizeof(int));
/* perform rest of ctx setup, create an ssl object, and connect it */
/* normal SSL I/O operations and application code go here */
/* if we want to upgrade client privilege, we enter the following code block */
SSL_set_verify(ssl, SSL_VERIFY_PEER | SSL_VERIFY_FAIL_IF_NO_PEER_CERT,
               verify_callback);
SSL_set_session_id_context(ssl, &admin_user, sizeof(int));
/* code fragment from Example 5-18 goes here.  the new session is made */
post_connection_check(ssl, host);
/* if everything is error-free, we have properly authenticated the client */
```

The code in Example 5-18 realizes the solution to the problem we laid out earlier for upgrading client authentication. By changing the session context ID to admin_user, we allow clients previously verified as admin users to resume connections, but no others. This is effective at keeping resumed sessions from being mistaken as privileged sessions. In addition, we set the verify options for the SSL object explicitly, forcing the renegotiation to demand a client certificate or fail. After renegotiation is complete, we call the post-connection check function. In some cases, we may want to tailor the post-connection function to meet application-specific needs.

Renegotiations in 0.9.7

Overall, renegotiation in Version 0.9.6 is inferior to the functions and simplicity that Version 0.9.7 promises. A new function has been added, SSL_regenotiate_pending. This function will return nonzero if a request is sent, but the handshake hasn't been finished. It will return zero once the handshake is complete. Using this function, we can eliminate most of the ugliness associated with renegotiations in 0.9.6. Before looking at forced renegotiations, we'll briefly return to passive renegotiations.

In most applications, renegotiations for changing the session key rather than upgrading client authentication are started by byte transfer thresholds. In other words, once our connection has transferred a certain number of bytes, we will renegotiate. Because of this new function, we can simply call SSL_renegotiate when the byte limit is reached. Then we periodically check the value of SSL_renegotiate_pending to determine if the renegotiation completed. Doing this, we can programmatically fail if the handshake isn't completed in a certain amount of time after the request.

Furthermore, a new SSL option to aid us has been added in Version 0.9.7. By setting SSL_OP_NO_SESSION_RESUMPTION_ON_RENEGOTIATION with a call to SSL_CTX_set_options, we can automatically prevent clients from being able to resume sessions when we ask for renegotiations, regardless of the session ID context. When our goal is to refresh session keys, this option is invaluable.

Using these two new additions will also allow us to make a much cleaner forced renegotiation for client authentication. We can call SSL_renegotiate to set the flag and make a single call to SSL_do_handshake to send the request out. Instead of setting internal state of the SSL object, we can now just call SSL_do_handshake until we either programmatically timeout or SSL_renegotiate_pending returns zero. If the latter condition is met, our renegotiation completed successfully. Ideally, we want to leave the session ID context changing and not set the new SSL option when performing renegotiation for client authentication. This is better because it allows authenticated users to resume authenticated sessions rather than always perform the full handshake.

Further notes

We've limited our discussion of renegotiations to server-side implementation. In general, applications will be made this way since servers dictate session caching, and a server almost always presents credentials. However, it is possible for a client to request or force renegotiation, though it is less common. Doing this is a logical extension of the methods used by a server. We now have a better understanding of renegotiations, why they occur, and why they're needed for certain operations. Forcing a renegotiation to force the client to provide a certificate to continue the connection is also a popular paradigm for implementing SSL applications. As we discussed early in this section, the alternatives to renegotiation for accomplishing this task are often too burdensome to be a general solution.

One major point that's been missing up to now is how to make an application react to renegotiation requests. The good news here is that it's all handled by the OpenSSL library for us. Recall the complications with I/O. The reason we had to handle all the different varieties of retries is that a renegotiation request could be received at any time. When an SSL connection is requested to renegotiate, the implementation automatically does so and completes the new handshake to generate a new session.

## CHAPTER 6

Symmetric Cryptography

So far, we've discussed how to use the OpenSSL programmatic interface for securing arbitrary TCP/IP connections using SSL. While SSL is a great general-purpose protocol, there are situations in which it is not appropriate. For example, SSL can't be used to store encrypted data, such as on a disk or in a cookie, nor can it encrypt UDP traffic. In these cases, you should use the OpenSSL API for symmetric cryptography.

As you have probably noticed, we've been careful to recommend using SSL instead of raw cryptographic primitives for securing your applications if at all appropriate. We do this because it is incredibly easy to apply cryptographic primitives in a way that is insecure. Even professional cryptographic protocol designers have a hard time writing "secure" cryptographic protocols built on these primitives, which is one reason peer-review is so important in the world of cryptography.

If you're planning to use this chapter to do real work, then we assume that you have some sort of need that SSL cannot fill, such as long-term data storage. We recognize that many people will want to design their own network protocols despite our recommendations. If you are considering such an option, we strongly urge you to prefer well-respected protocols, and even pre-existing implementations of those protocols, if possible. Nonetheless, this chapter is a reference for the basic API, and it is your responsibility to use that API in a secure manner.

Concepts in Symmetric Cryptography

Although we gave a brief overview of symmetric key cryptography in Chapter 1, there are some additional things we should discuss as background material for the rest of this chapter. Certainly, we don't wish to serve as a general-purpose textbook on cryptography. For such things, we recommend other books, such as Bruce Schneier's *Applied Cryptography* (John Wiley & Sons). For that reason, we'll avoid any topic that a developer need not care about, such as the internal workings of ciphers. Anything related to the choices you need to make, however, is fair game.

Block Ciphers and Stream Ciphers

Only two types of symmetric ciphers exist that are well-respected and see any sort of widespread use: *block ciphers* and *stream ciphers*. Block ciphers are traditionally the most popular. They operate by breaking up data into fixed-size blocks, and then encrypting each block individually, in which the encryption algorithm is a reversible function of the input. Leftover data is traditionally padded so that the length of the plaintext is a multiple of the cipher's block size. Stream ciphers are essentially just cryptographic pseudorandom number generators. They use a starting seed as a key to produce a stream of random bits known as the *keystream*. To encrypt data, one takes the plaintext and simply XORs it with the keystream. Stream ciphers don't need to be padded per se, though they are usually padded to byte-boundaries, since implementations usually operate on a per-byte level instead of a per-bit level.

The best block ciphers are a far more conservative solution than stream ciphers because they are better studied. Yet stream ciphers tend to be far faster than block ciphers. For example, RC4, currently the most popular stream cipher, runs about 4 times faster than Blowfish, which is among the fastest available block ciphers, and runs almost 15 times faster than 3DES, which is a very conservative cipher choice. AES is faster than 3DES and has more security in terms of a longer key size, but it is still generally slower than even Blowfish.

Neither block ciphers nor stream ciphers can give us *perfect security*, in which an attacker can never recover a message as long as the communicating parties use the algorithm properly. For each type of cipher, the security is, at best, a function of the key length. It's always possible to launch a brute-force attack, in which the attacker tries every possible key until the message properly decrypts. If the key length is long enough, the attack will take so long on average as to be infeasible in practice.

Even if there was no better attack on an individual cipher than brute force, there are other issues that plague naïve use of both types of cipher. Stream ciphers have the problem that a one-bit flip of the ciphertext causes a one-bit flip in the decrypted plaintext. Obviously, stream ciphers need to be supplemented with data integrity checks. For such purposes, we recommend message authentication codes (MACs— see Chapter 8).

When used directly, block ciphers always encrypt a given block of data in the same way, and thus do not effectively conceal patterns in a stream of data. An attacker can keep a dictionary of known plaintext blocks to known ciphertext blocks, which can often be useful in deciphering real messages. Additionally, an attacker can easily substitute one ciphertext block for another, often with great success. There are ways to use ciphers that can solve these problems to some degree, which we discuss in the next section. Additionally, MACs can be used to thwart actual modification attacks.

Stream ciphers are subject to a similar, more serious problem. Once you start encrypting using a given key, you must continue to generate new data in the keystream, or generate and exchange a new key. If you start over using the same key, the security of the stream cipher is effectively lost. The solution is to never reuse keys when using a stream cipher. Don't even use the same key across reboots.

Basic Block Cipher Modes

OpenSSL implements four common modes for block ciphers. Each of these modes can be used with every block cipher in the library, with the exception of DESX, which is defined as having only a single mode of operation.

- ECB (*Electronic Code Book*) mode is the basic mode of operation, in which the cipher takes a single block of plaintext and produces a single block of ciphertext. Data streams are broken into blocks that are individually processed. Usually, this mode is padded to accommodate messages that aren't a multiple of the cipher's block size length (in fact, you cannot avoid padding in OpenSSL prior to 0.9.7). Because of padding, the ciphertext can be up to a block longer than the plaintext. In addition, as previously mentioned, this mode is highly susceptible to dictionary attacks. ECB is almost always the wrong mode for the job, because it is so difficult to use securely. We strongly recommend that you not use it under any circumstances, unless you really know what you're doing. The biggest advantage of ECB over the other common modes is that messages can be encrypted in parallel. However, this is not an adequate reason to use ECB—an alternative mode that allows for parallelization is counter mode, which we discuss later in this chapter.

- CBC (*Cipher Block Chaining*) mode essentially solves ECB's dictionary problem by XORing the ciphertext of one block with the plaintext of the next block. Since block ciphertexts are interdependent, parallelization isn't possible. CBC is still a block-based mode, meaning that padding is generally used.

  CBC mode can be used to encrypt multiple data streams. However, dictionary attacks are possible if the data streams have common beginning sequences. For that reason, it is possible to set an *initialization vector* (IV), which is a block of data that gets XOR'd with the first block of plaintext before encrypting that block. The value of the IV need not be secret, but it should be random. The IV must be available to properly decrypt the ciphertext.

- CFB (*Cipher Feedback*) mode is one way of turning a block cipher into a stream cipher, though a complete block of plaintext must be received before encryption can begin. This mode isn't as prone to data manipulation attacks as most stream ciphers. Like CBC mode, CFB mode can use an initialization vector. The IV is more important than in CBC mode, because if two data streams are encrypted with the same key, and have the same IV, then both streams can be recovered. In practice, avoid reusing the same key when using CFB mode.

- OFB (*Output Feedback*) mode is another way of turning a block cipher into a stream cipher. OFB mode works more like a traditional stream cipher than CFB mode, and is therefore more susceptible to the same kind of bit-flipping attacks that affect stream ciphers (generally not a problem if you use a message authentication code). A compelling feature of OFB mode is that most of the work can be done offline. That is, you can generate a keystream before there is even data available to encrypt, while you have spare CPU cycles. The plaintext simply gets XOR'd into the keystream. OpenSSL doesn't directly support keystream precomputation. OFB mode can also use an IV. As with CBC mode, avoid using the same key to encrypt multiple data streams, particularly if you always use the same IV.

Encrypting with the EVP API

The OpenSSL API for symmetric cryptography is vast. Each cipher has its own set of routines for encryption and decryption. Fortunately, OpenSSL also provides a single API that serves as an interface to all symmetric encryption algorithms: the EVP interface, which can be accessed by including *openssl/evp.h*. The EVP API provides an interface to every cipher OpenSSL exports. Before using the EVP interface, we must know how to get a reference to the different ciphers we may wish to use. OpenSSL represents ciphers as data objects that generally get loaded behind the programmer's back. When you wish to use a particular cipher, you simply request a reference to the object associated with that cipher. There are two common methods for doing this. First, OpenSSL provides a method for each cipher in each mode of interest for that cipher, which loads the cipher data object into memory if necessary. For example, we can use the following code to get a reference to the Blowfish-CBC cipher object:

```
EVP_CIPHER *c = EVP_bf_cbc();
```

Second, OpenSSL provides the function EVP_get_cipherbyname, which returns the appropriate cipher object given a string representation of the cipher configuration, or NULL if no matching cipher is found. This function can be used only on cipher configurations that have previously been loaded. You can load all symmetric ciphers with the call OpenSSL_add_all_ciphers, which takes no parameters. OpenSSL_add_all_algorithms will also do the trick, but will load other kinds of cryptographic algorithms. The problem with using these functions is that they cause all ciphers to be linked into an executable at runtime, even when using dynamic loading. To avoid this overhead, avoid those calls, and manually add ciphers that you wish to use. If you want to add a small set of ciphers that you can then look up by name based on dynamic information, you can use EVP_add_cipher. For example:

```
EVP_add_cipher(EVP_bf_cbc());
```

Available Ciphers

OpenSSL provides implementations of an array of algorithms that meet most needs. The only significant lack in some versions is an implementation of the new Advanced Encryption Standard (AES). AES is supported in the long-awaited 0.9.7 release.

In addition to the actual cipher algorithms that OpenSSL provides, the null cipher is also supported, which passes data through untouched. You can access this cipher using EVP_enc_null. It is primarily useful for testing the EVP interface, so you should generally avoid using it in production systems.

AES

AES is the new Advanced Encryption Standard, also occasionally called Rijndael. It is available only in OpenSSL Versions 0.9.7 or later. AES is a block cipher that supports key and block sizes of 128, 192, and 256 bits. Unfortunately, as of this writing, OpenSSL does not provide support for using AES in CFB or OFB modes. See Table 6-1.

Table 6-1. Referencing the AES cipher (OpenSSL 0.9.7 only)

Cipher mode	Key/block size	EVP call for cipher object	String for cipher lookup
ECB	128 bits	EVP_aes_128_ecb( )	aes-128-ecb
CBC	128 bits	EVP_aes_128_cbc( )	aes-128-cbc
ECB	192 bits	EVP_aes_192_ecb()	aes-192-ecb
CBC	192 bits	EVP_aes_192_cbc()	aes-192-cbc
ECB	256 bits	EVP_aes_256_ecb()	aes-256-ecb
CBC	256 bits	EVP_aes_256_cbc()	aes-256-cbc

Blowfish

Blowfish is a block cipher designed by Bruce Schneier of *Applied Cryptography* fame. This algorithm has a good security margin and is the fastest block cipher OpenSSL provides. The key length of Blowfish is variable (up to 448 bits), but generally, 128-bit keys are used. The block-size for this cipher is fixed at 64-bits. Its biggest drawback is that key setup time is slow. As a result, Blowfish isn't a good choice when many different keys are used to encrypt short data items. Table 6-2 gives details.

Table 6-2. Referencing the Blowfish cipher

Cipher mode	EVP call for cipher object	String for cipher lookup
ECB	EVP_bf_ecb( )	bf-ecb
CBC	EVP_bf_cbc( )	bf-cbc
CFB	EVP_bf_cfb( )	bf-cfb
OFB	EVP_bf_ofb( )	bf-ofb

CAST5

The CAST5 algorithm, authored by Carlisle Adams and Stafford Tavares, is another cipher with variable-length keys and 64-bit blocks. The CAST5 specification allows for key lengths between 5 and 16 bytes (40 and 128 bits; keys must be a multiple of 8 bits in length). OpenSSL defaults to using 128-bit keys. CAST is a fast cipher with no known weaknesses. See Table 6-3.

Table 6-3. Referencing the CAST5 cipher

Cipher mode	EVP call for cipher object	String for cipher lookup
ECB	EVP_cast_ecb( )	cast-ecb
CBC	EVP_cast_cbc( )	cast-cbc
CFB	EVP_cast_cfb( )	cast-cfb
OFB	EVP_cast_ofb( )	cast-ofb

DES

DES, the *Data Encryption Standard*, uses fixed 64-bit blocks and 64-bit keys. Eight bits are parity bits, giving a maximum of 56 bits of strength. These days, the parity bits are usually completely ignored. DES dates back to the mid-1970s and is certainly the most widely scrutinized symmetric algorithm available. While no significant attacks better than brute force have ever been found, brute force is a very real attack, since a 56-bit keyspace is widely considered too small. Additionally, DES is the slowest of the ciphers OpenSSL supports, except for more secure DES variants. It is a good idea to avoid vanilla DES unless you are supporting legacy systems. See Table 6-4.

Table 6-4. Referencing standard DES

Cipher mode	EVP call for cipher object	String for cipher lookup
ECB	EVP_des_ecb( )	des-ecb
CBC	EVP_des_cbc( )	des-cbc
CFB	EVP_des_cfb( )	des-cfb
OFB	EVP_des_ofb( )	des-ofb

DESX

DESX is a DES variant that is resistant to brute-force attacks. It uses an additional 64 bits of key material to obscure the inputs and outputs of DES. The extra key material is used in a simple and efficient manner, resulting in a cipher that is not much slower than traditional DES, but is far more resistant to brute-force attacks. In fact, a brute-force attack is infeasible with DESX without a large number of known plaintexts. Other attacks against DESX may worry you if you think an attacker might be able to get 2^{60} plaintext/ciphertext pairs. Usually, that's not much of a worry. DESX runs only in CBC mode.

When speed is important and cryptographic acceleration is an option, DESX shines, because most such hardware supports DES (often exclusively), and DESX can be accelerated using standard DES acceleration. Nonetheless, triple DES offers a greater security margin, so is preferable if its performance can be tolerated. See Table 6-5 for details.

Table 6-5. Referencing DESX

Cipher mode	EVP call for cipher object	String for cipher lookup
CBC	EVP_desx_cbc( )	desx

Triple DES

Triple DES, often written as 3DES, is the most popular variant of DES and is probably the most conservative symmetric cipher available, due to the wide scrutiny DES has seen in the past quarter century. It is also the slowest algorithm available, though acceleration hardware can help. With 3DES, encryption is performed by encrypting data using DES, "decrypting" the ciphertext using a second key, then encrypting the data again, either with the original key (two-key 3DES) or with a third key (three-key 3DES). Three-key 3DES is always a better choice than two-key, as it is more secure and is no slower. The only drawback is that it requires a few extra bits for storing the additional key material. See Table 6-6.

Table 6-6. Referencing 3DES

Cipher mode	EVP call for cipher object	String for cipher lookup
ECB (3 key)	EVP_des_ede3( )	des-ede3
CBC (3 key)	EVP_des_ede3_cbc( )	des-ede3-cbc
CFB (3 key)	EVP_des_ede3_cfb( )	des-ede3-cfb
OFB (3 key)	EVP_des_ede3_ofb( )	des-ede3-ofb
ECB (2 key)	EVP_des_ede( )	des-ede
CBC (2 key)	EVP_des_ede_cbc( )	des-ede-cbc
CFB (2 key)	EVP_des_ede_cfb( )	des-ede-cfb
OFB (2 key)	EVP_des_ede_ofb( )	des-ede-ofb

IDEA

The IDEA cipher is a good all-around block cipher with 128-bit keys and 64-bit blocks. It is fast and is widely regarded as strong. Its major drawback is that it is covered by patent in the U.S. and Europe. Nonetheless, you can use the algorithm without paying a fee for noncommercial purposes.

IDEA is about 10 years old and has seen a fair amount of scrutiny. Bruce Schneier highly recommends the algorithm in *Applied Cryptography*, and it is commonly used with PGP. Table 6-7 gives more information.

Table 6-7. Referencing IDEA

Cipher mode	EVP call for cipher object	String for cipher lookup
ECB	EVP_idea_ecb( )	idea-ecb
CBC	EVP_idea_cbc( )	idea-cbc
CFB	EVP_idea_cfb( )	idea-cfb
OFB	EVP_idea_ofb( )	idea-ofb

RC2™

The RC2 algorithm is a block cipher from RSA Labs.

RC2 supports variable-length keys up to 128 bytes. OpenSSL's implementation uses a default length of 16 bytes (128 bits). There's an additional parameter for setting the "effective" key strength. What this means is you can take, say, a 128-bit key and cripple it to 40 bits worth of security. We strongly recommend against using this parameter.

RC2 is efficient and has no significant published weaknesses. However, the algorithm has not really seen a great deal of scrutiny, particularly compared to DES and AES. Table 6-8 gives the details.

Table 6-8. Referencing RC2

Cipher mode	EVP call for cipher object	String for cipher lookup
ECB	EVP_rc2_ecb( )	rc2-ecb
CBC	EVP_rc2_cbc( )	rc2-cbc
CFB	EVP_rc2_cfb( )	rc2-cfb
OFB	EVP_rc2_ofb( )	rc2-ofb

RC4™

RC4 is a stream cipher with variable-length keys that can be up to 256 bytes long. RC4 was previously a trade secret but is now in common use due to the publication of a reverse-engineered, third-party implementation. If you use RC4 in a commercial product, RSA Security might come after you legally, even though it would be unlikely to win. The name RC4 is also trademarked, and you should consult RSA Security before using it.

RC4 is a stream cipher and is blazingly fast compared to the available block ciphers in OpenSSL. It's certainly the fastest algorithm currently implemented in OpenSSL. RC4 is also well-regarded as an algorithm. For this reason, and due to its widespread use in SSL, it's vastly popular, though it is widely used with insecure 40-bit keys.

RC4 is difficult to use well. The encryption algorithm itself is good, but some problems with the way it sets up keys require care in using it. In particular, RSA Security recommends you take one of the following two steps when using this algorithm:

1. Make sure that all key material is cryptographically hashed before use. The problem necessitating this solution is most prominent when frequently rekeying RC4. A common approach to frequent rekeying is to use a base key, and then concatenate with a counter. In RC4, that turns out to be a bad thing to do. If you take the key material and the counter and hash them together to get the actual key, the weakness goes away. The general recommendation of hashing all key material before use is a good one, no matter which cipher you use in your applications.

2. Discard the first 256 bytes of the generated key stream before using it. The easy way to do this is to encrypt 256 bytes of random data and discard the results.

Additionally, as previously noted, it is particularly important to supplement use of RC4 with a MAC to ensure data integrity. See Table 6-9 for more information.

Table 6-9. Referencing RC4

Key length	EVP call for cipher object	String for cipher lookup
40 bits	EVP_rc4_40( )	rc4-40
128 bits	EVP_rc4( )	rc4

RC5™

RC5 is another block cipher from RSA Security. Its name is trademarked, and its algorithm is covered by an issued patent. You should certainly contact RSA Security before using this algorithm in any application.

RC5 is interesting because it is fast, well-regarded, and highly customizable. According to the RC5 specification, you can choose 64- or 128-bit blocks, use keys up to 255 bytes in size, and can use any number of cipher rounds, up to 255. However, OpenSSL's implementation uses 64-bit blocks and limits rounds to 8, 12, or 16, defaulting to 12. See Table 6-10.

Table 6-10. Referencing RC5

Cipher mode	Key bits	Rounds	EVP call for cipher object	String for cipher lookup
ECB	128	12	EVP_rc5_32_16_12_ecb( )	rc5-ecb
CBC	128	12	EVP_rc5_32_16_12_cbc( )	rc5-cbc
CFB	128	12	EVP_rc5_32_16_12_cfb( )	rc5-cfb
OFB	128	12	EVP_rc5_32_16_12_ofb( )	rc5-ofb

Note that nondefault parameters to RC5 cannot currently be accessed through EVP calls or through cipher lookup by name. Instead, you must first reference the default RC5 cipher object in the correct mode, and then use other calls to set parameters, as described below.

Initializing Symmetric Ciphers

Before we can begin encrypting or decrypting, we must allocate and initialize a cipher context. The cipher context is a data structure that keeps track of all relevant state for the purposes of encrypting or decrypting data over a period of time. For example, we can have multiple streams of data encrypted in CBC mode. The cipher context will keep track of the key associated with each stream and the internal state that needs to be kept between messages for CBC mode. Additionally, when encrypting with a block-based cipher mode, the context object buffers data that doesn't exactly align to the block size until more data arrives, or until the buffer is explicitly flushed, at which point the data is usually padded as appropriate.[*]

---

[*] This happens only if padding is turned on, of course.

The generic cipher context type is EVP_CIPHER_CTX. We can initialize one, whether it was allocated dynamically or statically, by calling EVP_CIPHER_CTX_init, like so:

```
EVP_CIPHER_CTX *x = (EVP_CIPHER_CTX *)malloc(sizeof(EVP_CIPHER_CTX));
EVP_CIPHER_CTX_init(x);
```

After allocating the context object and initializing it, we must set up the cipher context. At this point, we generally determine whether the particular context will be used for encrypting or decrypting. It is possible to set up a context to do both, but it's a bad idea in any mode other than ECB mode, because race conditions can easily occur that will desynchronize communication. Essentially, the internal cipher state of the two communicating parties needs to remain synchronized at all times. If both parties send data at the same time, they will likely end up trying to decrypt the data they receive using an incorrect state.

When we set up a cipher context, we not only choose whether we're encrypting or decrypting, but also do the following:

1. Choose the type of cipher we will be using, including the mode in which to use that cipher. We will be passing an EVP_CIPHER object to an initialization routine.

2. Set the key to be used for operations by passing it to the initialization routine as an array of bytes.

3. Specify an initialization vector for the cipher, if appropriate for the mode. A default IV will be used if not otherwise specified.

4. If using the "engine" release, we can specify whether we want to use hardware acceleration, if available. If we do, we must have previously specified an "engine" to use that supports our hardware. Specifying NULL as an engine tells OpenSSL to use its default software implementations. In 0.9.7, this functionality will be part of the library proper.

EVP_EncryptInit is the preferred method for setting up a cipher context for encryption. For decryption, it is EVP_DecryptInit. Both of these methods have the same signature, which includes four parameters.

```
int EVP_EncryptInit(EVP_CIPHER_CTX *ctx, const EVP_CIPHER *type,
                    unsigned char *key, unsigned char *iv);

int EVP_DecryptInit(EVP_CIPHER_CTX *ctx, const EVP_CIPHER *type,
                    unsigned char *key, unsigned char *iv);
```

ctx
> The EVP cipher context object to use.

type
> The cipher to use.

key
> The key to use for encrypting or decrypting.

iv
> The initialization vector to use.

Notice that the engine package prefers an extended API, `EVP_EncryptInit_ex` and `EVP_DecryptInit_ex`, which inserts a fifth argument before the key that is a pointer to the engine to use; it should be `NULL` when no hardware acceleration is being used. When Version 0.9.7 of OpenSSL is released, these versions of the calls will be the preferred API. When using engines, many calls can fail, so check error codes. We don't do this because we don't use the ENGINE API in our examples.

Let's consider an example in which we try to encrypt using Blowfish with 128-bit keys in CBC mode. CBC mode can use an initialization vector, which is always the size of one block (in this case, 8 bytes). We will use the OpenSSL pseudorandom number generator to provide a randomly generated key; however, distributing that key is not really covered in this example. For now, we'll assume that you will do it offline, perhaps by exchanging a disk, or reading the key over the phone (key exchange protocols are discussed in Chapter 8). To that end, we do print out the key to stdout in hexadecimal format. Note that doing this is not really the best idea for real applications. Example 6-1 shows how to do this.

Example 6-1. Preparing to use Blowfish in CBC mode for encryption

```
#include <openssl/evp.h>

void select_random_key(char *key, int b)
{
    int i;

    RAND_bytes(key, b);
    for (i = 0;  i < b - 1;  i++)
        printf("%02X:", key[i]);
    printf("%02X\n", key[b - 1]);
}

void select_random_iv(char *iv, int b)
{
    RAND_pseudo_bytes(iv, b);
}

int setup_for_encryption(void)
{
    EVP_CIPHER_CTX ctx;
    char           key[EVP_MAX_KEY_LENGTH];
    char           iv[EVP_MAX_IV_LENGTH];

    if (!seed_prng())
        return 0;
    select_random_key(key, EVP_MAX_KEY_LENGTH);
    select_random_iv(iv, EVP_MAX_IV_LENGTH);
    EVP_EncryptInit(&ctx, EVP_bf_cbc(), key, iv);
    return 1;
}
```

Note that multiple implementations of the seed_prng function are provided in Chapter 4. It returns 0 if the pseudorandom number generator cannot be seeded securely. We return an error status from our setup function in this case, so we don't need to check the return value of RAND_pseudo_bytes when we call it. Also, you may want to use raw entropy. See Chapter 4 for more information.

Another thing to note is that the party decrypting the data will need to initialize its cipher context with the same initialization vector created here. Passing the initialization vector in the clear is OK, but it should probably be MAC'd so that the receiver can detect tampering. If NULL is passed in for an IV, an array filled with zeros is used. Note that IVs can be used in all modes except ECB. In ECB mode, you can still pass in an IV, but block ciphers will ignore it.

Setting up for decryption is generally easier, because we already know the key and the IV used. Example 6-2 shows how to set up for decryption under the same configuration.

Example 6-2. Preparing to use Blowfish in CBC mode for decryption

```
#include <openssl/evp.h>

void setup_for_decryption(char *key, char *iv)
{
    EVP_CIPHER_CTX ctx;

    EVP_DecryptInit(&ctx, EVP_bf_cbc( ), key, iv);
}
```

Subsequent calls to EVP_EncryptInit or EVP_DecryptInit will change the value of any non-null parameter as long as the cipher type parameter is set to NULL. Otherwise, the context is completely reinitialized. Additionally, the key and the IV can both be set to NULL on the first call to these functions, and set separately later. This is necessary when you specify a cipher and then change the key length from the default. Of course, you will need to at least provide a valid key before encryption begins.

Specifying Key Length and Other Options

Many ciphers take a variable key length, which can be easily set after initialization using the call EVP_CIPHER_CTX_set_key_length. For example, we can set the Blowfish key length to 64 bits, as follows:

```
EVP_EncryptInit(&ctx, EVP_bf_ecb( ), NULL, NULL);
EVP_CIPHER_CTX_set_key_length(&ctx, 8);
EVP_EncryptInit(&ctx, NULL, key, NULL);
```

In this case, we set the key with a second call to EVP_EncryptInit after we specify the key length.

When using this functionality, make sure you only set the key length to a valid value for the cipher.

If we wish to check the default key length of a cipher object, we can use the call `EVP_CIPHER_key_length`. For example, the following will show us the default key length for Blowfish:

```
printf("%d\n", EVP_CIPHER_key_length(EVP_bf_ecb()));
```

We can also check to see the length of the keys a cipher context is using:

```
printf("%d\n", EVP_CIPHER_CTX_key_length(&ctx));
```

For other cipher parameters, OpenSSL provides a generic call, `EVP_CIPHER_CTX_ctrl`. Currently, this call can only set or query the effective key strength in RC2 or the number of rounds used in RC5.

```
int EVP_CIPHER_CTX_ctrl(EVP_CIPHER_CTX *ctx, int type, int arg, void *ptr);
```

ctx

> The cipher context object.

type

> The operation to perform, which can be one of the following constants:
>
> - EVP_CTRL_GET_RC2_KEY_BITS
> - EVP_CTRL_SET_RC2_KEY_BITS
> - EVP_CTRL_GET_RC5_ROUNDS
> - EVP_CTRL_SET_RC5_ROUNDS

arg

> The numerical value to set, if appropriate. If not appropriate, its value is ignored.

ptr

> A pointer to an integer for querying the numerical value of a property.

For example, to query the effective key bits in an RC2 cipher context, storing the result in a variable called kb:

```
EVP_CIPHER_CTX_ctrl(&ctx, EVP_CTRL_GET_RC2_KEY_BITS, 0, &kb);
```

And to set the effective key strength of RC2 to 64 bits:

```
EVP_CIPHER_CTX_ctrl(&ctx, EVP_CTRL_SET_RC2_KEY_BITS, 64, NULL);
```

Setting and querying RC5 rounds works the same way. Remember from our previous discussion that OpenSSL is limited to 8, 12, or 16 rounds for RC5.

Another desirable option to set in a cipher context is whether padding is used. Without padding, the size of the ciphertext will always be the same size as the plaintext. On the downside, the length of the data encrypted must be an exact multiple of the block size. With padding, any length in bytes is feasible, but the resulting ciphertext can be up to a block longer than the plaintext. Unfortunately, OpenSSL versions through 0.9.6c do not allow padding to be disabled. This changes in Version 0.9.7, which has a function called `EVP_CIPHER_CTX_set_padding` that takes a pointer to a cipher context, and an integer that represents a Boolean value (0 for no padding, 1 for padding).

Encryption

Once the cipher context is initialized, there are two steps to encryption with the EVP interface: *updating* and *finalization*. When you have data to encrypt, you pass the data to the update function, along with a pointer to where you'd like any output to go. There may or may not be output as the result of an update. If the cipher can encrypt one or more entire blocks of data, it will do so. Any leftover data will be buffered and processed either during the next call to the update function or during the call to finalize. When calling finalize, any leftover data is padded and encrypted. If there is no leftover data, a block of pad is encrypted.* As with updating, you must tell the routine where to store resulting data.

The update function is EVP_EncryptUpdate.

```
int EVP_EncryptUpdate(EVP_CIPHER_CTX *ctx, unsigned char *out, int *outl,
                      unsigned char *in, int inl);
```

> ctx
> > The cipher context to use.
>
> out
> > A buffer that will receive the encrypted data.
>
> outl
> > Receives the number of bytes written to the encrypted data buffer.
>
> in
> > A buffer that contains the data to be encrypted.
>
> inl
> > Specifies the number of bytes contained in the input data buffer.

When using a block-based cipher mode (ECB or CBC), the amount of output written can be both larger and smaller than the length of the input, due to internal buffering and padding. If you're using a cipher with 8-byte (64-bit) blocks, the output could be up to 7 bytes smaller than the input, or up to 7 bytes larger.† If you are encrypting incrementally with a single key, and are producing packets of data, this is good to keep in mind. If, instead, you're encrypting to a single buffer, you will always avoid overflow by making the output buffer an entire block bigger than the

---

* For the curious, here is how standard (PKCS) padding works. If *n* bytes of padding are needed, then *n* is used as the value of each byte. For example, the value of a one-byte pad (expressed in hexadecimal) is 0x01, and the value of an eight-byte pad is 0x0808080808080808. This way, the extent of the pad can be calculated unambiguously by looking at the last byte of the padded plaintext.

† Actually, the current implementation limits the output to six bytes longer than the input. However, you should not count on that behavior.

---

input buffer (the extra block may fill with padding). Optionally, you can manually keep track of exactly how much data will be output as a function of how much data was input.

The finalization function is `EVP_EncryptFinal`.

```
int EVP_EncryptFinal(EVP_CIPHER_CTX *ctx, unsigned char *out, int *outl);
```

> ctx
>> The cipher context to use.
>
> out
>> A buffer that will receive the encrypted data.
>
> outl
>> Receives the number of bytes written to the encrypted data buffer.

Currently, this function always outputs. However, in the forthcoming 0.9.7 release it will not place anything in the output buffer at all if padding is turned off. In such a case, if there is any buffered data, the function returns an error. Additionally, Version 0.9.7 adds an `EVP_EncryptFinal_ex` call that should be used when a context has been initialized by `EVP_EncryptInit_ex`.

Example 6-3 shows the implementation of a function that takes a pointer to an initialized EVP cipher context, a buffer to encrypt, an associated length, and a pointer to an integer. The function then encrypts the data 100 bytes at a time into a heap-allocated buffer, which is the function's return value. The length of the resulting ciphertext is passed back in the address specified by the final parameter.

Example 6-3. Encrypting plaintext 100 bytes at a time

```
#include <openssl/evp.h>

char *encrypt_example(EVP_CIPHER_CTX *ctx, char *data, int inl, int *rb)
{
    char *ret;
    int  i, tmp, ol;

    ol = 0;
    ret = (char *)malloc(inl + EVP_CIPHER_CTX_block_size(ctx));
    for (i = 0;  i < inl / 100;  i++)
    {
        EVP_EncryptUpdate(ctx, &ret[ol], &tmp, &data[ol], 100);
        ol += tmp;
    }
    if (inl % 100)
    {
        EVP_EncryptUpdate(ctx, &ret[ol], &tmp, &data[ol], inl%100);
        ol += tmp;
    }
    EVP_EncryptFinal(ctx, &ret[ol], &tmp);
    *rb = ol + tmp;
    return ret;
}
```

Factoring in the block length (done by calling `EVP_CIPHER_CTX_block_size`) is unnecessary when using a stream cipher, or when using the CFB or OFB cipher modes, since there is no padding in those cases. As a result, the cipher can output encrypted data as needed, without having to buffer any plaintext.*

The above example works well when we can afford to encrypt everything into a single buffer before processing the ciphertext. It doesn't work so well if we need to deal with ciphertext incrementally. For example, we might wish to send blocks of data as quickly as possible, and not wait for all data to be processed. Example 6-4 shows a solution for such a scenario. Data to be encrypted is sent to `incremental_encrypt` as needed. When there's data to be sent, `incremental_encrypt` calls `incremental_send`, which is simply a stub, but it can place those blocks currently encrypted on the network. When all data to be encrypted has been passed to `incremental_encrypt`, then `incremental_finish` is called.

Example 6-4. Performing incremental encryption

```
#include <openssl/evp.h>

/* Return the number of bytes actually written */
int incremental_encrypt(EVP_CIPHER_CTX *ctx, char *data, int inl)
{
    char *buf;
    int  ol;
    int  bl = EVP_CIPHER_CTX_block_size(ctx);

    /* Up to the block size - 1 chars can be buffered up.  Add that to the length
     * of the input, and then we can easily determine the maximum number of
     * blocks output will take by integer divison with the block size.
     */
    buf = (char *)malloc((inl + bl - 1) / bl * bl);
    EVP_EncryptUpdate(ctx, buf, &ol, data, inl);
    if (ol)
        incremental_send(buf, ol);
    /* incremental_send must copy if it wants to store. */
    free(buf);
    return ol;
}

/* Also returns the number of bytes written. */
int incremental_finish(EVP_CIPHER_CTX *ctx)
{
    char *buf;
    int  ol;

    buf = (char *)malloc(EVP_CIPHER_CTX_block_size(ctx));
    EVP_EncryptFinal(ctx, buf, &ol);
    if (ol)
```

---

* Strictly speaking, this isn't entirely true in CFB mode because the first block can be buffered.

Example 6-4. Performing incremental encryption (continued)

```
        incremental_send(buf, ol);
    free(buf);
    return ol;
}
```

Note that the number of bytes written by `EVP_EncryptFinal` should always be 8 when using 64-bit blocks and when padding is enabled.

Decryption

As expected, the decryption API looks similar to the encryption API. After cipher initialization, two methods are involved, `EVP_DecryptUpdate` and `EVP_DecryptFinal`. You can pass as much data as you want into `EVP_DecryptUpdate`.

When using a block-based mode (ECB or CBC), you can pass in partial blocks of text, but `EVP_DecryptUpdate` will output only whole blocks. The rest will be stored until there is more data to be processed, or until `EVP_DecryptFinal` is called. Moreover, if the context's cached ciphertext plus the length of the new ciphertext is exactly block-aligned, the entire final block will be held in the context instead of getting output. With CFB and OFB modes and with stream ciphers, there's no padding, so the size of the resulting ciphertext will be equal to the size of the plaintext.

If using a block-based mode, `EVP_DecryptFinal` first checks to see if the padding on the last block is in the right format. If not, the function returns 0, signifying failure. Otherwise, it flushes any remaining data to the buffer passed in as the second argument, and writes the number of bytes flushed into the third argument, a reference parameter. For other modes, this call does nothing.

Example 6-5 shows a simple function that decrypts a block of encrypted text into a dynamically allocated buffer and returns it. This function can be used to incrementally decrypt, and thus requires `EVP_DecryptFinal` to be called when a block-based mode is used. Of course, `EVP_DecryptInit` should always be called before passing a context to this function.

Example 6-5. Decrypting ciphertext

```
char *decrypt_example(EVP_CIPHER_CTX *ctx, char *ct, int inl)
{
    /* We're going to null-terminate the plaintext under the assumption it's
     * non-null terminated ASCII text.  The null can be ignored otherwise.
     */
    char *pt = (char *)malloc(inl + EVP_CIPHER_CTX_block_size(ctx) + 1);
    int  ol;

    EVP_DecryptUpdate(ctx, pt, &ol, ct, inl);
    if (!ol) /* there's no block to decrypt */
    {
```

Example 6-5. Decrypting ciphertext (continued)

```
        free(pt);
        return NULL;
    }
    pt[ol] = 0;
    return pt;
}
```

As is the case with encryption, factoring in the cipher's block length is strictly only necessary when using a block-based cipher mode.

Using the above function, and the ones we previously developed, let's look at Example 6-6, which encrypts a 15-byte string using Blowfish in CBC mode, then passes it into decrypt_example in two parts. Note, we use the macro EVP_MAX_BLOCK_LENGTH, which exists only in 0.9.7 and later. If you are using an earlier version of OpenSSL, you can define this macro to the value "64", which is the largest possible block size in 0.9.6c and earlier.

Example 6-6. Using the example encryption and decryption functions

```
int main(int argc, char *argv[])
{
    EVP_CIPHER_CTX ctx;
    char          key[EVP_MAX_KEY_LENGTH];
    char          iv[EVP_MAX_IV_LENGTH];
    char          *ct, *out;
    char          final[EVP_MAX_BLOCK_LENGTH];
    char          str[] = "123456789abcdef";
    int           i;

    if (!seed_prng())
    {
        printf("Fatal Error!  Unable to seed the PRNG!\n");
        abort();
    }

    select_random_key(key, EVP_MAX_KEY_LENGTH);
    select_random_iv(iv, EVP_MAX_IV_LENGTH);

    EVP_EncryptInit(&ctx, EVP_bf_cbc(), key, iv);
    ct = encrypt_example(&ctx, str, strlen(str), &i);
    printf("Ciphertext is %d bytes.\n", i);

    EVP_DecryptInit(&ctx, EVP_bf_cbc(), key, iv);
    out = decrypt_example(&ctx, ct, 8);
    printf("Decrypted: >>%s<<\n", out);
    out = decrypt_example(&ctx, ct + 8, 8);
    printf("Decrypted: >>%s<<\n", out);
    if (!EVP_DecryptFinal(&ctx, final, &i))
    {
        printf("Padding incorrect.\n");
        abort();
```

Example 6-6. Using the example encryption and decryption functions (continued)

```
    }
    final[i] = 0;
    printf("Decrypted: >>%s<<\n", final);
}
```

If we run this example, the first time we try to output decrypted plaintext, we will see nothing, even though we fed the decryption routine a full block of data. Note that when we feed the remainder of the data, we are passing in eight bytes, because the encryption routine padded the data to a block-aligned length. At that point, one block will be output, and the second block will be held in reserve until there is more data, or until `EVP_DecryptFinal` is called.

If we were to change the cipher to RC4, the above example would compile, but give slightly incorrect output. The length of the encrypted text would be 15 bytes, not 16, due to the lack of padding. As a result, passing in 16 bytes of ciphertext to the decrypt routine will cause a block of garbage to be decrypted. Changing the third argument in the second call to `decrypt_example` to seven fixes the problem.

Handling UDP Traffic with Counter Mode

It is almost never desirable to use ECB mode for encryption. Schneier recommends it for encrypting other keys or other situations in which the data is short and random. However, this advice applies only when the key length is no larger than the cipher block length. Additionally, if you wish to include an integrity check alongside your data (which is almost always a good idea), ECB again becomes undesirable.

Another occasion when people think to use ECB is when encrypting datagrams to be sent over a UDP connection. The problem is that packets may show up out of order, or not at all. All basic cipher modes besides ECB require an ordered, reliable stream of data.

CBC mode is much better suited to handling UDP traffic. A single key can be used to encrypt all data, but each packet gets initialized with a randomly chosen IV, which can be sent alongside the encrypted data.

Counter mode is slightly better suited than CBC for encrypting UDP traffic. One advantage of counter mode over OFB and other modes that simulate stream ciphers is that it can inherently survive data loss—the current state of the counter can be passed in the clear each time a packet is sent. Another major advantage of counter mode is that it allows for parallelization, which is not supported by any of the default modes, except for ECB (a CBC-based approach could parallelize at the packet level, but could not parallelize the processing of data within a single packet). Another feature unique to OFB is that most of the work can be done offline. That is, you can generate a keystream before there is even data available to encrypt, while you have spare CPU cycles.

Additionally, because counter mode essentially supports arbitrarily jumping around a data stream, it can enable file encryption where random access to the data is still possible. Moreover, in theory, counter mode should be able to handle the UDP encryption problem without a rekey for every packet. However, current limitations of the OpenSSL library make that goal difficult to achieve, although the forthcoming 0.9.7 release will fix the problem.

OpenSSL currently doesn't support counter mode, but it is simple to implement yourself. Counter mode effectively turns a block cipher into a stream cipher. For each block of plaintext, we encrypt a counter of exactly one block in length, which gets XOR'd with the corresponding block of plaintext. Then, the counter is incremented in some way. Increasing the counter by one or using a PRNG to increment the counter both work. The PRNG doesn't even need to be cryptographically secure, though it must not repeat items before enumerating all possible values.

We can prevent the attacker from seeing the counter if need be. Let's say that, in addition to an agreed-upon key, we share a second secret of the same length. Additionally, a sequence number is sent in the clear with each packet. To generate the counter used to encrypt the first data block in that packet, we concatenate the second shared secret with the sequence number, and cryptographically hash that. We show how to use cryptographic hashes in Chapter 7.

Counter mode is easily implemented by keeping track of a counter that is encrypted in ECB mode once for each block. In our UDP example, each packet would have several blocks. Only one counter should need to be sent per packet, because the receiving end should be able to recreate the counter values for the subsequent blocks.

Example 6-7 shows an implementation of counter mode that will work for any cipher in ECB mode. There is just one function, counter_encrypt_or_decrypt, as encryption and decryption are identical in counter mode.

```
int counter_encrypt_or_decrypt(EVP_CIPHER_CTX *ctx, char *pt, char *ct, int len,
                               unsigned char *counter);
```

ctx
>   The cipher context to use.

pt
>   A buffer containing the data to be encrypted or decrypted.

ct
>   A buffer that will contain the encrypted or decrypted data.

len
>   The number of bytes from the input buffer, pt, to process.

counter
>   The counter.

In this example, the counter must be the same size as the block size of the cipher we're using (we query the cipher's block size to specify that value). Cipher block sizes are usually bigger than 32 bits, so it is best to represent the counter as an array of unsigned bytes. This function also modifies the counter in place as it processes blocks. To increment the counter, we simply increment the leftmost byte until it rolls over, at which point we increment the byte next to it, and so on. Note that it's extremely important not to reuse counter values with a single key, not even across a reboot. If there is any chance of reusing a counter, be sure to change the key.

The next function will return −1 if it determines that the cipher is not in ECB mode (we need to use this mode in order to implement counter mode; do not take this example as an endorsement of ECB in general). This is accomplished by calling EVP_CIPHER_CTX_mode, which returns a number. If that number is equal to the constant EVP_CIPH_ECB_MODE, then we know the cipher was initialized improperly. See the documentation on the book's web site for a list of other valid mode constants.

Note that the code in Example 6-7 should not be used without also using a MAC to provide data integrity, as discussed in Chapter 7.

Example 6-7. Encryption and decryption using counter mode

```
int counter_encrypt_or_decrypt(EVP_CIPHER_CTX *ctx, char *pt, char *ct, int len,
            unsigned char *counter)
{
    int  i, j, where = 0, num, bl = EVP_CIPHER_CTX_block_size(ctx);
    char encr_ctrs[len + bl]; /* Encrypted counters. */

    if (EVP_CIPHER_CTX_mode(ctx) != EVP_CIPH_ECB_MODE)
        return -1;
    /* <= is correct, so that we handle any possible non-aligned data. */
    for (i = 0;  i <= len / bl;  i++)
    {
        /* Encrypt the current counter. */
        EVP_EncryptUpdate(ctx, &encr_ctrs[where], &num, counter, bl);
        where += num;
        /* Increment the counter. Remember it's an array of single characters */
        for (j = 0;  j < bl / sizeof(char);  j++)
        {
            if (++counter[j])
                break;
        }
    }
    /* XOR the key stream with the first buffer, placing the results in the
     * second buffer.
     */
    for (i = 0;  i < len;  i++)
        ct[i] = pt[i] ^ encr_ctrs[i];
    return 1; /* Success. */
}
```

As we discussed, the above example requires the state of the counter to be kept externally. Another option is to make a COUNTER_CTX data type that could hold a pointer to the underlying cipher context and the current state of the counter. However, this less-abstract API makes it easier to use in a situation in which the counter may need to be reset explicitly after desynchronization, such as when dealing with UDP traffic.

General Recommendations

So far, we have looked at how to use the EVP API to perform encryption and decryption. While we've examined some basic examples, we haven't looked at real-world examples. The primary reason is that we don't recommend using symmetric key encryption without a MAC; in cases where an attacker has read access to data, you should be worried about her also gaining write access. Therefore, we give real-world examples of using encryption along with MACs in Chapter 7.

When you do use MACs, use them with independent keys (that is, do not MAC with your encryption keys) and use them to validate all of the data, including anything sent in the clear. In particular, when using counter mode, make sure to include the counter value in the data that you include in the MAC calculation.

Extending this recommendation, whenever you design protocols based on encryption, avoid any communication in plaintext at all, and MAC anything that does need to be plaintext. In particular, if you do plaintext protocol negotiation before a key exchange, you should MAC the payloads of each message in the negotiation, so that after a key is agreed upon, both sides can validate the negotiation. For example, let's say that a client connects to the server and immediately asks to speak Version 2 of protocol X, and receives a response saying the server speaks only the insecure Version 1. If it turns out that a man in the middle told the server the client wanted Version 1, and fakes the response from the server, then neither the client nor the server would notice, and would wind up speaking an insecure version of the protocol.

Another recommendation is to design your protocol to be fault-tolerant. In particular, when using MACs to validate messages, be prepared to perform reasonable error handling if the data doesn't authenticate on the receiving end. If your protocol fails in such a situation, denial of service attacks will be quite easy.

Finally, be sure to protect yourself against dictionary and capture-replay type attacks. One thing you can do is add sequence numbers to the beginning of each message. It's also a good idea to place unique information per-user or per-connection near the beginning of each message.

## CHAPTER 7

Hashes and MACs

In the previous chapter, we looked at the most fundamental part of OpenSSL's cryptography library, symmetric ciphers. In this chapter, we look at the API for cryptographic hashing algorithms, also commonly called message digest algorithms or cryptographic one-way hash functions. Additionally, we will examine OpenSSL's interface to message authentication codes (MACs), also known as keyed hashes.

Overview of Hashes and MACs

We introduced the basic concepts behind cryptographic hashes and MACs in Chapter 1. Here, we describe the fundamental properties of these cryptographic primitives that you should understand before integrating them into your applications. As mentioned in Chapter 6, we provide only the minimum background information that you need to understand as a developer. If you need more background, or would like to see under the hood of any of the algorithms we discuss, refer to a general-purpose cryptography reference, such as Bruce Schneier's *Applied Cryptography*.

Cryptographic one-way hashes take arbitrary binary data as an input and produce a fixed-size binary string as an output, called the hash value or the message digest. Passing the same message through a single hash function always yields the same result. There are several important properties exhibited by cryptographic message digests. First, the digest value should contain no information that could be used to determine the original input. For that to be true, a one-bit change in the input data should change many bits in the digest value (on average, half). Second, it should be extremely difficult to construct a second message that yields the same resulting hash value. Third, it should also be difficult to find any two messages that yield the same hash value.

The most conservative characterization of the security afforded by a given hash function is measured by how hard it is to find two arbitrary messages that yield the same hash value. Generally, the security of a well-respected hash function that has a digest size of n bits should be about as secure as a well-respected symmetric cipher with half as many bits. For example, SHA1, which has a 160-bit digest size, is about as resistant to attack as RC5 with 80-bit keys. Some uses of these algorithms give security equal to their bit length that's just a good, conservative metric.

People frequently use cryptographic hash functions that they believe provide security, but that don't really provide very much. For example, it is common to release software along with an MD5 digest of the software package (MD5 is a common cryptographic hash function). The intention is to use the digest as a checksum. The person downloading software should also obtain the MD5 digest, and then calculate the digest himself on the downloaded software. If the two digests match, it would indicate that the downloaded software is unaltered.

Unfortunately, there are easy ways to attack this scheme. Suppose an attacker has maliciously modified a copy of the distribution of software package X, resulting in package Y. If the attacker can break onto the server and replace X with Y, then certainly, the checksum MD5(X) is also easily replaceable with the checksum MD5(Y). When a user validates the downloaded checksum, he will be none the wiser. Even without access to the actual server, attackers could replace X with Y and MD5(X) with MD5(Y) as they traverse the network.

The fundamental problem is that nothing in this scenario is secret. A much better solution for this kind of scenario is a digital signature, which anyone can verify, but only someone with the correct private key can generate (see Chapter 8).

Hash functions by themselves aren't often good for security purposes. The major exception is password storage. In such a situation, passwords are not stored, only hashes of passwords are stored, usually combined with a known "salt" value to avoid dictionary attacks in cases where the password database is stolen. When a user tries to log in, the hash of the entered password is compared against the one stored in the password database. If it's the correct password, the hashes will be identical.

Even this scenario works only if a trusted data source collects the authentication information through a trusted data path. If a client computes the hash and sends it in the clear over a network, an attacker can capture the hash and replay the information later to log in. Worse, if the server computes the hash, but the client sent the password in the clear over a network, an attacker could capture the transmission of the password.

One common use of hashes is as primitives in other cryptographic operations. For example, digital signature schemes generally work by hashing the input, then encrypting the hash with a private key. Doing so is generally far more efficient than performing public key encryption on a large input. Another frequent use is to remove any trace of patterns in data such as cryptographic keys. For example, you should hash your key material to make an RC4 key, instead of using the key material directly.

Another use of hashes is to ensure the message integrity of encrypted data, by encrypting the hash of a message along with the message itself. This is a primitive version of a *message authentication code* (MAC). A MAC generally uses a regular hash function as a primitive. The MAC algorithm produces a hash value from the data to protect a secret key. Only people with the correct secret key can forge the hash value, and only people with the secret key can authenticate the hash value.

One good thing about MACs is that they can provide integrity, even in the absence of encryption. Another good thing is that the best MACs tend to have provable security properties under reasonable assumptions about the strength of the hash algorithm in use. The algorithm we just described as an example doesn't have either of these advantages.

Like other cryptographic primitives, you should avoid creating your own MAC algorithm, even if it seems easy. There are good algorithms with provable properties, such as HMAC, which is currently the only MAC provided by OpenSSL. Why take the risk?

Hashing with the EVP API

Much like with symmetric cryptography, OpenSSL's cryptographic library has an API for each hash algorithm it provides, but the EVP API provides a single, simple interface to these algorithms. Just as with symmetric key encryption, there are three calls, one for initialization, one for "updating" (adding text to the context), and one for finalization, which yields the message digest.

At initialization time, you must specify the algorithm you wish to use. Currently, OpenSSL provides six different digest algorithms: MDC2, MD2, MD4, MD5, SHA1, and RIPEMD-160. The first four have digest sizes that are only 128 bits. We recommend that you avoid them except to support legacy applications. In addition, there are known attacks on MD4, and it is widely considered to be a broken algorithm. SHA1 is more common than RIPEMD-160 and is faster, but the latter is believed to have a slightly better security margin.

For each digest, at least one function returns an instance of the algorithm. Look up algorithms by name by calling OpenSSL_add_all_digests and EVP_get_digestbyname, and passing in an appropriate identifier. In both cases, a data structure of type EVP_MD represents the algorithm. Table 7-1 shows all of the message digest algorithms supported by OpenSSL, including the EVP call to get a reference to the algorithm, the digest name for lookup purposes, and the size of the resulting digests.

Table 7-1. Message digests and the EVP interface

Hash algorithm	EVP call for getting EVP_MD	String for lookup	Digest length (in bits)
MD2	EVP_md2( )	md2	128
MD4	EVP_md4( )	md4	128
MD5	EVP_md5( )	md5	128
MDC2	EVP_mdc2( )	mdc2	128
SHA1	EVP_sha1( )	sha1	160
	EVP_dss1( )	dss1	
RIPEMD-160	EVP_ripemd160( )	ripemd	160

The MDC2 algorithm is a construction for turning a block cipher into a hash function. It is usually used only with DES, and OpenSSL hardcodes this binding. The SHA1 and DSS1 algorithms are essentially the same; the only difference is that in a digital signature, SHA1 is used with RSA keys and DSS1 is used with DSA keys.

The EVP_DigestInit function initializes a context object, and it must be called before a hash can be computed.

```
void EVP_DigestInit(EVP_MD_CTX *ctx, const EVP_MD *type);
```

> ctx
>> The context object to be initialized.

> type
>> The context for the message digest algorithm to use. This value is often obtained using one of the EVP calls listed in Table 7-1.

The OpenSSL "engine" package and the forthcoming Version 0.9.7 have a preferred version of this call named EVP_DigestInit_ex, which adds a third argument that is a pointer to an engine object. Passing in NULL will get you the default software implementation. Its return value is also different; it is an integer indicating success (nonzero) or failure (zero). Be sure to check the return value from the function, because it can fail.

The EVP_DigestUpdate function is used to include data in the computation of the hash. It may be called repeatedly to pass more data than will fit in a single buffer. For example, if you're computing the hash of a large amount of data, it's reasonable to break the data into smaller bytes so that you needn't load an entire file into memory.

```
void EVP_DigestUpdate(EVP_MD_CTX *ctx, const void *buf, unsigned int len);
```

> ctx
>> The context object that is being used to compute a hash.

> buf
>> A buffer containing the data to be included in the computation of the hash.

> len
>> The number of bytes contained in the buffer.

Once all data to be considered for the hash has been passed to EVP_DigestUpdate, the resulting hash value can be retrieved using EVP_DigestFinal.

```
void EVP_DigestFinal(EVP_MD_CTX *ctx, unsigned char *hash, unsigned int *len);
```

> ctx
>> The context object that is being used to compute a hash.

> hash
>> A buffer into which the hash value will be placed. This buffer should always be at least EVP_MAX_MD_SIZE bytes in size.

> len
>> A pointer to an integer that will receive the number of bytes placed into the hash value buffer. This argument may be specified as NULL if you don't want or need to know this value.

Be sure to use `EVP_DigestFinal_ex` with `EVP_DigestInit_ex`, even though the arguments are no different. Once you've called `EVP_DigestFinal` or `EVP_DigestFinal_ex`, the context that you were using is no longer valid and must be re-initialized using `EVP_DigestInit` or `EVP_DigestInit_ex` before it can be used again. Also, be aware that the `EVP_DigestFinal_ex` function can fail.

Example 7-1 shows a function that performs message digests as an all-in-one operation. You pass in the name of an algorithm to use, a buffer of data to hash, an unsigned integer that denotes how much data to take from the buffer, and a pointer to an integer. The integer pointed to by the final argument gets the length of the resulting digest placed in it, and may be `NULL` if you're not interested in its value. The digest value is allocated internal to the function and is returned as a result. If there is any sort of error, such as the specified algorithm not being found, the function returns `NULL`.

Example 7-1. Computing a hash value using the EVP API

```
unsigned char *simple_digest(char *alg, char *buf, unsigned int len, int *olen)
{
    const EVP_MD   *m;
    EVP_MD_CTX     ctx;
    unsigned char *ret;

    OpenSSL_add_all_digests();
    if (!(m = EVP_get_digestbyname(alg)))
        return NULL;
    if (!(ret = (unsigned char *)malloc(EVP_MAX_MD_SIZE)))
        return NULL;
    EVP_DigestInit(&ctx, m);
    EVP_DigestUpdate(&ctx, buf, len);
    EVP_DigestFinal(&ctx, ret, olen);
    return ret;
}
```

Message digests cannot be printed directly because they are binary data. Traditionally, when there's a need to print a message digest, it is printed in hexadecimal. Example 7-2 shows a function that uses `printf` to print an arbitrary binary string in hexadecimal one byte at a time. It takes two parameters, the string, and an integer specifying the length of the string.

Example 7-2. Printing the hexadecimal representation of a hash value

```
void print_hex(unsigned char *bs, unsigned int n)
{
    int i;

    for (i = 0;  i < n;  i++)
        printf("%02x", bs[i]);
}
```

The code in Example 7-3 implements a simple sha1 command that is similar to the md5 command found on many systems. It gives SHA1 digests of files passed in on the command line. If the command is called with no arguments, then the standard input is hashed. Note that you can get the same results by running the command openssl sha1 (see Chapter 2).

Example 7-3. Computing SHA1 hashes of files

```
#define READSIZE 1024

/* Returns 0 on error, file contents on success */
unsigned char *read_file(FILE *f, int *len)
{
    unsigned char *buf = NULL, *last = NULL;
    unsigned char inbuf[READSIZE];
    int tot, n;

    tot = 0;
    for (;;)
    {
        n = fread(inbuf, sizeof(unsigned char), READSIZE, f);
        if (n > 0)
        {
            last = buf;
            buf = (unsigned char *)malloc(tot + n);
            memcpy(buf, last, tot);
            memcpy(&buf[tot], inbuf, n);
            if (last)
                free(last);
            tot += n;
            if (feof(f) > 0)
            {
                *len = tot;
                return buf;
            }
        }
        else
        {
            if (buf)
                free(buf);
            break;
        }
    }
    return NULL;
}

/* Returns NULL on error, the digest on success */
unsigned char *process_file(FILE *f, insigned int *olen)
{
    int             filelen;
    unsigned char *ret, *contents = read_file(f, &filelen);

    if (!contents)
```

Example 7-3. Computing SHA1 hashes of files (continued)

```
        return NULL;
    ret = simple_digest("sha1", contents, filelen, olen);
    free(contents);
    return ret;
}

/* Return 0 on failure, 1 on success */
int process_stdin(void)
{
    unsigned int  olen;
    unsigned char *digest = process_file(stdin, &olen);

    if (!digest)
        return 0;
    print_hex(digest, olen);
    printf("\n");
    return 1;
}

/* Returns 0 on failure, 1 on success */
int process_file_by_name(char *fname)
{
    FILE          *f = fopen(fname, "rb");
    unsigned int  olen;
    unsigned char *digest;

    if (!f)
    {
        perror(fname);
        return 0;
    }
    digest = process_file(f, &olen);
    if (!digest)
    {
        perror(fname);
        fclose(f);
        return 0;
    }
    fclose(f);
    printf("SHA1(%s)= ", fname);
    print_hex(digest, olen);
    printf("\n");
    return 1;
}

int main(int argc, char *argv[])
{
    int i;

    if (argc == 1)
    {
        if (!process_stdin())
```

Example 7-3. Computing SHA1 hashes of files (continued)

```
            perror("stdin");
    }
    else
    {
        for (i = 1;  i < argc;  i++)
            process_file_by_name(argv[i]);
    }
}
```

Using MACs

The OpenSSL library provides only one MAC implementation, HMAC. For this reason, there's no EVP interface to MACs. If all of the data to be MAC'd is available in memory at once (i.e., if you do not need to compute the MAC incrementally), then there is a single call named HMAC (include the header *openssl/hmac.h*) that takes care of everything.

```
unsigned char *HMAC(const EVP_MD *type, const void *key, int keylen,
                    const unsigned char *data, int datalen,
                    unsigned char *hash, unsigned int *hashlen);
```

type
> A message digest to use. See Table 7-1 for a list of digests and functions to obtain a suitable EVP_MD object.

key
> A buffer that contains the key that will be used.

keylen
> The number of bytes in the key buffer that should be used for the key.

data
> A buffer containing the data that an HMAC will be computed for.

datalen
> The number of bytes in the data buffer that should be used.

hash
> A buffer that the computed message digest will be placed in. It should always be at least EVP_MAX_MD_SIZE bytes in length.

hashlen
> A pointer to an integer that will receive the number of bytes of the hash buffer that were filled. This argument may be specified as NULL if you're not interested in this information.

The return value from the HMAC call will be a pointer to the hash buffer. The output buffer, hash, may also be specified as NULL, but we strongly recommend against it. When no output buffer is specified, an internal global buffer will be used. Use of this buffer is not thread-safe.

The key used can be of any size. We recommend your key be as long as any key you're using for a symmetric cipher (preferably 80 bits or more). However, we advise against using the same key for your MAC that you use for encryption. Instead, generate and exchange a second key.

Example 7-4 shows how to use the HMAC call to MAC files specified on the command line using a hardcoded key and the SHA1 digest algorithm. Of course, in a real application, you should be sure to choose a cryptographically strong key (see the function select_random_key from Chapter 6). Do not use the same key for encryption and MACing under any circumstances.

Example 7-4. Computing a MAC with the HMAC function

```
/* Warning: DO NOT USE THIS KEY.  Generate one randomly.  This is for
 * the sake of example only.
 */
static const char key[16] = { 0xff, 0xee, 0xdd, 0xcc, 0xbb, 0xaa, 0x99, 0x88,
                              0x77, 0x66, 0x55, 0x44, 0x33, 0x22, 0x11, 0x00 };

/* Returns 0 on failure, 1 on success */
int HMAC_file_and_print(unsigned char *fname)
{
    FILE          *f = fopen(fname, "rb");
    unsigned char *contents;
    unsigned char result[EVP_MAX_MD_SIZE];
    unsigned int  flen, dlen;

    if (!f)
        return 0;
    contents = read_file(f, &flen);
    fclose(f);
    if (!contents)
        return 0;

    HMAC(EVP_sha1(), key, sizeof(key), contents, flen, result, &dlen);

    printf("HMAC(%s, ", fname);
    print_hex(key, sizeof(key));
    printf(")= ");
    print_hex(result, dlen);
    printf("\n");

    return 1;
}
```

Validating MAC'd data is simple. Simply recompute the hash value and compare it against the transmitted hash value. If they are identical, then the message should not have been modified in transit. Example 7-5 shows a simple function that does a byte-for-byte comparison.

Example 7-5. A binary comparison function

```
/* Return 0 if equal, -1 if unequal */
int binary_cmp(unsigned char *s1, unsigned int len1,
               unsigned char *s2, unsigned int len2)
{
    int i, c, x;

    if (len1 != len2)
        return -1;

    c = len1 / sizeof(x);
    for (i = 0;  i < c;  i++)
    {
        if (*(unsigned long *)(s1 + (i * sizeof(x))) !=
            *(unsigned long *)(s2 + (i * sizeof(x))))
        {
            return -1;
        }
    }
    for (i = c * sizeof(x);  i < len1;  i++)
    {
        if (s1[i] != s2[i])
            return -1;
    }

    return 0;
}
```

If the data to be authenticated needs to be authenticated incrementally, the HMAC API provides a set of methods that works much the same way as the EVP message digest API with the addition of a key parameter.

The one major change that has been made in OpenSSL Version 0.9.7 is that you will need to zero out HMAC contexts explicitly before using them by passing them to HMAC_CTX_init. This function does not exist in previous versions of the library since HMAC_Init previously performed this initialization, although it was undocumented behavior. Once that is done, you can call HMAC_Init (HMAC_Init_ex in 0.9.7), which will properly initialize an HMAC context for use with HMAC_Update and HMAC_Final.

void HMAC_Init(HMAC_CTX *ctx, const void *key, int keylen, const EVP_MD *type);

> ctx
> > The HMAC context object that will be initialized.

> key
> > A buffer containing the key that will be used.

> keylen
> > The number of bytes in the key buffer to be considered valid key data.

> type
> > A message digest object that will be used. See Table 7-1 for a list of functions that return suitable values for this argument.

Once an HMAC context is initialized, it can be used to compute a MAC. Like the EVP API, data is passed incrementally to the `HMAC_Update` function.

```
void HMAC_Update(HMAC_CTX *ctx, const unsigned char *data, int len);
```

ctx
> The HMAC context object that is being used to compute a MAC.

data
> A buffer containing the data that will be MAC'd.

len
> The number of bytes in the data buffer that will be considered valid.

All of the data can be passed to `HMAC_Update` at once, or it can be passed incrementally by calling the function as many times as necessary. Once all of the data that will be MAC'd has been passed into the HMAC context via `HMAC_Update`, calling `HMAC_Final` will compute the MAC and return the hash.

```
void HMAC_Final(HMAC_CTX *ctx, unsigned char *hash, unsigned int *len);
```

ctx
> The HMAC context object that is being used to compute a MAC.

hash
> A buffer that will receive the computed hash value. This should be at least `EVP_MAX_MD_SIZE` bytes in length.

len
> A pointer to an integer that will receive the number of bytes written to the output hash buffer. This argument may be specified as `NULL` if you're not interested in the value.

Once `HMAC_Final` is called, the context must either be cleaned up using `HMAC_cleanup` or reinitialized for reuse. In other words, after a call to `HMAC_Final`, you cannot use the same HMAC context object in a call to `HMAC_Update` or `HMAC_Final` without first reinitializing it. When you are finished with an HMAC context, you should always call `HMAC_cleanup` to properly destroy the context object and free any resources that may be associated with it. `HMAC_cleanup` accepts only a single argument, which is the context object to be destroyed. Example 7-6 demonstrates how to compute a MAC using `HMAC_Init`, `HMAC_Update`, and `HMAC_Final`.

Example 7-6. Computing a MAC using HMAC_Init, HMAC_Update, and HMAC_Final

```
/* Warning: DO NOT USE THIS KEY.  Generate one randomly.  This is for
 * the sake of example only.
 */
static const char key[16] = { 0xff, 0xee, 0xdd, 0xcc, 0xbb, 0xaa, 0x99, 0x88,
                              0x77, 0x66, 0x55, 0x44, 0x33, 0x22, 0x11, 0x00 };

/* Returns 0 on failure, 1 on success */
int HMAC_file_and_print(unsigned char *fname)
{
```

```
FILE         *f = fopen(fname, "rb");
unsigned char *contents;
unsigned char result[EVP_MAX_MD_SIZE];
unsigned int  flen, dlen;
HMAC_CTX      ctx;

if (!f)
    return 0;
contents = read_file(f, &flen);
fclose(f);
if (!contents)
    return 0;

HMAC_Init(&ctx, key, sizeof(key), EVP_sha1());
HMAC_Update(&ctx, contents, flen);
HMAC_Final(&ctx, result, &dlen);
HMAC_cleanup(&ctx);

printf("HMAC(%s, ", fname);
print_hex(key, sizeof(key));
printf(")= ");
print_hex(result, dlen);
printf("\n");

    return 1;
}
```

Other MACs

OpenSSL has direct support only for HMAC, but there are several other kinds of MACs that are easily implemented. Some of the simplest and most useful are based on block ciphers. A large part of why HMAC is so popular is that it uses a cryptographic one-way hash as its underlying cryptographic primitive. A one-way hash was advantageous in the days when it was difficult to export strong cryptography, since true one-way functions were not restricted in any way.

However, MACs based on block ciphers can be compelling. First, such constructions can be faster, because HMAC must perform two hash operations. Second, those looking to keep total code size small will appreciate being able to reuse block cipher code (unless you specifically add the algorithm, the hash function won't get linked in if you don't use it). This advantage is especially appealing to people who wish to push cryptography into hardware.

HMAC does have provable security properties, but so do many cipher-based MACs, such as CBC-MAC, UMAC, and XCBC-MAC. In all cases, security proofs rely on an assumption of security in the underlying cryptographic primitive. For example, HMAC is secure, assuming that the underlying hash algorithm used with it is secure, and UMAC and XCBC-MAC are secure, assuming that the underlying block cipher is secure. It's smart to keep security assumptions to a minimum. For example, if you use a block cipher and a hash function, a break of either is likely to break the entire system. In such a case, your system is only as secure as its weakest link.

CBC-MAC is certainly unencumbered by patents, and XCBC-MAC and XOR-MAC are probably unencumbered. Some of the theoretical work UMAC is based upon might actually be covered by patent, so use it with caution.

CBC-MAC

The simplest MAC based on a block cipher is CBC-MAC. Basically, the message to be processed is encrypted using a block cipher in CBC mode. The authentication value is the last block of the ciphertext, or part thereof. This MAC is secure, assuming that the underlying block cipher is secure, and assuming that a single key processes only messages of a fixed size (the fixed size is calculated after padding is added; padding non-block–aligned messages is necessary).

The primary limitation of CBC-MAC is that it is not parallelizable (also true of HMAC), but this is not a significant issue except in the realm of gigabit networking. Another issue, one shared with all MACs based on block ciphers, is that any party with an authentication key and a resulting value can create new messages that yield the same MAC value. This problem is usually not considered a serious drawback, but if such a problem would be worrisome in a system you are designing, then stick with HMAC.

Many MAC constructions retain their provable security properties when used with a compression function instead of a block cipher. For example, XOR-MACs such as XMCC are frequently used with MD5 as the underlying cryptographic primitive. This can help solve the reversibility problem.

In Example 7-7, we provide a header file for a CBC-MAC implementation, which should be placed in a file named *cbcmac.h*.

Example 7-7. cbcmac.h

```
#ifndef CBC_MAC_H__
#define CBC_MAC_H__

#include <openssl/evp.h>
#include <stdlib.h>

#define CBCMAC_MAX_BYTES 64

typedef struct CBCMAC_CTX_st
{
    EVP_CIPHER_CTX cctx;
    char           cbcstate[CBCMAC_MAX_BYTES];
    char           workspace[CBCMAC_MAX_BYTES];
    short          worklen;
} CBCMAC_CTX;
```

Example 7-7. cbcmac.h (continued)

```
int CBCMAC_Init(CBCMAC_CTX *mctx, EVP_CIPHER *c, const unsigned char *k);
int CBCMAC_Update(CBCMAC_CTX *mctx, const char *data, int len);
int CBCMAC_Final(CBCMAC_CTX *mctx, unsigned char *out, int *outl);
int CBCMAC(EVP_CIPHER *c, const char *key, int key_len,
        unsigned char *str, int sz, unsigned char *out, int *outlen);

#endif
```

The above API is similar to the HMAC API. The context data type is obviously different, and the user is expected to pass in a block cipher object instead of a message digest object. Note that the block cipher must be in ECB mode, even though we're using CBC-MAC. The reason for this is that the above code implements the CBC mode itself, without saving encrypted blocks. Also, simply running a block cipher in CBC mode is not interoperable in cases in which messages need to be padded, because PKCS block cipher padding is different from the standard CBC-MAC padding. In this example, we're using ECB mode to implement a more secure mode of operation, so don't take this use of ECB mode as an endorsement in the general case!

Another difference between the CBC-MAC API and the HMAC API is that CBC-MAC does not require the user to pass in the key length explicitly. The implementation simply reads in the number of bytes that corresponds with the selected cipher.

Note that we recommend using AES when using CBC-MAC, assuming you are using OpenSSL 0.9.7 or later.

Example 7-8 shows the actual implementation of CBC-MAC.

Example 7-8. cbcmac.c

```
#include "cbcmac.h"

int CBCMAC_Init(CBCMAC_CTX *mctx, EVP_CIPHER *c, const unsigned char *k)
{
    int i, bl;

    EVP_EncryptInit(&(mctx->cctx), c, (unsigned char *)k, 0);
    if (EVP_CIPHER_CTX_mode(&(mctx->cctx)) != EVP_CIPH_ECB_MODE)
        return -1;
    mctx->worklen = 0;
    bl = EVP_CIPHER_CTX_block_size(&(mctx->cctx));
    for (i = 0;  i < bl;  i++)
        mctx->cbcstate[i] = 0;
    return 0;
}

/* We hand implement CBC-mode because of the requirements for the last block,
 * and to avoid dynamic memory allocation.
 */
int CBCMAC_Update(CBCMAC_CTX *mctx, const char *data, int len)
{
    int bl, i, n = 0, outl;
```

Example 7-8. cbcmac.c (continued)

```
    bl = EVP_CIPHER_CTX_block_size(&(mctx->cctx));

    if (mctx->worklen)
    {
        n = bl - mctx->worklen;
        if (n > len) /* Not enough bytes passed in to fill block buffer. */
        {
            for (i = 0;  i < len;  i++)
                mctx->workspace[mctx->worklen + i] = data[i];
            mctx->worklen += len;
            return 0;
        }
        else
        {
            for (i = 0;  i < n;  i++)
                mctx->workspace[mctx->worklen + i] = data[i] ^ mctx->cbcstate[i];
            EVP_EncryptUpdate(&(mctx->cctx), mctx->cbcstate, &outl,
                            mctx->workspace, bl);
        }
    }
    while (n < len)
    {
        for (i = 0;  i < bl;  i++)
            mctx->workspace[i] = data[n + i] ^ mctx->cbcstate[i];
        n = n + bl;
        EVP_EncryptUpdate(&(mctx->cctx), mctx->cbcstate, &outl,
                        mctx->workspace, bl);
    }
    mctx->worklen = len - n;
    for (i = 0;  i < mctx->worklen;  i++)
        mctx->workspace[i] = data[n + i];
    return 0;
}

int CBCMAC_Final(CBCMAC_CTX *mctx, unsigned char *out, int *outl)
{
    int i, bl = EVP_CIPHER_CTX_block_size(&(mctx->cctx));

    /* Pad with null bytes if necessary. In reality, we just copy in the
     * CBC state, since x ^ 0 = x.
     */
    if (mctx->worklen)
    {
        for (i = mctx->worklen;  i < bl;  i++)
            mctx->workspace[i] = mctx->cbcstate[i];
        EVP_EncryptUpdate(&(mctx->cctx), out, outl, mctx->workspace, bl);
    }
    else
    {
        for (i = 0;  i < bl;  i++)
            out[i] = mctx->cbcstate[i];
        *outl = bl;
    }
}
```

Example 7-8. cbcmac.c (continued)

```
    return 0;
}

int CBCMAC(EVP_CIPHER *c, const char *key, int key_len, unsigned char *str,
        int sz, unsigned char *out, int *outlen)
{
    CBCMAC_CTX x;
    int        e;

    if ((e = CBCMAC_Init(&x, c, key)))
        return e;
    if ((e = CBCMAC_Update(&x, str, sz)))
        return e;
    return CBCMAC_Final(&x, out, outlen);
}
```

XCBC-MAC

Black and Rogaway developed a simple modification to CBC-MAC that can process
varying length messages with a single key, called XCBC-MAC. The basic idea is to
run CBC-MAC as normal until it comes time to encrypt the last block. Before that
encryption occurs, one of two supplemental keys is XOR'd into the "plaintext,"
depending on the message length. This MAC is not noticeably slower than CBC-
MAC, since it requires only a single additional XOR operation. Example 7-9 demonstrates XCBC-MAC.

Example 7-9. xcbcmac.h

```
#ifndef XCBC_MAC_H__
#define XCBC_MAC_H__

#include <openssl/evp.h>
#include <stdlib.h>

#define XCBC_MAX_BYTES   32

typedef struct XCMAC_CTX_st
{
    EVP_CIPHER_CTX cctx;
    char           dk1[XCBC_MAX_BYTES];
    char           dk2[XCBC_MAX_BYTES];
    char           dk3[XCBC_MAX_BYTES];
    char           cbcstate[XCBC_MAX_BYTES];
    char           workspace[XCBC_MAX_BYTES];
    short          worklen;
    short          started;
} XCMAC_CTX;

int XCMAC_Init(XCMAC_CTX *mctx, EVP_CIPHER *c, const unsigned char *k);
int XCMAC_Update(XCMAC_CTX *mctx, const char *data, int len);
int XCMAC_Final(XCMAC_CTX *mctx, unsigned char *out, int *outl);
```

Example 7-9. xcbcmac.h (continued)

```
int XCMAC(EVP_CIPHER *c, const char *key, unsigned char *str, int sz,
          unsigned char *out, int *outlen);

#endif
```

Example 7-9 shows an API for XCBC-MAC, which is implemented in Example 7-10. The API is identical to our CBC-MAC API, with the exception of a different context type.

While XCBC-MAC uses three keys, it generates them from a single master key. The derived keys are computed by encrypting three fixed values with the original key, one value for each derived key. The output of each encryption is the same size as the cipher's block length. That's fine for the second two derived keys, because they are simply XOR'd into blocks of data. However, a single block may not be long enough for the first derived key because it is used in the block cipher, which may require a key that is longer than the block size.

The only specified instance of XCBC-MAC we've seen to date uses AES with 128-bit keys and 128-bit blocks, which obviously don't have this problem. The original description of XCBC-MAC describes what to do at a high level. Basically, you just perform more encryptions with the master key until enough data is generated. The only trick is that you need to use a unique plaintext for each encryption. In our implementation below, we allow for equal block and key sizes, as well as the common cases in which key length is twice the block length. Attempting to use any other block cipher will cause an error to be returned. When run with unequal block sizes and key sizes, this implementation is not guaranteed to interoperate with any other implementation you may find.

Example 7-10. xcbcmac.c

```
#include "xcbcmac.h"

/* These are recommended by Rogaway. */
static char g1[XCBC_MAX_BYTES] =
{
    0x01, 0x01, 0x01, 0x01, 0x01, 0x01, 0x01, 0x01, 0x01, 0x01, 0x01, 0x01, 0x01,
    0x01, 0x01, 0x01, 0x01, 0x01, 0x01, 0x01, 0x01, 0x01, 0x01, 0x01, 0x01, 0x01,
    0x01, 0x01, 0x01, 0x01, 0x01, 0x01
};

static char g2[XCBC_MAX_BYTES] =
{
    0x02, 0x02, 0x02, 0x02, 0x02, 0x02, 0x02, 0x02, 0x02, 0x02, 0x02, 0x02, 0x02,
    0x02, 0x02, 0x02, 0x02, 0x02, 0x02, 0x02, 0x02, 0x02, 0x02, 0x02, 0x02, 0x02,
    0x02, 0x02, 0x02, 0x02, 0x02, 0x02
};

static char g3[XCBC_MAX_BYTES] =
{
```

Example 7-10. xcbcmac.c (continued)

```
        0x03, 0x03, 0x03, 0x03, 0x03, 0x03, 0x03, 0x03, 0x03, 0x03, 0x03, 0x03, 0x03,
        0x03, 0x03, 0x03, 0x03, 0x03, 0x03, 0x03, 0x03, 0x03, 0x03, 0x03, 0x03, 0x03,
        0x03, 0x03, 0x03, 0x03, 0x03, 0x03
};

/* This is the extra plaintext for when generating the second half of a key
 * when the block size is half the key length.
 */
static char g4[XCBC_MAX_BYTES] =
{
        0x04, 0x04, 0x04, 0x04, 0x04, 0x04, 0x04, 0x04, 0x04, 0x04, 0x04, 0x04, 0x04,
        0x04, 0x04, 0x04, 0x04, 0x04, 0x04, 0x04, 0x04, 0x04, 0x04, 0x04, 0x04, 0x04,
        0x04, 0x04, 0x04, 0x04, 0x04, 0x04
};

int XCMAC_Init(XCMAC_CTX *mctx, EVP_CIPHER *c, const unsigned char *k)
{
    EVP_CIPHER_CTX tctx;
    int           i, outl, bl, kl;

    EVP_EncryptInit(&tctx, c, (unsigned char *)k, 0);

    kl = EVP_CIPHER_CTX_key_length(&tctx);
    bl = EVP_CIPHER_CTX_block_size(&tctx);

    if (kl != bl && bl * 2 != kl)
        return -1;
    EVP_EncryptUpdate(&tctx, mctx->dk1, &outl, g1, bl);

    if (kl != bl)
        EVP_EncryptUpdate(&tctx, &(mctx->dk1[bl]), &outl, g4, bl);
    EVP_EncryptUpdate(&tctx, mctx->dk2, &outl, g2, bl);
    EVP_EncryptUpdate(&tctx, mctx->dk3, &outl, g3, bl);

    EVP_EncryptInit(&(mctx->cctx), c, mctx->dk1, 0);

    if (EVP_CIPHER_CTX_mode(&(mctx->cctx)) != EVP_CIPH_ECB_MODE)
        return -2;

    mctx->worklen = 0;
    mctx->started = 0;
    for (i = 0; i < bl; i++)
        mctx->cbcstate[i] = 0;
    return 0;
}

int XCMAC_Update(XCMAC_CTX *mctx, const char *data, int len)
{
    int bl, i, n = 0, outl;

    if (!len)
        return 0;
```

Example 7-10. xcbcmac.c (continued)

```
    bl = EVP_CIPHER_CTX_block_size(&(mctx->cctx));
    for (i = 0;  i < len;  i++)
    {
        if (!mctx->worklen && mctx->started)
            EVP_EncryptUpdate(&(mctx->cctx), mctx->cbcstate, &outl,
                              mctx->workspace, bl);
        else
            mctx->started = 1;
        mctx->workspace[mctx->worklen] = data[n++] ^ mctx->cbcstate[mctx->worklen];
        mctx->worklen++;
        mctx->worklen %= bl;
    }
    return 0;
}

int XCMAC_Final(XCMAC_CTX *mctx, unsigned char *out, int *outl)
{
    int i, bl = EVP_CIPHER_CTX_block_size(&(mctx->cctx));

    if (!mctx->started)
        return -1;
    if (mctx->worklen)
    {
        /* Pad and XOR with K2, then encrypt */
        mctx->workspace[mctx->worklen] = 0x90 ^ mctx->cbcstate[mctx->worklen];
        for (i = mctx->worklen + 1;  i < bl;  i++)
            mctx->workspace[i] = mctx->cbcstate[mctx->worklen]; /* ^ 0 */
        for (i = 0;  i < bl;  i++)
            mctx->workspace[i] ^= mctx->dk2[i];
    }
    else
    {
        /* XOR with K3, then encrypt. */
        for (i = 0;  i < bl;  i++)
            mctx->workspace[i] ^= mctx->dk3[i];
    }
    EVP_EncryptUpdate(&(mctx->cctx), out, outl, mctx->workspace, bl);
    return 0;
}

int XCMAC(EVP_CIPHER *c, const char *key, unsigned char *str, int sz,
          unsigned char *out, int *outlen)
{
    XCMAC_CTX x;
    int       e;

    if ((e = XCMAC_Init(&x, c, key)))
        return e;
    if ((e = XCMAC_Update(&x, str, sz)))
        return e;
    return XCMAC_Final(&x, out, outlen);
}
```

Note that the padding scheme in the above implementation of XCBC-MAC is different from the one used by CBC-MAC, which pads to the nearest block length with null bytes. The one used here is the one that is recommended by the algorithm's authors and is used in other implementations. In this scheme, the pad is all zeros, except for the first bit, which is set to one.

XOR-MAC

XOR MACs are a family of message authentication algorithms that are based on a block cipher and are highly parallelizable, and thus suitable for authenticating traffic on a gigabit network. If you're not worried about potential parallelism, then you should probably use one of the other MACs we discuss in this chapter.

There are two specified XOR-MACs. The only one we have seen used is XMACC, which uses counter mode encryption. We provide a sequential implementation of this algorithm on the book's web site.

UMAC

UMAC is an incredibly fast MAC based on the mathematical concept of universal functions. It is provably secure if the underlying block cipher used by the algorithm is secure. UMAC is not parallelizable, but an implementation running on a current high-end processor can handle over half a gigabyte of data per second.

The IETF IPSec working group is considering adopting it as a standard, but its adoption is being held up due to potential intellectual property problems. The authors of UMAC have released any claims they have to intellectual property on that algorithm, but, as of this writing, there is significant concern that there may be a patent covering some of the underlying primitives. If that turns out to be the case, using UMAC would potentially require paying a licensing fee. If you do use this algorithm, be attentive to its status, and change quickly if you are unwilling to license. As we learn new information about this topic, we will update the book's web site.

See the UMAC home page for more information and reference code: *http://www.cs. ucdavis.edu/~rogaway/umac/*.

Secure HTTP Cookies

Let's pull our knowledge of symmetric cryptography and message authentication codes together in a real application, namely setting cookies over HTTP in a user's web browser from a server-side application. Web cookies are implemented by setting a value in the MIME header sent to the client in a server response. If the client accepts the cookie, then it will present the cookie back to the server every time the specified conditions are met.

A single MIME header is a header name followed by a colon, a space, and then the header value. The format of the header value depends on the header name. In this example, we're concerned with only two headers: the Set-Cookie header, which can be sent to the client when presenting a web page, and the Cookie header, which the client presents to the server when the user browses to a site for which a cookie is stored.

Let's consider an example in which we want to keep track of some history of the user's activity on our site, but we don't want the user to look at or modify the data. To do this, we should place a cookie on the user's machine that contains the history information. If this will be done in plaintext, we might send the following MIME header:

```
Set-Cookie: history=231337+13457;path=/
```

The path variable specifies the root page in the domain from which the cookie came. The cookie will be sent with a page request only if it is rooted under the specified path. In the above instance, the client will return this cookie to any page in the same domain. For the purposes of our example, our cookies will not persist. That is, once the user shuts down his browser, the cookies will be gone forever.

The problem with the above cookie is that the user can see and modify the contents. Instead, we should store two cookies, one containing the encrypted history information, and a second containing a MAC of the history information. The server does encoding and such when setting a cookie, then decrypts and validates whenever the cookie comes back. The server does not share its keys with any other entity—it alone uses them to ensure data has not been read or modified since it originally left the server.

It doesn't really matter if we use a MAC computed over the ciphertext or the plaintext. The primary difference between the two is that MACing the encrypted text would allow a third party with the MAC key to authenticate message integrity without being able to read the actual message. If you have no use for this feature, and you're at all afraid of the MAC key being stolen, then MAC the plaintext. You can even concatenate the MAC to the plaintext and encrypt everything.

One important thing when using MACs with encryption: you should never use the same key for encryption as for MACing. Indeed, in the following example, we will MAC the plaintext with one key, and encrypt the plaintext with a second key. Each result will be sent in its own cookie. The first will be called encrypted-history, and the second will be called history-mac.

The problem we encounter is that we can use only a limited character set in cookie headers, yet the output of our cryptographic algorithms is always binary. To solve this problem, we encode the binary data into the base64 character set. The base64 character set uses the uppercase letters, the lowercase letters, the numbers, and a few pieces of punctuation to represent data. Out of necessity, the length of data grows considerably when base64 encoded. We can use the EVP function EVP_EncodeBlock for base64 encoding to suit our purposes.

Example 7-11 shows part of a server-side infrastructure for setting these cookies. We assume that there is a single server process running continually that maintains state such as the global MAC key and the global encryption key. Our example produces the entire MIME-formatted cookie, but does not write the cookie into an actual message.

Example 7-11. Encrypting data for storage in a cookie

```
#include <stdio.h>
#include <string.h>
#include <openssl/evp.h>
#include <openssl/hmac.h>

#define MAC_KEY_LEN 16

static char bf_key[EVP_MAX_KEY_LENGTH];
static char iv[EVP_MAX_BLOCK_LENGTH] = {0,}; /* #define EVP_MAX_BLOCK_LENGTH
                                              * to 64 for OpenSSL 0.9.6c and
                                              * earlier.
                                              */
static char mac_key[MAC_KEY_LEN];

/* A helper function for base64 encoding */
unsigned char *base64_encode(unsigned char *buf, unsigned int len)
{
    unsigned char *ret;
    unsigned int  b64_len;

    /* the b64data to data ratio is 3 to 4.
     * integer divide by 3 then multiply by 4, add one for NULL terminator.
     */
    b64_len = (((len + 2) / 3) * 4) + 1;
    ret = (unsigned char *)malloc(b64_len);
    EVP_EncodeBlock(ret, buf, len);
    ret[b64_len - 1] = 0;
    return ret;
}

void init_keys(void)
{
    RAND_pseudo_bytes(bf_key, EVP_MAX_KEY_LENGTH);
    RAND_pseudo_bytes(mac_key, MAC_KEY_LEN);
}

static unsigned char *encrypt_input(unsigned char *inp, int *len)
{
    EVP_CIPHER_CTX ctx;
    unsigned char  *res = (unsigned char *)malloc(strlen(inp) +
                                          EVP_MAX_BLOCK_LENGTH);
    unsigned int    tlen;

    EVP_EncryptInit(&ctx, EVP_bf_cbc(), bf_key, iv);
    EVP_EncryptUpdate(&ctx, res, &tlen, inp, strlen(inp));
    *len = tlen;
```

Example 7-11. Encrypting data for storage in a cookie (continued)

```
        EVP_EncryptFinal(&ctx, &res[tlen], &tlen);
        *len += tlen;
        return res;
}

static char *fmt = "Set-Cookie: encrypted-history=%s;path=/\r\n"
                   "Set-Cookie: history-mac=%s;path=/\r\n";

char *create_cookies(char *hist)
{
        unsigned int  ctlen;  /* Length of cipher text in binary */
        unsigned int  maclen; /* Length of HMAC output in binary */
        unsigned char rawmac[EVP_MAX_MD_SIZE];
        unsigned char *buf, *ct, b64_hist, *b64_mac;

        /* Enough room for everything. */
        buf = (unsigned char *)malloc(strlen(fmt) + (strlen(hist) * 4) / 3 + 1 +
                                     (EVP_MAX_MD_SIZE * 4) / 3 + 1);
        ct = encrypt_input(hist, &ctlen);
        HMAC(EVP_sha1( ), mac_key, MAC_KEY_LEN, hist, strlen(hist), rawmac, &maclen);

        b64_hist = base64_encode(ct, ctlen);
        b64_mac  = base64_encode(rawmac, maclen);
        sprintf(buf, fmt, b64_hist, b64_mac);

        free(b64_mac);
        free(b64_hist);
        return buf;
}
```

The function init_keys should be called once at startup. The keys remain valid until the server is restarted. The function create_cookies takes the history string as an input, then dynamically allocates a string into which properly formatted, base64-encoded text is placed. That string is returned as the result from create_cookies. The server uses 128-bit Blowfish in CBC mode as the cipher, and HMAC-SHA1 for message authentication.

In Example 7-12, we show how to take the cookie data, remove the base64 encoding, decrypt the ciphertext, and authenticate the result. The function decrypt_and_auth takes the raw base64-encoded strings for the encrypted history string and the MAC value (not the full cookie—we assume the relevant data has been parsed out, for simplicity's sake), along with a pointer to an unsigned integer, into which the length of the decrypted results will be written. We recalculate the MAC, comparing against the returned one. The function returns the decrypted value on success, and NULL on error.

Example 7-12. Decrypting data stored in a cookie

```
unsigned char *base64_decode(unsigned char *bbuf, unsigned int *len)
{
        unsigned char *ret;
        unsigned int  bin_len;
```

Example 7-12. Decrypting data stored in a cookie (continued)

```
    /* integer divide by 4 then multiply by 3, its binary so no NULL */
    bin_len = (((strlen(bbuf) + 3) / 4) * 3);
    ret = (unsigned char *)malloc(bin_len);
    *len = EVP_DecodeBlock(ret, bbuf, strlen(bbuf));
    return ret;
}

static unsigned char *decrypt_history(unsigned char *ctext, int len)
{
    EVP_CIPHER_CTX ctx;
    unsigned int    tlen, tlen2;
    unsigned char   *res = (unsigned char *)malloc(len + 1);

    EVP_DecryptInit(&ctx, EVP_bf_cbc( ), bf_key, iv);
    EVP_DecryptUpdate(&ctx, res, &tlen, ctext, len);
    EVP_DecryptFinal(&ctx, &res[tlen], &tlen2);
    res[tlen + tlen2] = 0;
    return res;
}

unsigned char *decrypt_and_auth(unsigned char *b64_hist, unsigned char *b64_mac)
{
    unsigned char *ctext, *mac1, *res, mac2[EVP_MAX_MD_SIZE];
    unsigned int  mac1len, mac2len, ctextlen;

    if (!(ctext = base64_decode(b64_hist, &ctextlen)))
        return NULL;
    if (!(mac1 = base64_decode(b64_mac, &mac1len)))
    {
        free(ctext);
        return NULL;
    }

    res = decrypt_history(ctext, ctextlen);
    HMAC(EVP_sha1( ), mac_key, MAC_KEY_LEN, res, strlen(hist), mac2, &mac2len);
    if (binary_cmp(mac1, mac1len, mac2, mac2len))
    {
        free(res);
        res = NULL;
    }

    free(mac1);
    free(ctext);

    return res;
}
```

Note that when you are using this infrastructure for cookie encryption, you should place a user ID and potentially a sequence number at the beginning of any text that you encrypt, then check those on decryption. Doing so will help prevent capture-replay and dictionary attacks.

## CHAPTER 8

Public Key Algorithms

In the previous chapters, we discussed almost all of the algorithms used by the SSL protocol that make it secure. The one remaining class of algorithms is public key cryptography, which is an essential element of protocols like SSL, S/MIME, and PGP.

Depending on the algorithm employed, public key cryptography is useful for key agreement, digital signing, and encryption. Three commonly used public key algorithms are supported by OpenSSL: Diffie-Hellman (DH), DSA (Digital Signature Algorithm), and RSA (so named for its inventors, Rivest, Shamir, and Adleman). It's important to realize that these algorithms are not interchangeable. Diffie-Hellman is useful for key agreement, but cannot be used for digital signatures or encryption. DSA is useful for digital signatures, but is incapable of providing key agreement or encryption services. RSA can be used for key agreement, digital signing, and encryption.

Public key cryptography is expensive. Its strength is in the size of its keys, which are usually very large numbers. As a result, operations involving public key cryptography are slow. Most often, it is used in combination with other cryptographic algorithms such as message digests and symmetric ciphers.

Knowing when to use public key cryptography and how to combine it securely with other cryptographic algorithms is important. We'll begin with a discussion of when it is appropriate to use public key cryptography, and when it isn't. We'll continue our discussion of public key cryptography by introducing each of the three algorithms supported by OpenSSL. For each one, we'll discuss what they can and cannot do, as well as provide some examples of how to access their functionality at a low level. In addition, we'll discuss how they can be used together to compliment each other. Finally, we'll revisit our discussion of the EVP interface from Chapters 6 and 7, demonstrating how the interface can also be used with public key algorithms, which should be the preferred method, as long as it suits your needs.

When to Use Public Key Cryptography

Suppose that we want to create a secure communications system in which a group of people can send messages to one another. Using symmetric encryption, such a system can be easily devised. Everyone in the group agrees on a key to use when encrypting messages to each other. While this system provides data secrecy by limiting access to the messages to only those people in the group, it also has some serious drawbacks. For example, Alice cannot send a message to Bob without Charlie also being able to read it. Additionally, Charlie could forge a message so that it appears to have come from someone else in the group—or even worse, he could change a message that someone else sent.

In order to stop the threat of forgery or message corruption, we need to have some way to authenticate and verify the integrity of messages. At the same time, we need to provide for more granularity in encryption to allow private messages between individuals in the group. With symmetric encryption, these goals can be met by having each of our users share a unique key with each of the other users. With three members of the group, Alice, Bob, and Charlie, this would mean Alice has an Alice-Bob key and an Alice-Charlie key. When she receives a message from either Bob or Charlie, she decrypts it with the appropriate key, and if she recovers a message, she has authenticated the sender. Charlie is no longer able to forge or change a message from Alice to Bob because he does not have the Alice-Bob key.

While alleviating the original problems, we've managed to create new ones. The biggest problem is that this new system does not scale very well. If Dave is introduced into the group, he would need to agree on different keys to use with Alice, Bob, and Charlie. Every time that a new person joins the group, n-1 keys need to be created, in which n is the number of people now in the group. With 100 people in the group, there would have to be 4,950 different keys! Imagine, then, what would happen if Bob's computer was broken into and all of his keys were compromised. New keys would now have to be created for Bob to communicate with everyone else in the group. Finally, this system does not provide *non-repudiation*. Non-repudiation prevents either party involved in a communication from denying involvement in that communication. For example, Alice could receive a message from Bob encrypted with the Alice-Bob key, but Bob can credibly deny ever sending it by claiming Alice fabricated the message and encrypted it herself; non-repudiation guarantees that this is not possible.

The use of public key cryptography solves each of these problems, but it does not do so all by itself. It must be combined properly with message digests and symmetric encryption. Not only does public key cryptography tend to scale well, it also allows us to negotiate keys online, authenticate communications, maintain data integrity, and provide non-repudiation. Whenever any of these things is one of your goals, you should turn to public key cryptography for a solution.

Public key cryptography is not a magical solution to all things cryptographic. It can often be better and clearer not to use public key algorithms. As an example, in Chapter 7, we discussed storing data in a cookie. We used a symmetric cipher to encrypt the data and a MAC to maintain its integrity. It was not our intention to share the information with anyone, but only to protect it from prying eyes and tampering. In such a situation, the algorithms that we used were the right tools for the job. By themselves, they were able to do what was required. Had we used public key cryptography, we still would have required the use of a symmetric cipher and a message digest, in addition to requiring a private and public key. Using public key cryptography would have only introduced an unnecessary layer of complexity and required significantly more processing power from the server.

Because public key cryptography also depends on other cryptographic algorithms to be secure, if those algorithms can be used securely without public key cryptography, then you shouldn't be using public key cryptography. It may seem as though we're stating the obvious. All too often, inexperienced programmers tend to treat public key cryptography as though it was the one and only solution to all of their cryptographic needs. The fact of the matter is public key cryptography is frequently overkill for most situations. It's all about choosing the right tool for the job.

Diffie-Hellman

The Diffie-Hellman algorithm was the first public key algorithm ever invented. Introduced in 1976 by Whitfield Diffie and Martin Hellman, it is a simple algorithm that allows two parties to agree upon a key using an unsecured channel. In other words, it allows a shared secret to be created. The process is sometimes referred to as *key exchange*, but with Diffie-Hellman, it is more accurately called *key agreement*.

The primary use of Diffie-Hellman is shared-secret negotiation. The algorithm itself can be made to provide for authentication, but OpenSSL doesn't include any high level interfaces for using these features, so they must be implemented by the application if they're desired. For this reason, most OpenSSL applications that use this algorithm will also use another for authentication. For our purposes, we will discuss Diffie-Hellman mainly from the perspective of key agreement. Interested readers should refer to RFC 2631 for more information on using it for authentication.

Diffie-Hellman guarantees a shared secret will be created that is suitable to use as the key to a symmetric algorithm. Failing to provide authentication through some other means, either with authenticated extensions to the implementation or through use of another algorithm such as DSA, leaves the protocol susceptible to man-in-the-middle attacks. We'll discuss the details of this type of attack with regard to Diffie-Hellman toward the end of this section.

The Basics

The low-level interface to Diffie-Hellman provided by OpenSSL consists of a structure of the type DH and a set of functions that operate on that structure. The DH structure and functions are made accessible by including the *openssl/dh.h* header file. The DH structure itself contains many data members that are of little or no interest to us, but four members are important, as shown in the following abbreviated DH structure definition:

```
typedef struct dh_st
{
    BIGNUM *p;
    BIGNUM *g;
    BIGNUM *pub_key;
    BIGNUM *priv_key;
} DH;
```

The p and g members, known as Diffie-Hellman parameters, are public values that must be shared between the two parties using the algorithm to create a shared secret. Because they're public values, no harm will come from a potential attacker discovering them, which means that they can be agreed upon beforehand or exchanged over an insecure medium. Typically, one side of the conversation generates the parameters and shares them with the peer.

The p member is a prime number that is randomly generated. For temporary keys, it is typically at least 512 bits in length, whereas persistent keys should more appropriately be at least 1,024 bits. These sizes correspond to the notion of ephemeral and static keys presented in Chapter 5. The prime that will be used for p is generated such that (p-1)/2 is also prime. Such a prime is known as a *safe* or *strong prime*. The g member, also known as the *generator*, is usually a small number greater than one. OpenSSL functions best when this number is either two or five. A value of two is sometimes used for performance reasons, but keep in mind that faster key generation also means that an attacker can break the algorithm faster. In general, we recommend that a value of five be used.

Using the two public parameters, p and g, each pair chooses a random large integer for the priv_key member. A value for the pub_key member is computed from the priv_key member and shared with the peer. It is important that only the value of the pub_key member be shared. The value of the priv_key member should never be shared.

Using the values of priv_key and the peer's pub_key, each peer can independently compute the shared secret. The shared secret is suitable for use as the key for a symmetric cipher. The entire exchange between the peers can be done over an insecure medium. Even if someone captures the parameter and key exchange, the attacker will not be able to determine the shared secret.

Generating and Exchanging Parameters

Diffie-Hellman requires that both parties involved in the key exchange use the same parameters to generate public keys. This means the parameters either need to be agreed upon and exchanged before the conversation begins, or the parameters must be generated and exchanged as part of the key exchange. Either way, the parameters must first be generated by one party and given to the other, or perhaps generated by a third party and given to both. For the purposes of this discussion, we will assume that the generation of the parameters will be done as part of the key exchange process, although this is often not desirable because it can take a significant amount of time to generate the parameters.

The participants in the key agreement must first agree which party will be responsible for generating the parameters that they'll both use. In a client/server scenario, the parameters are usually generated by the server. Often, the server will generate the parameters when it starts up or retrieve them from a file that contains already generated parameters, and use the same parameters for each client that connects. It is also common for both the client and server to have a copy of the parameters built into the respective applications.

OpenSSL provides the function DH_generate_parameters, which will create a new DH object that is initialized with fresh values for p and g. The generation of the parameters generates a value only for p. The value of g is specified by the caller and is not chosen randomly by OpenSSL. The value of g should be a small number greater than one, usually either two or five.

```
DH *DH_generate_parameters(int prime_len, int generator,
                           void (*callback)(int, int, void *), void *cb_arg);
```

prime_len
> The size of the prime to be generated, specified in terms of bits.

generator
> The value to be used for g. In general, either DH_GENERATOR_2 or DH_ GENERATOR_5 should be used for this argument.

callback
> A pointer to a function that will be called during the prime generation process to report the status of the prime generation. The callback is the same as the callback used by BN_generate_prime, which we discussed in Chapter 4. In fact, DH_generate_parameters uses BN_generate_prime, and it is BN_ generate_prime that actually makes the calls to the callback function. This argument may be specified as NULL if no callbacks are desired.

cb_arg
> A pointer to application-specific data. OpenSSL does not use this value for anything itself. It is used only when passed as an argument to the specified callback function.

Using the generation function alone can be dangerous. While the generation function does have validity checks for the prime that it generates, it could generate a prime that is not suitable for use with the algorithm. For this reason, the function DH_check should always be used to ensure that the generated prime is suitable.

```
int DH_check(DH *dh, int *codes);
```

> dh
>
>> The DH object containing the parameters we wish to check.
>
> codes
>
>> An integer that will be treated as a bit mask by DH_check and will contain the results of the check when the function returns successfully.

If the function encounters an error unrelated to the validity of the generated prime, the return will be zero; otherwise, it will be nonzero. When the function returns successfully, the codes argument will contain a bit mask that indicates whether the parameters are suitable for use or not. If none of the bits is set, the parameters should be considered suitable for use. If any of the following bits are set, the parameters may not be suitable for use. In most cases, the parameters should be thrown away, and new ones should be generated.

DH_CHECK_P_NOT_PRIME

> If this bit is set, it indicates that the generated prime is not actually a prime number. Ordinarily, this bit should never be set when the parameters are generated using DH_generate_parameters, but it could very well be set when checking parameters retrieved from disk or from a peer.

DH_CHECK_P_NOT_SAFE_PRIME

> If this bit is set, it indicates that the generated prime is not safe. That is, (p-1)/2 is not also a prime number. As with DH_CHECK_P_NOT_PRIME, this bit should never be set when the parameters were generated using DH_generate_parameters, but it could very well be set when checking parameters retrieved from disk or from a peer.

DH_NOT_SUITABLE_GENERATOR

> If this bit is set, it indicates that the generated prime and the generator are not suitable for use together. The parameters don't necessarily need to be thrown away and regenerated if this bit is set. Instead, the generator could be changed and the check retried.

DH_UNABLE_TO_CHECK_GENERATOR

> If this bit is set, a nonstandard generator is being used, so the DH_check function is unable to check to see that the prime and the generator are suitable for use. If you know that you've set a nonstandard generator intentionally, it's up to you to decide whether it is safe to ignore this bit being set or not.

Once the parameters have been generated, they can be transmitted to the peer. The details of how the data is sent depend on the medium that is being used for the exchange. To transmit the parameters over a TCP connection, the BIGNUM functions BN_bn2bin and BN_bin2bn are obvious candidates.

The party that generates the parameters calls DH_generate_parameters to obtain a DH object. The party that is receiving the parameters must also obtain a DH object. This is easily done by calling the function DH_new, which will allocate and initialize a new DH object. The parameters that are received from the peer can then be directly assigned to the DH object's p and g data members, using the appropriate BIGNUM functions.

When we're done with a DH object, we must be sure to destroy it by calling the function DH_free, and passing the pointer returned by either DH_generate_parameters or DH_new as the only argument.

Computing Shared Secrets

Now that parameters have been generated and received by the two peers, each peer must generate a key pair and exchange their public keys. Remember that the private key must not be shared at all. Once this is done, each peer can independently compute the shared secret, and the algorithm will have done its job. With authenticated Diffie-Hellman, the public/private key pairs can persist beyond usage for a single key-agreement. In these cases, we must be wary of a special class of attack against Diffie-Hellman, which is discussed at the end of this section.

OpenSSL provides the function DH_generate_key for generating public and private keys. It requires as its only argument a DH object that has the parameters, p and g, filled in. If the keys are generated successfully, the return from the function will be nonzero. If an error occurs, the return will be zero.

Once the keys have been generated successfully, each peer must exchange their public key with the other peer. The details of how to exchange the value of the public key varies depending on the medium that is being used, but in a typical case in which the communication is taking place over an established TCP connection, the functions BN_bn2bin and BN_bin2bn will once again work for the exchange of the DH object's pub_key data member.

With the parameters and public key now exchanged, each party in the exchange can use his own private key and the peer's public key to compute the shared secret using the function DH_compute_key.

```
int DH_compute_key(unsigned char *secret, BIGNUM *pub_key, DH *dh);
```
    secret
        A buffer that will be used to hold the shared secret. It must be allocated by
        the caller and should be big enough to hold the secret. The number of bytes
        required to hold the secret can be determined with a call to DH_size, passing
        the DH object as the only argument.

pub_key

> The peer's public key.

dh

> The DH object that contains the parameters and the caller's private key.

After the shared secret is computed, the DH object is no longer needed unless more secrets will be generated and exchanged. It can be safely destroyed using the DH_free function.

In certain cases, Diffie-Hellman can be subject to a type of attack known as a *small-subgroup attack*. This attack results in a reduction of the computational complexity of brute-forcing the peer's private key value. Essentially, a small-subgroup attack can result in the victim's private key being discovered. There are several different methods of protecting Diffie-Hellman against this type of attack. The simplest method is to use ephemeral keying. If both parties stick to ephemeral keying and use a separate method of authentication, small-subgroup attacks are thwarted. This isn't always feasible, however, mostly due to computational expense. If static keys will be used, two simple mathematical checks can be performed on the public key received from a peer to ensure these attacks aren't possible. If the key passes both tests, it's safe to use. The first test verifies that the supplied key is greater than 1 and less than the value of the p parameter. The second test computes $y^q \bmod p$, in which y is the key to test and q is another large prime. If the result of this operation is 1, the key is safe; otherwise, it is not. The q parameter is not generated by OpenSSL even though there is a placeholder for it in the DH structure. An algorithm for generating q can be found in RFC 2631. If you're interested in the other methods or more detailed information on the attack, we recommend that you read RFC 2785.

Practical Applications

When we began our discussion of Diffie-Hellman, we mentioned that it provides key agreement and authentication. Use of the authentication features of this protocol is not very common; thus, pairing Diffie-Hellman with another algorithm for authentication is often done. The threat is that mistakenly leaving out authentication can lead to susceptibility to man-in-the-middle attacks. To execute such an attack, the attacker sits in between two hosts that are trying to communicate and intercepts all of the messages. For example, suppose that Alice and Bob plan to use Diffie-Hellman to make a shared secret. Charlie could intercept all messages from Alice to Bob and all messages from Bob to Alice. From this position, Charlie can agree upon a key with Alice and a different key with Bob. When the attacker receives a message from Alice, he decrypts it with the key he negotiated with her and reads the message. He can then encrypt the message using the key he negotiated with Bob and pass it along to him. Alice and Bob will believe that they're communicating securely. They'll be completely unaware that Charlie is eavesdropping and worse, possibly even altering their messages, inserting forged messages, or not passing the messages along at all.

To alleviate this problem, Diffie-Hellman should always be used with some method of authentication, most commonly from another algorithm. This is accomplished by authenticating the messages containing public values for the Diffie-Hellman agreement. Using signatures, each party would exchange their public keys to use for signing before the conversation begins, and then sign the public value before sending it. The details will be explained in the following section.

Digital Signature Algorithm (DSA)

The DSA algorithm was developed by the National Institute for Standards and Testing (NIST) and the National Security Agency (NSA). It was first proposed in 1991 and stirred up a significant amount of controversy. Finally, in 1994, it became a standard. As its name implies, the DSA algorithm is useful for computing digital signatures, but that is the only thing for which it can be used. It is not capable of providing key agreement or encryption without extension.

Using a private key, the user can compute a signature for an arbitrary piece of data. Anyone possessing the public key that corresponds to the private key used to compute a signature can then verify that signature. The algorithm works in conjunction with the Secure Hash Algorithm (SHA). Essentially, the hash of the data to be signed is computed, and the hash is actually signed, rather than the data itself. The public key that corresponds to the private key used to compute a digital signature can then be used to obtain the hash of the data from the signature. This hash is compared with the hash computed by the party verifying the signature. If they match, the data is considered authentic. If they don't match, the data is not identical to the data that was originally signed.

A digital signature is useful for verifying the integrity of data, ensuring that it has not been corrupted or tampered with. It also provides non-repudiation since only one person should have access to the private key used to compute a signature. The utility of a digital signature when combined with a key exchange algorithm such as Diffie-Hellman is easy to see. If the two parties performing a key exchange trust that the public key actually belongs to the party with which they're communicating, a digital signature can be used to prevent a man-in-the-middle attack.

The Basics

Similar to the low-level interface to Diffie-Hellman, the low-level interface to DSA provided by OpenSSL consists of a DSA structure and a set of functions that operate on that structure. The DSA structure and functions are made accessible by including the *openssl/dsa.h* header file. The DSA structure itself contains many data members that are of little or no interest to us, but five members are important, as shown in the following abbreviated DSA structure definition:

```
typedef struct dsa_st
{
    BIGNUM *p;
    BIGNUM *q;
    BIGNUM *g;
    BIGNUM *pub_key;
    BIGNUM *priv_key;
} DSA;
```

The p, q, and g members, known as DSA parameters, are public values that must be generated before a key pair can be generated. Because they're public values, no harm will come if a potential attacker discovers them. The same parameters can be safely used to generate multiple keys. In fact, RFC 2459 specifies a mechanism in which DSA parameters for a certificate can be inherited from the certificate of the issuer. Using parameter inheritance not only reduces the size of certificates, it also enforces the sharing of parameters.

The p member is a prime number that is randomly generated. Initially, the proposed standard fixed the length of the prime at 512 bits. Due to much criticism, this was later changed to allow a range between 512 and 1,024 bits. The length of the prime must be a multiple of 64 bits, however. OpenSSL does not enforce the 1,024-bit upper bound, but it's not a good idea to use a prime larger than 1,024 bits—many programs may not be able to use the keys that result from such a large prime. The q member is a prime factor of p-1. The value of q must also be exactly 160 bits in length. The g member is the result of a mathematical expression involving a randomly chosen integer, as well as p and q.

Using the three public parameters (p, q, and g), the public and private keys can be computed. Public parameters used to compute the keys are required to generate or verify a digital signature. The parameters must therefore be exchanged along with the public key in order for the public key to be useful. Of course, the private key should never be distributed.

Generating Parameters and Keys

Like Diffie-Hellman, DSA requires generation of parameters before keys can be generated. Once a set of parameters is generated, many keys can be created from it. This does not mean that only people with keys created from the same parameters can interoperate; it simply means that in order to do so, all of the parameter values must be included as part of the public key.

The interface for generating DSA parameters is similar to the interface for generating Diffie-Hellman parameters. The function DSA_generate_parameters will create a new DSA object that is initialized with fresh values for p, q, and g. Generation of DSA parameters is more complex than Diffie-Hellman parameter generation, although it is typically much faster, especially for large key lengths.

```
DSA * DSA_generate_parameters(int bits, unsigned char *seed, int seed_len,
                              int *counter_ret, unsigned long *h_ret,
                              void (*callback)(int, int, void *), void *cb_arg);
```

bits
> The size of the prime to be generated, specified in terms of bits. Remember that the maximum allowed by the standard is 1,024 bits.

seed
> An optional buffer containing data that gives the function a starting point to begin looking for primes. This argument can be specified as NULL, and generally should be.

seed_len
> The number of bytes contained in the seed buffer. If the seed buffer is specified as NULL, this argument must be specified as 0.

counter_ret
> An optional argument that will receive the number of iterations the function went through to find primes that satisfy the requirements for p and q. This argument may be specified as NULL.

h_ret
> An optional argument that will receive the number of iterations the function went through to find a value for h, which is the random number used to calculate g. This argument may be specified as NULL.

callback
> A pointer to a function that will be called during the prime generation process to report the status of the prime generation. The callback is the same as the callback used by BN_generate_prime, which we discussed in Chapter 4. This argument may be specified as NULL if no callbacks are desired.

cb_arg
> A pointer to application-specific data. OpenSSL does not use this value for anything itself. It is passed as an argument to the specified callback function.

Once parameters have been generated, key pairs can be generated. The function DSA_generate_key is provided by OpenSSL for doing just that. It requires as its only argument a DSA object that has the parameters p, q, and g filled in. If the keys are generated successfully, the return from the function will be nonzero. If an error occurs, the return will be zero. The generated public and private keys are stored in the supplied DSA object's pub_key and priv_key members, respectively.

Once the keys are computed, they can be used for creating digital signatures and verifying them. The DSA object containing the parameters and keys must remain in memory to perform these operations, of course, but when the DSA object is no longer needed, it should be destroyed by calling DSA_free and passing the DSA object as its only argument.

Signing and Verifying

Digital signatures must be computed over a message digest of the data that will be signed. The DSA standard dictates that the message digest algorithm used for this is SHA1, which has output of the same size as the DSA q parameter. This is no coincidence. In fact, the DSA algorithm cannot be used to compute a signature for data that is larger than its q parameter.

OpenSSL provides a low-level interface for computing signatures that does allow you to use DSA to sign arbitrary data. By this, we mean that OpenSSL does not enforce the requirement to use SHA1 as the message digest to sign, or even to sign a message digest at all! We strongly recommend against using the low-level interface for signing and verifying in favor of using the EVP interface, which we describe later in this chapter. However, we will briefly cover the three low-level functions for creating and verifying DSA signatures.

Computing a digital signature can be a processor-intensive operation. For this reason, OpenSSL provides a function that allows for the pre-computation of the portions of a signature that do not actually require the data to be signed.

```
int DSA_sign_setup(DSA *dsa, BN_CTX *ctx, BIGNUM **kinvp, BIGNUM **rp);
```

dsa

> The DSA object containing the parameters and private key that will be used for signing.

ctx

> An optional BIGNUM context that will be used in the pre-computation. If this argument is specified as NULL, a temporary context will be created and used internally.

kinvp

> Receives a dynamically allocated BIGNUM that will hold the pre-computed kinv value. This value can then be placed into the DSA object's kinv member so that it will be used when signing.

rp

> Receives a dynamically allocated BIGNUM that will hold the pre-computed r value. This value can then be placed into the DSA object's r member so that it will be used when signing.

Care must be taken when pre-computing the kinv and r values for signing. Both values must be placed in the DSA object. If only one is placed in the object, the memory used by the other will be leaked. Additionally, the values cannot be reused. They will be destroyed by the signing function. It may seem tempting to save a copy of the pre-computed values and reuse them for signing multiple pieces of data, but you must not. An integral part of a DSA signature is a 160-bit (actually, the same size as the q parameter, but that should always be 160 bits) random number known as k. If the same value for k is used more than once, it is possible for an attacker to discover the private key.

The function DSA_sign is provided for actually computing a digital signature using the DSA algorithm. If pre-computation of kinv and r has not been done, the function will perform the computation itself.

```
int DSA_sign(int type, const unsigned char *dgst, int len,
             unsigned char *sigret, unsigned int *siglen, DSA *dsa);
```

type
>   Ignored for DSA signing. The argument is present only for consistency with the RSA signing function.

dgst
>   The buffer of data that will be signed, which should always be an SHA1 hash.

len
>   The number of bytes in the data buffer for signing. It should always be the length of the message digest, but can never be larger than the size of the q parameter, which is fixed at 160 bits or 20 bytes.

sigret
>   A buffer that will receive the signature. It must be large enough to hold the signature. The minimum size for the buffer can be determined with a call to DSA_size, passing the DSA object that is being used for signing as the only argument.

siglen
>   Receives the number of bytes of the sigret buffer that were filled with the signature. This argument cannot be NULL.

dsa
>   The DSA object to use to sign the contents of the data buffer.

The function DSA_verify is used to verify signatures and is similar to the function used to create them.

```
int DSA_verify(int type, const unsigned char *dgst, int len,
               unsigned char *sigbuf, int siglen, DSA *dsa);
```

type
>   Ignored for DSA verification. The argument is present only for consistency with the RSA verification function.

dgst
>   The message digest of the data. This digest should be computed on the data prior to calling this function. This is used to compare with the digest in the signature.

len
>   The number of bytes in the digest buffer.

sigbuf
> The signature that will be verified.

siglen
> The number of bytes contained in the signature buffer.

dsa
> The DSA object to use to verify the signature.

Practical Applications

DSA does not provide a mechanism for key agreement. It cannot create a shared secret for us, whereas an algorithm such as Diffie-Hellman can. Thus, it is common to employ a protocol that uses Diffie-Hellman and DSA to deliver *two-way authentication*.

First, we need to establish that the client and server each have a public/private key pair and can exchange public keys offline, prior to beginning secure communications. At the same time, we need to assume they agree upon parameters for Diffie-Hellman key agreement. Overall, these assumptions are not egregious. A protocol might begin with each party computing public and private Diffie-Hellman keys. At this point, instead of sending that unauthenticated data to the opposite end, each party will sign the message containing the public value with their own private DSA key. After this is done, they can send the signed messages.

The value of that signature is that it assures both parties that the public keys actually came from their respective peer because only the server has the server's private key, and only the client has the client's private key. If both parties can verify the signature on the public key they've received, they can be sure that there is no man-in-the-middle. What we've just described is known as two-way authentication, because each party independently verifies the other.

RSA

Invented in 1977, RSA was the first public key algorithm capable of both digitally signing and encrypting data. Despite the fact that it was patented, it became the de facto public key algorithm. Almost any company that used public key cryptography in their products licensed the technology. It was patented only in the United States, and the patent expired on September 20, 2000.

Like other public key algorithms, RSA employs a public and private key pair. Although the mathematics behind the algorithm are easy to understand, we won't discuss them here. Many other texts explain the algorithm in detail. For our purposes, it is sufficient to say that the algorithm's strength lies in the infeasibility of factoring extremely big numbers, and after 25 years of extensive cryptanalysis, it remains unbroken.

The Basics

Just like the low-level interfaces to Diffie-Hellman and DSA, the low-level interface to RSA provided by OpenSSL consists of an RSA structure and a set of functions that operate on that structure. The RSA structure and functions are made accessible by including the *openssl/rsa.h* header file. The RSA structure itself contains many data members that are of little or no interest to us, but five members are important, as shown in the following abbreviated RSA structure definition:

```
typedef struct rsa_st
{
    BIGNUM *p;
    BIGNUM *q;
    BIGNUM *n;
    BIGNUM *e;
    BIGNUM *d;
} RSA;
```

The p and q members are both randomly chosen large prime numbers. These two numbers are multiplied together to obtain n, which is known as the public modulus. References to the strength of RSA actually refer to the bit length of the public modulus. Once the private key has been computed, p and q may be discarded, but they should never be disclosed. However, keeping the values for p and q around is a good idea; having them available increases the efficiency with which private key operations are performed.

The e member, also known as the public exponent, should be a randomly chosen integer such that it and (p-1)(q-1) are *relatively prime*. Two numbers are relatively prime if they share no factors other than one; they may or may not actually be prime. The public exponent is usually a small number, and in practice, is usually either 3 or 65,537 (also referred to as Fermat's F4 number). Using e, p, and q, the value of d is computed.

Together, the n and e members are the public key, and the d member is the private key.

Generating Keys

The RSA algorithm does not require parameters to generate keys, which makes key generation a much simpler affair. OpenSSL provides a single function to create a new RSA key pair, which will create a new RSA object that is initialized with a fresh key pair.

```
RSA *RSA_generate_key(int num, unsigned long e,
                void (*callback)(int, int, void *), void *cb_arg);
```

num

> Specifies the number of bits in the public modulus. The minimum this should be to ensure proper security is 1,024 bits, though we recommend 2,048 bits.

e

The value to use for the public exponent. OpenSSL does not attempt to generate this value randomly, but instead requires you to specify it. You may specify any number you like, but we recommend that you use one of the two constants, RSA_3 or RSA_F4.

callback

A pointer to a function that will be called during the prime generation process to report the status of the prime generation. The callback is the same as the callback used by BN_generate_prime, which we discussed in Chapter 4. This argument may be specified as NULL if no callbacks are desired.

cb_arg

A pointer to application-specific data. OpenSSL does not use this value for anything itself. It is used only when passed as an argument to the specified callback function.

Once keys are generated, it is a good idea to call RSA_check_key to verify that the keys generated by RSA_generate_key are actually usable. The function requires an RSA object as its only argument. The RSA object should be completely filled in, including values for its p, q, n, e, and d members. If the return value from the function is 0, it indicates that there is a problem with the keys, and that they should be regenerated. If the return value from the function is 1, it indicates that all tests passed, and that the keys are suitable for use. If the return value from the function is –1, an error occurred in performing the tests.

When the RSA key is no longer needed, it should be freed by calling RSA_free and passing the RSA object as its only argument.

Data Encryption, Key Agreement, and Key Transport

Now that we've explored key setup, we can look at the different methods of using those keys. The RSA algorithm allows for secrecy because it can encrypt data. Data encrypted with a public key can be decrypted only by an entity possessing the corresponding private key.

Before looking at the specifics of these operations, we must first discuss *blinding*. Any RSA operation involving a private key is susceptible to timing attacks. Given an RSA operation as a black box that we feed data into and collect results from, an attacker can discern information about our key material by measuring the amount of time it takes the various operations to complete. Blinding is essentially a change in the implementation that removes any correlation between the amount of time taken for an operation and the private key value.

The function RSA_blinding_on enables blinding for the RSA object passed into it as the first argument. This means that any operation on the RSA object involving the private key will be guarded from timing attacks. The second argument is an optional BN_CTX object, which may be specified as NULL. Likewise, the function RSA_blinding_off disables blinding for the RSA object passed into it. If you ever design a system that allows arbitrary operations on a private key, such as any system that automatically signs data, enabling blinding is important for the safety of the private key.

With RSA, it is most common to perform encryption with a public key and decryption with the corresponding private key. The functions RSA_public_encrypt and RSA_private_decrypt provide the means to perform these operations. It is also possible to perform encryption with a private key and decryption with the corresponding public key. Two functions, RSA_private_encrypt and RSA_public_decrypt, are provided by OpenSSL. They're intended for those who wish to implement signing at a very low level. In general, they should be avoided. Each of the four functions returns the number of bytes, including padding, that were encrypted or decrypted, or −1 if an error occurs.

```
int RSA_public_encrypt(int flen, unsigned char *from, unsigned char *to,
                       RSA *rsa, int padding);
```

flen
Specifies the number of bytes in the buffer to be encrypted.

from
A buffer containing the data to be encrypted.

to
A buffer that will be used to hold the encrypted data. It should be large enough to hold the largest possible amount of encrypted data, which can be determined by calling RSA_size and passing the RSA object that is being used to encrypt as its only argument.

rsa
The RSA object that contains the public key to use to perform the encryption.

padding
Specifies which of the built-in padding types supported by OpenSSL should be used when padding is necessary.

```
int RSA_private_decrypt(int flen, unsigned char *from, unsigned char *to,
                        RSA *rsa, int padding);
```

flen
Specifies the number of bytes of data in the buffer to be decrypted.

from
A buffer containing the data to be decrypted.

to
A buffer that will be used to hold the decrypted data. It should be large enough to hold the largest possible amount of decrypted data, which can be determined by calling RSA_size and passing the RSA object that is being used to decrypt as its only argument.

rsa

> The RSA object that contains the private key to use to perform the decryption.

padding

> Specifies which of the built-in padding types supported by OpenSSL was used when the data was encrypted. The padding for decryption must be the same as the padding used for encryption.

The encryption performed by RSA requires that the data to be encrypted be appropriately formed. If the data to be encrypted does not fit the requirements, it must be padded. OpenSSL supports several types of padding for RSA encryption:

RSA_PKCS1_PADDING

> If this type of padding is used, the length of the data to be encrypted must be smaller than RSA_size(rsa)-11. This is an older method of padding that has since been replaced by RSA_PKCS1_OAEP_PADDING. It should be used only for compatibility with older applications.

RSA_PKCS1_OAEP_PADDING

> If this type of padding is used, the length of the data to be encrypted must be smaller than RSA_size(rsa)-41. This type of padding is the recommended method for all new applications.

RSA_SSLV23_PADDING

> This type of padding is an SSL-specific modification to the RSA_PKCS1_PADDING type. Under normal circumstances, this type of padding is rarely used.

RSA_NO_PADDING

> This disables automatic padding by the encryption function, and assumes that the caller will perform the padding. It requires that the data to be encrypted is exactly RSA_size(rsa) bytes.

Signing and Verifying

As with DSA, RSA computes signatures over a chunk of data by first cryptographically hashing the data to obtain a digest value. This digest and the signer's private key are then used as input to the signing process. Verification can be performed by executing the same hash and using this digest value along with the signature value and the signing party's public key.

```
int RSA_sign(int type, unsigned char *m, unsigned int m_len,
             unsigned char *sigret, unsigned int *siglen, RSA *rsa)
```

type

> The message digest algorithm that obtains the cryptographic hash of the data to be signed. The algorithm is specified using NID_sha1 for SHA1, NID_ripemd160 for RipeMD-160, or NID_md5 for MD5.

m

> A buffer containing the data to be signed.

m_len

> The number of bytes in the data buffer that will be considered in the signature.

sigret

> A buffer that will receive the signature. It must be big enough to hold the largest possible signature, which can be determined with a call to RSA_size, passing the RSA object being used to sign as its only argument.

siglen

> Receives the number of bytes that were written to the signature buffer. This argument must not be NULL.

rsa

> The RSA object containing the private key to use to sign the data.

You will notice that the signature of the function is identical to the DSA signing function; however, the arguments are interpreted differently. The same is true for the signature verification function.

```
int RSA_verify(int type, unsigned char *m, unsigned int m_len,
               unsigned char *sigbuf, unsigned int siglen, RSA *rsa);
```

type

> The message digest algorithm used to obtain the cryptographic hash of the data that will be verified. The algorithm specified must be the same that was used to compute the signature that will be verified.

m

> A buffer containing the data that was signed and is to be verified.

m_len

> Specifies the number of bytes contained in the data buffer that will be considered.

sigbuf

> A buffer containing the signature to be verified.

siglen

> Specifies the number of bytes contained in the signature buffer.

rsa

> The RSA object containing the public key to use to verify the signature.

Practical Applications

It may be tempting to consider implementing a system in which we rely solely on RSA for secrecy. This is actually not a good idea for a variety of reasons, but most importantly because RSA is very slow compared to symmetric ciphers. Additionally, because we can encrypt only small chunks of data at a time with RSA keys alone, the best use for RSA's data encryption capabilities is for key exchange. There are several ways that RSA can be used in this manner.

One-way authenticating key transport

> The client chooses a random session key, encrypts it with the server's public key, and sends the encrypted data to the server. The server decrypts the message and recovers the session key. As with Diffie-Hellman, this shared secret can then be used with a symmetric cipher. This protocol is slightly better than Diffie-Hellman, though, because there is one-way authentication. The client has authenticated the server since no other party could have recovered the session key. This feature allows a party that knows someone's public key to compose an encrypted message for that person without any direct communication at the time of composition.

Two-way authenticating key transport

> Essentially, the client takes the same steps as in the protocol above, but before sending the message to the server, it signs the message. This way, the server can verify the signature using the client's public key, thus authenticating the client, and recover a session key. The client has authenticated the server because no other party could recover that session key.

Two-way authenticating key agreement

> Both the client and the server choose random data to use as key material, encrypt it with the opposite party's public key, sign the message with their own private key, and send the data to the opposite party. Because both parties have signed their messages, each one can authenticate the other. Additionally, each party has their own secret random number and the other party's number. Each party can then combine the two numbers in some well-known way, generally by XOR or by hashing the concatenation of the data, to obtain the shared secret.

While we've scratched the surface of the theory involved in designing secure protocols, we advise against trying to design your own, because doing it correctly and securely is very hard. Using a well-known and verifiably secure protocol such as SSL or TLS is highly recommended for all but academic situations.

The EVP Public Key Interface

In Chapters 6 and 7, we discussed OpenSSL's EVP interface, which is a high-level layer of abstraction that can be used with message digests and symmetric ciphers. It probably won't surprise you to learn that the interface can also be used with two of the public key algorithms that we've discussed in this chapter, DSA and RSA. Two sets of functions are provided for digital signatures and data encryption. They work very much like the functions that we've discussed in previous chapters.

The two new sets of EVP functions require the use of an EVP_PKEY object, used to hold the public or private key that is required. An EVP_PKEY object is therefore simply a container that can hold either a DSA or an RSA object. Actually, an EVP_PKEY object can also hold a DH object, but since Diffie-Hellman can be used only for key agreement, the EVP interface cannot actually make use of a DH object. With this in mind, we will limit our discussion to DSA and RSA keys.

An EVP_PKEY object is created by calling the EVP_PKEY_new function, which will return either a new EVP_PKEY object or NULL if an error occurred. Conversely, an EVP_PKEY object is destroyed by calling the EVP_PKEY_free function, passing the EVP_PKEY object to be destroyed as its only argument. When an EVP_PKEY object is first created, it is an empty container. Obviously, this is not very useful.

Two functions, EVP_PKEY_assign_DSA and EVP_PKEY_assign_RSA, are used to populate the EVP_PKEY object with either a DSA object or an RSA object. Each function requires exactly two arguments. The first is the EVP_PKEY object to assign to, and the second is the key object to be assigned. Once you assign a key object to an EVP_PKEY object, that object becomes "owned" by the EVP_PKEY object. In other words, the EVP_PKEY object takes responsibility for destroying the key object. You should never attempt to destroy a key object once it has been assigned to an EVP_PKEY object. An EVP_PKEY object can hold only a single object at a time; if you assign it multiple objects, the last one you assign to it is the one that it will contain, and all of the previous assignments will be destroyed.

Alternatively, either EVP_PKEY_set1_DSA or EVP_PKEY_set1_RSA can be used to populate the EVP_PKEY object with either a DSA object or an RSA object. The functions' signatures are identical to EVP_PKEY_assign_DSA and EVP_PKEY_assign_RSA. The difference between the two is that these two functions do not cause the EVP_PKEY object to assume ownership of the assigned key object. Instead, the key object's reference count is incremented when it is assigned, and decremented when it would otherwise be destroyed.

It is also possible to obtain a pointer to the key object contained by an EVP_PKEY object. If you know the type of key object the EVP_PKEY object contains, you can use the appropriate function for the key type, either EVP_PKEY_get1_DSA or EVP_PKEY_get1_RSA. These two functions increment the reference count on the key object that is returned, so you must be sure to call either DSA_free or RSA_free as appropriate when you're done with the object. If you don't know the type of key object the EVP_PKEY object contains, the function EVP_PKEY_type will return either EVP_PKEY_DSA or EVP_PKEY_RSA.

Signing and Verifying

The EVP interface provides a means to create and verify digital signatures using either DSA or RSA keys. Creating a digital signature requires a private key, while verifying one requires the public key that corresponds to the private key used to create the signature. When a digital signature is created for a piece of data, that same data is required to verify the signature.

The first step in creating a digital signature using the EVP interface is to initialize an EVP_MD_CTX object, discussed in Chapter 6. An EVP_MD_CTX object can be allocated dynamically using malloc or new, or it can be allocated statically as either a global or a local variable. In either case, EVP_SignInit must be called to initialize the object.

```
int EVP_SignInit(EVP_MD_CTX *ctx, const EVP_MD *type);
```

ctx
> The EVP_MD_CTX to be initialized.

type
> The message digest to use to compute the hash, which is actually signed instead of the data itself. The message digest is specified the same as the message digest is specified in a call to EVP_DigestInit. If you're using an RSA key for signing, you may choose from EVP_md2, EVP_md4, EVP_md5, EVP_sha1, EVP_mdc2, and EVP_ripemd160. If you're using a DSA key for signing, you must use EVP_dss1.

The "engine" release and Version 0.9.7 of OpenSSL deprecate the EVP_SignInit function. Instead, EVP_SignInit_ex should be used, which adds a third argument. The additional argument is a pointer to an engine object that has been initialized. It may also be specified as NULL, which causes the default software implementation to be used.

Once a context has been initialized, the data to be signed must be fed into it. This is done by calling EVP_SignUpdate as many times as necessary to feed in all the data. The function works identically to EVP_DigestUpdate and, in fact, is actually implemented as a preprocessor macro that simply calls EVP_DigestUpdate.

```
int EVP_SignUpdate(EVP_MD_CTX *ctx, const void *buf, unsigned int len);
```

ctx
> Specifies the context that is being used. It should be initialized using EVP_SignInit or EVP_SignInit_ex.

buf
> A buffer that contains the data to be signed. For each call to EVP_SignUpdate for the same context, the data from this buffer is concatenated with the data specified in previous calls.

len
> Specifies the number of bytes of data contained in the data buffer.

Once all of the data to be signed has been added into the context, the signature can be computed. This is done by calling EVP_SignFinal. Once EVP_SignFinal has been called, the context is no longer valid, and must be reinitialized with EVP_SignInit or EVP_SignInit_ex before it can be used to create another signature. Note that this does not mean that a dynamically allocated context object has been freed. OpenSSL has no way of knowing whether the context object was dynamically allocated or not, so it is up to the caller to free that memory as appropriate.

```
int EVP_SignFinal(EVP_MD_CTX *ctx, unsigned char *sig, unsigned int *siglen,
                  EVP_PKEY *pkey);
```

ctx
> The initialized context that contains the data to be signed.

sig
> A buffer that will receive the signature. This buffer must be large enough to hold the largest possible signature. The function EVP_PKEY_size can be used to find out how large the buffer must be. It requires a single argument, which is the EVP_PKEY object that will be used to compute the signature.

siglen
> Receives the number of bytes written into the signature buffer. This value must not be NULL, even if you're not interested in the information. Normally, this value is the same as the return from EVP_PKEY_size.

pkey
> The EVP_PKEY object that will be used to compute the signature. It must contain either a DSA or an RSA private key.

EVP_SignFinal will return zero if an error occurred in computing the signature, and nonzero if the signature computed successfully.

Verifying a signature is as simple as computing one. The set of functions to verify a signature match the functions to compute a signature, save for their names. Before a signature can be verified, a context must be initialized by calling EVP_VerifyInit. The "engine" release and Version 0.9.7 of OpenSSL deprecate EVP_VerifyInit in favor of EVP_VerifyInit_ex, which requires a third argument that is an engine object or NULL to use the default software implementation of the chosen message digest algorithm.

```
int EVP_VerifyInit(EVP_MD_CTX *ctx, const EVP_MD *type);
```

ctx
> The context object that will be initialized.

type
> The message digest algorithm to use. The message digest used for verification must be the same that was used for creating the signature that will be verified.

With an initialized context, EVP_VerifyUpdate should be called as many times as necessary to supply the context with all of the data that was purportedly used to create the signature. The data for verifying a signature should be the same data used to create the signature. If the signature and the data do not match, the verification will fail. This, of course, is the whole point of a digital signature—to verify that the data is intact and has not been modified in any way.

```
int EVP_VerifyUpdate(EVP_MD_CTX *ctx, const void *buf, unsigned int len);
```

ctx
> The context object that was initialized with EVP_VerifyInit or EVP_VerifyInit_ex.

buf
> A buffer that contains the data to be verified.

len
> Specifies the number of bytes contained in the data buffer.

Once all of the data has been passed into the context along with EVP_VerifyUpdate, EVP_VerifyFinal must be called to perform the actual verification of the signature. Its signature matches that of EVP_SignFinal, but its arguments and return value are interpreted differently.

```
int EVP_VerifyFinal(EVP_MD_CTX *ctx, unsigned char *sigbuf,
                    unsigned int siglen, EVP_PKEY *pkey);
```

ctx
> The initialized context that contains the data to be signed.

sigbuf
> A buffer containing the signature to be verified.

siglen
> Specifies the number of bytes contained in the signature buffer.

pkey
> The EVP_PKEY object that will be used to verify the signature. It must contain either a DSA or an RSA public key. The key should match the private key that was used to create the signature.

EVP_VerifyFinal will return −1 if an error occurs in verifying the signature. If the signature does not match the data, the return value will be 0, and if the signature is valid, the return value will be 1.

Encrypting and Decrypting

The EVP interface also provides an interface for enveloping data using RSA keys. *Data enveloping* is the process of encrypting a chunk of data with RSA, typically for securely sending it to a recipient. Initially, it may seem that enveloping is equivalent to using RSA to encrypt all of our data, but this is not correct. Because public key algorithms are inappropriate for encrypting large amounts of data, enveloping requires the sender to generate a random key, also called a session key, and encrypt that key using the public key of the intended recipient. The actual data is then encrypted with a symmetric cipher using the session key. Incorrectly implementing this process often causes bugs or vulnerabilities in programs. To avoid this, OpenSSL provides features in the EVP interface referred to as the "envelope" encryption/decryption interface that handles all of the subtleties correctly.

One of the features offered by the EVP interface for data encryption is the ability to encrypt the same data using several public keys. A single session key is generated and encrypted using each public key that is supplied. The recipients can then use their respective private keys to decrypt the session key, and thus decrypt the data using the appropriate symmetric cipher. The support for this feature is wholly contained by the context initialization function, which means the interface for encrypting for multiple recipients is the same as encrypting for a single recipient.

The act of encrypting data using a public key through the EVP interface is called sealing. A set of functions, EVP_SealInit, EVP_SealUpdate, and EVP_SealFinal, are provided to encrypt an arbitrary amount of data. Each of these functions requires an EVP_CIPHER_CTX object to maintain state. This object can be allocated either dynamically or statically and must be initialized prior to use. Initialization of the context object is achieved by calling EVP_SealInit. Unlike the other EVP context initialization functions that we've discussed, EVP_SealInit has not been deprecated in the "engine" release or Version 0.9.7 of OpenSSL.

```
int EVP_SealInit(EVP_CIPHER_CTX *ctx, EVP_CIPHER *type,
                 unsigned char **ek, int *ekl, unsigned char *iv,
                 EVP_PKEY **pubk, int npubk);
```

ctx

> The context to be initialized.

type

> The symmetric cipher used to perform the actual encryption. A large number of symmetric ciphers and variations are supported by OpenSSL; we don't list all of the options here. Chapter 6 discusses the supported ciphers in detail and provides a comprehensive list of suitable options for this argument.

ek

> An array of buffers. There must be as many elements allocated for the array as there are public keys specified for encryption. Each element in the array is a buffer that must be large enough to hold the encrypted session key. The size required for each buffer can be determined by calling EVP_PKEY_size, passing the EVP_PKEY object for each buffer as its only argument.

ekl

> An array that will receive the actual encrypted key length for each public key. Again, there must be as many elements allocated for the array as there are public keys specified for encryption.

iv

> A buffer that contains the initialization vector to use. If not specified as NULL, the initialization vector buffer should contain at least as many bytes as

defined by the constant `EVP_MAX_IV_LENGTH`. Not all ciphers require an initialization vector. For such ciphers, this argument can be specified as `NULL`.

pubk

> An array of public keys to use to encrypt the randomly generated session key. Each element in the array should be an `EVP_PKEY` object that contains an RSA public key.

npubk

> Specifies the number of public keys contained in the `pubk` array. It also determines the size requirements for the ek and ekl arrays.

Example 8-1 demonstrates how to call `EVP_SealInit`.

Example 8-1. Calling EVP_SealInit

```
ek = (unsigned char **)malloc(sizeof(unsigned char *) * npubk);
ekl = (int *)malloc(sizeof(int) * npubk);
pubk = (EVP_PKEY **)malloc(sizeof(EVP_PKEY *) * npubk);

for (i = 0;  i < npubk;  i++)
{
    pubk[i] = EVP_PKEY_new( );
    EVP_PKEY_set1_RSA(pubk[i], rsakey[i]);
    ek[i] = (unsigned char *)malloc(EVP_PKEY_size(pubk[i]));
}

EVP_SealInit(ctx, type, ek, ekl, iv, pubk, npubk);
```

Once initialization has been performed, the remainder of the sealing process is very much like encrypting with a symmetric cipher, as described in Chapter 6. In fact, it is identical, with the exception of the names of the functions that are used. The initialization function takes care of generating the session key and encrypting it using the public key of each recipient. It also prepares the context to perform the encryption of the actual data using the selected symmetric cipher.

```
int EVP_SealUpdate(EVP_CIPHER_CTX *ctx, unsigned char *out, int *outl,
                   unsigned char *in, int inl);
```

ctx

> The context previously initialized by `EVP_SealInit`.

out

> A buffer that will receive the encrypted data. Refer to Chapter 6 for the details of how to compute the size of this buffer.

outl

> Receives the number of bytes written to the encrypted data buffer.

in

> A buffer that contains the data to be encrypted.

inl

> Specifies the number of bytes contained in the unencrypted data buffer.

After the data to be encrypted has been fed into `EVP_SealUpdate`, `EVP_SealFinish` must be called to finish the job. It will perform any necessary padding and write any remaining encrypted data into its output buffer. Once `EVP_SealFinish` has been called, `EVP_SealInit` must be called again before the context can be reused.

```
int EVP_SealFinal(EVP_CIPHER_CTX *ctx, unsigned char *out, int *outl);
```

> ctx
>> The context previously initialized by `EVP_SealInit`. Used by `EVP_SealUpdate` to encrypt data.

> out
>> A buffer that will receive any final encrypted data.

> outl
>> Receives the number of bytes written to the encrypted data buffer.

When the seal process is complete, the encrypted session key, initialization vector (if any), and encrypted data must all be sent to the recipient in order for the recipient to decrypt the data successfully. The recipient can then use the EVP interface to unseal or open (decrypt) the data.

The function `EVP_OpenInit` initializes a context for decryption. Like `EVP_SealInit`, it has not been deprecated by the "engine" release or Version 0.9.7 of OpenSSL.

```
int EVP_OpenInit(EVP_CIPHER_CTX *ctx, EVP_CIPHER *type, unsigned char *ek,
                 int ekl, unsigned char *iv, EVP_PKEY *pkey);
```

> ctx
>> The context object that will be initialized.

> type
>> The symmetric cipher to use to decrypt the data. It should be the same cipher that was used to encrypt the data.

> ek
>> A buffer containing the public key–encrypted session key.

> ekl
>> Specifies the number of bytes contained in the encrypted session key buffer.

> iv
>> A buffer containing the initialization vector that was used with the symmetric cipher to encrypt the data.

> pkey
>> An `EVP_PKEY` object that contains an RSA private key that will be used to decrypt the session key.

Initializing the context decrypts the session key and prepares the context for decrypting the data using the specified symmetric cipher. The rest of the process is identical to decrypting data that has been encrypted with a symmetric cipher, i.e., the functions

EVP_OpenUpdate and EVP_OpenFinal are identical to the functions EVP_DecryptUpdate and EVP_DecryptFinal in every way, except for their names.

```
int EVP_OpenUpdate(EVP_CIPHER_CTX *ctx, unsigned char *out, int *outl,
                   unsigned char *in, int inl);
```

ctx
> The initialized context that will be used to decrypt the data.

out
> Specifies a buffer to which decrypted data will be written. It must be as large as the input buffer.

outl
> Receives the number of bytes written to the decrypted data buffer.

in
> Specifies a buffer from which encrypted data will be decrypted.

inl
> Specifies the number of bytes contained in the encrypted data buffer.

Once all of the data to be decrypted has been fed into EVP_OpenUpdate, EVP_OpenFinal should be called to complete the job. Remember from our discussion of ciphers in Chapter 6 that when a block cipher is being used, the final block of decrypted data will not be written to the output buffer until EVP_DecryptFinal is called (or, in this case, EVP_OpenFinal). Once EVP_OpenFinal is called, the context cannot be reused until EVP_OpenInit is called again.

```
int EVP_OpenFinal(EVP_CIPHER_CTX *ctx, unsigned char *out, int *outl);
```

ctx
> Specifies the context to finalize decryption for.

out
> Specifies a buffer to which decrypted data will be written.

outl
> Receives the number of bytes written to the decrypted data buffer.

Encoding and Decoding Objects

Generating key pairs and keeping them in memory all of the time isn't very useful. It's often desirable to generate a key pair and save it to a file. Conversely, if a key pair is saved in a file, it also needs to be readable from the file. One solution to the problem is simply to write the data members from the various objects that we've discussed to a format of our own design. Doing this will certainly work, but it has the major drawback of not being compatible with any other software with which we may want to use our keys.

As luck would have it, OpenSSL supports two standard formats for storing and exchanging key pairs. The first is binary form known as DER (*Distinguished Encoding Rules*). This type of file is suitable for use in binary files or for transfer over a network connection, but is not ideal for all situations, particularly text-based communications such as email. The second format that OpenSSL supports is known as PEM (*Privacy Enhanced Mail*), which is defined in RFCs 1421, 1422, 1423, and 1424. PEM data is base64-encoded and provides the ability to encrypt the data before encoding it.

Without delving into the details of the DER and PEM encodings, we need to know some of the properties of each. The biggest difference, as we've stated above, is that DER is a binary encoding and PEM is text-based. Due partially to this fact, a file may contain only a single DER-encoded object, but can contain many PEM objects. In general, if we need to write data to disk, we should use PEM; however, many third-party applications accept objects only in the DER encoding. For objects stored in files, the command-line utility allows for encoding conversion for most common object types.

Writing and Reading DER-Encoded Objects

OpenSSL provides functions for many types of objects that write the DER representation of the object into a buffer. Each of the functions has a similar signature: the OpenSSL object as the first argument and a buffer as the second. The functions return the number of bytes written to the buffer or, if the buffer is specified as NULL, the number of bytes that would have been written to the buffer is returned. In addition, if a buffer is specified, it is advanced to the byte after the last byte written in order to facilitate writing multiple DER objects to the same buffer.

```
int i2d_OBJNAME(OBJTYPE *obj, unsigned char **pp);
```

You'll note that the second parameter is specified as a pointer to the buffer. This is done so that the pointer can be advanced after the data is written to it. Example 8-2 demonstrates how these functions can be used by writing an RSA public key into a dynamically allocated buffer. The function returns the buffer that was allocated to hold the DER-encoded key and stores the length of the buffer in the second argument.

Example 8-2. DER-encoding an RSA public key

```
unsigned char *DER_encode_RSA_public(RSA *rsa, int *len)
{
    unsigned char *buf, *next;

    *len = i2d_RSAPublicKey(rsa, NULL);
    buf = next = (unsigned char *)malloc(*len);
    i2d_RSAPublicKey(rsa, &next);
    return buf;
}
```

Likewise, a function is provided for each type of object that reads the DER representation of the object from a buffer and creates the appropriate object in memory. Again, each of the functions has a similar signature. The first argument is an object to populate with the data obtained from the buffer, which is specified as the second argument. The third argument specifies the number of bytes contained in the buffer that should be used for constructing the object.

```
OBJTYPE *d2i_OBJNAME(OBJTYPE **obj, unsigned char **pp, long length);
```

If the first argument is specified as NULL, a new object of the appropriate type is created and populated with the data recovered from the buffer. If it is specified as a pointer to NULL, a new object of the appropriate type is created and populated in the same manner, but the argument is updated to receive the newly created object. Finally, if a pointer to an existing object is specified, the existing object is populated with the data recovered from the buffer. In all cases, the return value of the function is the object that was populated, or NULL if an error occurred in recovering the data. Example 8-3 demonstrates DER-decoding an RSA public key.

Example 8-3. DER-decoding an RSA public key

```
RSA *DER_decode_RSA_public(unsigned char *buf, long len)
{
    RSA *rsa;

    rsa = d2i_RSAPublicKey(NULL, &buf, len);
    return rsa;
}
```

The two functions d2i_PublicKey and d2i_PrivateKey have a different signature from the others. The first argument to these two functions is an integer that specifies the type of key (DH, DSA, or RSA), which is encoded in the buffer. One of the constants EVP_PKEY_DH, EVP_PKEY_DSA, or EVP_PKEY_RSA must be specified to indicate the type of key to expect. The rest of the arguments to these two functions are the same, except they are shifted to make room for the argument that specifies the type of key. The function d2i_AutoPrivateKey is provided to allow OpenSSL to attempt to guess the type of private key that is stored in the buffer. Table 8-1 lists some DER-encoding functions.

Table 8-1. Functions for reading and writing DER encodings of public key objects

Type of object	OpenSSL object type	Function to write the DER representation	Function to read the DER representation
Diffie-Hellman parameters	DH	i2d_DHparams	d2i_DHparams
DSA parameters	DSA	i2d_DSAparams	d2i_DSAparams
DSA public key	DSA	i2d_DSAPublicKey	d2i_DSAPublicKey
DSA private key	DSA	i2d_DSAPrivateKey	d2i_DSAPrivateKey
RSA public key	RSA	i2d_RSAPublicKey	d2i_RSAPublicKey
RSA private key	RSA	i2d_RSAPrivateKey	d2i_RSAPrivateKey

Table 8-1. Functions for reading and writing DER encodings of public key objects (continued)

Type of object	OpenSSL object type	Function to write the DER representation	Function to read the DER representation
EVP_PKEY public key	EVP_PKEY	i2d_PublicKey	d2i_PublicKey
EVP_PKEY private key	EVP_PKEY	i2d_PrivateKey	d2i_PrivateKey
EVP_PKEY private key	EVP_PKEY	N/A	d2i_AutoPrivateKey

The two classes of functions above are useful for reading and writing structures to flat memory, but they still require us to write them to or read them from either a file or BIO. To help with this task, OpenSSL provides functions and macros that handle writing to files and streams. Each of the function names listed in Table 8-1 can be used as a base for building a new name to read or write DER encodings to or from a file or BIO. By appending _bio or _fp to the names of the functions, names for functions for writing to or reading from a BIO or file can be made. For example, the function i2d_DSAparams_bio will write the DER representation of DSA parameters to the specified BIO. The definitions for the BIO and file interface functions are in the header file *openssl/x509.h*.

There are three exceptions to this rule. The first is that there is no BIO or file equivalent function for i2d_PublicKey or d2i_PublicKey. The second exception is that there is no equivalently named function for the d2i_AutoPrivateKey function. The third exception is that d2i_PrivateKey_bio and d2i_PrivateKey_fp both behave as though they were named d2i_AutoPrivateKey_bio and d2i_AutoPrivateKey_fp.

For the functions that write DER representations to a BIO or a file, the first argument is either a BIO or FILE object, depending on the function that is used. The second argument is the object that will be DER-encoded and written to the BIO or file. The return value from these functions is zero if an error occurs; otherwise, it is non-zero to indicate success.

The functions that read DER representations also require a BIO or FILE object as their first argument, depending on which function is used. The second argument is a pointer to an object of the type that is being read, which is treated just the same as the first argument to the base functions. That is, when NULL or a pointer to NULL is specified, a new object of the appropriate type is created; otherwise, the specified object is populated. The return value from these functions is NULL if an error occurs; otherwise, the return is the object that was populated. Example 8-4 demonstrates.

Example 8-4. Reading and writing DER-encoded objects using the BIO and file functions

```
BIO *bio = BIO_new(BIO_s_memory( ));
RSA *rsa = RSA_generate_key(1024, RSA_F4, NULL, NULL);
i2d_RSAPrivateKey_bio(bio, rsa);

FILE *fp = fopen("rsakey.der", "rb");
RSA *rsa = NULL;
d2i_RSAPrivateKey_fp(fp, &rsa);
```

Writing and Reading PEM-Encoded Objects

The same objects that can be read and written in DER format can also be read and written in PEM format. The interface to the PEM format is somewhat different from the DER interface. To begin with, it supports writing to and reading from a BIO or a file; it does not support memory buffers like the DER interface does. As it turns out, this isn't much of a limitation since you can just use a memory BIO. All of the function declarations can be found in the header file *openssl/pem.h*.

The functions for writing public keys and parameters all share the same basic signature. The functions for writing to a BIO require a BIO object as the first argument and the object type as the second argument. The functions for writing to a file require a FILE object as the first argument and the object type as the second argument. Each of the functions, regardless of whether they're writing to a BIO object or a FILE object, return zero if an error occurs and nonzero if the operation was successful.

The functions for writing private keys are a bit more complex because the PEM format allows them to be encrypted before they're encoded and written out. Each function requires a BIO or FILE object to write to, the object to be written, a password callback function, and symmetric cipher information.

```
int PEM_write_OBJNAME(FILE *fp, OBJTYPE *obj, const EVP_CIPHER *enc,
                      unsigned char *kstr, int klen, pem_password_cb callback,
                      void *cb_arg);
```

fp
> The file to write to.

obj
> The object that contains the data to be written. The type of this object can be DSA, EVP_PKEY, or RSA.

enc
> The optional cipher to use to encrypt the key data. This can be any symmetric cipher object supported by OpenSSL. Refer to Chapter 6 for a comprehensive list of the available options. If this is specified as NULL, the key data is written unencrypted, and the remaining arguments are ignored.

kstr
> An optional buffer that contains the password or passphrase to use for encryption. If this is specified as non-NULL, the password callback function is ignored, and the contents of this buffer are used.

klen
> Specifies the number of bytes contained in the kstr buffer.

callback
> A callback function to obtain the password or passphrase for encrypting the key data. Its signature is described below.

cb_arg

Application-specific data that is passed to the callback function. If the call-back function and the kstr buffer are specified as NULL, this is interpreted as a NULL-terminated, C-style string that is used as the password or passphrase to encrypt the key data. If it is also specified as NULL, the default password callback function is used. The default password callback function prompts the user to enter the password or passphrase.

The functions that are used to write to a BIO object have the same signature, except that the FILE object is replaced with a BIO object. The return values from functions that write private keys are the same as the values from functions that write public keys and parameters: zero if an error occurs, nonzero otherwise. The password call-back function, if one is used, has the following signature:

```
typedef int (*pem_password_cb)(char *buf, int len, int rwflag, void *cb_arg);
```

buf

A buffer that the password or passphrase will be written into.

len

The size of the password buffer.

rwflag

Indicates whether the password or passphrase will be used to encrypt or decrypt the PEM data. When writing PEM data, this argument will be non-zero. When reading PEM data, this argument will be zero.

cb_arg

Application-specific. It is passed from the function that caused the pass-word callback function to be called.

The functions for reading public keys, private keys, and parameters all share a similar signature. Each requires a BIO or a FILE object to read from, an object to populate with the data that was read, and a password callback function.

```
OBJTYPE *PEM_read_OBJNAME(FILE *fp, OBJTYPE **obj, pem_password_cb callback,
                          void *cb_arg);
```

fp

The file to read from.

obj

The object to populate with the data that is read. If it is specified as NULL, a new object of the appropriate type is created and populated. If it is specified as a pointer to NULL, a new object of the appropriate type is also created and populated. In addition, it receives a pointer to the newly created object.

callback

A callback function to obtain the password or passphrase if one is required. A password or passphrase is required only if the PEM data being read is encrypted. Normally, only private keys are encrypted. The callback function may be specified as NULL.

cb_arg

Application-specific data that is passed to the callback function. If the callback is specified as NULL, this argument is interpreted as a NULL-terminated, C-style string containing the password or passphrase to use. If both the callback and this argument are specified as NULL, the default password callback function is used.

The functions that are used to read from a BIO have the same signature, except that the FILE object is replaced with a BIO object. The return value from the reading functions is always a pointer to the object that was populated with the data that was read. If an error occurs reading the PEM data, NULL is returned. See Table 8-2.

Table 8-2. Functions for reading and writing PEM encodings of public key objects

Type of object	OpenSSL object type	Function to write the PEM representation	Function to read the PEM representation
Diffie-Hellman parameters	DH	PEM_write_DHparams	PEM_read_DHparams
		PEM_write_bio_DHparams	PEM_read_bio_DHparams
DSA parameters	DSA	PEM_write_DSAparams	PEM_read_DSAparams
		PEM_write_bio_DSAparams	PEM_read_bio_DSAparams
DSA public key	DSA	PEM_write_DSA_PUBKEY	PEM_read_DSA_PUBKEY
		PEM_write_bio_DSA_PUBKEY	PEM_read_bio_DSA_PUBKEY
DSA private key	DSA	PEM_write_DSAPrivateKey	PEM_read_DSAPrivateKey
		PEM_write_bio_DSAPrivateKey	PEM_read_bio_DSAPrivateKey
RSA public key	RSA	PEM_write_RSA_PUBKEY	PEM_read_RSA_PUBKEY
		PEM_write_bio_RSA_PUBKEY	PEM_read_bio_RSA_PUBKEY
RSA private key	RSA	PEM_write_RSAPrivateKey	PEM_read_RSAPrivateKey
		PEM_write_bio_RSAPrivateKey	PEM_read_bio_RSAPrivateKey
EVP_PKEY public key	EVP_PKEY	PEM_write_PUBKEY	PEM_read_PUBKEY
		PEM_write_bio_PUBKEY	PEM_read_bio_PUBKEY
EVP_PKEY private key	EVP_PKEY	PEM_write_PrivateKey	PEM_read_PrivateKey
		PEM_write_bio_PrivateKey	PEM_read_bio_PrivateKey

## CHAPTER 9

OpenSSL in Other Languages

So far, we've discussed OpenSSL in the context of the C programming language, but you don't have to use C to use OpenSSL! Language bindings are available for many different languages, including Java, Perl, PHP, Python, and others. Unfortunately, none of the non–C language bindings that we've come across are as complete as the C API; nonetheless, it is important to discuss at least a few of the more popular and best-supported language bindings that are available.

The first section of this chapter is a discussion of Net::SSLeay, the most popular and complete module that is widely available for Perl. Be careful not to confuse Net::SSLeay with Crypt::SSLeay. The latter package is intended only to add support for HTTPS to the LWP package (a popular WWW interface library for Perl) and does not provide the additional interfaces to OpenSSL that Net::SSLeay does. The second section of this chapter is a discussion of M2Crypto, the most popular and complete suite of modules that is widely available for Python. The third section of this chapter is a brief discussion of the experimental OpenSSL extensions available in PHP 4.0.4 and newer versions.

For the purposes of these discussions, we assume that you have a familiarity with the language that is being discussed and its accompanying tools. It is not our intent to guide you through the installation of the modules or the common usage of the language. The specific purpose of this chapter is to demonstrate how to use the modules and get you started with OpenSSL in your own programs.

Net::SSLeay for Perl

Net::SSLeay is the most complete OpenSSL module available for Perl. It is written and maintained by Sampo Kellomäki (*sampo@symlabs.com*) and can be found on the Web at *http://www.symlabs.com/Net_SSLeay*. As is the case with most Perl modules, it is also available from CPAN. Unfortunately, its installation is not as straightforward as one might hope, so take care in reading the accompanying installation instructions for guidance.

As its name suggests, the module has its roots in the old SSLeay library originally developed by Eric Young, which provides the foundation upon which OpenSSL has been built. SSLeay evolved into OpenSSL several years ago, and Net::SSLeay hasn't supported old versions of SSLeay since early 1999. At the time of this writing, the latest version of Net::SSLeay is Version 1.13 and requires OpenSSL 0.9.6c or later.

The module comes with a fair number of scripts that serve as examples to demonstrate how to use the module's basic functionality. It provides Perl bindings for many of the low-level OpenSSL library functions. Many convenience functions that are intended for use at a low level are also included. The module also contains several high-level functions that you can use to perform common tasks involving OpenSSL, such as obtaining a file securely from the Web or securely posting data to a CGI script.

A limited amount of documentation is also included with the module. A quick-reference file that contains a list of the functions that are exported is included, along with a simple one-line description of each. The main Perl module file, *SSLeay.pm*, also contains some documentation in perldoc format of the functions the module adds to the OpenSSL bindings. Aside from the quick-reference file, no additional documentation is provided for the OpenSSL bindings. In fact, the author refers you to the OpenSSL documentation and source code for more information.

Net::SSLeay Variables

Net::SSLeay exports several global variables that are useful for controlling the behavior of the modules. Some of them are useful only for debugging your programs, but most of them provide finer control over the behavior of OpenSSL itself or some of the utility functions that are provided by the module.

$linux_debug
: This variable should be set only when the module is being used on a Linux system. If it is set to a nonzero value, process information from */proc/pid/stat* will be displayed for each read and write.

$trace
: This variable sets the trace level that is used by the high-level utility functions. It is intended primarily for debugging, so it should generally be set to zero in production programs (the zero guarantees silence). Valid values for this variable are 0 for silence, 1 for only errors to be reported, 2 for cipher information to be reported, 3 to report progress, and 4 to display everything, including the data that is both sent and received.

$slowly
: This variable is used with the sslcat utility function. It controls the number of seconds that sslcat will sleep after sending data and before closing the sending side of the connection. It defaults to zero, which means that sslcat will not sleep

at all, but some servers may require a delay; otherwise, they won't be able to read all of the data that was sent.

$ssl_version

This variable sets the version of the SSL protocol that is used by the high-level utility functions. By default, it is set to 0, which indicates that the version should be guessed as SSLv2, SSLv3, or TLSv1. Valid values for this variable are 2 for SSLv2, 3 for SSLv3, 10 for TLSv1, and 0 to guess SSLv2, SSLv3, or TLSv1.

$random_device

This variable contains the name of a file that will be used to seed OpenSSL's PRNG. The default setting for this variable is */dev/urandom*, but not all operating systems have such a device. If your system does not have such a device, you should consider using a third-party program that can provide entropy, such as EGADS. You can optionally use */dev/random* if your system has it; however, that device can block if not enough randomness is available. See Chapter 4 for a discussion on the importance of properly seeding the PRNG.

$how_random

This variable specifies, in bits, how much entropy should be collected from the source specified by $random_device. The default value is 512 bits. If you change this, be sure that you collect enough entropy, but also be careful that you do not collect too much, especially if you're using */dev/random* as your entropy source, because it could block until more becomes available.

Net::SSLeay Error Handling

In addition to providing Perl bindings for many of OpenSSL's error handling functions, three utility functions are provded by Net::SSLeay to handle error conditions:

print_errs($msg)

This function returns a string containing a list of all of the OpenSSL errors that occurred since the OpenSSL function ERR_get_error( ) was last called. A newline character separates each error in the returned string, and each error is prefaced with the message string that you specify as an argument. Additionally, if the $trace variable is any nonzero value, the errors will be printed to stderr via Perl's warn function.

die_if_ssl_error($msg)

This function will cause your program to terminate immediately by calling die with the message that you pass as an argument if an OpenSSL error has occurred. The function simply calls print_errs to determine if any errors have occurred. If print_errs returns any errors, the program is terminated.

die_now($msg)

This function will cause your program to terminate immediately by calling die with the message that you pass as an argument. Before calling die, print_errs is called so that any errors will be printed to `stderr` if the `$trace` global variable is set to any nonzero value.

Net::SSLeay Utility Functions

Net::SSLeay provides many high-level utility functions that simplify the use of OpenSSL. They're mostly wrappers around the low-level OpenSSL functions for which the module also provides bindings. Several of the functions also provide a wrapper around the HTTPS protocol.

`make_headers(@headers)`

> This function converts an associative array into a string formatted for sending directly to an HTTP server. The array's keys should be the header identifier, and the values should be the value to be associated with each header identifier. Essentially, this function combines each key/value pair with a colon and joins all of the pairs with carriage returns and linefeeds. The return value from this function is the resulting string.

`make_form(@data)`

> This function converts an associative array into a string formatted for sending form data to a CGI script. The array's keys should be the field name, and the values should be the value to be associated with each field name. The values are encoded according to the rules governing special and reserved characters in URLs. Essentially, this function combines each key/value pair with an equal sign and joins all of the pairs with an ampersand. The return value from this function is the resulting string.

`get_https($site, $port, $path, $headers, $content, $mime_type, $crt_path, $key_path)`
`head_https($site, $port, $path, $headers, $content, $mime_type, $crt_path, $key_path)`
`post_https($site, $port, $path, $headers, $content, $mime_type, $crt_path, $key_path)`
`put_https($site, $port, $path, $headers, $content, $mime_type, $crt_path, $key_path)`

> These four functions are similar, so we'll describe them together. They take the same arguments and perform the HTTP request that is signified by their names. Not all of the arguments are appropriate for all of the functions, and in many cases empty values can be specified without any adverse effects. All of the functions establish a secure connection using SSL with the HTTPS protocol. You should not pass a URL to the functions, but instead pass the separate components that make up a URL as arguments, individually. These functions will build the URL for you, establish the connection, perform the requested operation with the data you've provided, and return the data from the server to your program. It's important to realize that these functions perform no real certificate verification, so the only protection they're providing is against passive eavesdropping attacks.

> The first argument, `$site`, should contain the hostname or IP address of the host you wish to contact. The second argument, `$port`, should be the port to connect to. For the HTTPS protocol, the default port is 443. The third argument, `$path`,

should be the path to the page as well as any variables you wish to pass as part of the URL. Essentially, this is the remainder of the URL.

The fourth argument, $headers, should contain any additional headers that you wish to send with your request. You can use the function make_headers to build a string of header information from an associative array. By default, Net::SSLeay will include the standard Host and Accept headers, so you do not need to include them yourself. The fifth argument, $content, is useful only for the put_https and post_https functions. Use it to specify the data to send to the server. In the case of the post_https, you can use the function make_form to build a string of data from an associative array to send to the server. The sixth argument, $mime_type, is used to specify the MIME type of the data contained in the $content argument. If you do not specify a MIME type, application/x-www-form-urlencoded is used by default.

The final two arguments, $crt_path and $key_path, are optionally used to specify the path and filename to the client certificate and RSA private key to be used in establishing the connection. Remember that if you request a private key to be used in the transaction, the passphrase for the key will be requested from the console by OpenSSL if it is encrypted. The certificate and key files must be in PEM format, which also means that they may both be contained in the same file.

All four functions will return an array containing the results of the transaction. If an error occurs, the returned array will have only two elements. The first element will be undef, and the second element will be a string representation of the error that occurred. If the transaction is successful, the array will have three elements. The elements will be (in this order): the data that makes up the page, the response code from the server, and the headers returned from the server. The headers will be returned in the form of an associative array.

sslcat($host, $port, $content, $crt_path, $key_path)

This function establishes an SSL-secured connection to another host, sends it some data, waits for a response, and returns the remote host's response to your program. The first two arguments, $host and $port, specify the hostname or IP address and the port number to connect to. The third argument, $content, specifies the data that you wish to send to the remote host.

The fourth and fifth arguments, $crt_path and $key_path, optionally specify the path and filename to the client certificate and RSA private key to be used in establishing the SSL connection. Remember that if you specify a key to be used, the passphrase for the key will be prompted for on the console if the key is encrypted.

The return value from this function will be the data returned by the remote host or undef if an error occurred. If you call the function to request an array as a return, the first element of the array will be the data that was received from the

remote host, and the second element will be a string containing error information if an error occurred.

randomize($seed_file, $seed_string, $egd_path)

This is a convenience function used to seed OpenSSL's PRNG. The first argument is the name of a file to be used as a seed file. The second argument is a
string to be used as a seed. The third argument is the name of a Unix domain
socket that is bound to a server that speaks the EGD protocol for gathering
entropy. If the argument is undefined, the environment variable EGD_PATH will be
consulted for the name of the socket to use. Additionally, if you've specified a
random device with the $random_device variable and it exists, the information will
be passed on to OpenSSL via RAND_load_file. This function has no return value.

set_cert_and_key($ctx, $cert_file, $key_file)

This is a convenience function for specifying the certificate and key to use for an
SSL context. All three arguments are required. Note that if the RSA key specified by $key_file is encrypted, OpenSSL will prompt you on the console for the
passphrase. This function returns 0 if an error has occurred; otherwise, the
return is nonzero.

ssl_read_all($ssl, $howmuch)

This function reads $howmuch bytes from SSL connection specified by $ssl. The
function will not return until the specified number of bytes has been read or
EOF is encountered, whichever happens first. The return from this function will
be the data that was received. If you call the function requesting an array return,
the first element of the array will be the data received, and the second element
will be the string representation of any errors that occurred.

ssl_read_CRLF($ssl, $max)

This function reads data from the SSL connection specified by $ssl until a car-
riage return and linefeed are received or the number of bytes equals $max if it is
specified. The carriage return and linefeed characters will be included in the
received data if they're read before the maximum byte limit is reached. The
return from this function will be the data that was received.

ssl_read_until($ssl, $delimiter, $max)

This function reads data from the SSL connection specified by $ssl until the
specified delimiter is received or the number of bytes equals $max if it is speci-
fied. If no delimiter is specified, $/ or a linefeed character will be used, depend-
ing on whether $/ is defined or not. If the delimiter is encountered, it will be
included in the data that is returned. The return from this function will be the
data that was received.

ssl_write_all($ssl, $data)

This function writes the data specified by $data to the SSL connection specified
by $ssl. The function will not return until all of the data has been written. The
data to be written may be passed as a reference. The return from this function

will be the number of bytes that were written. If you call the function requesting an array return, the first element of the array will be the number of bytes written, and the second element will be the string representation of any errors that occurred.

ssl_write_CRLF($ssl, $data)

> This function is a simple wrapper around ssl_write_all that makes an additional call to ssl_write_all to write both a carriage return and a linefeed after your data. The return from this function is the total number of bytes written. Remember that this byte count will include the carriage return and linefeed characters.

Net::SSLeay Low-Level Bindings

The Net::SSLeay module does not provide bindings for all of the functions that OpenSSL exports as part of its public API; however, it does provide a sizable subset of them. Certainly, the most commonly used functions have bindings, and the author has added bindings for a random splattering of other functions as needed. We don't provide a complete list of all of the bindings that are supported. There is a complete list contained in the Net::SSLeay package. If there is a function that is missing, you should consider adding it yourself or contacting the author of Net::SSLeay.

In general, the Perl bindings for OpenSSL match the C functions for which they provide bindings. That is, both the arguments and the return values are the same. As you would expect, there are some differences. The most significant difference is that the names of the Perl bindings are not prefixed with SSL_ as the OpenSSL C functions are. Instead, you should prefix the names with Net::SSLeay:: to get the function or constant that you want. If the function name does not start with SSL_ in the OpenSSL C library, the name is the same in Perl.

There are two notable exceptions to the rule that Perl bindings take the same arguments as OpenSSL C functions. Both read and write as exported by Net::SSLeay provide bindings to SSL_read and SSL_write; however, the Perl bindings are more intelligent about the data types that are passed through them. For example, write automatically figures out the number of bytes that need to be written.

For the most part, callbacks are not implemented in Net::SSLeay. Only one callback is implemented, and it does not come without a potentially severe restriction. The one callback that is implemented is the verify callback, which is used for verifying certificates. The restriction is that there can be only one callback across all SSL contexts, sessions, and connections. For most client applications, this restriction will probably never be encountered, but for server applications, the potential severity of the restriction increases significantly.

One final point to consider is that Net::SSLeay is not thread-aware. Given that threading is still experimental in Perl, it's not so surprising that Net::SSLeay isn't thread-aware. As Perl moves closer to fully supporting threading, this will become more of an issue, but for now it is something to keep in the back of your mind while designing and implementing your SSL-enabled applications in Perl using Net::SSLeay.

M2Crypto for Python

Although there are several solutions available for Python, M2Crypto is the most popular, the most complete, and not surprisingly, the most mature. It is written and maintained by Ng Pheng Siong (*ngps@post1.com*) and can be found on the Web at *http://www.post1.com/home/ngps/m2*. It requires SWIG, which can be found on the Web at *http://swig.sourceforge.net*. At the time of writing, the latest version of M2Crypto is Version 0.06 and requires OpenSSL 0.9.6 or later and SWIG 1.3.6. It's been tested and known to work on Unix and Windows with Python Versions 1.5.2, 2.0, and 2.1.

Although it is the most mature Python solution available, M2Crypto is barely a year old. Unfortunately, it is sorely lacking in documentation. Luckily, included in the distribution is a sizable collection of examples as well as a suite of unit test scripts that also serve as excellent examples of how to use the modules. M2Crypto contains not only a large set of low-level bindings to the OpenSSL C library functions, but a set of high-level classes that provide a far cleaner interface to SSL as well.

Low-Level Bindings

A significant number of the OpenSSL C library functions are directly bound. Many others are still available, although wrapped with a slightly different name, and their arguments may have changed slightly. These wrappers typically make the functions easier to use from Python and do a little extra work "under the hood" that may be necessary for everything to work properly for Python. You can make the low-level bindings to OpenSSL available in your program with the following statement:

```
from M2Crypto import m2
```

All of the low-level functions are named entirely in lowercase, and the OpenSSL C functions are normally named in a combination of uppercase and lowercase. For example, the OpenSSL C function named SSL_CTX_new would become m2.ssl_ctx_new in Python. We will not include a complete list of the low-level bindings in this chapter; however, the M2Crypto package contains one.

We don't recommend that you use the low-level bindings in your own programs, at least not without also using the high-level classes. The primary reason for this is that many of the SSL subsystems require some additional setup calls from Python to make them work properly. For example, to use the BIO functionality, you need to call m2.bio_init, an internal M2Crypto function, properly. If you're using the high-level classes, such calls are made for you, and you can generally feel free to extend the classes if you need to.

High-Level Classes

M2Crypto contains a reasonably complete set of high-level classes that you can use in your programs. Use of the high-level classes is encouraged over the low-level bindings for a couple of reasons. The primary reason that we cited in the earlier section on the low-level interface is a good one. As M2Crypto evolves and matures, it's possible that its internals will change, breaking your programs in the process. Another reason is because Python is primarily an object-oriented language, and the low-level interface is not object-oriented at all. A third reason is that OpenSSL's C library functions are often cumbersome to use. The high-level classes provide a much cleaner, easier-to-use interface to OpenSSL's functionality.

There are several submodules, all of which can be imported from the M2Crypto module to access the various groupings of functions that all make up the OpenSSL C API. Several of them are still works in progress, but the most commonly used SSL functionality is available.

M2Crypto.SSL

```
from M2Crypto import SSL
```

The SSL module contains several classes that provide the most basic interface to the OpenSSL C library. Included among them are Context, Connection, Session, SSLServer, ForkingSSLServer, and ThreadingSSLServer. The first, Context, is a wrapper around the C interface's SSL_CTX object. All of OpenSSL's connection-oriented services require a context on which to operate.

When a context is created, the version of the protocol that it will support must be supplied. You cannot change a context's protocol once it has been created. The Context class's constructor takes an optional parameter that specifies the protocol to use. The protocol can be sslv2, sslv3, tlsv1, or sslv23. If you do not specify a protocol, the default is sslv23, which indicates that SSLv2, SSLv3, or TLSv1 should be negotiated during the initial handshake. As we mentioned in Chapter 1, you should avoid supporting v2 in your applications.

Once a context object has been created, it can be used to establish an SSL connection. The class contains many methods that allow you to set and query the various attributes a context may have that are supported by OpenSSL itself. Operations include assigning a certificate and private key, loading CA certificates, and specifying criteria to determine whether a peer's certificate is acceptable or not.

The Connection class combines OpenSSL with sockets to provide an all-in-one object for establishing both client and server connections, as well as transferring data bidirectionally over the connection. This class is little more than a convenience object, since it does all of the tedious work of setting up a socket and establishing an SSL connection for you. All that you need to do is create a Context and set it up to meet your needs. For example, to establish a connection using TLSv1 for the protocol, your code might look a little something like this:

```
from M2Crypto import SSL

ctx = SSL.Context('tlsv1')
conn = SSL.Connection(ctx)
conn.connect(('127.0.0.1', '443'))
```

The Session class is not one that you would typically create yourself. There are two ways to get a Session object. The first is from an existing Connection object by calling its get_session method. The second is by loading a saved session from a file via SSL.load_session. Once you have a Session object, you can dump it to a file using its write_bio method.

The last three classes, SSLServer, ForkingSSLServer, and ThreadingSSLServer, are SSL versions of the Python TCPServer class found in the SocketServer module. They all work in the same manner, except the constructor for each class requires an additional argument that is a Context object. You are of course required to create the Context object and set it up to meet your needs.

M2Crypto.BIO

```
from M2Crypto import BIO
```

The BIO module provides interface classes to OpenSSL's BIO functions. The BIO class itself is an abstract class that provides the basic functionality of the other four classes that are built on top of it: MemoryBuffer, File, IOBuffer, and CipherStream. The BIO class itself is not intended to be instantiated. If you do, it'll be mostly useless, capable of doing little more than throwing exceptions when you try to use it.

There isn't much to be said for these four classes that we didn't already cover in Chapter 4. BIO is simply an I/O abstraction, and these four classes provide four different types of I/O. The MemoryBuffer class provides a wrapper around the OpenSSL BIO_s_mem type, which is an in-memory I/O stream. The File class provides a wrapper around the OpenSSL BIO_s_fp type, which is a disk file. The IOBuffer class provides a wrapper around the OpenSSL BIO_f_buffer type, and it is typically used only internally by a Connection object's makefile method. It essentially provides a wrapper around any other type of BIO.

Finally, the CipherStream class provides a wrapper around the OpenSSL BIO_f_cipher type, which is perhaps the most interesting of all four BIO wrappers that are supported by M2Crypto. It wraps around any other type of BIO of your choosing, encrypting data as it is written, and decrypting data as it is read. Some additional setup work is required to use this class, but all that is actually involved is setting the cipher to be used.

M2Crypto.EVP

```
from M2Crypto import EVP
```

The EVP module provides an interface to OpenSSL's EVP interface. Additionally, it provides an interface to OpenSSL's HMAC interface, which is not technically a part of the EVP interface. As we discussed in Chapters 6, 7, and 8, EVP is a high-level interface to message digests, symmetric ciphers, and public key algorithms. It provides a mechanism for computing cryptographic hashes, data encryption, and digital signatures.

The MessageDigest class provides the interface for computing cryptographic hashes. Its constructor requires an argument that is the string name of the algorithm to use. The available algorithms and their string names are listed in Chapter 7. Once a MessageDigest object is instantiated, its update method can be called as many times as necessary to supply it with the data to be hashed. A call to the final method computes the hash and returns it. Example 9-1 demonstrates.

Example 9-1. Computing the cryptographic hash of data

```
from M2Crypto import EVP

def hash(data, alg = 'sha1'):
    md = EVP.MessageDigest(alg)
    md.update(data)
    return md.final( )
```

The HMAC class provides one of two interfaces for the OpenSSL HMAC support. The constructor accepts two arguments, the second of which is optional. The first argument is the key to use, and the second optional argument is the string name of the message digest algorithm to use. The available algorithms and their string names are listed in Chapter 7. If no message digest algorithm is specified, SHA1 is used. Once an HMAC object is instantiated, its update method can be called as many times as necessary to supply it with the data to be MAC'd. A call to the final method computes the MAC and returns it. The hmac function provides the other interface and is simply a wrapper around the OpenSSL hmac function. It accepts three arguments, the third of which is optional. The first argument is the key to use, and the second is the data to be MAC'd. The third and optional argument is the message digest algorithm to use. Again, SHA1 is the default if one is not specified. The return from the function is the computed HMAC.

The Cipher class provides the interface to data encryption using a symmetric cipher. The class's interface is the same as the MessageDigest and HMAC classes. Once a Cipher object is constructed, the update method is used to supply it with the data to be encrypted or decrypted, and the final method completes the operation, returning the encrypted or decrypted data. The constructor requires four arguments, and accepts an additional four optional arguments.

```
class Cipher:
        def __init__(self, alg, key, iv, op, key_as_bytes = 0, d = 'md5',
                     salt = '', i = 1):
```

alg

> The symmetric cipher to use. It is specified using the string name of the desired cipher. Chapter 6 lists the available ciphers and their string names.

key

> The key to use to encrypt or decrypt the data.

iv

> The initialization vector to use to encrypt or decrypt the data.

op

> An integer that specifies whether encryption or decryption of the data should be performed. If op is specified as 1, encryption is performed. If it is specified as 0, decryption is performed.

key_as_bytes

> Specifies how to interpret the specified key. If it is specified as a nonzero value, the key is interpreted as a password or passphrase. In this case, an initialization vector is computed, and the iv argument is filled with the initialization vector that was used.

d

> Specifies the message digest algorithm that will be used to compute the key if key_as_bytes is specified as nonzero. The default is to use MD5.

salt

> Specifies the salt that will be used to compute the key if key_as_bytes is specified as nonzero.

i

> Specifies the number of iterations that will be performed to obtain the final key. In other words, it specifies the number of times the key data will be hashed.

Example 9-2 illustrates symmetric ciphers.

Example 9-2. Encrypting and decrypting with a symmetric cipher

```
from M2Crypto import EVP

def encrypt(password, data, alg):
    cipher = EVP.Cipher(alg, password, None, 1, 1, 'sha1')
    cipher.update(data)
    return cipher.final()

def decrypt(password, data, alg):
    cipher = EVP.Cipher(alg, password, None, 0, 1, 'sha1')
    cipher.update(data)
    return cipher.final()
```

Example 9-2. Encrypting and decrypting with a symmetric cipher (continued)

```
password = 'any password will do'
plaintext = 'Hello, world!'
ciphertext = encrypt(password, plaintext, 'bf-cbc')
print 'Decrypted message text: %s' % decrypt(password, ciphertext, 'bf-cbc')
```

The EVP module also provides a PKey class that is intended to be a wrapper around the OpenSSL EVP interface for digital signatures and data encryption; however, it is incomplete, providing only limited support for creating digital signatures. No mechanism exists for verifying digital signatures or data encryption in this class. The digital signature support is also nonfunctional. The class is essentially useless in its current form, and so we will not discuss it in any more depth here.

Miscellaneous crypto

```
from M2Crypto import DH, DSA, RSA, RC4
```

The DH, DSA, and RSA modules provide access to the three supported low-level, public key cryptographic algorithms known by the same names. The RC4 module provides direct access to the symmetric cipher by the same name. It's curious that RC4 is the only symmetric cipher that is supported directly with a class of its own, particularly since the EVP interface is exposed. We recommend that you avoid using it in favor of the EVP module's Cipher class.

The DH module provides a class by the same name that is generally instantiated by using one of the four functions provided by the module. The function DH.gen_params can be used to create a new DH object with randomly generated parameters. The functions DH.load_params and DH.load_params_bio can be used to create a DH object created from parameters stored in a file. DH.load_params accepts a filename from which the parameters will be loaded, and DH.load_params_bio accepts a BIO object from which the parameters will be loaded. Finally, DH.set_params allows you to create a DH object and specify the parameters yourself.

The DSA module provides a class by the same name that is generally instantiated by one of several module functions. The function DSA.gen_params can be used to create a new DSA object with randomly generated parameters. DSA.load_params and DSA.load_params_bio create a DSA object from a file or a BIO object. DSA.load_key and DSA.load_key_bio create a DSA object loaded from a file or BIO object containing a PEM representation of a private key. There is no mechanism to load public DSA keys.

The RSA module provides two classes: RSA and RSA_pub. The classes should be instantiated using one of the module's functions. RSA.gen_key returns an RSA object after generating a new key pair. RSA.load_key and RSA.load_key_bio both create an RSA object from a private key stored in PEM format from a file or BIO object. RSA.load_pub_key and RSA.load_pub_key_bio create an RSA_pub object from a public key stored in PEM representation from a file or BIO object. Finally, RSA.new_pub_key will instantiate an

RSA_pub object from the public exponent and composite of the primes that make up a private key.

The RC4 module provides an RC4 class as an interface to the RC4 symmetric cipher algorithm. This class is intended to be instantiated directly. It can be instantiated with or without a key, and the key can be changed with a call to its set_key method. Calling the update method with data to be encrypted will return the encrypted data.

Python Module Extensions

In addition to providing the low-level OpenSSL bindings and an object-oriented approach to OpenSSL in the high-level classes, M2Crypto also includes extensions to three of the modules that are part of Python itself. The extensions are what you might expect: SSL extensions to httplib, urllib, and xmlrpclib. The extensions to httplib and urllib simply support HTTPS. The extensions to xmlrpclib add an SSL_Transport class.

Extensions to httplib: httpslib

To use the httplib extensions, you'll need to import the M2Crypto.httpslib module:

```
from M2Crypto import httpslib
```

You don't need to import from httplib as well. M2Crypto's httpslib exports all of httplib in addition to its own extensions. The httplib interface changed drastically in Version 2.0 of Python. httpslib accounts for this and provides different extensions depending on the version of Python that you're using.

If you're using a version of Python earlier than 2.0, a single new class called HTTPS will be added. This class is a subclass of HTTP from httplib. The only detail that you need to concern yourself with is passing in an existing SSL context object to the constructor. For example, to connect to the local host on the default HTTPS port 443 using SSLv3, your code might look like this:

```
from M2Crypto import SSL, httpslib

context = SSL.Context('sslv3')
https = httpslib.HTTPS(context, '127.0.0.1:443')
```

If you're using Version 2.0 of Python or later, two new classes called HTTPSConnection and HTTPS will be added. HTTPSConnection is a subclass of HTTPConnection, and HTTPS is a subclass of HTTP. They both work similarly to their parent classes, but expect some extra information in their constructors in order to utilize SSL. All of the extra arguments are optional keyword arguments:

key_file
    Specifies the path and filename of an RSA private key file to be used in establishing the connection.

cert_file
> Specifies the path and filename of a certificate file to be used in establishing the connection.

ssl_context
> Specifies an existing SSL context object. If it is omitted, a context will be created using the sslv23 protocol.

The HTTPSConnection class accepts all three keyword arguments. The HTTPS class will recognize only ssl_context, silently ignoring the others. The code to connect to the local host on the default HTTPS port 443 using SSLv3 might look like this:

```
from M2Crypto import SSL, httpslib

context = SSL.Context('sslv3')
https = httpslib.HTTPSConnection('127.0.0.1:443', ssl_context = context)
```

It's important to realize that these functions do not perform any real certificate verification, so the only real protection they're providing is against passive eavesdropping attacks.

Extensions to urllib: m2urllib

To use the urllib extensions, you'll need to import the M2Crypto.m2urllib module:

```
from M2Crypto import m2urllib
```

You don't need to import urllib itself as well. The m2urllib module re-exports all of urllib along with its own extensions. Unlike httplib, the interface for urllib is the same for all currently supported versions of Python. The only addition is an open_https method added to the urllib.URLopener class. It works just the same as the existing open method does, taking the same arguments and returning the same values.

The open_https function does not take any additional arguments; it is responsible for creating the SSL context to be used, and you can't set up certificate or private key information either. The default protocol version that the SSL context is created with is controlled by the DEFAULT_PROTOCOL variable. By default, it is set to sslv3, but you can change it to any of the other supported values for creating an SSL context. For example, if you wanted either v2 or v3 to work, you might do the following:

```
from M2Crypto import m2urllib

m2urllib.DEFAULT_PROTOCOL = 'sslv23'
connection = m2urllib.URLopener().open_https('https://www.somesite.com')
```

Extensions to xmlrpclib: m2xmlrpclib

The xmlrpclib module is new in Python 2.2. If you're using an older version of Python, you can find this module from a third party. To use the xmlrpclib extensions, you'll need to import the M2Crypto.m2xmlrpclib module:

```
from M2Crypto import m2xmlrpclib
```

You don't need to import `xmlrpclib` as well. The `m2xmlrpclib` module re-exports all of `xmlrpclib` along with its own extensions. The only addition that the `m2xmlrpclib` module makes is a class named `SSL_Transport`. The class's constructor accepts a single optional argument that is an SSL context object. If you don't specify, one will be created that uses the `sslv23` protocol.

OpenSSL Support in PHP

PHP is a scripting language that is used primarily, if not exclusively, on the Web. It is normally HTML-embedded, although it is also capable of running as a CGI script. It boasts an extensive library of functions that provide interfaces to a wide variety of common external libraries and services, such as LDAP and MySQL. PHP-4.04pl1 introduced experimental support for OpenSSL. At the time of this writing, the current version of PHP is 4.1.1, and OpenSSL support is still considered experimental. Current versions of PHP require OpenSSL Version 0.9.5 or later.

Since PHP's support for OpenSSL is considered experimental, anything relating to the implementation could still change, including the function names, parameters, and return values. The support for OpenSSL in PHP is more limited than Perl or Python's support, but sufficient functionality does exist to make it moderately useful. Support for encryption, signing, S/MIME, key generation, and X.509 certificate manipulation is included.

PHP's OpenSSL functions are high-level abstractions from the OpenSSL API. Unlike Perl or Python, none of the low-level OpenSSL API is exposed directly. While this simplifies the usage of OpenSSL greatly, it also restricts its capabilities. As newer versions of PHP have been released, new OpenSSL functionality has been introduced. We recommend that you use the latest version of PHP available to you if you wish to make use of its OpenSSL functionality.

General Functions

The PHP OpenSSL extension provides four functions required for the more specific functionality offered by the extension. These functions provide a mechanism for error reporting as well as private and public key management. In particular, many of the more specific functions require a public or private key, which are often supplied as a key resource. Key resources can be obtained from any one of the sources listed below, but in all cases the key data obtained from an external source must be PEM-encoded because PHP provides no support for reading DER-encoded data:

- The resource retreived from a prior call to either `openssl_get_publickey` or `openssl_get_privatekey`
- An X.509 resource for public keys
- A string that specifies a filename to read the key from

- A string that contains the key data
- An array that contains the key as a string representing a filename or containing the key data and the passphrase required to decrypt the key

In Version 4.0.5 or later of PHP, any of the inputs to openssl_get_privatekey, openssl_get_publickey, or openssl_x509_read, which return key or certificate resources, can be used as the key or certificate resource to the function requiring the key or certificate resource. The earlier versions of the OpenSSL extension required the use of the three aforementioned functions, but versions that are more recent do not. If you'll be using the same key or certificate more than once, it is generally a good idea to use the functions to obtain a resource rather than obtaining it each time you need to use it.

mixed openssl_error_string(void)
> This function pops the most recent error from OpenSSL's error stack and returns a string representation of the error. If the stack is empty, the return from this function will be false. The string returned will be an English representation of the error as returned from the OpenSSL function ERR_error_string. Note that OpenSSL pushes errors onto a stack, and that this function pops only one error from that stack. Call this function repeatedly until it returns false in order to get all of the available error information when an error occurs.

resource openssl_get_privatekey(mixed key [, string passphrase])
> This function creates a key resource for a private key. The first argument, key, can be one of three representations of a public key: a string beginning with "file://" that contains the name of the file containing the private key data, a string that contains the private key data, or an array that contains the key information. If an array is used, the first element should be either a string that contains the name of the file containing the key data, or the key data. The second element should be the passphrase to decrypt the key. The optional argument, passphrase, should be a string containing the passphrase required to decrypt the key if one is necessary.

> The return from this function is false if an error occurs; openssl_error_string should be used to obtain error information. If the key is successfully loaded and decrypted, the return will be a PHP resource for the key. When you're done using the key resource, you should use openssl_free_key to release it.

resource openssl_get_publickey(mixed certificate)
> This function creates a key resource for a public key. The first argument, key, can be one of three representations of a certificate from which the public key will be extracted: a certificate resource, a string beginning with "file://" that contains the name of the file containing the certificate data, or a string that contains the certificate data.

> The return from this function is false if an error occurs; openssl_error_string should be used to obtain error information. If the key is successfully extracted

from the certificate, the return will be a PHP resource for the key. When you're done using the key resource, you should use openssl_free_key to release it.

void openssl_free_key(resource key)

> This function releases a key resource that was previously obtained from either openssl_get_privatekey or openssl_get_publickey. You should call this function to free any internal resources that are associated with a PHP key resource when you are through using it.

Certificate Functions

The PHP OpenSSL extension provides a limited number of functions useful for manipulating X.509 certificates. The functions allow you to create and free a certificate resource, verify that a certificate has permission to perform a specific function, and obtain information about the certificate. All certificate data that is provided to PHP must be PEM-encoded.

resource openssl_x509_read(mixed certificate)

> This function creates a certificate resource from X.509 certificate data. The certificate data may be supplied as one of two representations: a string beginning with "file://" that contains the name of the file containing the certificate data, or a string containing the certificate data.
>
> The return from this function is false if an error occurs; openssl_error_string should be used to obtain error information. If the certificate is successfully loaded, the return will be a PHP resource for the certificate. When you're done using the certificate resource, you should use openssl_x509_free to release it.

void openssl_x509_free(resource certificate)

> This function releases a certificate resource that was previously obtained from openssl_x509_read. You should call this function to free any internal resources that are associated with a PHP certificate resource when you are through using it.

bool openssl_x509_checkpurpose(mixed certificate, int purpose, array cainfo [, string untrusted_file])

> This function determines whether a certificate may be used to perform a specific function. The first argument, certificate, is a certificate resource obtained from openssl_x509_read. Table 9-1 lists the valid values for the second argument, purpose. Note that only one constant may be used at a time—the argument is not a bit mask. The third argument, cainfo, is a list of trusted certificate files or directories to be used in the verification of the certificate. If present, the optional argument, untrusted_file, is the name of the file containing any certificates of intermediate CAs required to verify the certificate. The extra certificates will not be trusted.

Table 9-1. Possible purpose values for openssl_x509_checkpurpose

Constant	Description
X509_PURPOSE_SSL_CLIENT	May the certificate be used for the client in an SSL session?
X509_PURPOSE_SSL_SERVER	May the certificate be used for the server in an SSL session?
X509_PURPOSE_NS_SSL_SERVER	May the certificate be used for a Netscape SSL server?
X509_PURPOSE_SMIME_SIGN	May the certificate be used for S/MIME signing?
X509_PURPOSE_SMIME_ENCRYPT	May the certificate be used for S/MIME encrypting?
X509_PURPOSE_CRL_SIGN	May the certificate be used to sign a certificate revocation list (CRL)?
X509_PURPOSE_ANY	May the certificate be used for any and all purposes?

The cainfo array should contain a list of files that will be used to verify the certificate. Directories may also be included in the list. Files should contain one or more certificates, and directories should contain certificates that would be accepted by the OpenSSL command-line tool commands that perform a similar function with the CApath option. Certificate files in a directory should contain one certificate per file and should be named with the hash value of the certificate subject's name and an extension of ".0". Any certificates made available via this function are trusted.

The return from this function will be true if the certificate may be used for the purpose that is being checked. If it may not, the return will be false. The integer value −1 will be returned if an error occurs in the verification process; openssl_error_string should be used to obtain error information.

array openssl_x509_parse(mixed certificate [, bool shortnames])

This function returns information about a certificate in an associative array. The keys for the array are currently undocumented, but easily discovered from the source code for the extension. We've listed them here in Table 9-2; however, due to the fact that they are undocumented, if anything in the OpenSSL extension is going to change in future versions, these keys have a high probability. If you can avoid it, we would advise against using this function for the time being until it stabilizes. If the second argument, shortnames, is omitted or specified as true, the keys in the returned array will use a shortened name.

Table 9-2. Keys for the array returned by openssl_x509_parse

Key name	Data type	Description
name	string	The name assigned to the certificate, if it has one. This key may not be present.
subject	array	An associative array that contains all of the fields comprising the subject's distinguished name, such as commonName, organizationName, etc. The shortnames argument affects the keys in this array.
issuer	array	An associative array that contains all of the fields comprising the issuer's distinguished name. The shortnames argument affects the keys in this array.
version	long	The X.509 version.

Key name	Data type	Description
serialNumber	long	The certificate's serial number.
validFrom	string	A string representation of the date the certificate is valid from.
validTo	string	A string representation of the date the certificate is valid to.
validFrom_time_t	long	A time_t integer representation of the date the certificate is valid from (number of seconds since Jan 1, 1970 00:00:00 GMT).
validTo_time_t	long	A time_t integer representation of the date the certificate is valid to.
alias	string	The alias assigned to the certificate, if it has one. This key may not be present.
purposes	array	Each element in this array represents a purpose that is supported by OpenSSL. The index values of this array correspond to the constants listed in Table 9-1. Each element of that array is another array containing three elements. The first two are bools. The first indicates whether the certificate may be used for that purpose, and the second indicates whether the certificate is a CA. The third is a string representation of the purpose name, which is affected by the shortnames argument.

Encryption and Signing Functions

The OpenSSL extension provides wrappers around OpenSSL's high-level EVP suite of functions, which can be used for data encryption as well as for digital signing. The functions provided are actually close mappings to the OpenSSL API functions; however, the PHP wrappers have imposed some limitations on them, most notably by limiting the cipher for encryption and decryption to RC4, and the digest for signing and verification to SHA1. We hope that future versions of the extension will remove these limitations, allowing for much more flexibility and security.

> There is another, potentially more serious problem with the encryption support in PHP. On systems in which the OpenSSL library cannot seed the PRNG itself, PHP provides no means to seed it. The problem exists particularly on Unix systems without a */dev/urandom* device. On such systems, we do not recommend that you use the PHP interface to OpenSSL unless there is another module loaded into the same server that does initialize the OpenSSL PRNG, such as mod_ssl. This warning also holds for the S/MIME functions that are described in the next section.

int openssl_seal(string data, string sealed_data, array env_keys, array pub_keys)
> This function is used for encrypting data. The data is encrypted using RC4 with a randomly generated secret key, which is then encrypted using a public key. The encrypted data is known as sealed data, and the encrypted secret key is known as an envelope. The recipient must have the envelope, the sealed data, and the private key matching the public key used to create the envelope to decrypt the sealed data. The function conveniently allows for multiple recipients by accepting an array of public keys.

The first argument, data, specifies the data that will be sealed. The second argument, sealed_data, receives the sealed data. The third argument, env_keys, receives the envelopes for each public key that is specified for the fourth argument, pub_keys. The public keys should be key resources returned by openssl_get_publickey. If an error occurs, the return value will be false; otherwise, it will be the length of the sealed data in bytes.

bool openssl_open(string sealed_data, string data, string env_key, mixed key)
This function is used for decrypting data that was previously encrypted using openssl_seal. The first argument, sealed_data, is the data to be decrypted. The decrypted data is placed into the second argument, data. The third argument, env_key, specifies the envelope containing the encrypted secret key required to decrypt the sealed data via RC4. The fourth argument, key, is the private key to use for decrypting the envelope to obtain the secret key. The private key should be specified as a key resource obtained from openssl_get_privatekey.

If the sealed data is decrypted successfully, the return from this function will be true, and the decrypted data will be placed into the second argument, data. If an error occurs, the return will be false, and you should use openssl_error_string to obtain error information. Note that encrypted data not created with the PHP OpenSSL extension can also be decrypted with this function, as long as it was encrypted using the RC4 cipher.

bool openssl_sign(string data, string signature, mixed key)
This function signs data using the SHA1 message digest algorithm. The first argument, data, is the data to be signed. The second argument, signature, receives the resultant signature. The third argument, key, is a private key resource to use to sign the data, and should be a key resource obtained from openssl_get_privatekey. Anybody who has the public key that matches the private key used to sign the data can then verify the signature.

If the data is successfully signed, the signature will be placed into the second argument, signature, and the return from the function will be true. If an error occurs, the return will be false, and openssl_error_string should be used to obtain error information.

int openssl_verify(string data, string signature, mixed key)
This function is used for verifying the signature of a chunk of data using the SHA1 message digest algorithm. The first argument, data, is the signed data to be verified. The second argument, signature, is the signature of that data. The third argument, key, is the public key that matches the private key used to compute the signature.

If the signature is valid, the return from this function will be the integer value 1. If it is incorrect, but no other errors occurred, the return will be the integer value 0. If an error occurs in the process of verifying the signature, the return will be the integer value −1, and openssl_error_string should be used to obtain error information. Note that data not signed with the PHP OpenSSL extension can also be verified with this function, as long as it was signed using the SHA1 message digest algorithm.

PKCS#7 (S/MIME) Functions

The final set of functions that the PHP OpenSSL extension offers is for PKCS#7, which are provided as structures encapsulated in MIME types defined by S/MIME. These functions provide for encryption, decryption, signing, and signature verification using X.509 certificates. The functions were added in PHP 4.0.6. They are not available in prior versions. These functions require use of the OpenSSL PRNG, and the PRNG must be seeded before you can use them safely. Unfortunately, there is no way to do this with PHP itself, as detailed in the warning in the previous section.

```
bool openssl_pkcs7_encrypt(string infile, string outfile, mixed certs,
array headers [, long flags])
```

> This function encrypts the data contained in the file named by the first argument, infile, and places it in the file named by the second argument, outfile. The encryption always uses a weak RC2 40-bit cipher, which is a limitation of the PHP interface. S/MIMEv2 supports both RC2 40-bit and 3DES, but the PHP implementation has unfortunately chosen to restrict the cipher to the weaker of the two. Public keys to use for encryption are obtained from the third argument, certs. The certificates to use for encryption are specified as an array, allowing for multiple recipients of the same message. The fourth argument, headers, is an array of data that will be prepended to the output file in plaintext. The array can be either indexed or associative. In the former case, each element of the array is a single line of text to be placed in the output file. In the latter case, each line is composed from the key and the value, joining them with a colon and a space. The fifth argument, flags, is optional and specifies options that can be used to control the encryption process. The argument is a bit mask, so you may specify multiple constants if they're appropriate. Table 9-3 lists the possible flag constants.

> If the function is successful, the return from the function will be true. If an error occurs in the encryption process, the return will be false and openssl_error_string should be used to obtain error information. On a successful run, the file specified by the second argument will contain the encrypted data. The process must have write access to the file, and it will be created if it does not exist. If it does exist, the existing file will be truncated before the output from this function is written to it.

Table 9-3. Flags: openssl_pkcs7_encrypt, openssl_pkcs7_sign, openssl_pkcs7_verify

Constant	Description
PKCS7_TEXT	When encrypting or signing, adds a Content-type: text/plain header to the output. When verifying a signature, the Content-type header is stripped.
PKCS7_BINARY	When encrypting or signing, prevents the conversion of bare linefeeds to carriage returns and linefeeds as required by the S/MIME specification to mark end of line.

Table 9-3. Flags: openssl_pkcs7_encrypt, openssl_pkcs7_sign, openssl_pkcs7_verify (continued)

Constant	Description
PKCS7_NOINTERN	When verifying a signature, only the certificates supplied to the function are trusted, causing any included certificates to be considered untrusted.
PKCS7_NOVERIFY	Prevents the verification of the signer's certificate of a signed message.
PKCS7_NOCHAIN	Prevents chained verification of the signer's certificate. Causes certificates in the signed message to be ignored.
PKCS7_NOCERTS	When signing a message, prevents the signer's certificate from being included in the output.
PKCS7_NOATTR	When signing a message, prevents attributes such as the signing time from being included in the output.
PKCS7_DETACHED	When signing a message, this is the default if no flags are specified. It causes the MIME type multipart/signed to be used. It's a good idea to include this option because some mail relays can't handle messages signed with this option turned off.
PKCS7_NOSIGS	Prevents verification of the signatures on a message

```
bool openssl_pkcs7_decrypt(string infile, string outfile, mixed certificate,
mixed key)
```

This function decrypts an encrypted message from the file named by the first argument, infile, and writes the plaintext into the file named by the second argument, outfile. The decryption is done using an RC2 40-bit cipher. The third argument, certificate, specifies the certificate to use, and the fourth argument, key, specifies the private key that matches the certificate.

If the function is successful, the return value will be true. If an error occurs, the return value will be false, and openssl_error_string should be used to obtain error information. The process must have write access to the output file. The file will be created if it does not exist, or if it does exist, it will be truncated before the output from this function is written to it.

```
bool openssl_pkcs7_sign(string infile, string outfile, mixed certificate,
mixed key, array headers [, long flags [, string extra_certificates]])
```

This signs the contents of the file named by the first argument, infile, and writes the result to the file named by the second argument, outfile. Unless PKCS7_NOCERTS is specified as part of the option flags argument, the certificate specified by the third argument, certificate, will be included in the result. The key specified by the fourth argument, key, should be a private key obtained from openssl_get_private, and will be used to sign the message. The fifth argument, headers, can be either an indexed or an associative array. The contents of the array will be prepended to the output after it has been signed. If the array is indexed, each element of the array is treated as a single line to be output. If the array is associative, one line will be written for each key, composed of the key and the value joined by a colon and a space. The sixth argument, flags, is optional and specifies signing options. It is a bit mask and can be composed of the constants described in Table 9-3. If the seventh argument, extra_certificates, is present, the certificates contained in the file that it names will also be included in the signed result.

If the function is successful, the signed message will be written to the output file named by the second argument, outfile, and the return from the function will be true. If an error occurs, the return will be false, and openssl_error_string should be used to obtain error information. The process must have write access to the output file, and it will be created if it does not exist. If the file does exist, it will be truncated before the output from this function is written to it.

```
bool openssl_pkcs7_verify(string infile, int flags [, string outfile
[, array cainfo [, string extra_certificates]]])
```

This function verifies the signature on the contents of the file named by the first argument, infile. The second argument, flags, specifies a bit mask of options that control the verification process. Table 9-3 lists the constant definitions and their meanings. If the third argument, outfile, is present and not null, it specifies the name of a file that the certificates contained in the signed message will be written to. The fourth argument, cainfo, if present, contains a list of trusted certificates that should be used in verifying the signature. The fifth argument, extra_certificates, if present, specifies the name of a file that contains any untrusted certificates that should be used in verifying the signature.

If a list of trusted certificates for verification is supplied, the array should contain the names of files and/or directories. Files that are specified as such may contain multiple certificates. Any directory that is specified should contain one file per certificate, and the file should have a name composed of the certificate subject's hash value and an extension of ".0". Symbolic links named in this manner referring to real files of any other name are acceptable.

The return from this function is true if the signature is valid. If the signature is not valid, but no errors otherwise occurred, the return from the function is false. If an error occurs in the verification process, the return value will be −1, and openssl_error_string should be used to obtain error information. If an output file is specified, the process must have write access to it, and it will be created if it does not already exist. If the file does exist, it will be truncated before the output of this function is written to it.

## CHAPTER 10

Advanced Programming Topics

We have explained quite a bit about using the OpenSSL library. Often, tasks such as certificate management are most easily accomplished with the command-line tool. For other tasks, such as SSL communications, we must flex our knowledge of the API. By this point it should be clear, though we have not explicitly stated it, that the command-line utilities all use various parts of the OpenSSL API, some of which we have not yet discussed in any detail.

In this chapter, we tackle some of the more advanced topics of programming with OpenSSL, including the programmatic interfaces to some features we've discussed only when using the command-line tool. In addition, we'll cover the interface for reading program variables at runtime. Using the details in this chapter, we will investigate how OpenSSL provides for a variety of other tasks, such as creating S/MIME secure email, importing certificates into common web browsers, and hooking into certificates to access public key components for more primitive cryptographic functions.

Object Stacks

OpenSSL has a large number of macros for dealing with stacks of typed objects. The API can perform only a small number of operations on a stack; however, there are a large number of macros to ensure type safety for objects on the stacks. For instance, if we had a stack of X509 objects and a generic push method for adding an object to the stack, nothing would prevent us from accidentally pushing a non-X509 object onto the stack. To alleviate this problem, OpenSSL provides type-specific macros on top of the generic operations. When manipulating stacks, the type-specific macros should always be used instead of the generic routines. Since the actual operations for a single type have the same behavior as the operations for any type, we will look at them generically. See Example 10-1.

Example 10-1. Stack manipulation functions in generic form

```
STACK_OF(TYPE) * sk_TYPE_new_null(void);
void sk_TYPE_free(STACK_OF(TYPE) *st);
```

Example 10-1. Stack manipulation functions in generic form (continued)

```
void sk_TYPE_pop_free(STACK_OF(TYPE) *st, void (*free_func)(TYPE *));
void sk_TYPE_zero(STACK_OF(TYPE) *st);
STACK_OF(TYPE) * sk_TYPE_dup(STACK_OF(TYPE) *st);

int sk_TYPE_push(STACK_OF(TYPE) *st, TYPE *val);
TYPE * sk_TYPE_pop(STACK_OF(TYPE) *st);
int sk_TYPE_unshift(STACK_OF(TYPE) *st, TYPE *val);
TYPE * sk_TYPE_shift(STACK_OF(TYPE) *st);
int sk_TYPE_num(STACK_OF(TYPE) *st);
TYPE * sk_TYPE_value(STACK_OF(TYPE) *st, int i);
TYPE * sk_TYPE_set(STACK_OF(TYPE) *st, int i, TYPE *val);
TYPE * sk_TYPE_delete(STACK_OF(TYPE) *st, int i);
TYPE * sk_TYPE_delete_ptr(STACK_OF(TYPE) *st, TYPE *ptr);
int sk_TYPE_insert(STACK_OF(TYPE) *st, TYPE *val, int i);
```

Example 10-1 shows the prototypes for some of the generic stack functions in OpenSSL. The type of a stack is implemented through the macro STACK_OF. Stacks are opaque types; an application should not check or set members directly. By replacing the **TYPE** placeholder used by the sample declarations in Example 10-1 with a specific object type, we get a good look at the prototypes of the actual stack manipulation calls for that type.

> The "functions" shown in Example 10-1, like many members of the OpenSSL API, are implemented via macros. Thus, it should be obvious that function pointer manipulation is not possible. In general, applications should use the API directly since the underlying implementation is subject to change in future versions.

The operations on the stack should be self-explanatory; we'll cover them briefly. The sk_TYPE_new_null function simply creates an empty stack, while the sk_TYPE_free function frees a stack; the latter frees only the stack, not the objects contained in the stack. To free a stack and all its members, the sk_TYPE_pop_free function should be used; we must pass in a function pointer to the free method for this to work correctly. The last of the general manipulation functions are sk_TYPE_zero to empty a stack and sk_TYPE_dup to copy a stack object.

There are also the general functions sk_TYPE_push and sk_TYPE_pop that we would expect in a stack implementation. Two that are less likely are sk_TYPE_unshift and sk_TYPE_shift; the former pushes an element to the bottom of the stack, and the latter pops the bottom item off the stack. The functions that add elements (sk_TYPE_push and sk_TYPE_unshift) return the total number of elements in the stack, and the other two functions return the item that was removed from the stack.

The last group of macros is a set of nontypical functions for a stack implementation; they add functionality that is more commonly found in lists. The first, sk_TYPE_num, returns the total number of items in the stack. To retrieve an item by index number (if the bottom item is zero) without changing the stack, we should use sk_TYPE_value.

In order to set an item in the stack explicitly, the function sk_TYPE_set will replace the ith item with the item passed to the call. The delete functions delete a single item from the stack. The item to delete can be selected by index or pointer value; the stack is shifted to fill the space left by the removed item. Finally, sk_TYPE_insert adds the indicated item to the ith position in the stack and moves all the items above it, including the ith item before the call, up one position.

As we'll see when we move into further topics of this chapter, proper stack handling is critical for setting up some data structures. While we'll probably put only a subset of this simple interface to use, we now have the tools to do more complex tasks.

Configuration Files

We learned how to create a CA by first creating a configuration file to hold our parameters in Chapter 3. The command-line tool used this file to perform as we had configured, such as obeying choices for algorithms, providing default values for fields in the subject name, etc. The public API has a suite of functions for processing and accessing values of configuration files. The files themselves simply organize and map keys to values. In general, the keys are strings, and the values can be either integers or strings, although all values are stored internally as strings.

The goal of the configuration file interface is to make the format of the file opaque to the code that processes it. This is done through NCONF objects. When such objects are created, a CONF_METHOD structure is specified that aggregates the routines to perform the low-level file parsing operations. OpenSSL most commonly uses the function NCONF_default to get the CONF_METHOD object. This method reads files of the format we described in Chapter 2. Because of the flexibility afforded by specifying the underlying CONF_METHOD, the NCONF interface may be extended in future versions of OpenSSL to include support for reading configuration files of new formats, such as XML.

There are only a few functions to this simple interface, and we'll explore them by looking at an example. Example 10-2 presents a small sample configuration file.

Example 10-2. A sample configuration file (testconf.cnf)

```
# The config file
GlobalVar = foo
GlobalNum = 12

[Params]
SectionName = mySection

[mySection]
myVar = bar
myNum = 7
```

Example 10-3 provides a test program to read the sample configuration file.

Example 10-3. Code to interact with the configuration file

```c
#include <stdio.h>
#include <stdlib.h>
#include <openssl/conf.h>

void handle_error(const char *file, int lineno, const char *msg)
{
    fprintf(stderr, "** %s:%i %s\n", file, lineno, msg);
    ERR_print_errors_fp(stderr);
    exit(-1);
}
#define int_error(msg)  handle_error(__FILE__, __LINE__, msg)

#define GLOB_VAR "GlobalVar"
#define GLOB_NUM "GlobalNum"
#define PARAMS   "Params"
#define SEC_NAME "SectionName"

#define CONFFILE "testconf.cnf"

int main(int argc, char *argv[])
{
    int                  i;
    long                 i_val, err = 0;
    char                 *key, *s_val;
    STACK_OF(CONF_VALUE) *sec;
    CONF_VALUE           *item;
    CONF                 *conf;

    conf = NCONF_new(NCONF_default());
    if (!NCONF_load(conf, CONFFILE, &err))
    {
        if (err == 0)
            int_error("Error opening configuration file");
        else
        {
            fprintf(stderr, "Error in %s on line %li\n", CONFFILE, err);
            int_error("Errors parsing configuration file");
        }
    }
    if (!(s_val = NCONF_get_string(conf, NULL, GLOB_VAR)))
    {
        fprintf(stderr, "Error finding \"%s\" in [%s]\n", GLOB_VAR, NULL);
        int_error("Error finding string");
    }
    printf("Sec: %s, Key: %s, Val: %s\n", NULL, GLOB_VAR, s_val);
#if (OPENSSL_VERSION_NUMBER > 0x00907000L)
    if (!(err = NCONF_get_number_e(conf, NULL, GLOB_NUM, &i_val)))
    {
        fprintf(stderr, "Error finding \"%s\" in [%s]\n", GLOB_NUM, NULL);
        int_error("Error finding number");
    }
#else
    if (!(s_val = NCONF_get_string(conf, NULL, GLOB_NUM)))
```

Example 10-3. Code to interact with the configuration file (continued)

```
    {
        fprintf(stderr, "Error finding \"%s\" in [%s]\n", GLOB_VAR, NULL);
        int_error("Error finding number");
    }
    i_val = atoi(s_val);
#endif
    printf("Sec: %s, Key: %s, Val: %i\n", NULL, GLOB_VAR, i_val);
    if (!(key = NCONF_get_string(conf, PARAMS, SEC_NAME)))
    {
        fprintf(stderr, "Error finding \"%s\" in [%s]\n", SEC_NAME, PARAMS);
        int_error("Error finding string");
    }
    printf("Sec: %s, Key: %s, Val: %s\n", PARAMS, SEC_NAME, key);
    if (!(sec = NCONF_get_section(conf, key)))
    {
        fprintf(stderr, "Error finding [%s]\n", key);
        int_error("Error finding string");
    }
    for (i = 0;  i < sk_CONF_VALUE_num(sec);  i++)
    {
        item = sk_CONF_VALUE_value(sec, i);
        printf("Sec: %s, Key: %s, Val: %s\n",
               item->section, item->name, item->value);
    }

    NCONF_free(conf);
    return 0;
}
```

In the example program, a new CONF object is created using the default method, and the file is loaded by the call to NCONF_load. There are also other functions for loading the file from open FILE or BIO objects: NCONF_load_fp and NCONF_load_bio. Three different functions are used to probe the configuration file for values. The first one that we use is NCONF_get_string, which returns the string of the value corresponding to the section and key values passed to it. If either the section or the key is undefined, it returns NULL. Our sample program uses a few preprocessor defines as shortcuts to the section and key strings:

```
    char *NCONF_get_string(const CONF *conf, const char *section,
                           const char *key);
    int NCONF_get_number_e(const CONF *conf, const char *section,
                           const char *key, long *result);
    STACK_OF(CONF_VALUE) *NCONF_get_section(const CONF *conf,
                                            const char *section);
```

One interesting point made in the example is the preprocessor conditionals around usage of the function NCONF_get_number_e. Versions of OpenSSL prior to 0.9.7 have a function, NCONF_get_number, that takes three arguments, the same as NCONF_get_string, except that NCONF_get_number returns an integer value instead of a string. This function should be avoided since it does not allow for error checking. The better way to read integer values from a configuration file is to get the value as a string, check for an error condition by checking for a NULL return value, and then convert the string to an integer ourselves. Of course, if the NCONF_get_number_e function is available, it can be used safely. This function writes the retrieved value to the last argument and returns nonzero on success.

 The function NCONF_get_number may be reimplemented in 0.9.7 simply as a macro for NCONF_get_number_e, requiring calling applications to be changed to account for the modified interface. Because of possible changes, it is safest to use NCONF_get_number_e.

The last NCONF function used in the example is NCONF_get_section. This function returns a stack of all the configuration parameters in the specified section. Our sample program iterates over the stack and prints all the pairs that it contains. This code actually manually accesses members of the CONF_VALUE structure; the declaration is provided in Example 10-4.

Example 10-4. The declaration of CONF_VALUE

```
typedef struct
{
    char *section;
    char *name;
    char *value;
} CONF_VALUE;
```

In general, the NCONF interface can provide a simple, readily available infrastructure for customized, application-specific configuration files. This interface is useful for other reasons, as well. For instance, we can build a custom CA application that shares configuration files with the command-line tool.

X.509

In the previous chapters, we discussed certificates in detail. We know how to perform all the common operations using the command-line tool, but we haven't discussed how to do this programmatically. Knowing this isn't strictly necessary, since applications aside from those implementing features similar to a typical CA will not need to do this programmatically. However, it can be useful in those cases.

We will cover several aspects of programmatically dealing with the X.509 family of operations. To do this most logically, we'll first look at the proper way to generate a certificate request. We'll also look at several common operations on the request itself. Once we know how to make a request, we'll look into the functions used to create a full-fledged certificate from a certificate request. Finally, we'll discuss how to verify a certificate chain. We've already discussed this process for SSL connections, but here we'll focus on verification when dealing with just X509 objects.

Generating Requests

Recall that an X.509 certificate is a public key packaged with information about the certificate owner and issuer. Thus, to make a request, we must generate a public and private key on which we'll base our certificate. We'll start our discussion assuming generation of the key pair has already been completed (see Chapter 8 for details).

An X.509 certificate request is represented by an X509_REQ object in OpenSSL. As we learned in Chapter 3, a certificate request's main component is the public half of the key pair. It also contains a subjectName field and additional X.509 attributes. In reality, the attributes are optional parameters for the request, but the subject name should always be present. As we'll see, creating a certificate is not a very difficult task.

Subject name

Before looking at an example, we need a little more background information on subject name manipulation with the API. The object type X509_NAME represents a certificate name. Specifically, a certificate request has only a subject name, while full certificates contain a subject name and an issuer name. The purpose of the name field is to fully identify an entity, whether it is a server, person, corporation, etc. To this end, a name field is composed of several entries for country name, organization name, and common name, just to name a few. Again, we can think of the fields in a name as key/value pairs; the key is the name of the field, and the value is its content.

In theory, there can be arbitrary fields in a name, but in practice, a few standard ones are expected. In OpenSSL, fields are internally identified through an integer value known as the NID. All of this information rapidly becomes relevant when it comes time to build the subject name of our request.

As we've already said, a certificate name is represented by an X509_NAME object. This object is essentially a collection of X509_NAME_ENTRY objects. Each X509_NAME_ENTRY object represents a single field and the corresponding value. Thus, our application needs to generate a X509_NAME_ENTRY object for each of the fields we'll put in the name of the certificate request.

The process is simple. First, we look up the NID of the field we need to create. Using the NID, we create the X509_NAME_ENTRY object and add our data. The entry is added to the X509_NAME, and we repeat the process until all the desired fields are entered. After the name is fully assembled, we can add it to an X509_REQ object.

OpenSSL provides many functions for manipulating X509_NAME and X509_NAME_ENTRY objects that enable us to perform the subject name assembly using many different methods. For instance, the function call X509_NAME_add_entry_by_txt automatically looks up the NID, creates the entry, and adds it to the X509_NAME. In the example below, we elected to show the explicit implementation instead of demonstrating the kinds of operations that are available.

X.509 Version 3 extensions

In previous chapters, we discussed the basics of X.509 Version 3 certificate extensions. In particular, in Chapter 5, we learned that the subjectAltName extension is very useful for SSL. This extension contains a field named dNSName that will hold the FQDN for the entity possessing the certificate. As far as certificate requests are concerned, we should add in the extension before sending the request to the CA for certification. Doing this programmatically is straightforward.

The X509_EXTENSION type object represents a single extension to an X509 object. The process of adding extensions to a request requires us to put all the requested extensions into a STACK_OF(X509_EXTENSION) object. After the stack is created, we can add the stack to the request, and our task is complete.

Putting it all together

Now we know how to create a certificate request: we have to create an X509_REQ object, add a subject name and public key to it, add all desired extensions, and sign the request with the private key. To represent the public and private key components, we should use the generic type EVP_PKEY and its corresponding functions. The slightly confusing part to this process is signing the request.

With OpenSSL, message digest algorithms are represented by EVP_MD objects. We need to specify a different EVP_MD object based on whether we're signing with an RSA or DSA key, but the public key algorithm isn't known when we do the signing, since we must use the abstract EVP_PKEY interface. We can probe the internals of an EVP_PKEY object to find out the underlying algorithm, but doing so isn't very clean since it requires directly accessing members of the structure. Unfortunately, this is the only solution to the problem. The example below shows how the EVP_PKEY_type function can be used in conjunction with a member of the type EVP_PKEY to perform this task.

We're ready to create a request now that we know the theory behind it. The code appears in Example 10-5.

Example 10-5. A program to generate a certificate request

```
#include <stdio.h>
#include <stdlib.h>
#include <openssl/x509.h>
#include <openssl/x509v3.h>
#include <openssl/err.h>
#include <openssl/pem.h>

void handle_error(const char *file, int lineno, const char *msg)
{
    fprintf(stderr, "** %s:%i %s\n", file, lineno, msg);
    ERR_print_errors_fp(stderr);
    exit(-1);
}
#define int_error(msg)  handle_error(__FILE__, __LINE__, msg)
```

Example 10-5. A program to generate a certificate request (continued)

```c
#define PKEY_FILE   "privkey.pem"
#define REQ_FILE    "newreq.pem"
#define ENTRY_COUNT 6

struct entry
{
    char *key;
    char *value;
};

struct entry entries[ENTRY_COUNT] =
{
    { "countryName",            "US"                },
    { "stateOrProvinceName",    "VA"                },
    { "localityName",           "Fairfax"           },
    { "organizationName",       "Zork.org"          },
    { "organizationalUnitName", "Server Division"   },
    { "commonName",             "Server 36, Engineering"   },
};

int main(int argc, char *argv[])
{
    int        i;
    X509_REQ   *req;
    X509_NAME  *subj;
    EVP_PKEY   *pkey;
    EVP_MD     *digest;
    FILE       *fp;

    OpenSSL_add_all_algorithms( );
    ERR_load_crypto_strings( );
    seed_prng( );

    /* first read in the private key */
    if (!(fp = fopen(PKEY_FILE, "r")))
        int_error("Error reading private key file");
    if (!(pkey = PEM_read_PrivateKey(fp, NULL, NULL, "secret")))
        int_error("Error reading private key in file");
    fclose(fp);

    /* create a new request and add the key to it */
    if (!(req = X509_REQ_new( )))
        int_error("Failed to create X509_REQ object");
    X509_REQ_set_pubkey(req, pkey);

    /* assign the subject name */
    if (!(subj = X509_NAME_new( )))
        int_error("Failed to create X509_NAME object");

    for (i = 0;  i < ENTRY_COUNT;  i++)
    {
        int             nid;
        X509_NAME_ENTRY *ent;
```

Example 10-5. A program to generate a certificate request (continued)

```
        if ((nid = OBJ_txt2nid(entries[i].key)) == NID_undef)
        {
            fprintf(stderr, "Error finding NID for %s\n", entries[i].key);
            int_error("Error on lookup");
        }
        if (!(ent = X509_NAME_ENTRY_create_by_NID(NULL, nid, MBSTRING_ASC,
                                        entries[i].value, -1)))
            int_error("Error creating Name entry from NID");
        if (X509_NAME_add_entry(subj, ent, -1, 0) != 1)
            int_error("Error adding entry to Name");
    }
    if (X509_REQ_set_subject_name(req, subj) != 1)
        int_error("Error adding subject to request");
    /* add an extension for the FQDN we wish to have */
    {
        X509_EXTENSION            *ext;
        STACK_OF(X509_EXTENSION) *extlist;
        char                     *name = "subjectAltName";
        char                     *value = "DNS:splat.zork.org";

        extlist = sk_X509_EXTENSION_new_null();

        if (!(ext = X509V3_EXT_conf(NULL, NULL, name, value)))
            int_error("Error creating subjectAltName extension");

        sk_X509_EXTENSION_push(extlist, ext);

        if (!X509_REQ_add_extensions(req, extlist))
            int_error("Error adding subjectAltName to the request");
        sk_X509_EXTENSION_pop_free(extlist, X509_EXTENSION_free);
    }

    /* pick the correct digest and sign the request */
    if (EVP_PKEY_type(pkey->type) == EVP_PKEY_DSA)
        digest = EVP_dss1();
    else if (EVP_PKEY_type(pkey->type) == EVP_PKEY_RSA)
        digest = EVP_sha1();
    else
        int_error("Error checking public key for a valid digest");
    if (!(X509_REQ_sign(req, pkey, digest)))
        int_error("Error signing request");

    /* write the completed request */
    if (!(fp = fopen(REQ_FILE, "w")))
        int_error("Error writing to request file");
    if (PEM_write_X509_REQ(fp, req) != 1)
        int_error("Error while writing request");
    fclose(fp);

    EVP_PKEY_free(pkey);
    X509_REQ_free(req);
    return 0;
}
```

Using the appropriate PEM call, we read in our private key. Recall that a public key is a subset of the information in a private key, so we need not read in anything more than the private key. Using the function X509_REQ_set_pubkey, we add the public key portion of the private key to the request:

```
int OBJ_txt2nid(const char *field);
X509_NAME_ENTRY *X509_NAME_ENTRY_create_by_NID(X509_NAME_ENTRY **ne, int nid,
                                       int type, unsigned char *value,
                                       int len);
int X509_NAME_add_entry(X509_NAME *name, X509_NAME_ENTRY *ne,
                        int loc, int set);
```

Using a loop, we read from our global array containing the fields and values, and add to our subject name. The function OBJ_txt2nid performs a lookup of the built-in field definitions. This function returns the integer NID value. After obtaining the NID, we use the X509_NAME_ENTRY_create_by_NID function to create the X509_NAME_ENTRY object properly. The third argument to this function must specify the type of character encoding; common specifications are MBSTRING_ASC for ASCII and MBSTRING_UTF8 for UTF8 encoding. The last argument is the length of the value of the field we are setting. By passing in a −1 for this argument, the data is interpreted as a C-style, NULL-terminated string. The length of the data is determined by searching the data for a NULL terminator. The last call used in the loop is X509_NAME_add_entry. This call adds the entry to the subject name. The third argument specifies the position at which we want to place the data. In essence, the X509_NAME is a stack of X509_NAME_ENTRY objects. Thus, there is an ordering to the fields in a name. Specifying −1 for this argument adds the new field after any other fields already in the X509_NAME. Alternatively, we could have passed in the return from X509_NAME_entry_count, but using −1 is better because it ensures that the field is added to the end of the list. The last argument to X509_NAME_add_entry specifies the operation to be performed on the item already in the location indicated by the third argument. For instance, if the X509_NAME object contained three fields, and we made a call to this function specifying 1 for the third argument and 0 for the last argument, the field in the middle would be replaced by the new data. Using −1 for the last argument will cause the new data to be appended to the previous data, while using 1 would cause it to be prepended.

After the subject name is fully built, we add it to the certificate request. Then we build and add our extension for the subjectAltName. This can be easily done through the X509V3_EXT_conf function:

```
X509_EXTENSION *X509V3_EXT_conf(LHASH *conf, X509V3_CTX *ctx,
                               char *name, char *value);
int X509_REQ_add_extensions(X509_REQ *req, STACK_OF(X509_EXTENSION) *exts);
```

The first two parameters to X509_EXT_conf aren't important for creating the simple extension we need. This function returns NULL on error and the built object otherwise. We revisit this function in more detail when we discuss creating certificates below. After the X509_EXTENSION object is created, it is added to the stack. The stack is then added to the request through the function X509_REQ_add_extensions. This function will return 1 on success.

Next, we perform the check for the key type to determine the correct `EVP_MD` object to pass to `X509_REQ_sign`. This check involves using `EVP_PKEY_type` to translate the member of the `EVP_PKEY` object to something we can test. If the key is RSA, we use `EVP_sha1`; if it is DSA, we use `EVP_dss1`. In either case, SHA1 is the algorithm used in the signing process.

Using what we've learned about parsing configuration files, this example could easily be extended to read the field names and values from an OpenSSL configuration file instead of the hardcoded information that we provided in the example. Doing this would allow the program to interact with the same configuration files as the command-line tools.

Making Certificates

We already know that creating a certificate requires a certificate request, a CA certificate, and a CA private key to match the CA certificate. However, we haven't discussed much beyond passing these elements into the command-line tool to produce a finished certificate. Programmatically, this process requires the programmer to perform several steps. We can break down the process into four essential steps.

1. Verify the certificate request and check its contents (`subjectName` and `subjectAltName` in this example) to decide if we wish to certify the data with our CA's certificate.

2. Create a new certificate and set all the necessary fields, such as public key, subject and issuer names, expiration date, etc.

3. Add applicable extensions to the certificate, including the requested `subjectAltName`.

4. Sign the certificate with the CA's private key.

Step 1 is perhaps the most important. To verify the request, we first check that the enclosed signature is valid; this helps to ensure the request was not modified after it was submitted for signing. More importantly, we need to determine if we actually want to certify the data in the request. Recall that signing a request into a certificate means that the CA has verified the identity of the requestor. This leaves the obligation of determining identity up to the application and, ultimately, the user of the application. It isn't a good idea to automatically sign any certificate presented. For instance, an attacker could create a request with the identity information for another user, submit it through the "normal" channels, and automatically be granted unauthorized privileges. For this reason, the application must prompt the user with all the information in the request and then ask whether it appears to be correct because the user is in the unique position to make that determination. For instance, we must somehow verify that the presenter of the request does indeed possess the FQDN in the `dNSName` of the request. Finally, the information in a request should not be altered in any way. In other words, if the CA does not authorize any part of the request, the whole request should be refused rather than changing the unacceptable portions.

In the second step, we create the certificate and assign all of its properties. These are generally some CA standard parameters for a new certificate. For example, the CA should determine the default certificate version to use and the default expiration time. In addition to the standard settings, we need to assign a subject name and an issuer name to the newly created certificate. The subject name for the certificate should be taken directly from the subject name of the certificate request, which we determined was valid in the previous step. For the issuer name, the CA certificate's subject name should be used. Lastly, the public key from the request must be added into the certificate.

One very important step in programmatically creating a certificate is the addition of certificate extensions; in step 3, we handle this process. As we discussed in Chapter 3, the use of X.509v3 certificates is nearly ubiquitous. As such, we need to add the relevant v3 fields. An important part of doing this correctly is knowing which extensions we actually want to give the certificate. For instance, we must determine if we wish to grant the new certificate the ability to act as a CA. In the example below, we simply use the default extensions for the OpenSSL command-line application and save the subjectAltName, which has been added.

The last step of creating a certificate is signing it with the CA private key. This process will prevent changes to any of the data we've placed in the certificate at this point; thus, it should be done last. A sample program that performs all of the actions described in this section appears in Example 10-6.

Example 10-6. Creating a certificate from a request and CA credentials

```
#include <stdio.h>
#include <stdlib.h>
#include <openssl/x509.h>
#include <openssl/x509v3.h>
#include <openssl/err.h>
#include <openssl/pem.h>

void handle_error(const char *file, int lineno, const char *msg)
{
    fprintf(stderr, "** %s:%i %s\n", file, lineno, msg);
    ERR_print_errors_fp(stderr);
    exit(-1);
}
#define int_error(msg)  handle_error(__FILE__, __LINE__, msg)

/* these are defintions to make the example simpler */
#define CA_FILE         "CA.pem"
#define CA_KEY          "CAkey.pem"
#define REQ_FILE        "newreq.pem"
#define CERT_FILE       "newcert.pem"
#define DAYS_TILL_EXPIRE 365
#define EXPIRE_SECS (60*60*24*DAYS_TILL_EXPIRE)

#define EXT_COUNT 5
```

Example 10-6. Creating a certificate from a request and CA credentials (continued)

```
struct entry
{
    char *key;
    char *value;
};

struct entry ext_ent[EXT_COUNT] =
{
    { "basicConstraints",    "CA:FALSE" },
    { "nsComment",           "\"OpenSSL Generated Certificate\"" },
    { "subjectKeyIdentifier", "hash" },
    { "authorityKeyIdentifier", "keyid,issuer:always" },
    { "keyUsage",            "nonrepudiation,digitalSignature,keyEncipherment" }
};

int main(int argc, char *argv[])
{
    int                      i, subjAltName_pos;
    long                     serial = 1;
    EVP_PKEY                 *pkey, *CApkey;
    const EVP_MD             *digest;
    X509                     *cert, *CAcert;
    X509_REQ                 *req;
    X509_NAME                *name;
    X509V3_CTX               ctx;
    X509_EXTENSION           *subjAltName;
    STACK_OF(X509_EXTENSION) *req_exts;
    FILE                     *fp;
    BIO                      *out;

    OpenSSL_add_all_algorithms();
    ERR_load_crypto_strings();
    seed_prng();

    /* open stdout */
    if (!(out = BIO_new_fp(stdout, BIO_NOCLOSE)))
        int_error("Error creating stdout BIO");

    /* read in the request */
    if (!(fp = fopen(REQ_FILE, "r")))
        int_error("Error reading request file");
    if (!(req = PEM_read_X509_REQ(fp, NULL, NULL, NULL)))
        int_error("Error reading request in file");
    fclose(fp);

    /* verify signature on the request */
    if (!(pkey = X509_REQ_get_pubkey(req)))
        int_error("Error getting public key from request");
    if (X509_REQ_verify(req, pkey)) != 1)
        int_error("Error verifying signature on certificate");

    /* read in the CA certificate */
```

```
    if (!(fp = fopen(CA_FILE, "r")))
        int_error("Error reading CA certificate file");
    if (!(CAcert = PEM_read_X509(fp, NULL, NULL, NULL)))
        int_error("Error reading CA certificate in file");
    fclose(fp);

    /* read in the CA private key */
    if (!(fp = fopen(CA_KEY, "r")))
        int_error("Error reading CA private key file");
    if (!(CApkey = PEM_read_PrivateKey(fp, NULL, NULL, "password")))
        int_error("Error reading CA private key in file");
    fclose(fp);

    /* print out the subject name and subject alt name extension */
    if (!(name = X509_REQ_get_subject_name(req)))
        int_error("Error getting subject name from request");
    X509_NAME_print(out, name, 0);
    fputc('\n', stdout);
    if (!(req_exts = X509_REQ_get_extensions(req)))
        int_error("Error getting the request's extensions");
    subjAltName_pos = X509v3_get_ext_by_NID(req_exts,
                                            OBJ_sn2nid("subjectAltName"), -1);
    subjAltName = X509v3_get_ext(req_exts, subjAltName_pos);
    X509V3_EXT_print(out, subjAltName, 0, 0);
    fputc('\n', stdout);

    /* WE SHOULD NOW ASK WHETHER TO CONTINUE OR NOT */

    /* create new certificate */
    if (!(cert = X509_new( )))
        int_error("Error creating X509 object");

    /* set version number for the certificate (X509v3) and the serial number */
    if (X509_set_version(cert, 2L) != 1)
        int_error("Error settin certificate version");
    ASN1_INTEGER_set(X509_get_serialNumber(cert), serial++);

    /* set issuer and subject name of the cert from the req and the CA */
    if (!(name = X509_REQ_get_subject_name(req)))
        int_error("Error getting subject name from request");
    if (X509_set_subject_name(cert, name) != 1)
        int_error("Error setting subject name of certificate");
    if (!(name = X509_get_subject_name(CAcert)))
        int_error("Error getting subject name from CA certificate");
    if (X509_set_issuer_name(cert, name) != 1)
        int_error("Error setting issuer name of certificate");

    /* set public key in the certificate */
    if (X509_set_pubkey(cert, pkey)) != 1)
        int_error("Error setting public key of the certificate");

    /* set duration for the certificate */
```

```
    if (!(X509_gmtime_adj(X509_get_notBefore(cert), 0)))
        int_error("Error setting beginning time of the certificate");
    if (!(X509_gmtime_adj(X509_get_notAfter(cert), EXPIRE_SECS)))
        int_error("Error setting ending time of the certificate");

    /* add x509v3 extensions as specified */
    X509V3_set_ctx(&ctx, CAcert, cert, NULL, NULL, 0);
    for (i = 0;  i < EXT_COUNT;  i++)
    {
        X509_EXTENSION *ext;

        if (!(ext = X509V3_EXT_conf(NULL, &ctx,
                                    ext_ent[i].key, ext_ent[i].value)))
        {
            fprintf(stderr, "Error on \"%s = %s\"\n",
                    ext_ent[i].key, ext_ent[i].value);
            int_error("Error creating X509 extension object");
        }
        if (!X509_add_ext(cert, ext, -1))
        {
            fprintf(stderr, "Error on \"%s = %s\"\n",
                    ext_ent[i].key, ext_ent[i].value);
            int_error("Error adding X509 extension to certificate");
        }
        X509_EXTENSION_free(ext);
    }

    /* add the subjectAltName in the request to the cert */
    if (!X509_add_ext(cert, subjAltName, -1))
        int_error("Error adding subjectAltName to certificate");

    /* sign the certificate with the CA private key */
    if (EVP_PKEY_type(CApkey->type) == EVP_PKEY_DSA)
        digest = EVP_dss1();
    else if (EVP_PKEY_type(CApkey->type) == EVP_PKEY_RSA)
        digest = EVP_sha1();
    else
        int_error("Error checking CA private key for a valid digest");
    if (!(X509_sign(cert, CApkey, digest)))
        int_error("Error signing certificate");

    /* write the completed certificate */
    if (!(fp = fopen(CERT_FILE, "w")))
        int_error("Error writing to certificate file");
    if (PEM_write_X509(fp, cert) != 1)
        int_error("Error while writing certificate");
    fclose(fp);

    return 0;
}
```

At the beginning of this program, we read the request and verify its signature using X509_REQ_verify. Like in Example 10-5, we use the shortcut for specifying the password to the deserialization routine for the private key; real-world implementations normally prompt the user for this in an application-specific way.

Once we've read in all the data for creating the certificate, we print the important data from the certificate request, namely the subjectName and the subjectAltName. The subjectName is retrieved using the function X509_REQ_get_subject_name and printed with X509_NAME_print. The last parameter of the print function controls whether the short name of the field or the OID is printed: 0 for the short name, 1 for the OID.

Extracting the subjectAltName extension is more complex than getting the subjectName. First, we must extract the stack of all the extensions in the request. With this stack, we use X509v3_get_ext_by_NID to get the integer indicating the position of the subjectAltName field. We can use this integer with the function X509v3_get_ext to get the actual X509_EXTENSION object. This object is then printed with X509V3_EXT_print. The third parameter to this call is identical to the last parameter of the X509_NAME_print call. The last parameter is the number of spaces to be indented before printing the data. After printing this crucial information, the application should query the CA administrator to determine if this data is correct and not a masquerading attempt.

After this process, we create an empty certificate and set the version of the new certificate. Since the version numbers start at 1, and the internal representation of versions starts at 0, using 2 in the call to X509_set_version really indicates Version 3 of X.509. Certificates must also bear a serial number assigned from the CA at the time of signing. To do this, we use a simple ASN.1 family function call.[*]

When signing certificates in applications, it is the application's responsibility to track serial numbers and assign them uniquely. Setting the subject and issuer names is performed as described above. After setting the names, we use X509_set_pubkey to assign the certificate the same public key we obtained from the request. Setting the certificate expiration time is performed by setting the notBefore and notAfter attributes. We use the X509_gmtime_adj function to set the starting time retrieved by calling X509_get_notBefore to 0. This sets the start time to the current time and date. By setting the notAfter parameter in a similar fashion, we specify the number of seconds for the lifetime of the certificate.

We use a previously unseen function, X509V3_set_ctx, to prepare a context for creating the extensions to the certificate:

```
void X509V3_set_ctx(X509V3_CTX *ctx, X509 *issuer, X509 *subject,
                    X509_REQ *req, X509_CRL *crl, int flags);
```

---

[*] ASN.1 (Abstract Syntax Notation 1) is a language that is used to describe data structures. For our purposes, this definition is sufficient. A complete discussion of ASN.1 is beyond the scope of this book.

This versatile function is called with several NULLs since we don't need to add extensions to any X509_REQ or X509_CRL objects. Additionally, we don't need any flags, so a 0 is used for the last argument. This X509V3_CTX object is used by the X509V3_EXT_conf to allow for some of the more complex extensions we wish to add. For example, the subjectKeyIdentifier extension is computed as a hash of part of the data in the certificate, and the X509V3_CTX object provides the routine access to this certificate (we added it to the context earlier).

We then loop through the array of extension data to create and add extensions to the new certificate. Unlike the process of adding extensions to a certificate request, we don't need to add the extensions to a stack before adding them to an X509 object. As we mentioned earlier, the extensions we add are the defaults for the OpenSSL command-line utility. After the loop is completed, we add the subjectAltName extension that we extracted from the request previously.

The last task we perform before writing our new certificate is to sign it. This is critical, since an unsigned certificate is essentially useless. The function X509_sign performs this for us. As in Example 10-5, we must perform a check to determine the type of the private key so that we can decide on a correct EVP_MD object to use as the hash algorithm.

We now have a complete, valid certificate. This is a big step. Using what we've learned, we are armed with enough knowledge to implement a minimal CA. Before leaving the topic of programming with X.509, however, one important topic remains to be discussed: certificate verification.

X.509 Certificate Checking

In Chapter 5, we discussed SSL server certificate verification extensively. Here, we'll discuss the layer just below SSL that performs certificate verification. Specifically, we'll discuss how OpenSSL's SSL functionality verifies a certificate against CRLs and other certificates in the certificate hierarchy. To do this, we'll require functions from the X.509 package. The SSL protocol implementation handles much of what we're about to discuss here for us; even so, some setup work is required on our part, particularly if we wish to include CRLs in the verification process, which we almost certainly do.

Knowing how to programmatically perform the verification of a certificate chain gives us valuable insight that we might not ordinarily have into what is actually involved in properly verifying a certificate. It also provides us with the information necessary to verify certificates on our own when we're not using the SSL protocol. Before delving into the verification process, however, it's helpful to understand the purpose of some of the objects that are involved.

In general, a certificate can be validated only against a collection of other certificate material, i.e., CA certificates and CRLs. OpenSSL uses the object type X509_STORE to represent a collection of certificates and certificate revocation lists to serve this purpose. Additionally, OpenSSL uses the type X509_STORE_CTX to hold the data used during an actual verification. This distinction is important; our implementations will look somewhat incongruous with respect to the context-object relationship we've seen with other OpenSSL packages. For certificate verification, we will create an X509_STORE first and populate it with all the available certificate and revocation list information. When it's time to verify a peer certificate, we will use the store to create an X509_STORE_CTX to perform the actual verification.

Along with the certificate stores and the associated contexts, the X509_LOOKUP_METHOD object is also important. Objects of this type represent a general method of finding certificates or CRLs. For instance, the X509_LOOKUP_file function returns a method to find certificate-related objects within a single file, and the X509_LOOKUP_hash_dir function returns a method to find objects within a properly set up OpenSSL CA directory. X509_LOOKUP_METHOD objects are important for creating X509_LOOKUP objects. These objects aggregate the collection of certificates accessible through the underlying method. For instance, if we have a certificate directory, we can create an X509_LOOKUP from an X509_STORE and the return value of X509_LOOKUP_hash_dir; this X509_LOOKUP object can then be assigned to a directory, and our X509_STORE will have access to all of the certificates and CRLs that the lookup aggregates.

To review: an X509_STORE holds X509_LOOKUP objects built on X509_LOOKUP_METHODs. This is how the store gains access to certificate and CRL data. The store can then be used to create an X509_STORE_CTX to perform a verification operation.

Knowing the relationships between some of these objects, we can begin to see the general form of what our code will have to do to verify a peer certificate. However, a few other important subtleties about correctly verifying a certificate have not yet been discussed. These can be made clear by analyzing Example 10-7, which demonstrates the whole process of validating a peer certificate.

Example 10-7. Verifying a client certificate

```
#include <stdio.h>
#include <stdlib.h>
#include <openssl/x509_vfy.h>
#include <openssl/err.h>
#include <openssl/pem.h>

void handle_error(const char *file, int lineno, const char *msg)
{
    fprintf(stderr, "** %s:%i %s\n", file, lineno, msg);
    ERR_print_errors_fp(stderr);
    exit(-1);
}
#define int_error(msg)  handle_error(__FILE__, __LINE__, msg)

/* these are defintions to make the example simpler */
#define CA_FILE     "CAfile.pem"
```

Example 10-7. Verifying a client certificate (continued)

```
#define CA_DIR      "/etc/ssl"
#define CRL_FILE    "CRLfile.pem"
#define CLIENT_CERT "cert.pem"

int verify_callback(int ok, X509_STORE_CTX *stor)
{
    if(!ok)
        fprintf(stderr, "Error: %s\n",
                X509_verify_cert_error_string(stor->error));
    return ok;
}

int main(int argc, char *argv[])
{
    X509            *cert;
    X509_STORE      *store;
    X509_LOOKUP     *lookup;
    X509_STORE_CTX *verify_ctx;
    FILE            *fp;

    OpenSSL_add_all_algorithms( );
    ERR_load_crypto_strings( );
    seed_prng( );

    /* first read the client certificate */
    if (!(fp = fopen(CLIENT_CERT, "r")))
        int_error("Error reading client certificate file");
    if (!(cert = PEM_read_X509(fp, NULL, NULL, NULL)))
        int_error("Error reading client certificate in file");
    fclose(fp);

    /* create the cert store and set the verify callback */
    if (!(store = X509_STORE_new( )))
        int_error("Error creating X509_STORE_CTX object");
    X509_STORE_set_verify_cb_func(store, verify_callback);

    /* load the CA certificates and CRLs */
    if (X509_STORE_load_locations(store, CA_FILE, CA_DIR) != 1)
        int_error("Error loading the CA file or directory");
    if (X509_STORE_set_default_paths(store) != 1)
        int_error("Error loading the system-wide CA certificates");
    if (!(lookup = X509_STORE_add_lookup(store, X509_LOOKUP_file( ))))
        int_error("Error creating X509_LOOKUP object");
    if (X509_load_crl_file(lookup, CRL_FILE, X509_FILETYPE_PEM) != 1)
        int_error("Error reading the CRL file");

    /* enabling verification against CRLs is not possible
       in prior versions */
#if (OPENSSL_VERSION_NUMBER > 0x00907000L)
    /* set the flags of the store so that CRLs are consulted */
    X509_STORE_set_flags(store, X509_V_FLAG_CRL_CHECK |
                                X509_V_FLAG_CRL_CHECK_ALL);
```

Example 10-7. Verifying a client certificate (continued)

```
#endif

    /* create a verification context and initialize it */
    if (!(verify_ctx = X509_STORE_CTX_new()))
        int_error("Error creating X509_STORE_CTX object");
    /* X509_STORE_CTX_init did not return an error condition
       in prior versions */
#if (OPENSSL_VERSION_NUMBER > 0x00907000L)
    if (X509_STORE_CTX_init(verify_ctx, store, cert, NULL) != 1)
        int_error("Error initializing verification context");
#else
    X509_STORE_CTX_init(verify_ctx, store, cert, NULL);
#endif

    /* verify the certificate */
    if (X509_verify_cert(verify_ctx) != 1)
        int_error("Error verifying the certificate");
    else
        printf("Certificate verified correctly!\n");

    return 0;
}
```

After reading in the peer certificate, we create our certificate store as expected. We also assign a verification callback function. The form and purpose of this callback is identical to the verification callback for SSL connections we saw in Chapter 5.

The following two function calls should also look familiar; we've already examined their mirrored functions for SSL_CTX objects. They behave just like the SSL-specific versions. To load the CRL file, however, we use the method described at the beginning of this section. The function X509_STORE_add_lookup will create the lookup object we need when we pass it the correct lookup method, given by X509_LOOKUP_file. After we've created the lookup (it's already added to the store), we need only assign the lookup the file from which to read. This is done by the call to X509_load_crl_file. In fact, the call to X509_STORE_load_locations could have been removed and done with lookups instead. For instance, the conditional clause using the function could be replaced by the following:

```
    if (!(lookup = X509_STORE_add_lookup(store, X509_LOOKUP_file())))
        fprintf(stderr, "Error creating X509_LOOKUP object\n");
    if (X509_LOOKUP_load_file(lookup, CA_FILE, X509_FILETYPE_PEM) != 1)
        fprintf(stderr, "Error reading the CA file\n");
    if (!(lookup = X509_STORE_add_lookup(store, X509_LOOKUP_hash_dir())))
        fprintf(stderr, "Error creating X509_LOOKUP object\n");
    if (X509_LOOKUP_add_dir(lookup, CA_DIR, X509_FILETYPE_PEM) != 1)
        fprintf(stderr, "Error reading the CRL file\n");
```

This code snippet simply follows the paradigm laid out above; we create a lookup and then set the lookup in an appropriate location. Using this expanded code can be useful in applications in which we want to do a more specific type of loading of the store, such as an application that has several CA files, each of which may contain more than one certificate.

Setting the flags for the certificate store is very important. By setting flags in the store, they are automatically copied to the store contexts created from it. Thus, setting the flag X509_V_FLAG_CRL_CHECK instructs the contexts to check client certificates for possible revocation. This flag will cause only the last item, the identity certificate itself, to be checked; the chain is not checked for possible revocation. To check the entire chain, we must also specify X509_V_FLAG_CRL_CHECK_ALL. As noted in the code, this capability is not available in versions of OpenSSL prior to Version 0.9.7.

After setting the flags, our store is adequately set up, and we are ready to begin the rather simple process of verifying the actual certificate. We create an X509_STORE_CTX, initialize it, and then call the verify function to determine the result. Looking at the initialization function in more detail is helpful, however.

```
int X509_STORE_CTX_init(X509_STORE_CTX *ctx, X509_STORE *store,
                        X509 *x509, STACK_OF(X509) *chain);
```

The last argument to this function optionally allows us to pass in the complete peer certificate chain for verification. This is often necessary, since the verifying party may not have a complete list of certificates that includes the identity certificate. This problem arises most commonly when CAs sign other CAs, as in the example SSL applications in Chapter 5. By passing the entire peer chain, we can attempt to verify the whole chain and have fewer errors because valid issuer certificates could not be found. Of course, in some applications—namely those that want only directly signed, authorized clients—this is inappropriate and should be left as NULL. In versions prior to 0.9.7, this function does not return an integer error code.

At the end of the main function, we can check the return value of X509_verify_cert and determine if the verification succeeded. As we would expect, our callback is used during this function call (it was passed on from the store to the store context).

PKCS#7 and S/MIME

PKCS#7 defines a standard format for data that has had cryptography applied to it. Like most standards, using this format will guarantee a level of interoperability with both existing and future applications. The standard itself is based on other PKCS standards for performing cryptographic operations. It is important to note that PKCS#7 specifies only a data format, not the choice of any specific algorithms.

Perhaps the most important trait of PKCS#7 is that it is the basis for Secure Multipurpose Internet Mail Extensions (S/MIME). S/MIME is a specification for sending secure email. Built on top of PKCS#7 and the former MIME standard, S/MIME allows us to email messages that can assure secrecy, integrity, authentication, and non-repudiation.

Using S/MIME, we can sign, verify, encrypt, and decrypt messages. This is very useful when developing mail applications, but it can also be used by programs that need to transmit data over a text-based medium, such as an instant-messaging implementation. As we'll see, programming with OpenSSL's PKCS#7 and S/MIME packages requires us to use much of our knowledge of the other packages.

A common misconception is that PKCS#7 and S/MIME are one in the same. In fact, they are not. S/MIME merely defines a specific encoding for PKCS#7 data. Using the S/MIME standard as implemented by OpenSSL, we can create applications that securely interact with other S/MIME-compliant applications, since the data encoding is standardized. It is also important to note here that OpenSSL's support for PKCS#7 and S/MIME is limited. Only S/MIMEv2 and PKCS#7 v1.5 are supported.

Signing and Verifying

The concept of signing and verifying is familiar by this point. Conceptually, to sign a message, we will need the sender's private key and the message to sign; the verification operation will require the sender's public key and the signed message. With S/MIME, the implementation is rather simple.

The signing process is opaque to the calling application. We simply provide all of the information with one function call to PKCS7_sign, and we get back a PKCS7 object. From there, we can use SMIME_write_PKCS7 to output the S/MIME armored message. Likewise, with verification, we obtain a PKCS7 object using SMIME_read_PKCS7 and perform the verification by calling the PKCS_verify function.

While the calls to the actual PKCS#7 and S/MIME family of functions are simple, we must perform some nontrivial setup for all of the arguments to these functions. In Example 10-8 below, our implementation focuses on that critical setup. Before we get ahead of ourselves, we should first look at these four functions in more detail.

```
PKCS7 *PKCS7_sign(X509 *signcert, EVP_PKEY *pkey, STACK_OF(X509) *certs,
                  BIO *data, int flags);
```

The first argument to PKCS7_sign is the certificate with which we'll sign the message. The second argument is the corresponding private key to the certificate. The third argument allows us to add other certificates to the S/MIME message. This is most useful when we have a long certificate chain and we wish to aid the receiving party's verification process. The fourth argument accepts a BIO object from which the message will be read. The last argument, flags, allows us to set properties of the resulting PKCS7 object. Its potential values are discussed at the end of this section.

```
int SMIME_write_PKCS7(BIO *bio, PKCS7 *p7, BIO *data, int flags);
```

The SMIME_write_PKCS7 function will write the PKCS7 object in the S/MIME encoding. The data is written to the BIO object passed in as the first argument. The object to write is the second. The other BIO object, the third argument, is the same object we used when calling `PKCS7_sign`. This allows the rest of the message data to be read and signed before writing the signature. The last argument is a set of flags of the same type as the signing function; they will be left for later discussion.

The verification process is, in essence, a reverse of the signing process. First, we read in a `PKCS7` object, and then we call `PKCS7_verify`.

```
PKCS7 *SMIME_read_PKCS7(BIO *bio, BIO **bcont);
```

This function simply reads an S/MIME-encoded `PKCS7` object from the `BIO` passed in as the first argument. The second argument is used to pass the caller back a pointer to a `BIO` that is opened for reading on the data in the `PKCS7` object. This passed-back `BIO` will be important for our verification process.

```
int PKCS7_verify(PKCS7 *p7, STACK_OF(X509) *certs, X509_STORE *store,
                 BIO *indata, BIO *out, int flags);
```

To verify a `PKCS7` object, pass the object as the first argument to the `PKCS7_verify`. The second argument specifies a chain of certificates that we can use to verify the signature. The validity of these certificates is checked against the `X509_STORE` specified as the third argument. This store must be set up fully before attempting to verify an S/MIME message. The setup is identical to that of Example 10-7. The `BIO` object that is passed as the fourth argument is the same object we retrieved from our call to `SMIME_read_PKCS7`. As the function `PKCS7_verify` processes the data read from this `BIO`, it writes the recovered message to the `BIO` used as the fifth argument. The flags are discussed below.

Now, using all we know about processing other types of OpenSSL objects and what we've just learned about PKCS#7 and S/MIME, we will dissect a small utility that can sign and verify text messages. The code appears in Example 10-8.

Example 10-8. A signing and verifying utility

```
#include <stdio.h>
#include <stdlib.h>
#include <openssl/crypto.h>
#include <openssl/err.h>
#include <openssl/pem.h>
#include <openssl/rand.h>

/*
 * This code appearing before the main function is all for X509_STORE setup.
 */

/* these are defintions to make the example simpler */
#define CA_FILE  "CAfile.pem"
#define CA_DIR   "/etc/ssl"
#define CRL_FILE "CRLfile.pem"

int verify_callback(int ok, X509_STORE_CTX *stor)
{
```

Example 10-8. A signing and verifying utility (continued)

```c
    if (!ok)
        fprintf(stderr, "Error: %s\n",
                X509_verify_cert_error_string(stor->error));
    return ok;
}

X509_STORE *create_store(void)
{
    X509_STORE  *store;
    X509_LOOKUP *lookup;

    /* create the cert store and set the verify callback */
    if (!(store = X509_STORE_new()))
    {
        fprintf(stderr, "Error creating X509_STORE_CTX object\n");
        goto err;
    }
    X509_STORE_set_verify_cb_func(store, verify_callback);

    /* load the CA certificates and CRLs */
    if (X509_STORE_load_locations(store, CA_FILE, CA_DIR) != 1)
    {
        fprintf(stderr, "Error loading the CA file or directory\n");
        goto err;
    }

    if (X509_STORE_set_default_paths(store) != 1)
    {
        fprintf(stderr, "Error loading the system-wide CA certificates\n");
        goto err;
    }
    if (!(lookup = X509_STORE_add_lookup(store, X509_LOOKUP_file())))
    {
        fprintf(stderr, "Error creating X509_LOOKUP object\n");
        goto err;
    }
    if (X509_load_crl_file(lookup, CRL_FILE, X509_FILETYPE_PEM) != 1)
    {
        fprintf(stderr, "Error reading the CRL file\n");
        goto err;
    }

    /* set the flags of the store so that CRLs are consulted */
    X509_STORE_set_flags(store, X509_V_FLAG_CRL_CHECK |
                        X509_V_FLAG_CRL_CHECK_ALL);

    return store;
err:
    return NULL;
}

int main(int argc, char *argv[])
```

Example 10-8. A signing and verifying utility (continued)

```c
{
    int             sign;
    X509            *cert;
    EVP_PKEY        *pkey;
    STACK_OF(X509)  *chain = NULL;
    X509_STORE      *store;
    PKCS7           *pkcs7;
    FILE            *fp;
    BIO             *in, *out, *pkcs7_bio;

    OpenSSL_add_all_algorithms( );
    ERR_load_crypto_strings( );
    seed_prng( );

    --argc, ++argv;
    if (argc < 2)
    {
        fprintf(stderr, "Usage: sv (sign|verify) [privkey.pem] cert.pem ...\n");
        goto err;
    }
    if (!strcmp(*argv, "sign"))
        sign = 1;
    else if (!strcmp(*argv, "verify"))
        sign = 0;
    else
    {
        fprintf(stderr, "Usage: sv (sign|verify) [privkey.pem] cert.pem ...\n");
        goto err;
    }
    --argc, ++argv;

    /* setup the BIO objects for stdin and stdout */
    if (!(in = BIO_new_fp(stdin, BIO_NOCLOSE)) ||
        !(out = BIO_new_fp(stdout, BIO_NOCLOSE)))
    {
        fprintf(stderr, "Error creating BIO objects\n");
        goto err;
    }

    if (sign)
    {
        /* read the signer private key */
        if (!(fp = fopen(*argv, "r")) ||
            !(pkey = PEM_read_PrivateKey(fp, NULL, NULL, NULL)))
        {
            fprintf(stderr, "Error reading signer private key in %s\n", *argv);
            goto err;
        }
        fclose(fp);
        --argc, ++argv;
    }
    else
```

Example 10-8. A signing and verifying utility (continued)

```
{
    /* create the cert store and set the verify callback */
    if (!(store = create_store( )))
        fprintf(stderr, "Error setting up X509_STORE object\n");
}

/* read the signer certificate */
if (!(fp = fopen(*argv, "r")) ||
    !(cert = PEM_read_X509(fp, NULL, NULL, NULL)))
{
    ERR_print_errors_fp(stderr);
    fprintf(stderr, "Error reading signer certificate in %s\n", *argv);
    goto err;
}
fclose(fp);
--argc, ++argv;

if (argc)
    chain = sk_X509_new_null( );
while (argc)
{
    X509 *tmp;

    if (!(fp = fopen(*argv, "r")) ||
        !(tmp = PEM_read_X509(fp, NULL, NULL, NULL)))
    {
        fprintf(stderr, "Error reading chain certificate in %s\n", *argv);
        goto err;
    }
    sk_X509_push(chain, tmp);
    fclose(fp);
    --argc, ++argv;
}

if (sign)
{
    if (!(pkcs7 = PKCS7_sign(cert, pkey, chain, in, 0)))
    {
        fprintf(stderr, "Error making the PKCS#7 object\n");
        goto err;
    }
    if (SMIME_write_PKCS7(out, pkcs7, in, 0) != 1)
    {
        fprintf(stderr, "Error writing the S/MIME data\n");
        goto err;
    }
}
else /* verify */
{
    if (!(pkcs7 = SMIME_read_PKCS7(in, &pkcs7_bio)))
    {
        fprintf(stderr, "Error reading PKCS#7 object\n");
```

Example 10-8. A signing and verifying utility (continued)

```
            goto err;
    }
    if (PKCS7_verify(pkcs7, chain, store, pkcs7_bio, out, 0) != 1)
    {
            fprintf(stderr, "Error writing PKCS#7 object\n");
            goto err;
    }
    else
            fprintf(stdout, "Certifiate and Signature verified!\n");
    }

    return 0;
err:
    return -1;
}
```

There should be no surprises in this code; it is a logical extension of what we already know about the various methods of processing private keys, certificates, and PKCS#7 objects.

This program is called with the first argument as either "sign" or "verify". If signing mode is used, we will expect the next argument to be the private key, the following argument to be the corresponding certificate, and the rest can be chain certificates that we'll add to the message. In verification mode, the third argument is expected to be the certificate, and the rest are extra certificates to check the signature.

We use the function create_store to represent the setup process for the certificate store abstractly. We read in the appropriate number of arguments based on the mode and add all the rest to a certificate stack. Finally, we either sign and emit the S/MIME message or read the S/MIME message and emit the original, verified message.

Encrypting and Decrypting

Again, we're familiar with the general process; we need a peer's public key to encrypt and our own private key to decrypt. The functions for reading and writing the PKCS#7 objects in the S/MIME encoding are unchanged, but we do have the new functions PKCS7_encrypt and PKCS7_decrypt. Before delving into the details of these two new functions, we should go back and think of the envelope interface we saw in Chapter 8. This interface allowed us to encrypt messages for other users with simple function calls and public key components, but in reality, the majority of the encryption was done using a symmetric cipher. These PKCS#7 functions do the same thing. They generate a random key and encrypt the data with it. Then the random key, or session key, is encrypted using the recipient's public key and included with the message. As an extension, PKCS#7 allows us to send a single encrypted message to multiple users by simply encrypting the session key with each of the recipient's public keys and including all of that data with the message. The example below will allow us to do this.

```
PKCS7 *PKCS7_encrypt(STACK_OF(X509) *certs, BIO *in, const EVP_CIPHER *cipher,
                    int flags);
```

The first argument is a collection of public keys for the recipients. Each public key will be used to encrypt the message's session key separately. The second argument specifies the BIO from which the message to encrypt will be read. The third argument specifies the symmetric algorithm to use, and the last are the flags, discussed below.

```
int PKCS7_decrypt(PKCS7 *p7, EVP_PKEY *pkey, X509 *cert, BIO *data, int flags);
```

The decryption function is equally simple. The PKCS7 object is passed in first; it is the product of a call to SMIME_read_PKCS7. The next two arguments are accounted for by the private key to perform the decryption and the corresponding certificate. The BIO object is used by the PKCS7_decrypt to write out the decrypted data. Again, the flags are discussed below.

We will look at another small utility, just as we did for signing and verifying, to make clear the kind of setup we need to do before calling these functions. Example 10-9 has that code.

Example 10-9. A utility to encrypt and decrypt S/MIME messages

```c
#include <stdio.h>
#include <stdlib.h>
#include <openssl/crypto.h>
#include <openssl/err.h>
#include <openssl/pem.h>
#include <openssl/rand.h>

int main(int argc, char *argv[])
{
    int             encrypt;
    PKCS7           *pkcs7;
    const EVP_CIPHER *cipher;
    STACK_OF(X509)  *certs;
    X509            *cert;
    EVP_PKEY        *pkey;
    FILE            *fp;
    BIO             *pkcs7_bio, *in, *out;

    OpenSSL_add_all_algorithms();
    ERR_load_crypto_strings();
    seed_prng();

    --argc, ++argv;
    if (argc < 2)
    {
        fprintf(stderr, "Usage: ed (encrypt|decrypt) [privkey.pem] cert.pem "
                        "...\n");
        goto err;
    }
    if (!strcmp(*argv, "encrypt"))
```

Example 10-9. A utility to encrypt and decrypt S/MIME messages (continued)

```
        encrypt = 1;
    else if(!strcmp(*argv, "decrypt"))
        encrypt = 0;
    else
    {
        fprintf(stderr, "Usage: ed (encrypt|decrypt) [privkey.pem] cert.pem "
                        "...\n");
        goto err;
    }
    --argc, ++argv;

    /* setup the BIO objects for stdin and stdout */
    if (!(in = BIO_new_fp(stdin, BIO_NOCLOSE)) ||
        !(out = BIO_new_fp(stdout, BIO_NOCLOSE)))
    {
        fprintf(stderr, "Error creating BIO objects\n");
        goto err;
    }

    if (encrypt)
    {
        /* choose cipher and read in all certificates as encryption targets */
        cipher = EVP_des_ede3_cbc( );
        certs = sk_X509_new_null( );

        while (argc)
        {
            X509 *tmp;

            if (!(fp = fopen(*argv, "r")) ||
                !(tmp = PEM_read_X509(fp, NULL, NULL, NULL)))
            {
                fprintf(stderr, "Error reading encryption certificate in %s\n",
                        *argv);
                goto err;
            }
            sk_X509_push(certs, tmp);
            fclose(fp);
            --argc, ++argv;
        }

        if (!(pkcs7 = PKCS7_encrypt(certs, in, cipher, 0)))
        {
            ERR_print_errors_fp(stderr);
            fprintf(stderr, "Error making the PKCS#7 object\n");
            goto err;
        }
        if (SMIME_write_PKCS7(out, pkcs7, in, 0) != 1)
        {
            fprintf(stderr, "Error writing the S/MIME data\n");
            goto err;
        }
    }
```

```
    else
    {
        if (!(fp = fopen(*argv, "r")) ||
            !(pkey = PEM_read_PrivateKey(fp, NULL, NULL, NULL)))
        {
            fprintf(stderr, "Error reading private key in %s\n", *argv);
            goto err;
        }
        fclose(fp);
        --argc, ++argv;
        if (!(fp = fopen(*argv, "r")) ||
            !(cert = PEM_read_X509(fp, NULL, NULL, NULL)))
        {
            fprintf(stderr, "Error reading decryption certificate in %s\n",
                    *argv);
            goto err;
        }
        fclose(fp);
        --argc, ++argv;

        if (argc)
            fprintf(stderr, "Warning: excess parameters specified. "
                            "Ignoring...\n");

        if (!(pkcs7 = SMIME_read_PKCS7(in, &pkcs7_bio)))
        {
            fprintf(stderr, "Error reading PKCS#7 object\n");
            goto err;
        }
        if (PKCS7_decrypt(pkcs7, pkey, cert, out, 0) != 1)
        {
            fprintf(stderr, "Error decrypting PKCS#7 object\n");
            goto err;
        }
    }

    return 0;
err:
    return -1;
}
```

This program is similar to the one in Example 10-8. When in encryption mode, it expects all the arguments after the word "encrypt" to be certificate files for the recipients. In decryption mode, the argument after "decrypt" must be the private key filename. The following argument should be the corresponding certificate; all further arguments are ignored, and a warning is emitted.

Analyzing this program, we can see several similarities to the previous example. When encrypting, we create the recipient stack, create the PKCS7 object with it and the message, and then write the product out. Decryption requires us to get the private key and certificate before performing the PKCS#7 and S/MIME operations.

Combined Operations

Often, we will want to both sign and encrypt an S/MIME message. As it turns out, we can do this easily using the two utilities we've created. First, we sign the message, and then we encrypt it for the recipients. Take the following example. Assume we have a proper root certificate in the file *CAfile.pem* and a CRL in the file *CRLfile.pem*. We will further assume that we have two users: foo with certificate in *foocert.pem* and private key in *fookey.pem*, and bar with certificate and key files named similarly. Using the following command, foo can prepare his message for bar.

```
$ cat msg.txt | ./sv sign fookey.pem foocert.pem \
> | ./ed encrypt barcert.pem > msg.smime
```

This command line reads the original message from the file *msg.txt* and begins by signing it with foo's private key. After this, the message is encrypted with the public key in the certificate of the recipient, i.e., bar's certificate. We could easily add more certificate files to this part of the command line if we wish to send the message to multiple targets.

Upon receiving this S/MIME message, bar would execute the following command.

```
$ cat msg.smime | ./ed decrypt barkey.pem barcert.pem \
> | ./sv verify foocert.pem
```

This command will use bar's private key first to decrypt the message. At this point, the verify routine uses foo's certificate to verify the signature, and the message is displayed.

Of course, this is an elementary example, but it gives us some idea of how S/MIME messages can be nested. This is the simplest way of sending a signed and encrypted message.

PKCS#7 Flags

We delayed our discussion of the PKCS#7 flags until we had shown a real implementation using the functions. In addition, we're now in a better position to understand the flags since we are more aware of the capabilities of PKCS#7 and S/MIME. The flags are all bit-valued and can be combined through the logical OR operation. Each of these PKCS7_... flags have SMIME_... aliases as well. We will limit our discussion to the more common and useful flags.

PKCS7_NOINTERN

> The verification process will not use the certificates embedded in the object for signature verification, i.e., the peer's certificate must be known beforehand for successful verification.

PKCS7_NOVERIFY

> When verifying a PKCS#7 object, do not try to verify the signer's certificate. The signature will still be checked.

PKCS7_NOCERTS
    The signing process will not add any extra certificates to the generated object.

PKCS7_DETACHED
    Do not include the signer's certificate in the generated object when signing data.

PKCS7_NOSIGS
    Do not verify the signature on the PKCS#7 object.

Some of these flags are dangerous, since they undermine security. We should strictly limit usage of the flags to applications running for testing or academic purposes.

PKCS#12

The PKCS#12 standard specifies a format for secure transportation of user identity information. This can be any sort of information, including certificates, passwords, and even private keys. The purpose for this standard is to allow user credentials to be portable while remaining secure.

The PKCS#12 standard allows for many different levels of security ranging from the use of a hardware security token to simpler password-based protection. For our purposes, we need only discuss a small subset of the features. The reason PKCS#12 is important to us is that many applications, namely common web browsers, use PKCS#12-formatted credentials.

For instance, if we develop an SSL-enabled web server, we want to be able to allow user authentication via client certificates. Using PKCS#12, we can generate the client credentials using OpenSSL and then import the data into a third-party web browser. This allows the browsing application to present the certificate to our SSL server and thus properly authenticate. The primary benefit of knowing how to perform this task is simple—we gain interoperability. We will limit our discussion of PKCS#12 to simply performing this task.

Wrapping Information into a PKCS#12 Object

This process is rather simple. It requires only one function call. The function takes all of the data presented and creates a password-protected PKCS12 object. With the created PKCS12 object, we can safely transport the data to a PKCS#12-compliant application. The application can then import the data, provided the password under which it was protected is supplied.

```
PKCS12 *PKCS12_create(char *pass, char *name, EVP_PKEY *pkey, X509 *cert,
                STACK_OF(X509) *ca, int nid_key, int nid_cert,
                int iter, int mac_iter, int keytype);
```

    The PKCS12_create function takes many arguments, but only the first five are important; the rest can be safely left as 0. The first argument is the password to use in protecting the data. The second argument specifies a general name to identify the created set of credentials. The following three arguments are the main parts of the object, the private key, the certificate, and the certificate's CA chain.

This function returns a properly formed PKCS12 object on success and NULL if an error occurs. To use this function successfully, we need only use the knowledge we already have to read in the data programmatically and then make this call. Once we've created the PKCS12 object, we will write it out to a file, in the most common case. The convention for PKCS#12 objects is to write them in DER format; thus, i2d_PKCS12_fp should be used.

```
int i2d_PKCS12_fp(FILE *fp, PKCS12 *p12);
```

Once we have the file, we can use it to import our credentials into any application that supports PKCS#12 objects. As a final note, we should use this method of exporting credentials only for user/client information. If we wanted to do something simpler, like add a CA certificate to a browser, we should just use i2d_X509_fp to write the single X509 object.

Importing Objects from PKCS#12 Data

Another common feature, the last we'll discuss on the topic of PKCS#12, is building applications that can import user identity information via PKCS#12. For all of the reasons mentioned, it is a good idea to build this support into applications in which it's appropriate. Again, OpenSSL provides one simple function call to serve our needs.

The first issue is reading the PKCS#12 file in from disk. The function d2i_PKCS12_fp performs this task.

```
PKCS12 *d2i_PKCS12_fp(FILE *fp, PKCS12 **p12);
```

We can simply use a NULL for the second argument, and a newly allocated and populated PKCS12 object is returned, as long as no errors are encountered in the file. Once we have this object, we can call PKCS12_parse to unwrap all of the identity objects that are encoded in it.

```
int PKCS12_parse(PKCS12 *p12, const char *pass, EVP_PKEY **pkey, X509 **cert,
                 STACK_OF(X509) **ca);
```

The second argument must be the same passphrase under which the file was protected. The last arguments are all used to pass back pointers to the indicated objects: the private key, the certificate, and the certificate chain file. After this call is completed, the PKCS12 object can be freed, and we can use the unwrapped objects normally.

In the end, PKCS#12 provides a solid foundation to safely write and read user credentials and, at the same time, affords a degree of interoperability for user identity information.

Command-Line Reference

This Appendix is a reference for all of the commands supported by the OpenSSL command-line tool. We've made an effort to provide complete documentation for each of the commands based on the information contained in the OpenSSL documentation and the source code.

asn1parse

The asn1parse command is a diagnostic utility that parses ASN.1 structures. It can also be used to extract data from ASN.1-formatted data.

Options

-inform PEM|DER

    Specify the format of the input data, which may be either DER or PEM. The default is PEM.

-in filename

    Specify the name of a file to read for input. The default is to read from stdin.

-out filename

    Specify the name of a file to write output to. The default is to write to stdout.

-noout

    Cause all output except for error messages to be suppressed.

-offset number

    Specify the byte offset of the input data to start parsing at.

-length number

    Specify the number of bytes to include in the parse.

-i

    Cause the output to be indented for readability.

-oid filename

    Specify the name of a file containing extra OID definitions. See the "Notes" section below for more information on the format of this file.

-strparse offset

> Cause the content octets starting at the specified byte offset to be parsed. This option may be specified multiple times.

-dump

> Cause unknown data to be displayed in hexadecimal form.

-dlimit number

> Specify the maximum number of bytes of unknown data to be displayed. The default is to display all of it.

Notes

Data in the ASN.1 format is composed of objects, some with an assigned object identifier (OID). An object identifier is a sequence of numbers that is normally represented by separating each number in the sequence with a period. Because object identifiers are often composed of many numbers, they can be difficult to remember. For this reason, object identifiers are given names. OpenSSL defines many object identifiers internally and displays them with their names, but if an unknown object identifier is encountered, it is represented by this command in its numerical form. The oid option allows you to specify the name of a file that additional OID definitions will be read from so that they may be displayed using their names when they're encountered by this command.

The format of a file containing object identifier definitions is quite simple. Each OID definition appears on its own line and consists of three columns. The first column is the numerical representation of the OID. The second column is a short name of the OID, which should be a single word composed of only upper- and lowercase letters. The third column is a long name of the OID, which may contain multiple words and characters other than letters. The long name is the name that will be displayed by the asn1parse command.

---

ca

The ca command is a basic certification authority that can be used to issue X.509 certificates and certificate revocation lists.

Options

-config filename

> Specify the name of a file to be used as a configuration file. If omitted, the system-wide default configuration file is used. Use of this option overrides the OPENSSL_CONF environment variable.

-verbose

> Cause more information to be displayed than normal.

-name section

> Specify the name of a section in the configuration file being used that contains the default settings for the CA. The default is to use the section specified by the default_ca key in the ca section of the configuration file.

-in filename

Specify the name of a file containing a certificate request to be signed by the CA, causing a certificate to be created.

-ss_cert filename

Specify the name of a file containing a self-signed certificate to be signed by the CA.

-spkac filename

Specify the name of a file containing a Netscape Signed Public Key and Challenge.

-infiles

If this option is present, it must be the last option on the command line. Each argument after it is assumed to be a file containing a certificate request to be signed by the CA, and certificates will be created for each one.

-out filename

Specify the name of a file to write the certificate or certificates created by the CA to. The default is to write certificates to stdout. If the gencrl option is used, this option specifies the name of the file to which the generated certificate revocation list will be written.

-outdir directory

Specify the directory where certificates will be written. Each certificate that is issued will be written with a filename composed of the certificates serial number in hexadecimal and an extension of ".pem". This option overrides the configuration file's new_certs_dir key.

-cert filename

Specify the name of the file containing the CA's certificate. This option overrides the configuration file's certificate key.

-keyfile filename

Specify the name of the file containing the CA's private key. This option overrides the configuration file's private_key key.

-key password

Specify the password that is required to decrypt the CA's private key. This option does not conform to the guidelines outlined in Chapter 2 for passwords and passphrases. Use of this option is not recommended. The passin option should be used instead.

-passin password

Specify the password or passphrase that is required to decrypt the CA's private key. The password or passphrase specified with this option follows the guidelines outlined in Chapter 2.

-notext

Cause the text form of a certificate to be excluded from the output file.

-startdate date

Specify the start date on which the issued certificate or certificates will be valid. If this option is omitted, the default is to use the current system time. This option overrides the configuration file's default_startdate key.

-enddate date

Specify the end date on which the issued certificate or certificates will be valid. If this option is omitted, the default is to use the start date plus the number of days specified with the days option. Use of this option will override the days option if both are used. This option overrides the configuration file's default_enddate key.

-days number

Specify the number of days for which issued certificates will be valid. This option overrides the configuration file's default_days key.

-md digest

Specify the message digest algorithm to use. The default is to use MD5, but valid options include MD5, SHA1, and MDC2. This option overrides the configuration file's default_md key.

-policy section

Specify the name of a section in the configuration file being used that contains a policy definition to be used. This option overrides the configuration file's policy key.

-msie_hack

Specify this option if you need to issue certificates that will work with very old versions of the Internet Explorer certificate enrollment control "certenr3". Avoid using this option unless you know that you absolutely need it.

-preserveDN

Cause the order and components of the distinguished name from a certificate request to be preserved in the issued certificate. Ordinarily, the certificate will be created using only the components from the policy that is in use by the CA.

-batch

Cause verification prompts to be suppressed, allowing the command to do its work without any human intervention.

-extensions section

Specify the name of a section in the configuration file being used that contains the extensions to be added to certificates that are issued. If no extension section is used, an X.509v1 format certificate will be issued; otherwise, an X.509v3 certificate will be issued. This option overrides the configuration file's x509_extensions key.

-gencrl

Cause a certificate revocation list to be generated.

-crldays number

Specify the number of days before the next certificate revocation list will be generated. This option is used to compute the date that is used to fill in the nextUpdate field. This option overrides the configuration file's default_crl_days key.

-crlhours number

Specify the number of hours before the next certificate revocation list will be generated. This option computes the date that is used to fill in the nextUpdate field. This option may be used in combination with the crldays option. This option overrides the configuration file's default_crl_hours key.

-revoke filename

Specify the name of a file containing a certificate that will be revoked.

-crlexts section

Specify the name of a section in the configuration file being used that contains the extensions to be added to the certificate revocation list that is issued. If no extension section is used, a v1 CRL is created; otherwise, a v2 CRL is created. This option overrides the configuration file's crl_extensions key.

Configuration Options

oid_file

Specify the name of a file that contains object identifier definitions. The format of this file is one definition per line, each line consisting of three columns. The first column is the numerical representation of the OID. The second column is the OID's short name, which should be a single word composed of only upper- and lowercase letters. The third column is the OID's long name, which may be composed of multiple words and characters other than letters.

oid_section

Specify the name of a section that contains object identifier definitions. Key names in the section should be the OID's short name, and the corresponding value should be the OID's numerical representation. Long names are the same as short names for OIDs that are defined in this manner.

new_certs_dir

Specify the directory where issued certificates will be stored. This is the same as the outdir command-line option.

certificate

Specify the name of a file containing the CA's certificate. This is the same as the cert command-line option.

private_key

Specify the name of a file containing the CA's private key. This is the same as the keyfile command-line option.

RANDFILE

Specify the name of a file that will be used to seed the PRNG. On Unix systems, the filename may be the name of an EGD socket.

default_days

Specify the number of days for which issued certificates will be valid. This is the same as the days command-line option.

default_startdate

Specify the default starting date for which issued certificates will be valid. This is the same as the startdate command-line option.

default_enddate

Specify the default ending date for which issued certificates will be valid. This is the same as the enddate command-line option.

default_crl_days

Specify the default number of days until a new certificate revocation list is generated. This is the same as the crldays command-line option.

default_crl_hours

Specify the default number of hours until a new certificate revocation list is generated. This is the same as the crlhours command-line option.

default_md

> Specify the default message digest to be used for signing certificates and certificate revocation lists. This is the same as the md command-line option.

database

> Specify the name of a file that will be used to keep track of certificates that are issued by the CA. This setting is mandatory and has no corresponding command-line option.

serialfile

> Specify the name of a file that will be used to keep track of the next serial number that will be assigned to a certificate when it is issued. This setting is mandatory and has no corresponding command-line option.

x509_extensions

> Specify the name of a section in the configuration file that contains the set of extensions to be included in certificates that are issued by the CA. This is the same as the extensions command-line option.

crl_extensions

> Specify the name of a section in the configuration file that contains the set of extensions to be included in certificate revocation lists that are issued by the CA. This is the same as the crlexts command-line option.

preserve

> If this is set to yes, the order and components of the distinguished name contained in a certificate request will be preserved in the issued certificate. This is the same as the preserveDN command-line option.

msie_hack

> If this is set to yes, certificates that are issued will work with very old versions of the Internet Explorer certificate enrollment control "certenr3". Avoid using this option unless you know that you absolutely need it.

policy

> Specify the name of a section in the configuration file that defines the policy for this CA. This option is the same as the policy command-line option.

Notes

For the options that require a date as a parameter or configuration file keys that require a date as a value, the date should be specified in the same format as an ASN.1 UTC Time structure, which is YYMMDDHHMMSSZ, in which Z is the actual capital letter Z.

The use of a configuration file is strongly encouraged. In fact, unless the settings in the system-wide default configuration file are acceptable, a configuration file is required because there are mandatory configuration options that have no equivalent command-line options.

Each key in a policy definition section should be named for the short name of each object identifier present in a distinguished name. The value for each key should be match, supplied, or optional. OIDs that are marked as match must be present in the certificate request and must match the same OID in the CA's distinguished name. OIDs that are marked as supplied must be present in the certificate request, and OIDs that are marked as optional may or may not be present in the certificate request.

The ca command is intended to be an example certification authority. It has several limitations that make it unsuitable for use in a production environment. This command is discussed in detail in Chapter 3.

ciphers

The ciphers command is used to obtain a list of the ciphers that are supported for the different versions of the SSL protocol. It is primarily useful as a test tool to determine the appropriate cipher lists for the version of the protocol that you wish to use. The command's output is a list, separated by colons, of the supported cipher strings matching the criteria specified by the command's options.

Options

-ssl2

Include only the ciphers that are supported by SSLv2.

-ssl3

Include only the ciphers that are supported by SSLv3.

-tls1

Include only the ciphers that are supported by TLSv1.

-v

Produce a more verbose list of cipher strings that includes the protocol version, key exchange, authentication, encryption, and MAC algorithms.

Notes

By default, cipher strings for all of the supported protocol versions are included. Only one of the version options may be specified at a time. Additional arguments on the command line are interpreted either as ciphers to be added to the list or as modifiers to refine the list.

crl

The crl command is used to examine and verify the validity of certificate revocation lists. The command can be used to display the contents of a CRL in human-readable form. It can also be used to convert CRLs between DER and PEM formats.

Options

-in filename

Specify the name of the file containing a CRL to be examined or verified. If this option is omitted, stdin is used.

-inform DER|PEM

Specify the format of the CRL that will be examined or verified. Possible formats are DER or PEM. If this option is omitted, PEM is the default format.

-out filename

Specify the name of a file to which the command's output will be written. If this option is omitted, stdout is used.

-outform DER|PEM

Specify the format of the CRL that will be written out by the command. If this option is omitted, the default is PEM.

-text

Cause a human-readable text representation of the CRL to be written to the output destination.

-noout

Suppress the output of the CRL in DER or PEM format. By default, the input CRL is also output, except when the CRL's signature is being verified.

-hash

Cause a hash of the CRL's issuer name to be written to the output destination. The hash can be used to look up CRLs in a directory by issuer name in which the standard filename for each CRL is the hash of the issuer's name and an extension of ".0".

-issuer

Cause the CRL issuer's name to be written to the output destination.

-lastupdate

Cause the CRL's lastUpdate field to be written to the output destination.

-nextupdate

Cause the CRL's nextUpdate field to be written to the output destination.

-fingerprint

Cause a fingerprint of the CRL to be written to the output destination. The fingerprint is a hash of the CRL computed using a message digest algorithm. By default, MD5 is used.

-CAfile filename

Verify the CRL's signature using the certificate contained in the specified file.

-CApath directory

Verify the CRL's signature using the certificates contained in the specified directory. Each certificate file in the directory should be named with the hash of the issuer's name and an extension of ".0".

Notes

When computing a fingerprint of a CRL, the default message digest that is used is MD5. Any other message digest algorithm supported by OpenSSL can also be used by specifying the name of the algorithm to use as an option. The message digest names are the same as those used by the dgst command.

crl2pkcs7

The crl2pkcs7 command is used to combine certificates and an optional certificate revocation list into a single PKCS#7 structure.

Options

-in filename

Specify the name of a file from which to read a CRL for inclusion in the resulting PKCS#7 structure. If this option is omitted, the CRL will be read from stdin.

-inform DER|PEM

>Specify the format of the CRL that will be read. Valid formats are either DER or PEM. If this option is not specified, the default is PEM.

-out filename

>Specify the name of a file to write the resulting PKCS#7 structure to. If this option is omitted, output is written to stdout.

-outform DER|PEM

>Specify the format of the PKCS#7 that will be written. Valid formats are either DER or PEM. If this option is not specified, the default is PEM.

-certfile filename

>Specify the name of a file containing one or more certificates in PEM format. This option may be specified multiple times to include multiple certificates from multiple files.

-nocrl

>Do not include a CRL in the resulting PKCS#7 structure. If this option is specified, the in and inform options are ignored, and no CRL is read from stdin.

Notes

The PKCS#7 structure that is created is not signed. It will contain only the certificates and CRL that are specified for inclusion. The PKCS#7 structure that results from this command can be used to send certificates and CRLs to Netscape as part of the certificate enrollment process. To do so, the PKCS#7 structure that is created must be DER-encoded and sent as MIME type application/x-x509-user-cert. The header and footer lines can be removed from the PEM output from this command to send user certificates and CRLs to Microsoft Internet Explorer using the "Xenroll" control.

dgst

The dgst command is used to compute the hash of a block of data using a message digest algorithm. It can also be used to sign data and verify signatures.

Options

-dss1, -md2, -md4, -md5, -mdc2, -rmd160, -sha, -sha1

>Specify the message digest algorithm to use. If this option is omitted, the default is to use MD5.

-out filename

>Specify the name of a file to write the results from the command to. If this option is omitted, stdout is used.

-hex

>Cause the output to be written in hexadecimal format. When computing a hash, this is the default.

-c

>Cause the hexadecimal output to be grouped by two digits, each group separated by a colon. This option is ignored if the output format is not hexadecimal.

-binary

>Cause the output to be written in binary format. When signing, this is the default.

-rand filename
> Specify the name of a file or files to use to seed the pseudorandom number generator. This option uses the format described in Chapter 2.

-sign filename
> Sign the contents of the specified file. The hash value of the data computed using the specified message digest algorithm is actually the only data that is signed.

-verify filename
> Verify a signature using the public key contained in the specified file.

-prverify filename
> Verify a signature using the private key contained in the specified file.

-signature
> Specify the name of a file containing the signature to be verified. This option is ignored unless used with the verify or prverify options.

Notes

Any arguments remaining on the command line after the last option are interpreted as the names of files, for which hashes will be computed, signed, or verified. When a signature is to be generated or verified, only one file should be used at a time. If a DSA key is used for signing or verification, the DSS1 message digest must be used, and the PRNG must be seeded.

dhparam

The dhparam command is used to generate Diffie-Hellman parameters. It can also be used to examine previously generated parameters.

Options

-in filename
> Specify the name of a file from which parameters should be read. If no file is specified, stdin is used—unless new parameters will be generated, in which case no input is required.

-inform DER|PEM
> Specify the format, DER or PEM, of the input data. If this option is omitted, the default format is PEM.

-out filename
> Specify the name of a file to which the generated parameters will be written. If no file is specified, stdout is used.

-outform DER|PEM
> Specify the format, DER or PEM, of the output data. If this option is omitted, the default format is PEM.

-rand filename
> Specify the name of a file or files to use to seed the pseudorandom number generator. This option uses the format described in Chapter 2.

-dsaparam
> When this option is specified, the input data is expected to be DSA parameters. The parameters are converted to Diffie-Hellman parameters.

-2, -5

Specify the generator to use, either 2 or 5. If this option is omitted, a generator of 2 is the default. If this option is present, input files are ignored and new parameters are generated.

-noout

Cause output of the DSA parameters in DER or PEM format to be suppressed. This option is useful when viewing previously generated parameters.

-text

Cause a human-readable representation of the input parameters to be written to the output destination.

-C

Cause a C code representation of the input parameters to be written to the output destination.

Notes

The length of the primes to generate is specified as the last argument to the command. If a length is not specified, a default of 512 bits is used.

dsa

The dsa command is used modify DSA private keys or examine their contents. The command may be used to remove encryption from a private key, add it to a private key, or change the encryption that is used on a private key. The command can also be used to compute a public key from a private key.

Options

-in filename

Specify the name of a file from which a DSA private key will be read. If no file is specified, stdin is used.

-inform DER|PEM

Specify the format, DER or PEM, of the key that is read as input. If this option is omitted, the default format is PEM.

-out filename

Specify the name of a file to which the output from this command will be written. If this option is omitted, stdout will be used.

-outform DER|PEM

Specify the format, DER or PEM, of the key that is written. If this option is omitted, the default format is PEM.

-pubin

Cause the input key to be interpreted as a public key.

-pubout

Cause the output key to be interpreted as a public key.

-passin password

Specify the password to use to decrypt the input key. This option follows the password and passphrase guidelines outlined in Chapter 2.

-passout password

> Specify the password to use to encrypt the output key. This option follows the password and passphrase guidelines outlined in Chapter 2.

-des, -des3, -idea

> Specify the cipher to use to encrypt the private key. If this option is omitted, the private key that is written out by this command will not be encrypted.

-noout

> Cause the output of the key in DER or PEM format to be suppressed.

-text

> Cause the input key, public or private, to be output in a human-readable form.

-modulus

> Cause the modulus of the public key to be written to the output destination.

dsaparam

The dsaparam command is used to generate new DSA parameters. It can also be used to examine previously generated parameters.

Options

-in filename

> Specify the name of a file from which existing DSA parameters will be read. If no file is specified, stdin is used.

-inform DER|PEM

> Specify the format, DER or PEM, of the parameters that are read as input. If this option is omitted, the default format is PEM.

-out filename

> Specify the name of a file to which the output from this command will be written. If this option is omitted, stdout will be used.

-outform DER|PEM

> Specify the format, DER or PEM, of the parameters that are generated. If this option is omitted, PEM is the default.

-rand filename

> Specify the name of a file or files to be used to seed the PRNG. This option follows the format outlined in Chapter 2.

-genkey

> Cause a private key to be generated using the generated parameters or the parameters read from the input source. The private key will not be encrypted.

-noout

> Cause the output of the parameters in DER or PEM format to be suppressed.

-text

> Cause the parameters to be output in a human-readable form.

-C

> Cause the parameters to be output in C code form.

Notes

The length of the parameters to be generated is specified as the last argument to the command. If the length is specified, the input source is ignored, and new parameters are generated.

---

enc

The enc command is used to perform encryption or decryption using symmetric ciphers. The command can also be used to perform base64 encoding.

Options

-in filename
> Specify the name of the file to be used as input. If this option is omitted, stdin is used.

-out filename
> Specify the name of the file to be used as output. If this option is omitted, stdout is used.

-pass password
> Specify the password to be used for encryption or decryption. The password is used to generate an initialization vector (iv) and a key to be used by the cipher. This option follows the guidelines for passwords and passphrases outlined in Chapter 2.

-e
> Cause the input to be encrypted. This is the default operation to be performed.

-d
> Cause the input to be decrypted.

-salt
> Cause a salt to be used in the key derivation routines. This option should always be used unless you need backward compatibility with versions of OpenSSL older than 0.9.5.

-nosalt
> If this option is specified, no salt will be used in the key derivation routines. This is the default.

-a
> Cause the data to be base64-encoded after it is encrypted, or base64-decoded before it is decrypted.

-A
> Cause the base64 encoding to be produced on a single line when it is being encoded and expected on a single line when it is being decoded. This option is ignored unless the a option is specified.

-p
> Cause the derived key and initialization vector to be output.

-P
> Cause the derived key and initialization vector to be output. No encryption or decryption is performed when this option is specified.

-k password

Specify the password from which the key and initialization vector should be derived. This option is for backwards compatibility only, and the use of the pass option is preferred.

-kfile filename

Specify the name of a file containing the password from which the key and initialization vector should be derived. Only the first line of the file is read. This option is for backwards compatibility only, and the use of the pass option is preferred.

-K key

Specify the key to use in hexadecimal form. If this option is used along with a password option, then only the initialization vector is derived from the password, and this key is used. If no password is specified, the initialization vector must also be specified.

-iv vector

Specify the initialization vector to use in hexadecimal form.

-S salt

Specify the salt to use in hexadecimal form.

-bufsize number

Specify the size of the buffers to use for I/O.

Notes

The name of the cipher to use should be specified either as an option or as the name of the command instead of enc. A large number of ciphers are supported by this command. Additionally, base64 encoding is also supported. Note that base64 is an encoding, not a cipher. The ciphers are summarized in Table A-1.

Table A-1. Ciphers supported by the enc command

Cipher name	Description
base64	Base64 encoding
bf, bf-cbc, bf-cfb, bf-ecb, bf-ofb	128-bit Blowfish
cast, cast-cbc, cast5-cbc, cast5-cfg, cast5-ecb, cast5-ofb	CAST5
des, des-cbc, des-ofb, des-ecb	DES
des-ede, des-ede-cbc, des-ede-cfb, des-ede-ofb	Two-key triple DES
des-ede3, des-ede3-cbc, des3, des-ede3-cfb, des-ede3-ofb	Three-key triple DES
desx	DESX
idea, idea-cbc, idea-cfb, idea-ecb, idea-ofb	IDEA
rc2, rc2-cbc, rc2-cfg, rc2-ecb, rc2-ofb	128-bit RC2
rc2-64-cbc	64-bit RC2
rc2-40-cbc	40-bit RC2
rc4	128-bit RC4
rc4-64	64-bit RC4
rc4-40	40-bit RC4
rc5, rc5-cbc, rc5-cfb, rc5-ecb, rc5-ofb	128-bit RC5 with 12 rounds

errstr

The errstr command will convert a 32-bit integer error code into a human-readable error message.

Option

-stats
  Cause statistical information about the error tables to be displayed on stdout.

Notes

Each argument on the command line is interpreted as a 32-bit integer error code to be converted into a human-readable error message. The error code should be specified in hexadecimal form.

gendsa

The gendsa command is used for generating DSA keys from DSA parameters.

Options

-des, -des3, -idea
  Specify the cipher to use to encrypt the generated key. If none of these options is specified, the key will not be encrypted.

-rand filename
  Specify the name of a file or files to use to seed the PRNG. The parameter for this option follows the guidelines outlined in Chapter 2.

Notes

The parameters to use for generation of the private key should be contained in a file in PEM format. The name of the file to read the parameters from should be specified as the last argument on the command line without any option. No option is available with this command to specify a password, so one must be entered when the command prompts for it.

genrsa

The genrsa command is used for generating RSA keys.

Options

-out filename
  Specify the name of the file to write the generated key to. If this option is omitted, the key will be written to stdout.

-rand filename
  Specify the name of a file or files to use to seed the PRNG. The parameter for this option follows the guidelines outlined in Chapter 2.

-passout password

    Specify the password or passphrase to use to encrypt the generated key. The parameter for this option follows the guidelines for passwords and passphrases outlined in Chapter 2.

-des, -des3, -idea

    Specify the cipher to use to encrypt the generated key. If none of these options is specified, the key will not be encrypted.

-F4, -3

    Specify the public exponent to be used by the generated key. If F4 is specified, 65537 will be used; otherwise, 3 will be used. If neither of these options is specified, the default is 65537.

Notes

The length of the key to generate is specified as the last argument on the command line. If no length is specified, a default length of 512 bits will be used.

---

nseq

The nseq command is used to create or examine a Netscape certificate sequence.

Options

-in filename

    Specify the name of the file from which a Netscape certificate sequence or X.509 certificates will be read. If this option is omitted, stdin will be used.

-out filename

    Specify the name of the file to which a Netscape certificate sequence or X.509 certificates will be written. If this option is omitted, stdout will be used.

-toseq

    Cause the input file to be treated as X.509 certificates rather than as the default of a Netscape certificate sequence. The output will be a Netscape certificate sequence created from the X.509 certificates.

Notes

By default, this command will take a file containing an arbitrary number of X.509 certificates and produce a Netscape certificate sequence. Use of the toseq option reverses the process.

---

passwd

The passwd command is used to compute common password hashes that are typically used for system passwords on various Unix systems.

Options

-1

    Use BSD's MD5-based algorithm.

-apr1

Use an Apache variant of the `apr1` algorithm.

-quiet

Suppress warning messages when passwords are truncated.

-salt salt

Specify the salt to use.

-in filename

Specify the name of a file from which plaintext passwords should be read. Each line contains one password, and a hash will be computed for each.

-stdin

Cause passwords to be read from `stdin` without prompting or suppressing echo.

-table

Cause both the plaintext password and the generated hash to be output in tabular form.

Notes

By default, the standard Unix crypt hash will be used, which limits the length of plaintext passwords to eight characters. The other two supported hash algorithms have no limit on password length.

---

pkcs7

The `pkcs7` command is used to examine PKCS#7-formatted files. It can also be used to convert them from DER to PEM format, and vice versa.

Options

-in filename

Specify the name of a file containing a PKCS#7 structure. If this option is omitted, a PKCS#7 structure is read from `stdin`.

-inform DER|PEM

Specify the format, DER or PEM, of the input PKCS#7 structure. If this option is omitted, PEM is the default format.

-out filename

Specify the name of the file to which output from the command will be written. If this option is omitted, `stdout` will be used.

-outform DER|PEM

Specify the format, DER or PEM, of the PKCS#7 structure that is written by the command. If this option is omitted, the default format of PEM will be used.

-noout

Cause output of a PKCS#7 structure to be suppressed.

-text

Cause a human-readable representation of the input PKCS#7 structure to be output.

-print_certs

Cause any certificates or certificate revocation lists contained in the PKCS#7 structure to be output.

Notes

This command is not capable of printing out the various fields that can be contained in a PKCS#7 structure. Only PKCS#7 v1.5 structures as defined by RFC2315 are understood.

pkcs8

The pkcs8 command is used to create, examine, and manipulate PKCS#8-formatted files.

Options

-in filename

Specify the name of a file from which either a PKCS#8 structure or a private key will be read. If this option is omitted, stdin will be used.

-inform DER|PEM

Specify the format of the input data, either DER or PEM. If this option is omitted, PEM is the default format.

-out filename

Specify the name of a file to which the output from the command will be written. If this option is omitted, stdout will be used.

-outform DER|PEM

Specify the format of the output data, either DER or PEM. If this option is omitted, PEM is the default format.

-passin password

Specify the password to decrypt the input PKCS#8 structure or private key. This option follows the guidelines outlined in Chapter 2.

-passout password

Specify the password to encrypt the output PKCS#8 structure or private key. This option follows the guidelines outlined in Chapter 2.

-topk8

If this option is specified, a private key, either DSA or RSA, will be the expected input data, and the output will be a PKCS#8 structure. Otherwise, a PKCS#8 structure will be the expected input, and a private key will be the output.

-nocrypt

Cause the PKCS#8 structure that is output from this command to be unencrypted. If the input is a PKCS#8 key, it will be expected to be unencrypted.

-nooct

Cause the RSA private key output from this command to be written in a broken format that is required by some software. This option is ignored if the private key is not RSA or the input data is a PKCS#8 structure.

-embed

Cause the DSA private key output from this command to be written in a broken format that is required by some software. This option is ignored if the private key is not DSA or the input data is a PKCS#8 structure. With this option, the DSA parameters used to generate the private key are embedded in the output's PrivateKey structure.

-nsdb

Cause the DSA private key output from this command to be written in a broken format that is required by Netscape private key databases. This option is ignored if the private key is not DSA or the input data is a PKCS#8 structure.

-v1 algorithm

Specify the PKCS#5 v1.5 or PKCS#12 algorithm to use for encryption in the PKCS#8 structure that is output. Valid algorithms are `PBE-MD2-DES`, `PBE-MD5-DES`, `PBE-SHA1-RC2-64`, `PBE-MD2-RC2-64`, `PBE-MD5-RC2-64`, `PBE-SHA1-DES`, `PBE-SHA1-RC4-128`, `PBE-SHA1-RC4-40`, `PBE-SHA1-3DES`, `PBE-SHA1-2DES`, `PBE-SHA1-RC2-128`, and `PBE-SHA1-RC2-40`.

-v2 algorithm

Specify the PKCS#5 v2.0 algorithm to use for encryption in the PKCS#8 structure that is output. Valid algorithms are `des`, `des3`, and `rc2`. The recommended algorithm is 3DES.

pkcs12

The `pkcs12` command is used to create, examine, and manipulate PKCS#12-formatted files.

Options

-in filename

Specify the name of a file from which a PKCS#12 structure in PEM format will be read. If this option is omitted, `stdin` will be used.

-out filename

Specify the name of a file that will be used to write a PKCS#12 structure in PEM format. If this option is omitted, `stdout` will be used.

-password password, -passin password

Specify the password or passphrase that is required to decrypt the input PKCS#12 structure. This option follows the guidelines for passwords and passphrases outlined in Chapter 2.

-passout password

Specify the password or passphrase that will be used to encrypt the output PKCS#12 structure. This option follows the guidelines for passwords and passphrases outlined in Chapter 2.

-des, -des3, -idea

Specify the cipher that will be used to encrypt the output PKCS#12 structure. If this option is omitted, the default is to use 3DES.

-nodes

Cause the output PKCS#12 structure to be unencrypted.

-noout

Cause the output of a PKCS#12 structure to be suppressed. This option is useful when extracting the various structures that are contained by a PKCS#12 structure.

-clcerts

Cause only the client certificates contained in the input PKCS#12 structure to be output.

-cacerts

Cause only the CA certificates contained in the input PKCS#12 structure to be output.

-nocerts

> Suppress the output of any certificates, whether they are client or CA certificates.

-nokeys

> Suppress the output of any private keys.

-info

> Cause a human-readable form of the PKCS#12 structure to be output, which includes information such as the algorithms used.

-nomacver

> Inhibit the verification of the PKCS#12 structure's MAC integrity when reading it in.

-twopass

> Cause separate prompts for the integrity and encryption passwords. Normally, these two passwords are the same, and most software using PKCS#12 structures expect them to be, so this option may render PKCS#12 structures that are created unreadable by some software. Use of this option is not recommended.

-export

> Cause a PKCS#12 object to be created instead of examined or manipulated. When this option is specified, no PKCS#12 object is read as input. Instead, the input data is expected to be a combination of private keys and certificates. At least one certificate and matching private key must be present in the input data.

-inkey filename

> Specify the name of a file from which a private key will be read. If this option is specified, the input data read from either stdin or the file specified with the in option is not required to contain a key.

-certfile filename

> Specify the name of a file containing additional certificates that will be included in the output PKCS#12 structure.

-CAfile filename

> Specify the name of a file containing additional certificates that will be included in the output PKCS#12 structure.

-CApath directory

> Specify the name of a directory containing certificates that will be included in the output PKCS#12 structure. The files in the directory are expected to be named by each certificate issuer's hash and an extension of ".0".

-name name

> Specify the "friendly name" for the primary certificate and private key contained in the PKCS#12 structure. This "friendly name" is ordinarily used for display purposes in programs that use the PKCS#12 structure.

-caname name

> Specify the "friendly name" for any extra certificates contained in the PKCS#12 structure. This option may be specified once for each additional certificate that will be contained in the PKCS#12 structure. The names should be specified in the order that certificates are included. It should be noted that not all software uses these names. Some use only the primary certificate's "friendly name."

-chain
> Cause the entire certificate chain of the primary certificate to be included in the output PKCS#12 structure. If this option is not specified, the CAfile and CApath options are ignored. If not all of the certificates in the chain are available, it is considered a fatal error, and no PKCS#12 structure will result.

-descert
> Cause the primary certificate to be encrypted using 3DES instead of 40-bit RC2, which is the default. Note that some old export grade software will not be able to read the PKCS#12 structure if the certificate is this strongly encrypted.

-keypbe algorithm
> Specify the algorithm to use to encrypt the private key. Any PKCS#5 v1.5 or PKCS#12 algorithm is valid, but we recommend that you use only PKCS#12 algorithms. The pkcs8 command reference lists the algorithms that may be used.

-certpbe algorithm
> Specify the algorithm to use to encrypt the primary certificate. Any PKCS#5 v1.5 or PKCS#12 algorithm is valid, but we recommend that you use only PKCS#12 algorithms. The pkcs8 command reference lists the algorithms that may be used.

-keyex
> Mark the private key to be usable for exchange purposes only. By default, the key may be used for either exchange or signing. This option is mutually exclusive with the keysig option.

-keysig
> Mark the private key to be usable for signing purposes only. By default, the key may be used for exchange or signing. This option is mutually exclusive with the keyex option.

-noiter, -nomaciter
> Cause the MAC and key algorithms not to use iteration counts.

-maciter
> This option is normally enabled by default, but is present for backwards compatibility. It causes the MAC and key algorithms to use iteration counts, thus strengthening the protection on the PKCS#12 structure.

-rand filename
> Specify the name of a file or files to be used to seed the PRNG. This parameter for this option follows the guidelines outlined in Chapter 2.

rand

The rand command is used to obtain random output from the OpenSSL PRNG.

Options

-out filename
> Specify the name of a file to which output from this command will be written. If this option is omitted, stdout will be used.

-rand filename
> Specify the name of a file or files that will be used to seed the PRNG. This option follows the guidelines outlined in Chapter 2.

-base64
> Cause the output generated from this command to be base64-encoded.

Notes

The number of random bytes to be produced must be specified as the last argument on the command line.

---

req

The req command is used to create, examine, and manipulate PKCS#10-formatted certificate requests. It can also be used to create self-signed certificates suitable for use in setting up a root certification authority.

Options

-config filename
> Specify the name of a file to use as a configuration file. If this option is omitted, the system-wide default configuration file is used. Use of this option overrides the OPENSSL_CONF environment variable.

-in filename
> Specify the name of a file from which a certificate request will be read. If this option is omitted, stdin is used.

-inform DER|PEM
> Specify the format of the input certificate request, either DER or PEM. If this option is omitted, PEM is the default format.

-out filename
> Specify the name of a file to which the resulting self-signed certificate or certificate request will be written. If this option is omitted, stdout will be used.

-outform DER|PEM
> Specify the format, DER or PEM, which will be used to write the self-signed certificate or certificate request. If this option is omitted, PEM is the default.

-passin password
> Specify the password or passphrase that will be used to decrypt the private key corresponding to the input certificate or certificate request. This option follows the guidelines outlined in Chapter 2 for passwords and passphrases.

-passout password
> Specify the password or passphrase that will be used to encrypt the private key that may be generated with the certificate or certificate request. This option follows the guidelines outlined in Chapter 2 for passwords and passphrases.

-rand filename
> Specify the name of a file or files that will be used to seed the PRNG. This option follows the guidelines outlined in Chapter 2.

-noout

Cause output of a certificate or certificate request to be suppressed. This option is useful when examining a certificate request.

-text

Cause a human-readable representation of the input certificate request to be output.

-modulus

Cause the modulus of the public key contained in the request to be output.

-verify

Verify the signature on the certificate request.

-new

Cause a new certificate request to be generated. When this option is used, no data is read from either stdin or the file specified with the in option. If the key option is not also specified, a new RSA key pair will be generated.

-newkey rsa:length, -newkey dsa:filename

Cause a new certificate request to be generated with a new key pair. For an RSA key pair, the length of the primes must be specified. For a DSA key pair, the name of a file containing the DSA parameters must be specified. The parameters are expected to be in PEM format.

-key filename

Specify the name of a file containing the private key to use in the certificate request.

-keyform DER|PEM

Specify the format, DER or PEM, of the private key specified using the key option. If this option is omitted, the default is PEM.

-keyout filename

Specify the name of a file to which the private key that was used will be written.

-nodes

If a new key pair is generated, this option causes the output private key to be unencrypted.

-md2, -md5, -mdc2, -sha1

Specify the message digest algorithm to use to sign the certificate request. If this option is omitted, the default is MD5. These options are ignored when a DSA key is being used because DSS1 must always be used with DSA keys.

-x509

Cause a self-signed certificate to be output instead of a certificate request. The resulting self-signed certificate is suitable for use with a root certification authority.

-days number

When a self-signed certificate is being generated, this option specifies the number of days for which the certificate will be valid.

-extensions section

Specify the name of a configuration file section containing the extensions to be included in a self-signed certificate.

-reqexts section

Specify the name of a configuration file section containing the extensions to be included in a certificate request.

-asn1-kludge

> Cause empty attribute sets to be omitted from the resulting certificate request. This invalid format is required by some CA software. Use of this option is not recommended unless you know that you need it.

-newhdr

> Cause the word "new" to be added to the PEM header and footer lines when a certificate request is being generated. Most software does not require this.

Configuration Options

RANDFILE

> Specify the name of a file that will be used to seed the PRNG for private key generation. This setting is overridden by the rand command-line option.

input_password

> Specify the password to use for the private key that is used as input. This setting is overridden by the passin command-line option.

output_password

> Specify the password to use for encrypting a generated private key. This setting is overridden by the passout command-line option.

default_bits

> When an RSA key is generated, this setting specifies the default key length. It can be overridden using the newkey command-line option.

default_keyfile

> Specify the name of a file that will be used to write a generated private key. This setting is overridden by the keyout command-line option.

encrypt_key, encrypt_rsa_key

> Setting the value for this key to no will cause any generated private key to be unencrypted. This setting is equivalent to specifying the nodes command-line option.

default_md

> Specify the default message digest algorithm to use for signing certificates and certificate requests. This setting is overridden by the md2, md5, mdc2, or sha1 command-line options.

oid_file

> Specify the name of a file containing object identifier definitions. The file should contain one definition per line, with each line consisting of three columns. The first column is the numerical representation of the OID. The second column is the OID's short name, and the third column is the OID's long name. The short name should be a single word and composed of only upper- and lowercase letters.

oid_section

> Specify the name of a configuration file section that contains object identifier definitions. In this section, each key should be the short name of the OID, and the corresponding value should be the OID's numerical representation. When OIDs are defined this way, the short and long names are the same.

string_mask

> This setting is used to mask out certain string types for certain fields. The default setting is normally appropriate and shouldn't need to be changed.

req_extensions

> Specify the name of a configuration file section that contains the extensions to be included in a certificate request. This setting is overridden by the reqexts command-line option.

x509_extensions

> Specify the name of a configuration file section that contains the extensions to be included in a self-signed certificate. This setting is overridden by the extensions command-line option.

prompt

> Setting the value for this key to no will cause all prompting for distinguished name information to be suppressed. It also causes the section specified by the distinguished_name key to be interpreted differently.

attributes

> Specify the name of a section containing any attributes that should be included in a generated certificate request.

distinguished_name

> Specify the name of a section containing the fields to be included in a generated certificate request.

Notes

The sections named by the attributes and distinguished_name keys in the configuration file can follow one of two possible formats, depending on the setting of the prompt key. If prompting is disabled, each key in the section should be the name of a field to be included in the certificate request, and the corresponding value should be the value for each field. This is the simplest format for these sections.

If prompting is enabled, four keys are required for each field that will be included in the generated certificate request. Each key uses the name of the field as a base. The key using the name of the field alone is the prompt that is displayed to the user. For the other three keys, _default, _min, and _max are appended to the field name, and the corresponding values are the default value for the field in the generated certificate request, the minimum length of data that can be entered by the user, and the maximum length of data that can be entered by the user.

Some fields can appear more than once in a distinguished name, but the format described does not allow for more than one field of the same name. To allow for this situation, any characters up to and including a period at the beginning of a field name are ignored, thus allowing for multiple definitions for a field in the configuration file, but including only the proper field name in the generated certificate request. For example, 1.organizationName and 2.organizationName are separate definitions in a configuration file, but in the generated certificate request, two fields named organizationName will be included.

rsa

The rsa command is used modify RSA private keys or examine their contents. The command may be used to remove encryption from a private key, add it to a private key, or change the encryption that is used on a private key. The command can also be used to compute a public key from a private key.

Options

-in filename
> Specify the name of a file from which an RSA private key will be read. If no file is specified, stdin is used.

-inform DER|NET|PEM
> Specify the format—DER, NET, or PEM—of the key that is read as input. If this option is omitted, the default format is PEM.

-out filename
> Specify the name of a file to which the output from this command will be written. If this option is omitted, stdout will be used.

-outform DER|NET|PEM
> Specify the format—DER, NET or PEM—of the key that is written. If this option is omitted, the default format is PEM.

-pubin
> Cause the input key to be interpreted as a public key.

-pubout
> Cause the output key to be interpreted as a public key.

-passin password
> Specify the password to use to decrypt the input key. This option follows the password and passphrase guidelines outlined in Chapter 2.

-passout password
> Specify the password to use to encrypt the output key. This option follows the password and passphrase guidelines outlined in Chapter 2.

-des, -des3, -idea
> Specify the cipher to use to encrypt the private key. If this option is omitted, the private key that is written out by this command will not be encrypted.

-noout
> Cause the output of the key in DER or PEM format to be suppressed.

-text
> Cause the input key, public or private, to be output in a human-readable form.

-modulus
> Cause the modulus of the public key to be written to the output destination.

-check
> Specify this option to check the consistency of an RSA private key.

-sgckey
> Cause a modified form of the NET format used by some versions of Microsoft IIS and old Netscape servers to be used for the output key. This format is not very secure, so it should be used only if necessary.

Notes

When producing private keys using the sgckey option, the passout option is currently ignored. The command will not read some forms of an unmodified NET format private key because they contain additional data. To use these keys with this command, try editing the key with a binary editor and removing all of the data in the file prior to the byte sequence 0x30, 0x82. Do not remove this byte sequence; it should be included in the resulting file.

---

rsautl

The rsautl command is used to utilize RSA keys for encryption and signing. It can be used to encrypt and decrypt data, as well as sign and verify signatures.

Options

-in filename
> Specify the name of a file from which data will be read. If this option is omitted, stdin will be used.

-inkey filename
> Specify the name of a file containing the public or private key to use. By default, the file should contain a private key unless the pubin or certin option is specified.

-pubin
> Indicate that the file specified by the inkey option contains a public key.

-certin
> Indicate that the file specified by the inkey option contains a certificate, which contains a public key.

-out filename
> Specify the name of a file to which data will be written. If this option is omitted, stdout will be used.

-hexdump
> Cause the output data to be output in a hexdump format.

-asn1parse
> Cause the output data to be ASN.1-parsed and output in the same format as the one that the asn1parse command emits.

-sign
> Cause the input data to be signed and the output to be the result. Signing requires a private key. Note that because signing uses the RSA algorithm directly, only small pieces of data can be signed.

-verify
> Cause the input data to be interpreted as a signature and verified. The output is the original input data that was signed. Verifying requires the public key matching the private key that was used to sign the data.

-encrypt
> Cause the input data to be encrypted. Encryption requires a public key.

-decrypt
> Cause the input data to be decrypted. Decryption requires that the private key match the public key that was used to encrypt the data.

-pkcs, -oaep, -ssl, -raw
> Specify the type of padding to use: PKCS#1 v1.5, PKCS#1 OAEP, SSLv2-compatible, or no padding at all. The default is to use PKCS#1 v1.5 padding.

s_client

The s_client command is a basic SSL client that can be used to connect to an SSL-enabled server. It provides functionality not unlike the standard Telnet program, although it does not support the telnet protocol. The command is useful primarily as a diagnostic tool when building and setting up SSL-enabled servers.

Options

-connect host:port
> Specify the host and port that should be used to establish a connection. Separate the host and port with a colon. The host may be an IP address or a hostname. The port may be a number or a service name. If this option is omitted, "127.0.0.1:443" is used.

-cert filename
> Specify the name of a file that contains the certificate to use for the connection. Most servers do not require a client certificate, but if the server requests one, this certificate will be used.

-key filename
> Specify the name of a file that contains the private key matching the certificate to use for the connection. If this option is not specified and a certificate is requested, the command will expect to find the private key in the same file as the certificate.

-verify depth
> Specify the maximum certificate chain depth. Use of this option enables verification of the server's certificate and causes verification to fail if more than the specified number of certificates is in the chain. Even if verification of the server's certificate fails, the connection will be allowed to proceed.

-CAfile filename
> Specify the name of a file containing one or more trusted certificates that will be used to verify the server's certificate if the verify option is specified.

-CApath directory
> Specify the name of a directory containing trusted certificates that will be used to verify the server's certificate if the verify option is specified. Each file should contain only one certificate, and the files should be named with the certificate issuer name's hash and an extension of ".0".

-reconnect
> Cause five connections to be made to the server using the same session ID. This option is a diagnostic tool to ensure that session caching is working properly on the server.

-pause
> Cause a one-second pause between each read and write operation.

-showcerts
> Cause every certificate in the server certificate's chain to be displayed rather than just the server's certificate.

-prexit
> Cause session information to be printed when the connection is terminated. Information will be displayed even if the connection fails. If the connection fails, some of the output from this command may not be accurate.

-state
> Cause SSL session states to be printed.

-debug
> Cause extensive debugging information, including a hexdump of all traffic, to be printed.

-nbio_test
> Cause tests of non-blocking I/O to be run.

-nbio
> Cause non-blocking I/O to be enabled.

-crlf
> Cause translation of bare linefeeds to be translated in carriage return and linefeed sequences, which is required by some servers.

-ign_eof
> Prevent the connection from being shut down when end of file is reached on `stdin`.

-quiet
> Cause printing of session and certificate information to be suppressed. This option also enables the ign_eof option.

-ssl2, -ssl3, -tls1, -no_ssl2, -no_ssl3, -no_tls1
> Specify the version or versions of the SSL protocol that should be used to attempt a connection with the server. By default, all protocols are enabled.

-bugs
> Enable workarounds for several known bugs in various server implementations of SSL and TLS.

-cipher list
> Specify a list of ciphers that the client will indicate to the server that it supports. Normally, the server chooses the first cipher on the list, so you should arrange ciphers in order of preference if you supply more than a single cipher.

-rand filename
> Specify the name of a file or files that will be used to seed the PRNG. This option follows the guidelines outlined in Chapter 2.

Notes

When a connection is established, any data received from the server is displayed on `stdout`, and any data read from `stdin` is sent to the server. If neither `quiet` nor `ign_eof` are specified, the client operates in interactive mode, which means that the session will be renegotiated if a line begins with the capital letter R, or the connection will be shut down if a line begins with the capital letter Q.

s_server

The s_server command is a basic SSL-enabled server that can be used as a diagnostic tool when building, setting up, and debugging SSL clients.

Options

-accept port

Specify the port on which to listen for connections. If this option is not specified, the default of 4433 is used.

-context ID

Specify any string that will be used as the SSL context ID.

-cert filename

Specify the name of a file containing the certificate to use. If this option is not specified, the command will look for a file called *server.pem* in the directory from which the command-line tool was started.

-key filename

Specify the name of a file containing the private key to use. The private key must match the certificate that is being used. If this option is not specified, the command will expect to find the private key in the same file as the certificate.

-dcert filename

Specify the name of a file containing an additional certificate that the server can use. This is useful for providing both RSA and DSA keys for connecting clients. There is no default if this option is not specified.

-dkey filename

Specify the name of a file containing the private key that matches the certificate specified with the dcert option. If the dcert option is specified without this one, the key should be in the same file as the certificate.

-nocert

Cause no certificate to be used. Use of this option severely restricts the ciphers that are available for use. This means that only anonymous Diffie-Hellman ciphers may be used. Operating a server without a certificate provides very little actual security.

-dhparam filename

Specify the name of a file containing Diffie-Hellman parameters. The parameters will be used by the ephemeral DH ciphers to generate keys. If this option is not specified, the command will attempt to find Diffie-Hellman parameters in the same file as the server's certificate.

-no_dhe

Disable the use of the ephemeral DH ciphers. No Diffie-Hellman parameters will be searched for if this option is specified.

-no_tmp_rsa

Disable the use of ciphers that require the use of temporary RSA keys.

-verify depth
> Cause the server to request a certificate from the client and perform verification on it. The connection will be allowed to proceed if the client does not provide a certificate. The client's certificate chain will not be allowed to be more than the specified depth.

-Verify depth
> Cause the server to demand a certificate from the client and perform verification on it. The connection will not be allowed to proceed if the client does not provide a certificate. The client's certificate chain will not be allowed to be more than the specified depth.

-CAfile filename
> Specify the name of a file containing trusted certificates that will be used to verify the client's certificate if one is received when it's requested.

-CApath directory
> Specify the name of a directory containing trusted certificates that will be used to verify the client's certificate if one is received when it's requested. Each file in the directory should contain only one certificate, and the files should be named with the certificate issuer name's hash and an extension of ".0".

-state
> Cause SSL session states to be printed.

-debug
> Cause extensive debugging information, including a hexdump of all traffic, to be printed.

-nbio_test
> Cause tests of non-blocking I/O to be run.

-nbio
> Cause non-blocking I/O to be enabled.

-crlf
> Cause translation of bare linefeeds to be translated in carriage return and linefeed sequences, as is required by some servers.

-quiet
> Cause printing of session and certificate information to be suppressed.

-ssl2, -ssl3, -tls1, -no_ssl2, -no_ssl3, -no_tls1
> Specify the version or versions of the SSL protocol that should be supported by the server. By default, all protocols are enabled.

-bugs
> Enable workarounds for several known bugs in various server implementations of SSL and TLS.

-hack
> Enable an additional workaround required by some early versions of Netscape.

-cipher list
> Specify a list of ciphers that the server will indicate to the client that it supports. Normally, the server chooses the cipher to use based on the order received from the client, so the ordering of the ciphers specified with this option is ignored.

-rand filename
> Specify the name of a file or files that will be used to seed the PRNG. This option follows the guidelines outlined in Chapter 2.

-www
> Cause an HTML-formatted status message to be sent to the client when it connects.

-WWW
> Cause the server to emulate a simple HTTP server. Requested pages will be resolved relative to the directory from which the server was started.

Notes

When a connection is established with a client and neither the www nor the WWW options are specified, the server runs in interactive mode, displays all data received from the client, and sends all data received from stdin to the client. In addition, certain commands are recognized as input from stdin, as enumerated in Table A-2. The commands are recognized only when they are entered at the start of a line.

Table A-2. Commands recognized by the server

Command	Function performed by the server
q	Terminates the current connection, but continues to accept new connections.
Q	Terminates the server.
r	Renegotiates the SSL session.
R	Renegotiates the SSL session and requests a client certificate.
P	Sends plaintext to the underlying TCP connection, which is a protocol violation and should cause the client to disconnect.
S	Displays session cache status information.

s_time

The s_time command can be used to connect to SSL-enabled servers and measure the performance of the OpenSSL library's implementation of the SSL protocol.

Options

-cipher cipher
> Specify the cipher to use. Use the ciphers command to obtain a list of acceptable ciphers.

-time seconds
> Specify the maximum number of seconds to collect timing information. If this option is omitted, the default is 30 seconds.

-nbio
> Run the timing test using non-blocking I/O.

-ssl2
> Run the timing test using SSLv2 only.

-ssl3
> Run the timing test using SSLv3 only.

-bugs
> Enable SSL bug compatibility.

-new
> Run the timing test for new connections only.

-reuse
> Run the timing test for connection reuse.

-verify depth
> Enable verification of peer certificates up to the specified depth.

-cert filename
> Specify the name of a file containing the certificate to use. The certificate is expected to be in PEM format.

-key filename
> Specify the name of a file containing the private key to use. The key is expected to be in PEM format.

-CAfile filename
> Specify the name of a file containing one or more trusted certificates in PEM format that will be used to verify the peer certificate.

-CApath directory
> Specify the name of a directory containing trusted certificates that will be used to verify the peer certificate. Each file in the directory should be named with the certificate issuer name's hash value and an extension of ".0". Only one certificate should be present in each file.

-connect host:port
> Specify the host and port that should be used to establish a connection. Separate the host and port with a colon. The host may be an IP address or a hostname. The port may be a number or a service name.

-www url
> Specify a URL from which data will be obtained. This option does not replace the connect option. The address contained in the URL is not used to make the connection. It is only passed to the server in an HTTP 1.0 GET request.

sess_id

The sess_id command is a diagnostic tool that can be used to display SSL session information in human-readable form.

Options

-in filename
> Specify the name of a file containing session information. If this option is omitted, stdin will be used.

-inform DER|PEM
> Specify the format—DER or PEM—of the input session information. If this option is omitted, the default format is PEM.

-out filename
> Specify the name of a file to which output from this command will be written. If this option is omitted, stdout will be used.

-outform DER|PEM

>   Specify the format—DER or PEM—of the output session information. If this option is omitted, the default format is PEM.

-noout

>   Cause the output of session output in DER or PEM format to be suppressed.

-text

>   Cause a human-readable representation of the session information to be output.

-cert

>   Cause the certificate contained in the session information to be output, if one is present.

-context ID

>   Specify the session ID that will be used in the output session information. The ID may be specified as any string of characters.

smime

The smime command is used to encrypt, decrypt, sign, and verify S/MIME format messages. It supports versions of S/MIME up to v2 and can be used to S/MIME-enable mail readers that do not natively support it.

Options

-in filename

>   Specify the name of a file from which data will be read. If this option is omitted, stdin will be used by default.

-inform DER|PEM|SMIME

>   Specify the format of the input data. If this option is omitted, the default is to use SMIME. This option is ignored if data is being encrypted or signed.

-out filename

>   Specify the name of a file to which data will be written. If this option is omitted, stdout will be used by default.

-outform DER|PEM|SMIME

>   Specify the format of the output data. If this option is omitted, the default is to use SMIME. This option is ignored if data is being decrypted or verified.

-encrypt

>   Cause the input data to be encrypted.

-decrypt

>   Cause the input data to be decrypted.

-sign

>   Cause the input data to be signed.

-verify

>   Cause the input data to be verified.

-pk7out

>   Cause the input data to be written out as a PEM-encoded PKCS#7 structure.

-content filename

Specify the name of a file containing the detached content. This option is valid only when verifying data.

-text

Cause plaintext MIME headers to be added to the output if the input data is being encrypted or signed. Cause plaintext MIME headers to be stripped from the input if the input data is being decrypted or verified.

-CAfile filename

Specify the name of a file containing trusted certificates for use in verifying.

-CApath directory

Specify the name of a directory containing trusted certificates for use in verifying. Each file in the directory should contain a single certificate and be named with the certificate issuer name's hash and an extension of ".0".

-nointern

When verifying data, cause any certificates included in the data to be considered untrusted.

-noverify

Do not verify the signer's certificate of a signed message.

-nochain

Do not perform chain verification of the signer's certificate or certificates.

-nosigs

Do not attempt to verify the signatures on the input data.

-nocerts

Do not include certificates in the signed data when signing.

-noattr

Do not include attributes like the time the data was signed in the output when signing.

-binary

Do not perform canonical translation.

-nodetach

Use opaque signing when signing data. Using this option requires that any mail agents encountering this message must be S/MIME-enabled. If this option is not specified, cleartext signing with the MIME type multipart/signed is used.

-certfile filename

Specify the name of a file containing one or more certificates. When signing, these certificates will be included in the signed data. When verifying, these certificates will be searched for the signer's certificate.

-signer filename

Specify the name of a file that the signer's certificate will be written to when verifying a signature. When signing, this file should contain the signer's certificate.

-recip filename

Specify the name of a file that contains the recipient's certificate. The certificate must match one of the recipients of the data.

-inkey filename

Specify the name of a file containing the private key to use when signing or decrypting data. The private key must match the public key contained in the certificate. If this option is omitted, the private key must be included in the certificate file specified with the recip or signer options.

-passin password

Specify the password or passphrase required to decrypt the private key when signing or decrypting data. This option follows the guidelines outlined in Chapter 2 for passwords and passphrases.

-rand filename

Specify the name of a file or files that will be used to seed the PRNG. This option follows the guidelines outlined in Chapter 2.

-to recipient

Specify the address of the recipient. If this is specified, it is included as part of the headers written outside the encrypted or signed data.

-from sender

Specify the address of the sender. If this is specified, it is included as part of the headers written outside the encrypted or signed data.

-subject subject

Specify the subject of the message. If this is specified, it is included as part of the headers written outside the encrypted or signed data.

Notes

When encrypting a message, files containing the certificates of the recipients in PEM format are also required on the command line. The filenames should be included after all other options are specified in free form.

When sending S/MIME messages using this command, it is important that no blank line be inserted between the message's headers and the output from this command. Some mail programs add a blank space, so care must be taken to avoid that.

This command allows only a single signer per message when signing. When verifying a signed message, the command does support multiple signers. Some S/MIME clients do not deal well with messages that have multiple signers. It is possible to sign an already signed message to achieve a similar effect.

The command sets the exit code (or errorlevel on Windows) according to the status of the command's requested operation. Exit codes are as follows:

0. The operation was completed successfully.
1. An error occurred when parsing the command's options.
2. One of the input files could not be read.
3. An error occurred creating the PKCS#7 file or when reading the MIME message.
4. An error occurred decrypting or verifying the message.
5. The message was verified correctly, but an error occurred when attempting to write out the signer's certificate or certificates.

speed

The speed command can be used to measure the performance of OpenSSL's crypto library. It performs benchmark tests on the ciphers supported by OpenSSL and reports on their speed.

Notes

The arguments for this command are the algorithms that will be tested. If no arguments are specified, all algorithms are tested. Valid algorithms are md2, mdc2, md5, hmac, sha1, rmd160, idea-cbc, rc2-cbc, rc5-cbc, bf-cbc, des-cbc, des-ede3, rc4, rsa512, rsa1024, rsa2048, rsa4096, dsa512, dsa1024, dsa2048, idea, rc2, des, rsa, and blowfish.

spkac

The spkac command is used to create, examine, and manipulate Netscape-signed public keys and challenge (SPKAC) formatted files.

Options

-in filename
>   Specify the name of a file from which data will be read. If this option is omitted, stdin is used by default.

-out filename
>   Specify the name of a file to which data will be written. If this option is omitted, stdout is used by default.

-passin password
>   Specify the password or passphrase that will be used to decrypt the private key if one is required. This option follows the guidelines for passwords and passphrases in Chapter 2.

-key filename
>   Specify the name of a file containing a private key to use when creating an SPKAC file. If this option is specified, the in, noout, spksect, and verify options are ignored.

-challenge string
>   Specify a challenge string to be included in an SPKAC file that is created.

-spkac name
>   Specify an alternative name for the variable containing the SPKAC. If this option is omitted, the default is to use the name "SPKAC". This option affects both generated and input SPKAC files.

-spksect section
>   Specify an alternative name for the section containing the SPKAC. If this option is omitted, the default is to use the default section.

-noout
>   Cause the output of an SPKAC file to be suppressed.

-pubkey
>   Cause the public key of an SPKAC to be output.

-verify
>   Verify the signature on the supplied SPKAC.

verify

The verify command is used to verify the validity of X.509 certificates. It performs an exhaustive check on a certificate, including validation of each certificate in a chain of certificates.

Options

-CAfile filename
> Specify the name of a file containing one or more trusted certificates.

-CApath directory
> Specify the name of a directory containing trusted certificates. There should be one certificate per file in the directory, and each file should be named by the certificate issuer name's hash and an extension of ".0".

-untrusted filename
> Specify the name of a file containing one or more untrusted certificates.

-purpose purpose
> Specify the purpose for the certificate being verified. If this option is omitted, no chain verification of certificates is performed. Valid purposes are sslclient, sslserver, nssslserver, smimesign, and smimeencrypt.

-issuer_checks
> Cause diagnostic messages relating to searches for issuer certificates to be printed.

-verbose
> Cause extra information about the operations that are being performed to be printed.

Notes

An argument consisting only of a dash (-) is considered a marker that means each argument that follows is the name of a file containing a certificate to be verified. It may be omitted, but is useful when a filename begins with a dash. Each argument that is not an option or parameter to an option is interpreted as the name of a file containing a certificate to be verified.

version

The version command displays information about the version of OpenSSL that is installed.

Options

-a
> Include all version information in the output. Specifying this option is equivalent to specifying all of the other available options.

-b
> Output the date when OpenSSL was built.

-c
> Output the compilation flags that were used to build OpenSSL. These flags are compiler-specific flags.

-o

Output the compile-time options that were used to build OpenSSL. These are OpenSSL-specific option flags that control the built-in features.

-p

Output the platform for which OpenSSL was built.

-v

Output the OpenSSL version.

x509

The x509 command is used to create, examine, and manipulate X.509 certificates. It is a complex command that accepts a large number of options. We've broken the options up into separate sections based on their function.

General Options

-in filename

Specify the name of a file from which data will be read. The expected data varies depending on the type of operation being performed, but usually an X.509 certificate is expected. If this option is omitted, stdin is used by default.

-inform DER|PEM|NET

Specify the format of the input data. If this option is omitted, the default is normally PEM, but may vary depending on the operation being performed.

-out filename

Specify the name of a file to which data will be written. Output is normally an X.509 certificate. If this option is omitted, stdout is used by default.

-outform DER|PEM|NET

Specify the format of the output data. If this option is omitted, the default is normally PEM, but may vary depending on the operation being performed.

-md2, -md4, -md5, -mdc2, -sha, -sha1, -rmd160, -dss1

Specify the message digest to use for signing. If this option is omitted, the default is to use MD5 for certificates and certificate requests containing RSA keys. For certificates and certificate requests containing DSA keys, DSS1 is always used, regardless of which algorithm is specified on the command line.

Display Options

-noout

Cause output of the certificate in encoded form to be suppressed.

-text

Output a human-readable representation of the certificate.

-modulus

Output the value of the modulus of the public key contained in the certificate.

-serial

Output the certificate's serial number.

-hash

> Output the hash of the certificate issuer's name. This value is used by any command that accepts a CApath option to name the certificates in the directory specified by the option.

-subject

> Output the certificate's subject name.

-issuer

> Output the certificate's issuer name.

-nameopt option

> Specify how the subject or issuer names are displayed. This option may be specified more than once. See the section below for a list of valid options and what they mean.

-email

> Output the certificate's email address or addresses if any are present.

-startdate

> Output the certificate's start date.

-enddate

> Output the certificate's end date.

-dates

> Output the certificate's start and end dates.

-checkend seconds

> Check whether the certificate will expire within the number of seconds specified as a parameter to this option.

-pubkey

> Output the certificate's public key in PEM format.

-fingerprint

> Output the certificate's fingerprint, which is the digest of a DER-encoded form of the whole certificate.

-C

> Output a C code representation of the certificate.

Trust Options

The trust options described in this section are experimental and subject to change in future releases of OpenSSL. The information presented here is current for Version 0.9.6 of OpenSSL.

-trustout

> Cause a trusted certificate to be output. Either a trusted or untrusted certificate is accepted as input to the command, but only untrusted certificates are normally output. If any trust settings are modified on a certificate, a trusted certificate is automatically output, regardless of whether this option is specified.

-alias

> Output the certificate's alias. Technically, this is a display option, but it is listed as a trust option because a certificate's alias is a trust setting.

-setalias alias

> Specify the alias for the certificate. Allows a certificate to be referred to by its alias.

-purpose

> Cause a series of tests to be performed on the certificate's extensions. The results of the test are output.

-clrtrust

> Cause all permitted or trusted uses of the certificate to be cleared.

-clrreject

> Cause all prohibited or rejected uses of the certificate to be cleared.

-addtrust OID

> Add a permitted or trusted use to the certificate. Any object identifier's short name may be used as a parameter for this option. OpenSSL itself uses only `clientAuth`, `serverAuth`, and `emailProtection`.

-addreject OID

> Add a prohibited or rejected use to the certificate. Any object identifier's short name may be used as a parameter for this option.

Signing Options

The X509 command is capable of signing certificate requests, thus creating certificates. The command can be used to create self-signed certificates and to behave like a mini-CA.

-req

> Cause the input data to be treated as a certificate request. This option is required with many of the other options described in this section.

-signkey filename

> Specify the name of a file containing the private key that will be used to create a self-signed certificate. If the input data is a certificate, its issuer name will be set to its subject name, and the public key that it contains will be replaced with the public key that matches the private key specified by this option. The certificate's start date will be set to the current date, and its end date will be computed using the days option. If the input data is a certificate request, a self-signed certificate is created using the specified private key and the subject name contained in the request.

-keyform DER|PEM

> Specify the format of the key that is specified with the `signkey` option. If this option is omitted, PEM is the default.

-passin password

> Specify the password required to decrypt the private key specified with the `signkey` or `CAkey` options. This option follows the guidelines for passwords or passphrases outlined in Chapter 2.

-days number

> Specify the number of days to make a certificate valid. The default is 30 days.

-CA filename

> Specify the name of a file containing a certificate that will be used for signing. This certificate's subject name is used as the issuer name for the resulting certificate, and the certificate is signed using the private key that matches this certificate. This option is normally used with the `req` option, but may be used with an existing self-signed certificate as well.

-CAform DER|PEM

> Specify the format—DER or PEM—of the certificate specified with the CA option. If this option is omitted, PEM is the default.

-CAkey filename

> Specify the name of a file containing the private key that matches the certificate specified with the CA option. If this option is omitted, the private key is expected to be in the same file as the certificate.

-CAkeyform DER|PEM

> Specify the format—DER or PEM—of the private key specified with the CAkey option. If this option is omitted, PEM is the default.

-CAserial filename

> Specify the name of a file containing the certificate's serial number information. This file uses the same format as the serial-number file for the ca command, which is a single line containing an even number of hexadecimal digits representing the next serial number to use. If this option is omitted, the filename specified with the CA command is used with its extension stripped and replaced with *.srl*.

-CAcreateserial filename

> Specify the name of a file containing the certificate's serial number information. If the file doesn't exist, it will be created using the number "02" as the next serial number to issue.

-extfile filename

> Specify the name of a file containing extensions that should be included in the new certificate. This file is essentially a configuration file, although the configuration file's only use with this command is for certificate extensions.

-extensions section

> Specify the name of the section to use from the file specified with the extfile option that contains the extensions to include in the new certificate.

-clrext

> Cause all extensions present in a certificate to be removed. This option should be used when a new certificate is being created from another existing certificate, using either the signkey or the CA options.

-x509toreq

> Convert a certificate into a certificate request. The signkey option should be used in combination with this option to specify the name of the file containing the private key that matches the certificate.

Name Options

The nameopt display option accepts a variety of options that control how the issuer and subject names of a certificate are displayed. The option may be specified multiple times to specify multiple options. Each of the supported option keywords is enumerated in this section. Any of the options can be optionally preceded with a dash (-) to turn that option off.

compat

> The default format. It is equivalent to specifying no nameopt options at all.

RFC2253

> Cause names to be displayed in a format compatible with RFC 2253. It is equivalent to specifying the options esc_2253, esc_ctrl, esc_msb, utf8, dump_nostr, dump_unknown, dump_der, sep_comma_plus, dn_rev, and sname.

---

oneline

A single-line format that is more readable than the RFC 2253 format. It is equivalent to specifying the options esc_2253, esc_ctrl, esc_msb, utf8, dump_nostr, dump_der, use_quote, sep_comma_plus_spc, spc_eq, and sname.

multiline

A multiline format that is equivalent to specifying the options esc_ctrl, esc_msb, sep_multiline, spc_eq, and lname.

esc_2253

Cause special characters required by RFC 2253 to be escaped. The characters that are escaped are comma (,), plus (+), double quotes ("), less than (<), greater than (>), and semi-colon (;). In addition, a hash mark (#), a space at the beginning of a string, or a space at the end of a string are also escaped.

esc_ctrl

Cause control characters to be escaped. Escaped characters have an ASCII value less than a space (0x20) or equal to the delete character (0x7F).

esc_msb

Cause characters that have their most significant bit (MSB) set to be escaped.

use_quote

Cause some characters to be escaped by surrounding the entire string with double-quotes characters.

utf8

Cause all strings to be converted to the UTF8 character encoding.

no_type

Cause multibyte characters to be uninterpreted. In other words, each byte of a multi-byte character is treated as if it was a character of its own.

show_type

Cause the ASN.1 type of the string to be prepended to the output.

dump_der

Cause any fields that need to be hexdumped to be dumped using the DER encoding of the field. If this option is not used, just the content octets will be displayed.

dump_nostr

Cause noncharacter string types to be displayed. If this option is not used, noncharacter string types will be displayed as though each content octet was a single character.

dump_all

Cause all fields to be displayed.

dump_unknown

Cause any field that has an OID unknown to OpenSSL to be displayed. Without this option, unknown fields are not included in the output.

sep_comma_plus, sep_comma_plus_space, sep_semi_plus_space, sep_multiline

Specify how fields will be separated in the output.

dn_rev

Cause the fields to be displayed in the reverse order that they are present in the name.

nofname

Cause the field name to be suppressed.

sname
    Cause the field name to be displayed using the field object identifier's short name.

lname
    Cause the field name to be displayed using the field object identifier's long name.

oid
    Cause the field name to be displayed using the field object identifier's numerical representation.

spc_eq
    Cause spaces to be placed around the equals sign (=) that is used to separate the field name from its value.

Index

We'd like to hear your suggestions for improving our indexes. Send email to *index@oreilly.com*.

encrypted messages, sending to multiple
    users, 302
encryption, 2, 184–187
engine, 109
ENGINE object type, 109
ENGINE_by_id( ), 110
ENGINE_set_default( ), 110
    flags for, 110
entropy, 18, 97
    EGADS, harvesting with, 19
    Unix systems, sources on, 100
Entropy Gathering and Distribution System
    (see EGADS)
Entropy Gathering Daemon (see EGD)
entropy sources, 44
environment variables for RANDFILE, 43
env:<variable> option, 42
ephemeral keying, 15, 144–146
    security advantages of, 144
equals sign (=), 31
ERR package, 81
    functions, 81–84
error handling, 81–86, 149
    error messages, displaying, 84
        format, returned messages, 85
error queues, 81
    destroying, 86
errstr command, 323
ERR_error_string( ), 84, 85
ERR_error_string_n( ), 84
ERR_get_error_line_data( ), 85
ERR_load_crypto_strings( ), 84
ERR_load_SSL_strings( ), 84
ERR_print_errors( ), 85
ERR_print_errors_fp( ), 85
ERR_remove_state( ), 86, 116
EVP interface, 174–192
    computing a hash value, 197
    data encryption with multiple keys, 241
    encrypting and decrypting, 240–244
        envelope encryption/decryption
            interface, 241
        sealing, 241
    finalization, 184
    hashing algorithms, 195–200
        function calls to, 195
    M2Crypto.EVP module, 261
    public key cryptography, 236–245
    signing and verification, 237–240
    updating, 184
EVP_add_cipher( ), 174
EVP_CIPHER_CTX, 180

EVP_CIPHER_CTX object, 241
EVP_CIPHER_CTX_ctrl( ), 183
EVP_CIPHER_CTX_init( ), 180
EVP_CIPHER_CTX_mode( ), 191
EVP_CIPHER_CTX_set_key_length( ), 182
EVP_CIPHER_CTX_set_padding( ), 183
EVP_CIPHER_key_length( ), 183
EVP_DecryptFinal( ), 187
EVP_DecryptInit( ), 180, 187
EVP_DecryptUpdate( ), 187
EVP_DigestFinal( ), 196
EVP_DigestFinal_ex( ), 197
EVP_DigestInit( ), 196
EVP_DigestInit_ex( ), 196
EVP_DigestUpdate( ), 196, 238
EVP_EncodeBlock( )
    base64 encoding, 213
EVP_EncryptFinal( ), 185
EVP_EncryptFinal_ex( ), 185
EVP_EncryptInit( ), 111, 180
EVP_EncryptInit_ex( ), 111
EVP_EncryptUpdate( ), 184
EVP_get_cipherbyname( ), 174
EVP_get_digestbyname( ), 195
EVP_MD objects, 282
EVP_MD_CTX objects, 237
EVP_OpenFinal( ), 244
EVP_OpenInit( ), 243
EVP_OpenUpdate( ), 244
EVP_PKEY object, 236
EVP_PKEY objects, 282
EVP_PKEY_assign_DSA( ), 237
EVP_PKEY_assign_RSA( ), 237
EVP_PKEY_free( ), 237
EVP_PKEY_get1_DSA( ), 237
EVP_PKEY_get1_RSA( ), 237
EVP_PKEY_new( ), 237
EVP_PKEY_set1_DSA( ), 237
EVP_PKEY_set1_RSA( ), 237
EVP_PKEY_size( ), 241
EVP_SealFinish( ), 243
EVP_SealInit( ), 241
    calling the function, 242
EVP_SealUpdate( ), 242
EVP_SignFinal( ), 238, 239
EVP_SignInit( ), 238
EVP_SignUpdate( ), 238
EVP_VerifyFinal( ), 240
EVP_VerifyInit( ), 239
EVP_VerifyInit_ex( ), 239
EVP_VerifyUpdate( ), 239
example code web site, xii

key_file (M2Crypto keyword), 264
keys, 2
    CAs, legal values for, 61
    DER encoding and decoding of, 245–247
    key agreement, 36, 219
    key exchange and RSA, 235
    length
        default length, checking, 183
        security, and, 172
        specifying, 182
    length and security, 20
    pairs, storage and exchange, 244
    PEM format, encoding and
        decoding, 248–250
    securing, 14
    security and PRNGs, 98
    session keys, replacing via
        renegotiation, 166
    stolen, 16
keystream, 172
keyUsage extension, 49–51
    common bit settings, 50

L

libcrypto, error messages, 84
libssl, error messages, 84
line parameter
    dyn_create_function( ), 78
    dyn_destroy_function( ), 79
    dyn_lock_function( ), 79
    locking_function( ), 76
Linux, 19
    (see also Unix)
$linux_debug variable, 252
locking_function( ), 75
locks, OpenSSL, 75
logging, error messages, 84
LOW keyword, 146

M

m2.bio_init( ) (M2Crypto), 258
M2Crypto, 258–266
    BIO module, 260
    case-sensitivity, 258
    DH algorithm, and, 263
    DSA alogorithm, and, 263
    EVP module, 261
        symmetric ciphers, encryption and
            decryption with, 262
    high-level classes, 259
    httpslib module, 264

low-level bindings, 258
    m2urllib module, 265
    m2xmlrpclib module, 265
    OpenSSL, supported versions, 258
    Python module extensions, 264–266
    Python, supported versions, 258
    RC4 cipher, and, 264
    RSA algorithm, and, 263
    SSL module, 259
    SWIG, supported versions, 258
    versions, 258
MACs (Message Authentication Codes), 9,
        194, 200–212
    block cipher MACs, 204
    CBC-MAC, 205–208
    HMAC, 200–204
    security properties, 204
    symmetric encryption, and, 192
    UMAC, 212
    validating MAC'd data, 201
    weaknesses, block-cipher based
        MACs, 205
    XCBC-MAC, 208–212
    XOR-MAC, 212
make test script, 23
make_form( ) (Net::SSLeay), 254
make_headers( ) (Net::SSLeay), 254
man-in-the-middle attacks, 11
    Certification Authorities, and, 17
    digital signatures, prevention with, 225
    OCSP, and, 54
    public key cryptography, and, 45
mathematical operations, functions for, 106
MD5, insecurity of, 194
MD5 keyword, 146
MDC2 algorithm, 196
memory BIOs, 91
    creating, 91
memory leaks, preventing, 134, 152
message digest algorithms, 32–33
    command-line, accessing through, 32
    (see also MACs)
message digests, 8, 193
    algorithms, supported in OpenSSL, 195
    EVP_MD objects, 282
    hexadecimal, printing in, 197
    keyed hashes, 9
    sha1 command, 198–200
    (see also MACs)
MessageDigest class (M2Crypto.EVP
        module), 261

software, code-signing certificates for, 57
software engines, support in OpenSSL, 110
source BIO, 90
source/sink BIOs (see BIO package)
speed command, 345
spkac command, 345
spoofing, 3
s_server command, 338–340
SSL (Secure Sockets Layer), ix, 1, 10–14, 112
   application software flaws, and, 21
   BIO specification, 125
   certificate preparation, 119–121
   cipher suites, 146
   drawbacks of, 12–14
   efficiency, 12
   general data security, and, 21
   impractical applications of, 20–21
   incompatibility, UDP and IPX, 20
   input/output methods, specification, 125
   load balancing, 14
   non-repudiation, and, 20
   options, 143–146
   programming, 113
      example applications, 113
   references, 2
   sessions (see sessions)
   SSL connections, input and
      output, 155–166
   SSL handshake, 130
   SSL object, 119
   v2, security flaws, 112
   Version 2, flaws in, 18
      risks of supporting, 19
   version selection, 118
   (see also public key cryptography)
sslcat( ) (Net::SSLeay), 255
SSLeay, 21, 252
SSLServer class (M2Crypto), 260
SSLv23_method( ), 143
SSL_accept( ), 128
SSL_connect( ), 125
SSL_CTX objects, 118, 119
   trusted certificates, loading to, 129
SSL_CTX_flush_sessions( ), 153
SSL_CTX_get_cert_store( ), 133
SSL_CTX_load_verify_locations( ), 129, 140
   X509_STORE object, and, 133
SSL_CTX_sess_set_get_cb( ), 154
SSL_CTX_sess_set_new_cb( ), 153
SSL_CTX_sess_set_remove_cb( ), 154
SSL_CTX_set_cert_verify_callback( ), 130
SSL_CTX_set_cipher_list( ), 146

SSL_CTX_set_default_passwd_cb( ), 120
SSL_CTX_set_default_passwd_cb_
   userdata( ), 121
SSL_CTX_set_default_paths( )
   X509_STORE object, and, 133
SSL_CTX_set_default_verify_paths( ), 130,
   140
SSL_CTX_set_mode( ), 158
SSL_CTX_set_options, 119
SSL_CTX_set_session_cache_mode( ), 153
SSL_CTX_set_session_id_context( ), 153
SSL_CTX_set_timeout( ), 153
SSL_CTX_set_tmp_dh( ), 145
SSL_CTX_set_tmp_dh_callback( ), 145
SSL_CTX_set_verify( ), 130–133
   flags, 131
SSL_CTX_set_verify_depth( ), 132
   security vulnerability, 133
SSL_CTX_use_certificate_chain_file( ), 120,
   121
SSL_CTX_use_PrivateKey_file( ), 120, 121
SSL_do_handshake( ), 168
SSL_ERROR_WANT_READ, 158
SSL_ERROR_WANT_WRITE, 158
SSL_free( ), 126
SSL_get_error( ), 156
   common return values, 156
SSL_get_peer_certificate( ), 134
SSL_get_session( ), 151
SSL_get_shutdown( ), 128
SSL_get_verify_result( ), 135–137
SSL_get0_session( ), 152
SSL_get1_session( ), 152
SSL_load_error_strings( ), 84, 114
SSL_METHOD objects and accessor
   methods, 118
SSL_OP_SINGLE_DH_USE, 146, 149
   conversion, DSA parameters to DH,
   and, 150
SSL_read( ), 156
SSL_regenotiate_pending( ), 169
SSL_renegotiate( ), 166, 169
SSL_renegotiate_pending( ), 169
SSL_SESSION objects, 151
   security requirements, 154
SSL_set_bio( ), 125
SSL_set_mode( ), 158, 164
SSL_set_session( ), 152
SSL_set_session_id_context( ), 168
SSL_shutdown( ), 128
SSL_VERIFY_FAIL_IF_NO_PEER_
   CERT, 150

SSL_VERIFY_PEER, 140, 150
SSL_write( ), 156
$ssl_version variable, 253
ssl_context (M2Crypto keyword), 265
ssl_read_all( ) (Net::SSLeay), 256
ssl_read_CRLF( ) (Net::SSLeay), 256
ssl_read_until( ) (Net::SSLeay), 256
ssl_write_all( ) (Net::SSLeay), 256
ssl_write_CRLF( ) (Net::SSLeay), 257
stacks, 275–277
    generic stack functions, 275–277
        sk_TYPE_dup( ), 276
        sk_TYPE_free( ), 276
        sk_TYPE_insert( ), 277
        sk_TYPE_new_null( ), 276
        sk_TYPE_num( ), 276
        sk_TYPE_pop( ), 276
        sk_TYPE_pop_free( ), 276
        sk_TYPE_push( ), 276
        sk_TYPE_set( ), 277
        sk_TYPE_shift( ), 276
        sk_TYPE_unshift( ), 276
        sk_TYPE_value( ), 276
        sk_TYPE_zero( ), 276
    type safety, macros for, 275
standard error messages, 84
static keying, 144
static locking callbacks, 75–77
    POSIX systems, 76
    Win32 systems, 76
static locks, 75
stdin option, 42
s_time command, 340
stolen keys, 16
stream ciphers (see ciphers)
@STRENGTH keyword, 146
strong primes, 220
Stunnel, 23–28
subject names, 281
subjectAltName extension, 282
    dNSName field, 124, 134
SureWare acceleration hardware, ID
        string, 110
SWIG, 258
symmetric ciphers, 34–35
    command-line access, 34
    commands, 35
symmetric cryptography, 5–6
    OpenSSL API for, 171
    (see also ciphers; EVP interface)

T

tampering, 3
testconf.cnf, 277
text files, encoding and decoding keys
        to, 244–250
    DER format, 245–247
    PEM format, 248–250
third-party software, securing with
        OpenSSL, 23
THREAD_cleanup( ), 77
threading, error check calls, 156
ThreadingSSLServer class (M2Crypto), 260
thread-local storage, 85
thread-safety, OpenSSL, 75, 85
THREAD_setup( ), 77
TLS (Transport Layer Security), ix, 1, 112
tmp_dh_callback( ), 149
$trace variable, 252
Transport Layer Security protocol (TLS), ix,
        1, 112
Triple DES cipher, 177
trust, establishing, 45
trusted certificate files, 129
    on multiuser systems, 130
trusted certificates, loading to an
        application, 129
two-way authenticating key agreement, 236
two-way authenticating key transport, 236
two-way authentication, 149, 230

U

UDP traffic, encryption of, 189–192
UMAC, 212
Unix
    config script, 22
    EGADS, entropy harvesting with, 19
    entropy, sources of, 100
    make test script, 23
    random number seeding, 43
unordered data streams and encryption
        modes, 189
updating, 184
urllib extensions (Python), 265
user identity information, secure
        transport, 307

V

verification mode, SSL_VERIFY_PEER, 140
    behavior on the server, 142

About the Authors

John Viega, Chief Scientist and founder of Secure Software Solutions, is a well-known security expert, and co-author of *Building Secure Software* (Addison-Wesley). John is responsible for numerous software security tools, and is the original author of Mailman, the GNU mailing list manager. He holds a B.A. and M.S. in Computer Science from the University of Virginia. John has never been to Cleveland.

Matt Messier is a founder and Director of Windows Development at Secure Software Solutions. Matt has co-authored security tools such as RATS and EGADS, and leads development of AttackShield, a solution for protecting third-party applications from unknown security vulnerabilities. Matt has also built tools for automatically finding security vulnerabilities in binary applications. Matt doesn't care so much for Cleveland.

Pravir Chandra, Research Scientist at Secure Software Solutions, is an expert in language-level security. Most recently, he co-authored the DARPA-funded "catscan" tool for static security analysis of C source code. Pravir holds a B.S. in Computer Science from Case Western Reserve University, and wants you to know that Cleveland rocks!

Colophon

Our look is the result of reader comments, our own experimentation, and feedback from distribution channels. Distinctive covers complement our distinctive approach to technical topics, breathing personality and life into potentially dry subjects.

The animals on the cover of *Network Security with OpenSSL* are seals and sea lions. Seals and sea lions are related; both are marine mammals belonging to the order Pinnipedia. Sea lions, along with fur seals, are members of the eared seal family. Eared seals, as their name implies, have external ears on either side of the head. These ears are covered by small flaps. All other seals, or true seals, lack external ears, having only small, wrinkled openings where their ears would otherwise be. Another principle difference between eared seals and true seals is the functionality of their rear flippers. Eared seals can turn their rear flippers forward to move about on land. True seals cannot, and can move on land only by rolling, sliding, or wriggling from place to place. Despite the awkwardness of both seals and sea lions on land, both swim very gracefully using undulating motions of their front flippers. Fish and squid are the main staples of the seal and sea lion diet. These mammals can dive to great depths—up to 2,000 feet in some species—in search of food.

Seals and sea lions have long been hunted for their blubber and their fur. There are eighteen living species of seal and four major species of sea lion in existence. Some species are endangered or threatened. All are currently protected.

Colleen Gorman was the production editor and the copyeditor for *Network Security with OpenSSL*. Matt Hutchinson, Linley Dolby, and Jane Ellin provided quality control. Sue Willing, Sarah Sherman, and Phil Dangler provided production support. John Bickelhaupt wrote the index.

Ellie Volckhausen designed the cover of this book, based on a series design by Edie Freedman. The cover image is a 19th-century engraving from the Dover Pictorial Archive. Emma Colby produced the cover layout with QuarkXPress 4.1 using Adobe's ITC Garamond font.

David Futato designed the interior layout. This book was converted into FrameMaker 5.5.6 with a format conversion tool created by Erik Ray, Jason McIntosh, Neil Walls, and Mike Sierra that uses Perl and XML technologies. The text font is Linotype Birka; the heading font is Adobe Myriad Condensed; and the code font is LucasFont's TheSans Mono Condensed. The illustrations that appear in the book were produced by Robert Romano and Jessamyn Read using Macromedia FreeHand 9 and Adobe Photoshop 6. The tip and warning icons were drawn by Christopher Bing. This colophon was written by Clairemarie Fisher O'Leary.